MARTYRS
MIRROR

YOUNG CENTER BOOKS IN ANABAPTIST & PIETIST STUDIES

Donald B. Kraybill, *Series Editor*

MARTYRS MIRROR

A Social History

David L. Weaver-Zercher

JOHNS HOPKINS UNIVERSITY PRESS

Baltimore

The author and publisher are grateful to Mennonite Central Committee (MCC) for its generous support of this book. A worldwide ministry that responds to basic human needs and works for peace and justice in the name of Christ, MCC brings together Anabaptist churches and people to share God's love and compassion.

Johns Hopkins University Press
2715 North Charles Street
Baltimore, Maryland 21218-4363
www.press.jhu.edu

Library of Congress Cataloging-in-Publication Data

Weaver-Zercher, David, 1960–
Martyrs mirror : a social history / David L. Weaver-Zercher.
pages cm. — (Young center books in Anabaptist and pietist studies)
Includes bibliographical references and index.
ISBN 978-1-4214-1882-7 (hardcover : alk. paper) — ISBN 978-1-4214-1883-4 (electronic)
— ISBN 1-4214-1882-7 (hardcover : alk. paper) — ISBN 1-4214-1883-5 (electronic)
1. Braght, Thieleman J. van (Thieleman Janszoon), 1625–1664. Bloedig toneel.
2. Anabaptists—Europe—Biography. 3. Christian martyrs—Europe—Biography.
4. Persecution. I. Title.
BR1600.B833W43 2016
272—dc23   2015012592

A catalog record for this book is available from the British Library.

Special discounts are available for bulk purchases of this book. For more information, please contact Special Sales at 410-516-6936 or specialsales@press.jhu.edu.

Johns Hopkins University Press uses environmentally friendly book materials, including recycled text paper that is composed of at least 30 percent post-consumer waste, whenever possible.

To my mother, Alice Grace Zercher,
and to my late father, John Engle Zercher

Contents

Preface

F our hundred years have passed since Hans Landis, the last Anabaptist executed in Switzerland, was put to death. An irrepressible
preacher from near Zurich, Landis had been imprisoned numerous times before his final arrest and subsequent beheading in 1614. According to one eyewitness, Landis's executioner led the seventy-year-old
minister toward the execution site with a rope, pausing long enough to
beg his victim's forgiveness. Landis comforted the man, assured him that
he had already forgiven him, and added that "God would forgive him
too." A second account of Landis's execution reports that his wife and
children arrived "with mournful crying" to bid their husband and father
goodbye. When Landis saw them, he implored them to leave, so that his
"tranquility of heart for the death awaiting him might not be disturbed."[1]

These accounts of Landis's execution can be found in *The Bloody Theater of the Baptism-Minded and Defenseless Christians,* a massive collection of Christian martyr stories compiled by the Dutch Mennonite minister Thieleman van Braght and published in 1660.[2] Unlike some of his
Anabaptist contemporaries, van Braght lived in tolerant surroundings
that afforded him the luxury of sustained historical reflection. Making
the most of this indulgence, and with previous Anabaptist martyrologies at his service, van Braght succeeded in crafting a grand narrative
of what he considered authentic Christianity, a narrative that ran from
biblical times to his own times. To fashion that narrative, van Braght included martyr accounts from the church's first fifteen centuries, thereby
creating a bloodstained prologue that set the stage for the emergence of

Anabaptism in the sixteenth century. In van Braght's portrayal of Christian history, the persecution of faithful people in the name of heresy-hunting was nothing new in the sixteenth century, and neither were the convictions for which the Anabaptists died. The Anabaptist martyrs, van Braght averred, stood in good company.

Van Braght's *Bloody Theater*, which today is more commonly known as *Martyrs Mirror*, remains in print in both English and German.[3] Because its stories focus primarily on the experiences of sixteenth-century Anabaptists, whose theological descendants include Mennonites and Amish, copies of *Martyrs Mirror* can be found in many North American Amish and Mennonite homes. Rare is the person who has read *Martyrs Mirror* from cover to cover, though some people do read in it, using it as a reference book, and even more encounter its contents through sermons, Sunday school lessons, grade-school texts, history books, and abridgments of modest size. In some Anabaptist communities, copies of *Martyrs Mirror* are treasured possessions, passed down from earlier generations or given as wedding or graduation gifts.

What is *Martyrs Mirror*, and how did it come to be? Why and how has this stout martyrology remained in print for more than 350 years? For what purposes has it been used, and how does it function in the present? These are the questions I explore in this book. To answer them I draw on the work of many others, particularly those who have written about the book's European roots. In addition to synthesizing their work into a survey of *Martyrs Mirror*'s production and reproduction, I trace the influence of *Martyrs Mirror* in North American Anabaptist life past and present, an influence both multiplied and verified by the array of texts van Braght's work has inspired. Indeed, my primary interest is this: how has a book detailing sixteenth-century martyrdom continued to hold sway over people whose lives bear so little resemblance to those of the martyrs?

My thesis is relatively straightforward: *Martyrs Mirror* has functioned, and continues to function, as a measure of Christian faithfulness. What does it mean to live a faithful Christian life? Anabaptists past and present have often looked to the martyrs—their martyrs—to answer that question, for in addition to being exemplars of spiritual resolve, the martyrs conveyed the content of authentic faith, at least as they understood it. For instance, Hans Landis not only remained true to his convictions, but he also forgave the man who was charged with lopping off his Anabaptist head. More particular to the Anabaptist tradition, Landis exemplified what Anabaptists have traditionally called *nonresistance* or, in some settings, *defenselessness:* the Christlike refusal to respond to one's enemies in an eye-for-an-eye fashion.[4] It was therefore no coincidence that, nearly four centuries after his death, Landis's specter loomed large at a conciliatory meeting of twenty-first-century Anabaptist and Reformed church leaders. At this meeting, held in 2004 near the site of Landis's execution, Swiss Mennonite leader Ernest Geiser received a Reformed Church apology for persecuting sixteenth-century Anabaptists and then responded in a Landis-like way: "We accept your confession with a spirit of forgiveness."[5] Conference participants also heard a poem, written and read by James Landis, a fourteenth-generation descendant of the executed Hans.[6]

Given *Martyrs Mirror*'s dramatic content, church leaders in some Anabaptist communities have frequently sought to expand its reach. Along with making van Braght's accounts accessible to new generations of readers, these leaders have used the book and its gripping details to advance the faith for which the martyrs died. In particular, leaders have employed *Martyrs Mirror* in the spiritual instruction of adolescents, schooling them in key tenets of the faith—chief among them adult baptism and nonresistance—and impressing upon them the necessity of being faithful in difficult circumstances. To be sure, remaining faithful in twenty-first-century North America is a very different proposition from what it was in sixteenth-century Europe, where Anabaptist youth sometimes suffered the same fate as Hans Landis. Still, these leaders believe, if sixteenth-century Anabaptist teens could defy their inquisitors, surely their examples can inspire their successors to live faithfully in the present.

Martyrs Mirror has often been effective in this regard, for the text is, to many who read it, both awe-inspiring and spiritually compelling. Nonetheless, its patrons' spiritual objectives have often been hindered by at least four factors. First, the book's sheer size has made it a challenging text to reproduce and a difficult text to read, intimidating publishers and readers alike. Second, in addition to being a spiritual resource, *Martyrs Mirror* has always existed as a commodity, one that potential consumers have not always been convinced is worth the price. Third, the takeaway messages of *Martyrs Mirror* are not always clear, especially in times of ease and in contexts where non-Anabaptists treat their Anabaptist neighbors with love and respect. Finally, some readers have questioned the wisdom of esteeming a text that not only commemorates suffering but also seems to valorize it; that not only criticizes Roman Catholics but also calls them devils; that not only praises steadfastness but also lauds fathers who spurn their families' farewells. That some Anabaptist readers have voiced these concerns, whereas others have never considered them, offers insight into the way different Anabaptist communities have approached *Martyrs Mirror* as a spiritual resource.

Whatever contemporary Anabaptists think about *Martyrs Mirror*—and some think of it rarely, if at all—it is not unusual to find some who claim Hans Landis, or one of the other martyrs, as an ancestor. Of course, Landis's twenty-first-century relatives are more likely to be struck by lightning than by an executioner's sword, and in most cases their ancestral line runs more directly to Hans's brother Rudolph than it does to the martyr himself. Still, it is the connection to Hans that continues to carry cachet in some Anabaptist circles. For instance, when historian John L. Ruth published his history of Lancaster County Mennonites in 2001, he devoted the bulk of his first chapter to Landis's life and death, even though that death occurred a century before Mennonites first settled in Lancaster County. Significantly, Ruth chose for his book's title a Bible passage that Landis quoted to his captors just days before his execution: "The earth is the Lord's."[7] In Ruth's telling, the words and deeds of this renowned martyr provided a useful frame for plotting the entire history of Lancaster County Mennonitism. Ruth even took pains to convey his own link to the Landis line: whereas his earlier books were attributed to "John L. Ruth," *The Earth Is the Lord's* identified its author as "John Landis Ruth."[8]

That Ruth would highlight this genealogical connection four hundred years after the fact reveals much about the martyrological memory of twenty-first-century Anabaptists, particularly in North America. This memory cannot be attributed to *Martyrs Mirror* alone, but its prevalence through the centuries is hard to imagine apart from the book that van Braght so painstakingly compiled. Especially in an age when faith-inspired beheadings can no longer be dismissed as a bad medieval memory, and the ensuing calls for vengeance are both loud and insistent, the staying power of a seventeenth-century martyr book that repudiates retaliation demands our close consideration and careful analysis.

Anabaptism and Related Terms

An overview of sixteenth-century Anabaptism occupies chapter 1, though some basic terminology is useful even at this point. The term *Anabaptist* literally means "rebaptizer." It was a term assigned to those who, during the European Reformation, rejected infant baptism in favor of adult baptism. For the Anabaptists, baptism was meant to signify one's commitment to Jesus Christ. Only adults could make that kind of commitment, so baptizing infants, in their view, made no sense. In their adversaries' view, the men and women who pursued adult baptism were Anabaptists, because they were undergoing a second baptism as adults. The Anabaptists, however, considered their adult baptism their first authentic baptism. To them adult baptism was the only baptism that counted.

In addition to being called *Anabaptists,* the adult-baptizing Christians in early modern Europe assumed other labels. One common designation for Anabaptists in the Netherlands, and therefore in van Braght's *Bloody Theater,* was *Doopsgesinde,* which literally means "the baptism-minded."[9] Another common designation for Dutch Anabaptists was *Mennists* or *Mennonites,* derived from the name of an early Dutch Anabaptist leader, Menno Simons. Four centuries later these terms continue to be used: Anabaptist groups in the Netherlands carry the name *Doopsgesinde,* and many Anabaptist groups in contemporary North America are called *Mennonites.*

Like Mennonites, other European Anabaptist groups derived their names from early leaders. For instance, in sixteenth-century Moravia, one Anabaptist group came to be known as *Hutterites,* a label derived from the revered Jacob Hutter. Another group, the *Amish,* emerged a century and a half later, in 1693, in the Alsace region of present-day France. Named for their founder Jakob Ammann, the Amish sought to reinstitute the practice of shunning, a stringent form of church discipline that had fallen out of favor among many of their Anabaptist counterparts.[10] Although no Hutterites or Amish continue to live in Europe, both groups continue today in North America. All told, nearly 750,000 members identify with Anabaptist churches in North America, their members distributed among 100 subgroups and 7,500 congregations.[11] Together these churches continue to espouse key elements of sixteenth-century Anabaptism, including adult baptism and nonresistance.

Despite sharing some core convictions, however, contemporary Anabaptists demonstrate significant theological and sociological diversity. Some of these differences reach back centuries, but others have developed more recently. The different churchly names—Mennonites, Amish, Hutterites, and Brethren—hint at the historic diversity within the Anabaptist tradition, but the diversity that exists today often cuts across these long-standing ecclesial categories. For instance, tradition-minded Mennonite groups often share more in common with Amish groups than they share with more progressive Mennonite groups. These commonalities that cut across ecclesial lines have led some scholars to suggest that it makes more sense to classify North American Anabaptist groups by three types—Old Order, conservative, and assimilated—based on their levels of assimilation to the larger society.[12]

We will revisit the issue of diversity within the Anabaptist tradition throughout this book, particularly in parts 2 and 3. For now it is important to know two things. First, *Martyrs Mirror* has been, and continues to be, an esteemed resource for a wide array of Anabaptist groups. In fact, among the attributes that are widely shared among North American Anabaptists, mindfulness of a persecuted past is high on the list. Nonetheless, and this is the second thing to know, Anabaptists in different social locations have often thought about this persecuted past differently. More specifically, readers in one Anabaptist group have often read and reacted to the contents of *Martyrs Mirror* differently from readers in another Anabaptist group. In the final analysis, this book is interested in both questions: not only *whether* people read *Martyrs Mirror,* but *how* they read it.

Citations and Spelling Considerations

The focus of this book is a martyrology compiled by Thieleman van Braght and published in 1660. Commonly called *Martyrs Mirror,* the martyrology carries a long title that actually begins with the words *The Bloody Theater (Het Bloedigh Tooneel),* not *Martyrs Mirror (Martelaers Spiegel).* To complicate matters even more, an earlier Anabaptist martyrology, produced in 1631 by Hans de Ries and a handful of colleagues, begins its title with the words *Martyrs Mirror* (*Martelaers Spiegel*).[13] Although de Ries's volume will receive consideration in chapter 2, the bulk of this book deals with van Braght's 1660 martyrology, which, unlike de Ries's work, remains in print. Because van Braght's martyrology is commonly called *Martyrs Mirror*, I will typically refer to it as such. In fact, unless I indicate that I am referring to de Ries's 1631 martyrology, each mention of *Martyrs Mirror* in the pages that follow refers to van Braght's 1660 work or a subsequent edition of it.

In most of the book I have chosen to quote from Joseph F. Sohm's English translation of *Martyrs Mirror*, first published by the Mennonite Publishing Company (later the Mennonite Publishing House) in 1886. This is the translation that the Mennonite publisher, now called Herald Press, continues to keep in print. Significantly, the pagination of the Sohm text has remained constant since 1938, through many Mennonite Publishing House and Herald Press reprints and slightly revised editions. Because the vast majority of people who own an English translation of *Martyrs Mirror* own a Mennonite Publishing House or Herald Press edition dated 1938 or later, I cite the 1938 edition unless otherwise noted (again, the wording and the page references would be the same had I instead chosen to cite Herald Press's 1950 edition or one of the many editions that Herald Press has published since then). When considering a pre-1886 edition of *Martyrs Mirror*, I cite that edition in the notes, often complementing that citation with corresponding page references to the 1938 English edition.

Throughout the main text I have tried to harmonize the spellings of people's names and place names. Unless there is a reason to do it otherwise, I spell early Anabaptists' names as they appear in the 1938 English edition of *Martyrs Mirror*. With respect to geographical locations, I spell towns, cities, and regions as they are typically spelled today. In the notes, I have tried to be faithful to how authors' names and publication place names were spelled in the original publications. For instance, Thieleman van Braght sometimes appears as Thielem van Braght if that is how his name was spelled on the title page of a given work. When referring to *Martyrs Mirror* in the main text, I do not apostrophize the word *martyrs* (*Martyrs' Mirror*) unless I am quoting a source that uses the apostrophe.

Chapter Summary

This book is organized chronologically. Part 1 begins with the sixteenth-century emergence of the Anabaptist movement and the persecution its adherents suffered (chapter 1), then tracks the collection of martyr accounts into martyr books that anticipated *The Bloody Theater* (chapter 2). Chapter 3 introduces readers to Thieleman van Braght, his historical context, and his reasons for producing yet another Anabaptist martyrology. Chapter 4 charts the overall organization of *The Bloody Theater* and, in broad strokes, introduces readers to the martyrology's contents.

Part 2 moves beyond the production and content of *The Bloody Theater,* and beyond the 1660s, to consider the work's most significant editions and translations. Chapter 5 explores the culminating embodiment of van Braght's book, the 1685 Dutch edition that included 104 copper etchings by artist Jan Luyken. Chapter 6 brings the story of *Martyrs Mirror* to North America, where the volume was translated into German in the late 1740s by the Ephrata communitarians. The next two chapters continue the volume's North American story by examining various German and English translations and their place in nineteenth- and twentieth-century Anabaptist life. These chapters underscore various themes that run through the rest of the book, including the desire of various individuals and groups to marshal the martyrs' witness for their own ends, and the interplay between the book's production and its consumption.

Part 3 examines the place of *Martyrs Mirror* in contemporary North American Anabaptist life, which, for the purposes of this book, means 1990 to the present. Chapters 9 and 10 make distinctions between tradition-minded Anabaptist groups and assimilated Anabaptist groups and explore the ways the book is used and cited in these respective contexts. Chapter 11 takes a longer historical view by examining the life and legacy of one particular Anabaptist martyr, Dirk Willems. More specifically, the chapter seeks to answer two questions: How and why did Dirk's martyrological image become so pervasive, and what messages do people imbibe when they ponder it? Chapter 12 refocuses on more contemporary events but expands the geographical scope by probing the place of *Martyrs Mirror* in a global Anabaptist context. In addition, chapter

12 considers the recent call by some Mennonites leaders to reopen the canon of Anabaptist martyrs, a canon that has more or less been closed since 1660.

It is too early to say whether this call to reopen the canon of Anabaptist martyrs will affect the way North American Anabaptists think about the worlds they inhabit. Those who are assembling an updated set of martyr stories express some hope in this regard, supposing that, at least in some circles, these newer stories will inspire greater reflection on both the cost and the possibility of being faithful. In that sense, these contemporary martyrologists, while far too humble to claim van Braght's mantle, are assuming his mantle nonetheless. His work gives shape to theirs, and his enduring influence on Anabaptist spirituality provides them with an example of using history in the service of faith. How and to what extent van Braght and his work established this influence are the questions this book seeks to address.

CH. 01 : ANABAPISM: ORIGINS, SPREAD, AND PERSECUTION

CH. 02: MEMORIALIZING BEFORE THE BLOODY THEATRE

CH. 03: VAN BRAGT & THE PUBLICATION OF T.B.T

CH. 04: T.B.T: MARTYR STORIES

CH. 05: T.B.T ILLUSTRATED: THE 1685 MARTYRS MIRROR

CH. 06: A N. AMERICAN EDITION: THE 1748-49 EPHRATA

CH. 07: MARTYRS MIRROR IN 19TH c. AMERICA

CH. 08: MARTYRS MIRROR IN 20TH c. AMERICA

CH. 09: THE TRADITION-MINDED & THE USE OF M.M.

CH. 10: THE ASSIMILATED & THE DILEMMA OF M.M.

CH. 11: MOST USABLE MARTYR: DIRK WILLEMS

CH. 12: MARTYRS MIRROR IN THE 21ST c.

PART I

The Prehistory and Production of The Bloody Theater

CHAPTER 1

Anabaptism

Origins, Spread, and Persecution

By the time *The Bloody Theater* was published in 1660, the Anabaptist movement was more than a hundred years old. Filled with colorful personalities, competing visions, and martyred bodies, the movement's history was less than tidy. Neither the center nor the boundaries of the Anabaptist movement were beyond debate, even among those who claimed a commitment to radical reform. Contemporary historians continue to find much complexity in the radical reform movements of the sixteenth century. Who were the Anabaptists? Where, how, and why did they come to prominence? And why did so many people wish to see them dead?

Regardless of how they draw the lines, historians typically begin the Anabaptist story in the early 1520s, in the context of the German Reformation.[1] This reformation, spurred by Martin Luther and his demands for ecclesiastical reform, was itself a messy process, involving religious and political authorities, reform-minded theologians and clerics, and lay people with a jumble of economic, political, and religious concerns. We therefore begin this chapter with a look at the broader Reformation before training our lenses on the more radical elements that birthed the Anabaptist movement.

Europe in 1500: The Social and Religious Context

To describe Europe in 1500 as early modern, one must place the accent squarely on the word *early.*[2] Many modern assumptions and practices, some of which still hold sway in today's postmodern world, had not yet arrived. For instance, a specialized economy, in which workers would parlay discrete skills into income that could then be spent on goods and services, lay well into the future. Indeed, the vast majority of Europeans in 1500 labored alongside household members in work that focused on meeting basic needs of food and shelter.[3] Much like economic life, political life in 1500 was more medieval than modern. The notion of equal rights expressed via impersonal political processes was scarcely imaginable to most citizens. Instead, political life "was a matter of feudal and dynastic superiority," in which particular people, by virtue of heredity or special favor, held specific social roles and political privileges.[4] Village assemblies consisting of the most prominent landowners met regularly to determine local policies, as well as to devise punishments for those who violated these policies. Kings and princes ruled over larger regions, coordinating efforts to ward off the advances of competing interests. Empire building, in which "larger states [would] consume the smaller and digest them in a slow process of internal consolidation," was the order of the day, and it gradually gave shape to what became the map of modern Europe.[5]

Religion also had a distinctly premodern character. Although the rites of the institutional church carried weight, many Europeans "were less worried about saving their souls than about everyday life," which was always tenuous owing to illness, drought, and pestilence.[6] Untreatable diseases such as influenza, dysentery, and smallpox were common, and one-third of infants died before the age of five.[7] In this environment, people understandably participated in folk practices intended to ward off danger. Incantations to protect crops and animals, charms to secure one's fertility, and potions to ward off illness were common. These "ineffective techniques" for protecting life and limb, frequently criticized by church leaders as groundless superstition, nonetheless served an important role in people's lives, for they allayed their anxieties "when effective [techniques were] not available."[8]

Although popular religion had its place, so too did institutional religion, which in western Europe was the preserve of the Roman Catholic Church. Headed by the pope and led by sanctioned bishops and priests, the Catholic Church wished to be the sole provider of spiritual services. These services took various forms, all with the goal of making available to the masses the gracious salvation of Jesus Christ. More specifically, the services took the form of the church's sacraments, including infant baptism, penance, and the Eucharist. According to Catholic theologians, individuals were saved "not in a once-for-all act of redemption, but by a lifelong course through a cycle of sin, absolution, and penance."[9] In other words, human beings, however pious they might be, would inevitably sin and would therefore stand in need of God's forgiveness. Fortunately, this forgiveness was always available from the church. If the sinner would confess his or her sin to the local Catholic priest and demonstrate proper contrition, the priest would grant absolution and then assign works of satisfaction (penance), which might include good deeds, prayers, fasts, or pilgrimages to sacred sites. Although some people were more inclined to sin than others, only at death would a person escape this cycle once and for all.

The penitential cycle constituted the heart of the church's religious system, but other elements of the system offered supporting roles. Infant baptism, typically administered by the priest within days of a child's birth, freed the baptized child from the damnable consequences of original sin. The parish mass, in which the priest repeated the sacrifice of Christ on the cross, made Christ's body—and God's grace—available to those who ate the Communion bread. Finally, at the end of life, many people received last rites from the local priest that prepared their souls for death. By participating in these practices—baptism, Communion, penance, and last rites—late medieval Christians believed they would eventually find eternal rest in heaven, though not without a stopover in purgatory, where sinners' works of satisfaction were completed. Popular views varied on what purgatory entailed, though almost all people believed it included some degree of suffering. The less time spent in purgatory, the better.

Some historians have alleged that this penitential system, which required people to recount their sins to their priests, placed burdens on people that were too heavy to bear. To the contrary, writes Euan Cameron, the Catholic Church went to great lengths to lighten this spiritual load. In particular, the late medieval church devised a system of indulgences through which penitent persons, by almsgiving or purchase, could shorten their time (or their deceased relatives' time) in purgatory. This system was based on the notion that the church itself had surplus merit to offer, merit that had been accumulated by the church's saints. The most saintly person in this regard was Mary, Jesus's virgin mother. According to late medieval theology, this surplus merit could be made available to sinners, including people who had already died, in lieu of their own works of satisfaction. In some cases, the indulgence granted was a plenary indulgence that abolished *all* punishments for one's past sins. Not surprisingly, these indulgences grew popular with the masses. Many people were willing to pay good money to buy such indulgences for themselves or their loved ones suffering in purgatory.

Not everyone was satisfied with the religious status quo, however. On the one hand, some observers found the church unwilling to address its moral and bureaucratic shortcomings. Church leaders who were more concerned with career advancement than spiritual life; priests who violated their vows of poverty and chastity; an institution that required huge amounts of money to sustain itself—all these failures, though sometimes overstated by the church's critics, were widely discussed in late medieval Europe. In addition to citing the church's moral failings, some well-educated people challenged its theological claims. These complaints took various forms and addressed various aspects of Catholic theology, though some critics eventually landed on the most fundamental question possible: was it true, as the church's leadership claimed, that there was no salvation outside the Catholic Church? Or might there be another way to be reconciled to God, one that did not depend on the church's penitential system? Before long, answers to this question set Catholics against reform-minded Protestants throughout western Europe.

The German Reformation

Calls for church reform were hardly novel in 1500. In fact, reform-minded Christians can be found in every era of the church's history. Still, the intensity of these calls grew as the fifteenth century gave way to the sixteenth, owing in part to the rise of Christian humanism. Although lines from the humanist Erasmus to Martin Luther and other early Protestants can be overdrawn, Erasmus's writings took aim at many religious practices that Luther challenged with more profound results. For instance, in his *Handbook of the Christian Soldier,* written in 1501, Erasmus criticized those who went through the motions of religious activity without the proper understanding, and he correspondingly extolled Bible reading as a vital spiritual practice.[10] Later, in his satire *The Praise of Folly* (1509), Erasmus took aim at "forged pardons" and other "charms" that had become the foundation of many people's religious lives. He even took a swipe at Mary, "to whom," he said, "the common people tend to attribute more than to the Son."[11] All of these complaints found later resonance in Luther's writings, though none of them persuaded Erasmus, who continued to venerate Mary and respect the church's teaching authority, to break with the Catholic Church.[12]

Neither did Luther anticipate a break with Rome, though he did hope to effect far-reaching reforms. A Catholic priest and professor of theology at the University of Wittenberg, Luther grew increasingly disenchanted with the church's practice of granting indulgences. In Luther's view, only God could absolve a person's sins, by a pardon that was entirely unconnected to human effort or activity. In 1517 the Wittenberg theologian went public with his opinions, posting his now famous Ninety-Five Theses on the door of the city's cathedral. "Any truly repentant Christian has a right to full remission of penalty and guilt, even without indulgence letters," wrote Luther. Taking aim directly at the Catholic hierarchy, Luther argued that "Christians are to be taught that papal indulgences are useful only if they do not put their trust in them, but are very harmful if they lose their fear of God because of them."[13]

Through these statements we see that Luther believed both in a God who punished sinful people and in the possibility of avoiding that punishment. To Luther, however, escaping God's wrath had nothing to do with performing works of satisfaction and everything to do with demonstrating the proper attitude toward God. In time Luther's views on these matters came to be summarized by the Latin term *sole fide:* only by faith in Jesus Christ's gracious activity, and not by one's works, can one be saved. In his 1519 sermon "Two Kinds of Righteousness," Luther described in detail how sinful human beings can be clothed in the righteousness of Jesus Christ that covers their unrighteousness. "Although we have rather deserved wrath and condemnation," wrote Luther, "everything which Christ has is ours, graciously bestowed on us unworthy men out of God's sheer mercy."[14] Luther later wrote that "this one and firm rock, which we call the doctrine of justification," is "the chief article of the whole Christian doctrine."[15]

Luther's willingness to challenge the church's penitential system met quick condemnation from many quarters, including the pope himself. Rather than backing down, Luther upped the ante by fashioning more thoroughgoing critiques of the church's penitential system. Still, to reduce the German Reformation to Luther's theological audacity would miss an important confluence of factors that reshaped the religious world of early modern Europe. Complaints about a corrupt clergy, concerns about the church's hunger for wealth, the desire of lay people to read the Bible on their own, and objections to the proliferation of relics, pilgrimages, and other ritualized forms of righteousness—all these factors contributed to reforming desires and activities. Some reformers went further, pinpointing social problems in need of remedy, including the inequitable distribution of power and wealth among the various classes. In some circles, these religious and social concerns went hand in hand as a challenge to all traditional authority. In these places, the political struggle against lords and magistrates correlated with the laity's struggle against clerical domination.[16]

One reformer who represented the convergence of religious and social reform was Andreas Bodenstein von Karlstadt, who, along with Luther, taught at the University of Wittenberg. Initially skeptical of Luther's arguments, Karlstadt eventually joined Luther in his attacks on the penitential system and, like his more renowned colleague, found himself excommunicated by the Catholic Church. When Luther went into hiding in 1521, Karlstadt remained in Wittenberg to advance their work, though he soon enacted reforms that Luther could not abide. In a worship service on Christmas Day in 1521, Karlstadt wore secular clothing, refused to use the word "sacrifice" during the mass, pronounced the words "This is my body" in German instead of Latin, and offered communicants both bread and wine, departing from the tradition of restricting the wine to clergy. According to historian Hans-Jürgen Goertz, this "consciously staged departure from the church's most important ritual practice" constituted a blatant challenge to the notion that the clerical hierarchy *was* the church.[17] Not surprisingly, it was a challenge that endeared Karlstadt to the common people.

Karlstadt's Christmas Day actions foreshadowed his trajectory as a reformer more radical than Luther. When Luther returned to Wittenberg, he praised the intent behind Karlstadt's actions, but he warned against moving too quickly, before people's hearts could be prepared for change. Karlstadt shot back: "Every single congregation, whether it be great or small, should see to it that it does what is right and good, without tarrying for anyone."[18] Finding little political support in Wittenberg for his populist agenda, Karlstadt withdrew from academic life, moved to the countryside, and assumed the role of a simple peasant, identifying himself as "Brother Andreas." Before long, however, he was drawn back into religious life, elected as pastor to the congregation in Orlamünde. There he continued to advocate reform, going so far as to abolish infant baptism. He later refuted the notion of the real presence of Christ in the Communion elements, advocating instead a symbolic understanding of the Lord's Supper.

Along with advancing these ecclesiastical reforms, many of which enhanced the status of the laity vis-à-vis the clergy, Karlstadt sought to remedy the economic plight of the lower classes. By the mid-1520s, a loose confederation of German-speaking peasants had decided the only way to remedy an oppressive political-economic system was by armed revolt, an uprising that came to be known as the German Peasants' War. Karlstadt expressed his solidarity with the peasants in both word and practice, visiting a peasant encampment in 1525 to deliver weapons to them. According to historian William W. McNiel, Karlstadt's support of the peasants was both theologically and politically motivated. "Karlstadt was not prone to violence, even in the defense of the gospel," writes McNiel, "but he was willing to excuse its perpetrators if the cause was right and the probable outcome seemed likely to further the Reformation."[19]

Karlstadt later disavowed his support of the revolt, but another reformer, Thomas Müntzer, gave his life for the peasant cause. Like Karlstadt, Müntzer spent time in Wittenberg, where he became familiar with Luther's ideas. Later, as interim priest in the nearby town of Zwickau, Müntzer sought to institute a litany of reforms, but the town council found his efforts too polarizing and dismissed him from his post. Müntzer then traveled to Prague, where he published a fiery letter known as his "Prague Manifesto." In this letter, Müntzer attacked the clergy and "donkey-fart doctors of theology," contrasting them to ordinary Christians who were willing to be led by the Holy Spirit. Casting himself as a Spirit-led prophet who would restore the church to God's intentions, Müntzer warned his readers that his restored church would be used by God to judge the sinful world, separating the elect from the damned.[20]

Müntzer is best known, however, for his willingness to link his religious reform to the power of the peasant class. In his "Sermon to the Princes," delivered in 1524, Müntzer warned civic leaders that they would be overthrown unless they supported his vision. This vision was theological, but it was also social, for once God's order was restored, Müntzer said, people would live in relationships characterized by brotherly love, not hierarchical domination. In this renewed society, he wrote, "the people shall be free and God alone will rule over them."[21] Increasingly convinced that the overthrow of ecclesiastical and political domination demanded violence, he ultimately cast his lot with the peasant forces, serving as their leader-chaplain. "God goes ahead of you," he assured his troops in early 1525. "You shall not be put off by the numbers against you, for it is not your battle but the Lord's."[22] Müntzer's apocalyptic hope that God would intervene on the side of his righteous army went unfulfilled. In 1525, in the last major battle of the Peasants' War, the peasants were routed and their leader was captured and beheaded.

Long before Müntzer lost his head for sedition, Luther had distanced himself from Müntzer's politics. In his "Letter to the Princes of Saxony," penned in 1524, Luther wrote that Müntzer was inspired not by the Holy Spirit but by Satan.[23] A year later, Luther harshly condemned the warring peasants in his tract *Against the Robbing and Murdering Hordes of Peasants*. In that tract Luther charged the peasants with "sins against God and man . . . [that] merited death in body and soul," for not only had the peasants rebelled against God's ordained rulers, but they had also committed blasphemy by claiming their rebellion was divinely inspired. In light of their actions, Luther pledged his political support even to those rulers who did not support his reforms, assuring them that they were doing God's work by crushing the "faithless, perjured, disobedient, rebellious murderers, robbers, and blasphemers."[24]

In this respect, at least, Luther and Müntzer agreed: using the sword to defend God's work in the world was justifiable, perhaps not in every instance, but at least in some. This view was practically universal in early modern Europe, where it accorded with late medieval conceptions of state-sponsored religion. Nearly all Christian leaders at that time, including the Protestant reformers, believed that the gospel must be supported by Christian rulers who bore the sword to punish heretics and infidels. To forgo that support, they thought, would be both socially irresponsible and theologically suicidal. In Switzerland, however, a band of radical reformers was emerging at this very time that would challenge these reigning assumptions about the gospel, the sword, and the state.

Anabaptism: Zurich and Beyond

Even as Luther was advancing his reforms in Germany, Ulrich Zwingli was pressing for change in Switzerland. Zwingli, who had been ordained a Catholic priest in 1506, assumed the preaching post at a leading Zurich church in 1518. Influenced by the writings of Erasmus and perhaps by Luther as well, Zwingli came to believe that the scriptures could be accessible to all, and he therefore encouraged the formation of lay Bible study groups, some of which included craftsmen and peasants. Over time, Zwingli departed from Catholic teaching and practice in various ways, rejecting the efficacy of indulgences, condemning the veneration of saints, and raising questions about the church's power of excommunication. In 1522 he publicly transgressed the church's Lenten fast, and he petitioned his bishop to abolish the requirement of clerical celibacy, a requirement he had already violated by secretly marrying.[25]

Zwingli's actions drew censure from the Catholic Church, and before long the Zurich city council felt constrained to respond. In 1523 the council organized two disputations between Zwingli and his Catholic adversaries, the second of which focused on the use of sacred images (which Zwingli opposed) and the meaning of the Lord's Supper (Zwingli advocated a symbolic understanding of the meal). Zwingli emerged victorious in both debates—that is, the city council deemed his views to be biblically sound—but because of its concerns about social unrest, it cautioned him against introducing ecclesial reforms too quickly. Concluding that slow-paced change was better than none at all, and realizing that the support of the council was fundamental to his success, Zwingli opted for a go-slow approach.

Zwingli's pragmatism alienated some of his supporters, many of whom later became the first Anabaptists. Led by Conrad Grebel, the young adult son of a Zurich city councilman and a brother-in-law to the humanist reformer Vadian, Zwingli's followers accused their reform-minded mentor of obeying human authorities instead of God.[26] By early 1524 some of these radicals had added infant baptism to their list of grievances, and Zurich's city council had begun to hear reports of people refusing to baptize their newborns. When private conversations between advocates and opponents of infant baptism failed to resolve the conflict, one of the radicals, Felix Mantz, forwarded a petition to the city council. In his petition Mantz contended that true baptism must be restricted to those who "take on a new life, lay aside sins, are buried with Christ, and rise with him from baptism in newness of life."[27] The council was not convinced, however, and in January 1525, it responded to Mantz's petition by threatening to banish from Zurich all those who failed to baptize their infants. The council also instructed Grebel and Mantz to keep silent on the issue.[28]

Grebel and Mantz were not deterred. On January 21, 1525, they and a few of their like-minded friends baptized one another with what an early Anabaptist chronicler called "true Christian baptism."[29] This, according to historian C. Arnold Snyder, constituted the "earliest documented baptism of adults in the sixteenth century."[30] Literally speaking, the Anabaptist movement had begun.

Centuries later, Mennonite historians would point to these events to establish Anabaptist origins and, more importantly, to serve as a blueprint by which to guide twentieth-century Mennonite life. In addition to highlighting believers' baptism, historians in the Bender School (named for Harold S. Bender, a mid-twentieth-century Mennonite historian and church leader) underscored two other features they saw in the radicals' reform agenda. First, they pointed to the radicals' view of the church as a voluntary community. The practice of infant baptism assumed that all members of society were church members by virtue of their birth in a particular place and time period. To the contrary, the radicals said, joining the church was a voluntary decision that could be made only according to an individual's conscience. Since not every person was willing to make that choice, only those who committed themselves to Christian discipleship should be considered Christians, and only committed Christians should be entitled to church membership.[31]

Along with the voluntary church, the Bender School underscored the early Anabaptists' rejection of the sword. The early Anabaptists were nonresistant, wrote Bender, for they rejected "all warfare, strife, and violence, and . . . the taking of human life." In fact, he said, this principle "was thoroughly believed and resolutely practiced by all the original

Anabaptist Brethren and their descendants throughout Europe from the beginning until the [nineteenth] century."[32] These early Anabaptists did not condemn the use of the sword by civic authorities—law and order needed to be maintained, they said—but they believed that Christians should not assume sword-bearing roles. Moreover, they rejected the notion that the church should look to the state to defend its cause. In that respect, said Bender, early Anabaptists not only rejected the sword as an unchristian instrument, but they also rejected the centuries-old assumption that the gospel was best served by linking it to the state.

The Bender School got much of early Anabaptism right, but historians have since challenged its views as too simplistic. One challenge points to evidence that Bender and others ignored or downplayed in their accounts of Anabaptist origins. For instance, at least some of the earliest Anabaptists did not envision a church free from political involvements but in fact looked for governmental or rebel support to advance their goals. Correspondingly, some early Anabaptists were not principled pacifists. The most prominent example in this regard was Balthasar Hubmaier, an Anabaptist leader who, during his time as pastor of an Anabaptist congregation in Waldshut, supported armed resistance against the Austrian government.[33] A second challenge to the Bender school came from the "polygenesis" historians of the 1970s. According to their critique, Bender had focused too narrowly on the events in and around Zurich and had thus ignored the complex realities of a geographically dispersed Anabaptism. They noted that, in addition to the circle of Anabaptists in and around Zurich, two other influential circles emerged quite independently around the same time, one in southern Germany (where Hans Hut, a former partisan of the Peasants' War, emerged as a prominent leader) and another in northern Germany and Holland. Over time, these different Anabaptisms grew, merged, and migrated, producing a shifting mélange of European Anabaptist expressions, some of which departed theologically from the normative Anabaptist vision that Bender saw in early Anabaptism.[34]

This intramural complexity enabled the sixteenth-century critics of Anabaptism to caricature the movement in ways that best served their purposes. Ulrich Zwingli's successor, Heinrich Bullinger, published two lengthy treatises condemning Anabaptism, the first of which pegged Thomas Müntzer as the Anabaptists' founding patriarch, this despite the fact that Müntzer himself never underwent rebaptism. By the time Bullinger published his second diatribe in 1560, he could point to the northern German city of Münster as evidence of the Anabaptists' violent tendencies. In 1534–35, Anabaptists in and around Münster had become captivated by the apocalyptic visions of German Anabaptist Melchior Hoffman, who preached that God would pave the way for Christ's return by destroying the ungodly.[35] Hoffman's message was one that many Dutch and northern German Anabaptists embraced in the early 1530s, but in Münster Anabaptist leader Jan Matthijs modified Hoffman's message to say that Christians could themselves hasten the return of Christ by annihilating the wicked. When Matthijs declared Münster the New Jerusalem and forced its unconverted citizens to leave, the local Catholic bishop rallied an army to retake the city. In the end, Matthijs and many other Anabaptists died in a lengthy siege. For centuries thereafter, the excesses of Münster, which included not only violence but polygamy, were frequently used by the Anabaptists' detractors to malign the movement.[36]

To define the early Anabaptist movement as a product of Thomas Müntzer's apocalypticism, or to cast the Münster debacle as Anabaptism's logical conclusion, is even less in line with the historical record than is Bender's account. Many, and perhaps most, early Anabaptists were nonresistant Christians who sought to create a pure church unsullied by alliances with political powers. Even if these were not majority opinions from the beginning, they quickly emerged as such and were thus the views that subsequent generations of Anabaptists ultimately embraced.[37] In that sense, the earliest Anabaptists did pose a significant—and lasting—challenge to the assumption that the church and the state must work together to defend the gospel.

The point of our consideration, however, is not to identify the essence of early Anabaptism. Rather, it is to establish the complexity of a group of people who shared a commitment to adult baptism, a complexity that forced all the subsequent chroniclers of Anabaptism to make decisions about the story they would tell. Thieleman van Braght was one of those later chroniclers, and when he decided in the mid-seventeenth century to publish a new Anabaptist martyrology, he encountered two questions he could not ignore: what did it mean to be an Anabaptist, and what did it mean to be a martyr? We will explore van Braght's answers to these questions in chapter 3. First, however, we will consider what contemporary historians tell us about the scope of Anabaptist martyrdom in the sixteenth and early seventeenth centuries and the reasons why killing Anabaptists made perfect sense to those who killed them.

Persecution, Martyrdom, and Mennonites

For many people living in twenty-first-century North America, the notion of church and government authorities working hand in hand to exterminate a competing religion seems both uncivilized and unnecessary. Even those who claim to possess the unblemished truth and who truly fear the consequences of other people's flawed theology typically affirm the idea of religious toleration. Whether that commitment is principled or pragmatic, most North Americans find the historical record of Christians killing Christians regrettable and the historical actors foolhardy.

In contrast, many late medieval church and civic leaders found the notion of religious toleration both foolhardy and contemptible. Their views rested in part on their desire to foster theological rectitude, a desire that was linked to their belief in God's coming judgment. In short, they believed that erroneous religious beliefs would result in the damnation of those who held them. Moreover, these leaders knew that many heretics worked overtime to convey their views, which meant that other peoples' eternal destinies lay in the balance. The longer a heretic's opinions were abided, the more likely it would be that the heretic would lead others straightaway to hell. Medieval leaders embraced the responsibility of safeguarding their subjects from this spiritual threat. For them, going soft on heretics was not a sign of gracious leadership but was rather a "misplaced mercy" that put other peoples' souls at risk.[38]

In addition to fearing the eternal consequences of heretical teaching, late medieval leaders also feared the temporal consequences of religious division. Those who advocated novel theologies were often accused of sedition, whether or not they mounted a direct challenge to the political order. The Edict of Paris (1543) is instructive in this regard, for it described France's Protestant heretics as "disturbers of the peace and tranquility of our republic and subjects, and secret conspirators against the prosperity of our state."[39] Issued during the reign of Francis I, this edict was one of many statements fashioned by France's Catholic leadership to condemn Calvinists bent on reform. But it wasn't just Catholic authorities who bemoaned the effects of religious diversity. Protestants also argued that religious diversity in a given region would result in social and political unrest.

Charges of sedition, applied to heretics in general, fell most heavily on Anabaptists, for at least four reasons. First, some Anabaptists *were* violent revolutionaries, as events at Münster and a few other locales revealed.[40] Second, Anabaptists frequently sought to enact their ecclesiastical reforms on their own terms, often proceeding in ways or at speeds that rebuffed the desires of governing officials. Third, Anabaptists were the only sixteenth-century reformers who rejected infant baptism in favor of adult baptism. More than simply a theological innovation, their renunciation of infant baptism struck at the very heart of the social order, for it "undermined the claim to universal inclusiveness that was the foundation of both ecclesiastical and secular order." In other words, "the volunteerism of adult baptism seemed to make participation in the Christian polity a choice rather than a responsibility."[41] Fourth, some Anabaptists provided evidence that they were indeed opting out of the political order, refusing to serve in government offices, bear the sword, or swear oaths in court.[42] In all these ways, the Anabaptists gave their sixteenth-century opponents compelling reasons to brand them as politically dangerous revolutionaries.

Condemned by Protestants and Catholics alike, Anabaptists suffered a level of judicial persecution that outpaced the persecution of all other religious groups in sixteenth-century Europe.[43] This persecution took many forms—from fines and confiscation of property to imprisonment, torture, and execution—and in some regions of Europe lasted more than a century. Meted out by civic authorities with the religious leaders' blessing, persecution sought to silence Anabaptist leaders and intimidate commoners who might consider embracing their cause. This goal was never fully achieved, and some Anabaptists went on to claim that the authorities' brutality actually advanced the movement by generating sympathy for the Anabaptist point of view. No doubt this occurred in some instances, but it is nonetheless true that the Anabaptist movement was severely challenged by those who sought to eradicate it. Most of the movement's early leaders, including Conrad Grebel, Felix Mantz, and others who participated in the first rebaptisms in 1525 suffered persecution, and many of them lost their lives before 1530. Other Anabaptists, fearing the same fate, did exactly what the authorities wanted them to do: they renounced their heretical views and returned to the bosom of the state-sponsored church.[44]

All told, about twenty-five hundred Anabaptists lost their lives in the sixteenth and early seventeenth centuries, mostly in Switzerland and the Netherlands, but also in other regions.[45] Compared to the scope of twentieth-century genocides, the number of sixteenth-century Anabaptist martyrs was small. By sixteenth-century standards, however, it was large, exceeding the combined numbers of Catholic martyrs executed in Protestant realms and Lutheran or Calvinist martyrs executed in Catholic realms.[46] The persecution of Anabaptists was particularly intense in the movement's early years. One historian has estimated that more than half of the eight-hundred-plus Anabaptists executed in Switzerland, southern and central Germany, Austria, Bohemia, and Moravia were killed in the movement's first five years, a number that "represents about 10 percent of all the Christians judicially executed for heterodoxy or religious treason over the entire sixteenth and seventeenth centuries."[47] Although the persecution of Anabaptists waned in some areas as the sixteenth century ran its course, the fact remains that Anabaptists suffered an outsized share of persecution in Europe's post-Reformation century.

The intensity of persecution suffered by Anabaptists shaped the movement's identity and its historical trajectory. Simply put, Anabaptists assumed a "martyrological mentality" to an extent that other Reformation movements did not.[48] For Anabaptists, following Jesus meant embracing the prospect of pain and suffering. This view appeared even before the first Anabaptist martyrdom took place in 1525. In a letter to Thomas Müntzer in 1524, Conrad Grebel wrote, "True believers are sheep among wolves, sheep for the slaughter," people who will inevitably face "anguish and tribulation, persecution, suffering, and death."[49] Whether or not Grebel foresaw the intense persecution to come, his words foreshadowed an attitude that many Anabaptists soon assumed. Before long, other Anabaptists were speaking in similar cadences, sometimes tying their experiences to the crucifixion of Jesus Christ. Arrested by Zurich authorities in 1525, George Blaurock testified that, like Jesus the Good Shepherd, he offered his "body and life and soul" for his sheep. He therefore expected his blood to be "pressed from [his] flesh like Christ on the cross."[50] Blaurock's expectation eventually came to pass. Although he avoided execution in Zurich, he was arrested in Austria for preaching the Anabaptist heresy to anyone who would listen. He was burned at the stake in 1529.

Even before Blaurock lost his life, Swiss Anabaptists had formalized their view of the Christian's place in the world. In 1527 Anabaptist leaders from various regions gathered in Schleitheim in hopes of resolving some theologically divisive issues. The result was the seven-article Schleitheim Confession, which summarized Anabaptist positions on baptism, church discipline, church leadership, the sword, and the Lord's Supper. Significantly, one entire article addressed the need for Christians to separate themselves from "the wickedness which the devil has planted in the world." Positing a sharply dualistic view of the world ("there is nothing else in the world and all creation than good or evil"), the article asserted that none of these oppositional elements could "have part with the other." The article then proceeded to identify a host of worldly enticements—idolatry, taverns, weapons of violence, and so on—and concluded that Christians should "have no part with such." To do so would reveal an evil heart uncommitted to God.[51]

Persecution of the faithful is not an explicit theme in the Schleitheim Confession, but its influence can be divined on nearly every page. Shaped by their experiences of persecution, the confession's writers saw evidence of the battle between good and evil everywhere they looked, and they warned the confession's readers that every person needed to decide which kingdom to serve. The perils were great, they said, for "the worldly are armed with steel and iron," but the reward for faithfulness was even greater: "The Lord will be your God, and you will be His sons and daughters."[52] This assurance sustained the gathering's chief organizer, Michael Sattler, who was arrested and executed a few months after the assembly's conclusion. A song later attributed to Sattler outlined the tribulations and the rewards of Christian faithfulness:

> When you are slandered and abused now,
> persecuted and beaten for [Christ's] sake,
> be joyful, for see, your reward
> is prepared for you on heaven's throne.[53]

The martyrological mentality that took hold in Swiss Anabaptism in the late 1520s soon came to characterize Anabaptism in other regions. Beginning in 1527, Anabaptists in Moravia and Austria joined the growing list of martyrs, leading some Anabaptists to make connections between their "baptism in water" and "baptism by blood."[54] When Sicke Freerks was executed in 1531, martyrdom likewise became part of the Anabaptist experience in the Netherlands. This fate became much more commonplace in the years following the siege of Münster in 1535.[55]

In the aftermath of Münster, as nonviolent Anabaptists sought to pick up the pieces of a shattered movement, they faced the dual challenges of distancing themselves from Münster's legacy and avoiding the executioner's sword. No Dutch Anabaptist was more important in this process than Menno Simons.[56] Ordained a priest in 1524, Menno soon grew skeptical of the Catholic Church's sacramental system, in particular the doctrine of transubstantiation. By 1531 he had also grown skeptical of infant baptism, ultimately deciding that adult baptism was the only true baptism. Even then Menno did not leave his priestly post, however. Not until 1536 did he break with the Catholic Church and join the Anabaptist movement, a movement that had recently been sullied by the sordid events in Münster. Menno was undeterred by this challenge, and over the next ten years he became the most influential leader in the Dutch Anabaptist movement, spreading the Anabaptist gospel through his preaching and writing, all the while opposing Anabaptist leaders with more apocalyptic tendencies. By 1545 at least some Dutch Anabaptists were being referred to as *Mennists,* a precursor to the more lasting label *Mennonites.*[57]

When Menno died in 1561, he had been an Anabaptist for nearly twenty-five years. Unlike many other early Anabaptist leaders, Menno did not die a martyr's death, but he did spend much of his time underground or on the run. This experience informed his understanding of the Christian life, which he expressed in his most important theological work, *Foundation of Christian Doctrine.* "If the Head [Jesus] had to suffer such torture, anguish, misery, and pain," observed Menno, "how shall His servants, children, and members expect peace and freedom as to their flesh?"[58] Citing Paul's warning to Timothy, Menno reminded his readers that all who "live godly in Christ Jesus . . . must suffer persecution."[59] A few years later, in a tract on Christ's incarnation, Menno wrote that true believers can expect nothing from worldly rulers "but the stake, water, fire, wheel, and sword." These rulers demonstrate their opposition to God's kingdom, he said, for they do nothing but "persecute, banish, burn, murder, and destroy all those who teach and uphold the glory, praise, honor, will, and commandments of the Lord."[60]

All told, the persecution of early Anabaptists marked the nascent movement—in Switzerland, Austria, Moravia, the Netherlands, and elsewhere—with a unique martyrological identity that set it apart from other Christian traditions in early modern Europe. To be sure, other Christians suffered persecution in the sixteenth century when they advocated views that incensed the ruling authorities. Moreover, not every Anabaptist convert suffered persecution. Even early on, some Anabaptists found out-of-the-way places to live, regions overseen by rulers who tolerated their heterodox views. Still, as historian Brad Gregory has noted, whereas for other Christians martyrdom was sporadic, for Anabaptists it was "a part of life—and confirmation of the very meaning of being Christian."[61] Before long, the witness of these Anabaptist martyrs was memorialized by their surviving brothers and sisters in songs, stories, and books.

CHAPTER 2

Memorializing Martyrdom
before *The Bloody Theater*

The theme of martyrdom tracks a long history in Christian memory-making. Sixteenth-century Anabaptists could easily recount
the miseries inflicted upon Old and New Testament heroes, and
they could also name Christians who had suffered in the centuries that
followed. These stories, from the Bible and from subsequent church history, provided comfort to Anabaptists in an age when, in their view,
most self-identified Christians were theologically misguided, if not allied with Satan. At the same time, this pre-Reformation cloud of witnesses forced Anabaptists to answer questions about Anabaptism's place
in the larger Christian story.

Those questions eventually fell to Thieleman van Braght, who in
the mid-seventeenth century found himself assuming a role that other
Christians, including other Anabaptists, had filled before him: martyrologist. Van Braght's efforts in this regard were extraordinary, but they
were not sui generis. He lived in an age of prolific martyrological writing, with Catholics and Protestants alike assembling detailed catalogs
of heroes and antiheroes.[1] Historian, memory shaper, prosecuting at-
torney, and preacher—the martyrologist was all of these things at once,
and like other martyrologists who preceded him, van Braght sought to
fashion history in a way that would both defend and advance his movement's cause. In doing so he drew on the work of other martyrologists,
some Anabaptist, some not. In the next chapter, we will see how van
Braght reshaped earlier texts in order to write his own account of Chris-

tian martyrdom. The current chapter looks at these preexisting sources, which constituted the textual soil from which *The Bloody Theater* would spring, on their own terms.

Martyrdom in the Christian Scriptures

No book was more important to the early Anabaptists than the Bible: the Old Testament, the New Testament, and the Apocrypha.[2] The Anabaptists followed Luther's lead in giving primacy to the Bible over church tradition, though the Anabaptists proved more exacting than other Protestants in rejecting church tradition on biblical grounds. Indeed, the distinguishing practice of the Anabaptist movement, adult baptism, was based largely on Anabaptists' view that the Bible offered no support for infant baptism and a wealth of support for believers' baptism.[3] The earliest Anabaptists did not formulate an explicit doctrine of scripture, but their commitment to biblical authority was never far from the surface.[4] The testimonies of Anabaptist martyrs, given in courts and execution sites, reveal that even ordinary Anabaptists knew the Bible well. In its pages they found instructions for how to live. They also found confirmation that godly people endangered their bodies when they chose the path of faithfulness.

The Old Testament offered the early Anabaptists some of their most inspiring examples of faithful suffering. Moses, appointed by God to free the Hebrews from Egyptian slavery, was harried by Pharaoh and threatened with death. Prophets such as Elijah and Jeremiah faced similar perils, though in their cases the harassment came from authorities closer to home. The willingness to suffer for one's faith was perhaps best exemplified in the Old Testament by the prophet Daniel, who was thrown into the lions' den for praying to God, and by Shadrach, Meshach, and Abednego, who were placed in a fiery furnace for refusing to worship Nebuchadnezzar's image. Some of these stories concluded happily. Daniel and his three friends all escaped death, protected by a God more powerful than any earthly authority. In other cases, however, the faithful found their lives cut short. Jesus later said that the blood of God's messengers was shed throughout the Hebrew scripture, "from the blood of righteous Abel to the blood of Zechariah son of Barachiah."[5]

The Apocrypha likewise included stories of righteous suffering that the early Anabaptists knew well and recounted to one another often.[6] Perhaps the most important story in this regard was that of an unnamed mother and her seven sons who were ordered by the king to eat pork in violation of Jewish law. Despite being tortured, they refused the king's directive, whereupon the king ordered his minions to kill the sons one by one as their mother looked on. The Maccabean narrator concluded that the mother "was especially admirable and worthy of honorable memory," for "although she saw her seven sons perish within a single day, she bore it with good courage because of her hope in the Lord."[7] Less tragic but nonetheless instructive to the Anabaptists was the story of Susanna, a married woman who spurned the sexual advances of two community elders. Hoping to coerce the beautiful young woman into having sex with them, the elders threatened to accuse her of extramarital relations with another man. Knowing full well that she would die if the elders succeeded in their plot, Susanna opted to remain chaste, a faithful decision that eventually came to light—but only in the nick of time, after she was condemned to death and was being led off to her execution.[8]

Of course, it was Jesus himself who provided the Anabaptists with their most vital example of faithful suffering.[9] Here was a person full of truth who nonetheless faced opposition everywhere he turned. Early in Jesus's ministry, the opposition was mostly theological, as he sparred with Jewish religious authorities. Later, however, the opposition turned political, and at Pilate's behest Jesus was executed for sedition. According to some New Testament writers, Jesus's suffering was more than just an undeserved execution; it was absolutely necessary for the redemption of the world.[10] Still, in spite of its uniqueness, Jesus's suffering was deemed exemplary for those who wished to share in his reward. His followers are "joint heirs with Christ," wrote Paul, "if, in fact, we suffer with [Jesus] so that we may also be glorified with him."[11] "We are afflicted in every way," Paul observed in another letter, "carrying in the body the death of Jesus, so that the life of Jesus may also be made visible in our bodies."[12]

Paul's writings on this topic were particularly apt in light of his own experience. According to Acts 8, Paul stood watch over the stoning of Stephen, the first Christian martyr. His presence at this event represented a larger pattern: a fanatical Jew, Paul was "ravaging the church" by entering Christians' homes, arresting converts, and committing them to prison.[13] Before long, however, this enemy of the church underwent a dramatic conversion and committed himself to Christ. Formerly the hunter, Paul became the hunted, and he soon found his life in danger. The New Testament does not describe Paul's death, but according to Christian tradition he was beheaded during the reign of Nero. In any case, Paul's writings carry a clear martyrological theme, one that the early Anabaptists found compelling. In fact, Paul's warning to the young Timothy that "all who want to live a godly life in Christ Jesus will be persecuted" appears no less than twenty-five times in accounts that made their way into Thieleman van Braght's *Bloody Theater*.[14]

Anabaptists fixed upon martyrological themes in other New Testament books as well, most notably Hebrews and Revelation. Hebrews provides a litany of Old Testament figures who lived by faith, concluding with reference to the unnamed multitudes who were flogged, imprisoned, stoned to death, sawn in half, and otherwise persecuted. These people, "of whom the world was not worthy," remained steadfast in their faith "in order to obtain a better resurrection."[15] This blessed future takes center stage in the book of Revelation, when the visionary writer sees in heaven "a great multitude" offering praises to God. When the writer asks a bystander who the worshippers are, he learns that they are faithful Christians who have emerged from the "great ordeal."[16]

To call the Bible a martyrology is an overstatement, although one that van Braght would make in his preface to *The Bloody Theater*.[17] Comprising many kinds of literature and containing many different messages, the Bible was used by early Anabaptists for a myriad of purposes. Still, the Bible's martyrological messages struck a chord with persecuted Anabaptists, who frequently compared their lives to the experiences of their biblical heroes. Anabaptist martyrologists, not least van Braght, developed this theme more fully, using it to place the Anabaptist martyrs firmly on the side of God.

Martyrdom in Christian History

The persecution experienced by New Testament Christians continued in various forms in the Roman Empire until the early fourth century. Persecution was sporadic and in most cases localized, but when it came, it was often brutal. Not until 313 CE, when the co-emperors Constantine and Licinius issued their Edict of Milan, did Christians enjoy official governmental toleration throughout the empire. Even then, however, intolerance continued, though it was now dressed in Christian attire: heterodox Christians who departed from the church's officially sanctioned theology bore the authorities' wrath. In both of these environments, when Christians suffered at the hands of pagan rulers and when they suffered at the hands of other Christians, theologians and memorialists weighed in on the meaning of their suffering.[18]

For their part, Anabaptist memorialists had to discern the relationship between their own martyrs and pre-Reformation Christian martyrs and, correspondingly, the relationship between their movement and the various ecclesial expressions that predated theirs. Early Anabaptists did not show much interest in undertaking that task. As Geoffrey Dipple has written, only in the aftermath of intense persecution could the Anabaptists "afford the luxury of elaborate historical reflection."[19] Until then, Anabaptist memorialists were mostly content to connect Anabaptist history, and the stories of their martyrs, to people and events they encountered in the Bible. As time passed, however, and especially in places where persecution waned, Anabaptist martyrologists began to take notice of others who had suffered and died for their faith. In time, some of these pre-Reformation martyrs found their way into Anabaptist martyrologies.

For sixteenth-century Anabaptists undergoing persecution, and for the seventeenth-century martyrologists who wrote about them, the best source for learning about early Christian martyrdom was Eusebius of Caesarea. In his ten-chapter *Ecclesiastical History,* written in the late third and early fourth centuries, Eusebius chronicled the challenges and triumphs of the early church, beginning with Jesus's life and concluding with Constantine's unification of the empire in 324 CE.[20] Like other historians of his time, Eusebius structured his narrative around the Roman emperors' reigns, but his primary characters were Christians who sustained the church during perilous times. Of the eight objectives Eusebius identifies at the outset of his book, two focus explicitly on martyrdom: to record "the hostilities waged by heathen against the divine Word and the heroism of those who fought to defend it," and to record "the martyrdoms of our own time and the gracious deliverance provided by our Savior and Lord."[21] In subsequent chapters, Eusebius runs through a host of Christian martyrs from the time of Christ to the reign of Diocletian

(284–305 CE): Stephen; the apostles Peter, John, and Paul; Justin Martyr; Polycarp—the list goes on and on.

Centuries later, Anabaptist martyrologists would mine Eusebius's *History* for source material and historical themes.[22] Complicating their efforts was the fact that Eusebius's work was much more than a martyrology: it was also an account of Christian triumph, trumpeting the church's "deliverance" by the emperor Constantine.[23] In his concluding chapter, Eusebius describes Constantine's defeat of his former ally Licinius, who had "determined to make war on God."[24] Fortunately, wrote Eusebius, Constantine took God's side, and with Jesus as his ally, he easily dispatched Licinius's armies. Heretofore divided between east and west, the Roman Empire was now unified. More importantly, it now enjoyed the fruits of Constantine's beneficent rule. In all places, Eusebius concludes, "the victorious emperor published human ordinances and laws that reflected liberality and true piety."[25]

Later historians have rightly criticized Eusebius's assessment of Constantine's reign, including his rose-colored view of the emperor's machinations. Still, Constantine's reign brought about a decisive transformation in the church's development, for he quickly moved beyond toleration to Christian patronage. In his view, the empire was best served by linking its fortunes to Christianity in a tit-for-tat relationship: in exchange for bolstering the power and prestige of the church's leaders, Constantine looked to the church to offer his empire its theological backing. On the surface, at least, the church benefited from this patronage; before long, "vast churches, glittering with gold and mosaics, were to be found in the major cities of the empire."[26] Of course, for the church to be the politically unifying force the emperors wanted it to be, church divisions needed to be overcome. Emperors knew that the church was ill prepared to achieve unity on its own, for it had no effective mechanism to bring about consensus on nagging ecclesiastical issues. Emperors, in contrast, could employ the sword to enforce unity. They could threaten heretics and other religious troublemakers with a variety of punishments, lest these infidels fuel the disunity that threatened both church and empire. Moreover, emperors could insert themselves into the church's theological disputes, as Constantine did at the Council of Nicaea in 325 CE.[27] The emperors' involvements in these matters did not bring perfect unity to the church, but they did bring a greater unity than the church could have achieved on its own.

The task of justifying Christian complicity in this messy, sometimes violent work fell to Augustine of Hippo, who provided the church's most thoroughgoing rationale for persecuting so-called heretics. A North African bishop, Augustine developed this rationale in the fifth century as he sparred with the Donatists, who comprised the majority of North African Christians. In Augustine's view, the Donatists held an overly rigorous view of the church, and they threatened the church's unity by their unwillingness to acknowledge the validity of other bishops' baptisms.[28] In the course of this dispute, Augustine argued that the authorities had the responsibility to deal harshly with those who spouted dangerous ideas. "What then is the function of brotherly love?" he asked. "Does it, because it fears the short-lived fires of the furnace for a few, therefore abandon all to the eternal fires of hell?"[29] This rationale for persecuting the Donatists—that it is better to persecute a few than to allow those few to lead others to hell—for centuries informed church and civic leaders' thinking on how to deal with heretics.

This shift from the persecuted church to the persecuting church complicated the work of martyrology, or at least made it more contested. As early as the second century, church leaders debated the question of who could be counted as true Christian martyrs. What about professing Christians who died for *spurious* beliefs? Building on the work of others, Augustine offered a dictum in answer to this question: "Not the punishment, but the cause, makes a martyr."[30] In other words, those who identify themselves as Christians, but who espouse false views for which they die, cannot be counted as true martyrs. Of course, Augustine's dictum assumed assent to a particular set of doctrines as true and another set of doctrines as false, an assumption that ran headlong into the reality of a factious church. Still, even as it begged important questions about the possibility of discerning truth, Augustine's dictum proved useful to subsequent martyrologists, including van Braght, enabling them to draw lines that needed to be drawn when memorializing martyrs.

Augustine's dictum also enabled the church in power to write narratives that cast some who died on account of their faith not as noble martyrs, but rather as reprobates getting their due. This was the case, for instance, with the Catholic-sponsored *Ecclesiastical Annales,* which appeared in stages between 1588 and 1607. Written by the Italian priest Caesar Baronius, *Ecclesiastical Annales* sought to contradict the *Magdeburg Centuries,* a Lutheran-written history that had appeared a few decades earlier. The Lutheran writers, echoing their namesake, argued that Catholic leadership had fallen prey to the Antichrist, who led it away from the beliefs of the early church. In response, Baronius's *Annales* sought to show how the Catholic Church had successfully preserved the gospel in the face of attacks by heretical influences. In Baronius's recounting, the Catholic Church was a heroic protector of the truth, meting out God's wrath upon those who led the masses astray.[31]

Neither Eusebius nor Baronius, Catholic historians separated by twelve hundred years, would have been sympathetic to the Anabaptists' cause. Similarly, Anabaptist martyrologists would have found much to dispute in the two men's histories, including their respective catalogs of heroes and heretics. Nonetheless, when seventeenth-century Anabaptist martyrologists assembled their works, they drew upon the ecclesiastical sources that were available to them, including Eusebius and Baronius, using what they found in an effort to sketch a history of faithful Christianity that stretched back to biblical times. Furthermore, in the manner of Augustine, they sought to devise criteria for distinguishing between true and false martyrs. For his part, Thieleman van Braght, a relative latecomer to the work of Anabaptist memory-making, stood on the shoulders of Anabaptist martyrologists who came before him, martyrologists who provided much of the material that eventually constituted his book.

Martyr Hymns, Pamphlets, and German-Language Collections

Even before particular Anabaptist martyrs were memorialized in song and prose, suffering for the faith constituted a key theme in Anabaptist hymnody. Some of the earliest hymns were composed by or attributed to Anabaptists who anticipated their own deaths, including Anabaptist leaders such as Felix Mantz, George Blaurock, and Michael Sattler, all of whom died before 1530. One of Blaurock's hymns, written before he was burned at the stake in 1529, acknowledges that the

> Antichrist asserts himself with sharpness
> Over those who fear God,

but such a fate is made tolerable by the knowledge that Jesus suffered as well:

As He Himself did suffer
While hanging on the cross
Thus it fares with the righteous presently
They suffer great violence.[32]

A hymn attributed to Michael Sattler fixes on the same theme, with words of admonition coming straight from Jesus's mouth:

The world will lie in wait for you
And bring you much mockery and dishonor,

says Jesus.

Yet fear not such a man
Who can kill only the body
But far more fear the faithful God
Whose it is to condemn both.[33]

The largest collection of death-anticipating hymns emerged from a prison in Passau in the late 1530s. In 1535 a group of Moravian Anabaptists was captured on its way to Germany and imprisoned in a castle near Passau. In captivity for two years, the Passau prisoners composed fifty-three songs to provide one another with spiritual encouragement. Their hymns spoke of loneliness, torture, and imminent death, costs of discipleship that the prisoners knew well.[34] Some of the Passau prisoners, unhinged by torture and the prospect of lifelong imprisonment, eventually recanted their convictions. In the meantime, the group produced a corpus of song that promised eternal rewards for those who remained steadfast:

Come here, all you Christians
who are dedicated to God,
Let us with a rich shout
be witnesses of the Lord
and of his word with our blood,
This will come to good for us
so that we obtain the crown.[35]

As the number of Anabaptist martyrs increased, the movement's song repertoire grew to include actual martyr ballads, that is, narrative accounts that detailed the arrests, interrogations, and deaths of particular Anabaptists.[36] Composed in Switzerland, Moravia, the Netherlands, and elsewhere, these ballads sometimes ran more than forty stanzas in length; but despite their length, they were frequently memorized and taught to others. It is likely that some of these memorized martyr hymns never reached the printed page and were essentially lost to history. In dozens of cases, however, the words were recorded, collected for posterity's sake, and later published in hymnals or songbooks.

The lengthy hymn detailing the arrest and death of a young Dutch woman is illustrative in this regard. From it singers learn that Elisabeth, a "maid of tender limbs," was taken captive in the city of Leeuwarden. She was imprisoned and "pressed . . . from all sides" to swear an oath regarding her marital status. Following the Anabaptists' injunction against oath-swearing, Elisabeth responded that she was willing only to offer her "yea" and her "nay." Elisabeth's Catholic interrogators proceeded to press her on other issues, including the mass, infant baptism, and priestly absolution. In all these cases, Elisabeth offered biblically informed responses summarizing the Anabaptists' views. In the end, the stubborn Elisabeth was banished to the torture chamber, where her fingers were clamped until "blood spurted out from her nails." Urged to recant her views, she instead prayed for God's help to withstand the pain. A few months later, she was executed by drowning.[37]

Ballads like this one served at least three functions in early Anabaptism. Along with commemorating a particular person, ballads offered an admonition to other Anabaptists to remain steadfast in every circumstance. "Let us make note of Elisabeth's manly courage," enjoins the ballad's final stanza, and

> how she, in need, bore pain and sorrow
> And called upon the Lord so good.[38]

Martyr ballads also gave those who sang them instructions on how to respond to inquisitors' questions, should they find themselves in similar circumstances. Could a priest forgive a person's sins? ask Elisabeth's inquisitors. Elisabeth responds in the negative, for "Christ is the only priest exalted," and "He alone purifies us of our base sins."[39] In an age when less than 10 percent of the European population was literate, and the transmission of doctrine was mostly an oral/aural process, these rhyming, rhythmic ballads functioned as easy-to-memorize training manuals, providing those who sang them with words by which to challenge their inquisitors, and perhaps also the words they needed to persuade themselves to remain true to the Anabaptist faith.[40]

Anabaptist songwriters composed martyr ballads throughout the years when Anabaptists suffered martyrdom, and they appear to have been widely shared and sung. To be sure, many of these ballads exist without attribution, so it is sometimes difficult to know when they were written. However, Ursula Lieseberg's study of sixty-five German-language martyr songs suggests that many were composed by eyewitnesses shortly after the executions took place or by persons who had attended the martyrs' judicial proceedings.[41] It is therefore likely that some martyr ballads were composed as early as 1527 and that the corpus continued to grow for almost a century, through the first decades of the seventeenth century.[42] These hymns served an important role in congregational singing, especially in times and places where Anabaptists were still being hounded. Indeed, some sixteenth-century adversaries of the Anabaptists complained about the fervor with which Anabaptist communities sang about their martyrs. According to one antagonist, the Anabaptists "always put their drowned and burned, obstinate and impervious, alleged martyrs into a song."[43]

Hymn singing was not the only means by which early Anabaptists remembered their martyrs' sacrifices. Letters containing martyr accounts circulated through congregations, and stories passed by word of mouth from one sympathizer to another. At least two Anabaptist martyrs executed before 1530 were memorialized in pamphlet form, including the Swiss leader Michael Sattler, who led the confessional gathering at Schleitheim in 1527 and was executed three months later.[44] The most influential Sattler pamphlet, printed in Zurich within a few weeks of his execution, was attributed to Klaus von Graveneck, a Protestant nobleman who was likely an eyewitness to Sattler's trial and execution.[45] Much like those who sang martyr ballads, those who read von Graveneck's pamphlet (or had it read to them) would have encountered rationales for views that the authorities considered heretical. In addition they would have been introduced to a man who, in the face of certain death, maintained a serene trust in God.[46]

Sixteenth- and seventeenth-century Anabaptist martyrologists would incorporate letters and pamphlets into their works; they would also use a written chronicle produced by the Hutterites, a communal Anabaptist group that formed in Moravia around 1527 as Anabaptists sought refuge there.[47] No sixteenth-century Anabaptist group was more attuned to its history or more attentive to its martyrological identity than were the Hutterites, whose hopes of finding toleration in Moravia were dashed in a crackdown following the Münster debacle in 1535. Leader Jacob Hutter was among the first to die. Captured in Austria in 1536, Hutter was brutally tortured before being burned at the stake. Other Moravian Anabaptist groups, some with close connections to Hutter's group, likewise suffered severely. In time Hutter's followers found a greater degree of toleration in Moravia. In the meantime, however, their missionary work in other regions of Europe made martyrdom a frequent reality.

Even as they experienced persecution, the Hutterites recorded and re-iterated it. Almost from the beginning of their movement, the Hutterites established something akin to an archive in which they collected literary materials, including prison letters, doctrinal statements, and martyr accounts, not simply of Hutterite martyrs but of other Anabaptist martyrs as well. Sometime in the 1560s, Hutterite historians began compiling these materials into a chronologically ordered and ever-expanding volume that has since become known as the *Great Chronicle*. Handwritten and hand-copied in German (it remained unpublished until the nineteenth century), the *Great Chronicle* contains stories of Anabaptism's Swiss origins as well as events in Hutterite history. Gruesomely detailed tortures and executions appear frequently in the volume's first stages, including the execution of Jacob Hutter, "a Christian hero steadfast in faith."[48] Accounts from the *Great Chronicle* eventually found their way to the Netherlands, where Dutch Mennonite martyrologists included them in their martyrologies.

A second German-language book that informed Dutch martyrological writing was the *Ausbund,* a collection of hymns that carried a strong theme of martyrdom. The *Ausbund*'s precursor, a slimmer volume titled *Etliche schöne christliche Gesäng* (Genuinely beautiful Christian songs), consisted of the fifty-three hymns composed by the Passau prisoners in the 1530s. First published in 1564, *Etliche schöne christliche Gesäng* was reissued in 1583 (or earlier) in an expanded form, this time carrying the title *Ausbund*, meaning "paragon."[49] In the *Ausbund*, the Passau hymns make up the songbook's second half, and eighty other songs constitute its first half. Of these eighty additional songs, twenty-one are Anabaptist martyr ballads. Many other songs in the *Ausbund's* first half were written by martyrs-to-be, including the songs by George Blaurock and Michael Sattler cited above. All told, forty-two consecutive songs in the *Ausbund's* first half "are either about, or were written by or attributed to martyrs."[50]

Although both the *Great Chronicle* and the *Ausbund* included non-martyrological material, it is fair to say that they were the Anabaptist movement's first German-language martyrologies. One hundred years after these works took shape, van Braght would avail himself of Dutch martyrologies that drew on these German-language works as he compiled his *Bloody Theater*. Even more foundational to van Braght's project, however, was a Dutch-language martyr book that appeared in the Netherlands just as the *Great Chronicle* and the *Ausbund* were materializing in Moravia and Germany. First published in 1562, *Het Offer des Heeren* (The sacrifice of the Lord) provided the literary core around which much of van Braght's *Bloody Theater* would be built.

A Dutch Martyrology: *The Sacrifice of the Lord*

By 1562, the year *The Sacrifice of the Lord* was published, the Anabaptist movement had been in existence for almost forty years. Dutch Anabaptism began slightly later than its Swiss and Moravian counterparts, with the first rebaptisms taking place in 1530. Almost as soon as the baptismal waters began to flow, persecution rained down on Anabaptist heads. The first Dutch Anabaptist martyr, Sicke Freerks, was executed in early 1531, and other executions followed that same year. In 1535, after the mayhem at Münster, the drive to rid the country of the Anabaptist scourge assumed greater urgency among the authorities. For much of the sixteenth century, Dutch Anabaptists were shadowed by persecution in various forms, instigated by the Catholic Church, which was simultaneously battling the advance of Dutch Calvinism. The last Anabaptist executed in the northern provinces of the Netherlands lost his life in 1574; the last

Anabaptist executed in the southern provinces (now Belgium) died in 1597.[51] The exact number of Anabaptists executed in sixteenth-century Netherlands is unknown, though most historians estimate it at well over one thousand.[52]

In the decades prior to *The Sacrifice of the Lord*'s appearance, Dutch Anabaptists faced not only external threats but internal challenges as well. Even after the revolt in Münster was put down, some Anabaptists remained who wished to establish God's kingdom by the sword. Other Anabaptists forswore violence but continued in an apocalyptic mode, relying on prophetic visions to direct their cause. Menno Simons may have helped to save the movement from itself, but even he faced on-going "management problems," particularly with respect to meting out church discipline in appropriate ways. In particular, Simons found him-self caught up in debates, sometimes with himself, over the propriety of shunning wayward church members. Simons worked hard to bring Dutch Anabaptists into agreement on this issue, but he never fully suc-ceeded. By the time he died in 1561, Dutch Anabaptism had been rent into two main factions: the Dutch Mennonites, who were stricter in the application of the ban, and the Waterlanders (named for the Waterland region north of Amsterdam, where they were most concentrated), who were more lenient on the issue.[53]

Despite this divisive issue, the Dutch Anabaptist movement grew in the 1540s and 1550s, creating an expanding market of Anabaptist readers. Even though Anabaptist-related publications had been deemed illegal by the Catholic Inquisition, a handful of Dutch printers took the risk of producing Anabaptist literature. In 1554 a Bible translation favored by the Anabaptists, the Biestkens New Testament, was printed by Nikolaes Biestkens, a member of the Mennonite congregation in Emden. Four years later, in 1558, Biestkens printed the entire Bible, which, like his New Testament, enjoyed many new editions in subsequent decades.[54] Around the same time, Biestkens printed a songbook containing mostly Ana-baptist hymns that likewise went through many subsequent editions.[55]

This was the context—a context that included ongoing persecution, underground printing, and a growing but divided Dutch Anabaptist community—that framed the production of *The Sacrifice of the Lord*, a principal sixteenth-century precursor to van Braght's *Bloody Theater*. The book appeared without attribution to an editor, and it listed no printer or place of publication. These informational lacunae would have protected its producers, but another result was that for centuries historians could only hazard guesses about the printer's identity. In the late twentieth century, however, Paul Valkema Blouw established the printer to be Jan Hendricksz, who until 1556 printed Catholic religious writings in the city of Utrecht.[56] By comparing the type and punctuation habits of Hendricksz's earlier works with the type and habits in the unattributed *Sacrifice of the Lord,* Blouw ascertained that the same printer was responsible for the early Catholic works and the later Anabaptist martyr book. According to Blouw, these characteristics can also be found in other unattributed Anabaptist publications from 1556 and beyond, suggesting that Hendricksz converted to Anabaptism about that time. After his conversion, Hendricksz likely moved his printing business eighty miles north, to the city of Franeker. Not only did Franeker have a relatively large Anabaptist population, but it was also known for being a more tolerant city than Utrecht, so much so that no Anabaptist was ever executed there.[57]

The title page of the 1562 edition reveals a much longer title than the one commonly used, a title that outlines both the content and the purpose of the volume. "This book has been named 'The Sacrifice of the Lord,'" begins the title page, "because its content pertains to some sacrificed children of God." These sacrificed children, continues the writer, "have brought forth from the good treasure of their hearts confessions, letters, and testaments, which they spoke with their mouths and have sealed with their blood." The martyrs included in the volume offered their testimonies for two purposes, says the title page, one temporal ("for the comfort and strengthening" of the faithful) and the other eternal ("to the praise, glory, and honor of Him who created all things").[58] In other words, like the martyr ballads before it, *The Sacrifice of the Lord* had an inspirational purpose: to bolster would-be martyrs with the thought that eternal reward far exceeded the cost of earthly suffering.[59] At the same time, *The Sacrifice of the Lord* had a very practical purpose, one it also shared with the earlier martyr ballads: to provide its readers with responses if and when the inquisitors came knocking.[60]

More than sharing common purposes with Anabaptist martyr ballads, *The Sacrifice of the Lord* included many ballads within its pages. Its first edition contained only prose materials, including letters and interrogation accounts, that together detailed the experiences of twenty-three different martyrs. One year later, however, a supplementary song-book was bound to the prose component, adding twenty-five martyr songs that, according to historian Brad Gregory, mentioned 131 different martyrs.[61] All subsequent editions of the book (ten more editions were issued between 1566 and 1599) included the songbook, which from the printer's perspective was no longer an afterthought.[62] In 1570 even more songs were added to the volume, though these new songs were not added to the songbook section but were rather printed alongside previously included prose materials from which their lyrics were drawn. This rendering of prose material into rhyming songs, writes Gregory, "suggests how integral the latter were in the transmission of the memory of the martyrs" throughout the sixteenth century.[63]

Who were the martyrs remembered in *The Sacrifice of the Lord*? By and large, both in the prose and the songbook sections, they were Dutch Mennonites who suffered martyrdom in the 1550s. That said, the first edition, in addition to including a song about Jesus Christ and a prose account of the apostle Stephen's death, contained an account of Swiss Anabaptist leader Michael Sattler's death. The inclusion of Sattler in *The Sacrifice of the Lord* is significant, especially in retrospect: not only did it indicate that the Dutch martyrologist(s) considered Sattler as part of their movement, but it also signaled the beginning of what later grew into a pan-European Anabaptist martyrology. Still, Sattler's appearance constituted a clear exception to the book's Dutch predilection. Subsequent editions of *The Sacrifice of the Lord* added other martyrs to the mix (the 1599 edition has thirty-three prose entries), but in general the book remained what it was in its first incarnation: a Dutch Mennonite martyrology that skipped almost entirely from early Christianity to the Dutch Mennonite experience of the 1550s.[64] Why the volume's editor did not include more martyrs from Anabaptist movements in other regions is not entirely clear; it is unlikely that materials pertaining to these other martyrs were entirely unavailable to him. The most reasonable answer to this question pertains to the anticipated readership: published for fellow Dutch Mennonites, *The Sacrifice of the Lord* focused almost exclusively on the Dutch Mennonite experience.

The process by which the editor of *The Sacrifice of the Lord* came into possession of his martyrological material cannot be known in detail, though it was almost certainly a combination of methods. The editor likely knew some martyr songs by memory, and in other cases the songs he incorporated into the volume would have already been written down. Moreover, evidence exists that prison letters and other martyrological resources were being hand-copied by the Anabaptist faithful, circulated in their communities, and in some cases collated into simple codices. These handwritten resources were frequently annotated; in some instances readers appear to have added biblical references in the margins before forwarding the materials to other readers. In this way the memorialization process was a collaborative effort, one that no doubt benefited the editor of *The Sacrifice of the Lord.*[65]

Ultimately, however, the book's editor needed to organize the materials at hand. In addition to dividing his material into prose and song sections, he placed the entries in chronological order according to the martyrs' respective years of death. He rarely added commentary to his collected material, though he did pen a preface and a concluding statement. The preface, like the expansive title, identifies the book's purpose to be "for the comfort and strengthening of all lovers of the truth." It then proceeds to list a host of biblical characters—Abraham, Moses, Elijah, Daniel, Susanna, Paul, and many others—who experienced God's comfort in times of need. In this way, the editor aligns the Anabaptist martyrs with biblical heroes, assuring his readers that, with God on their side, they need not fear. By annotating his preface with a myriad of biblical citations, the editor further assured his readers that the work they were reading carried God's stamp of approval.[66]

In light of the many editions issued between 1562 and 1599, it appears that *The Sacrifice of the Lord* was widely read among sixteenth-century Dutch Mennonites, offering them encouragement in trying times. To be sure, being an Anabaptist in the Netherlands became easier as the century passed. Especially in the realm's northern provinces, which seceded from Spanish Catholic control in 1581 to become the Dutch Republic, political toleration became the norm in the century's closing decades. Still, this frequently reprinted martyr book continued to carry signs of originating in an age of persecution. Most notably, the final edition's dimensions had increased only modestly from the 1562 edition, which was roughly four inches high, three inches wide, and an inch and a half thick.[67] Originally the book's small size had nothing to do with paper costs or printing methods and everything to do with the ability of owners to hide the book in their clothing, for those who were caught with an Anabaptist martyr book would likely have faced arrest or something worse. By the turn of the seventeenth century, this fear of being apprehended with a forbidden martyrology was a thing of the past, at least for Dutch Mennonites living in the north.[68] Their subsequent martyr books were much more expansive, in both size and scope.

Early-Seventeenth-Century Anabaptist Martyrologies

By the dawn of the seventeenth century, religious toleration had taken root in the northern regions of the Netherlands, as a corollary of Dutch independence from Spain and the consequent decline of the Catholic Church's authority. In this more tolerant environment, superintended by Dutch Calvinists, Dutch Anabaptists had both the freedom and the resources to memorialize Anabaptist martyrs in new ways and for new purposes. Up to this point, a primary reason for publishing martyr books was to instruct readers on how to respond to their inquisitors' questions. Going forward, however, the primary purpose was to help readers resist more subtle pressures that could poison their faith. Even if temporal life was no longer at stake, eternal life still hung in the balance. The gift of salvation could easily be lost in a world filled with devilish enticements.

In addition to inspiring faithfulness, seventeenth-century Anabaptist martyrologists sought to address and resolve divisions in their midst. By 1700 the Dutch Anabaptist world had divided into a variety of factions, divisions that were often rooted in divergent views on church purity and ecclesiastical discipline.[69] The most lenient Anabaptists in this intramural squabble were the Waterlanders. Separating from the stricter Dutch Mennonites in 1557, the Waterlanders even sought to distance themselves from Menno Simons, rejecting the increasingly common label *Mennists* in exchange for a new label, *Doopsgesinde,* meaning "baptism-minded."[70] To the extreme side of the Waterlanders were the Hard Frisians (sometimes called Old Frisians), a Mennonite faction that maintained a robust understanding of church discipline, including the practice of shunning wayward church members. Another prominent party in early-seventeenth-century Dutch Anabaptism was the Flemish church, a union of congregations rooted in the emigration of persecuted Mennonites from Flanders in the 1550s. Divergent ethnic and cultural sensibilities made for ongoing tensions between the more established Frisian Mennonites and Flemish immigrants, who felt that their world-denying faith had been authenticated through persecution. Despite frequent attempts at reconciliation, these divisions within Dutch Mennonitism remained and in some cases multiplied.[71] Underneath this diversity, however, all shared an interest in maintaining and appropriating the martyrs' legacy.

In 1615 Waterlander Hans de Ries took the lead in publishing a new Anabaptist martyrology, the first one published in the seventeenth century. Titled *History of the Martyrs or Genuine Witnesses of Jesus Christ*, de Ries's martyrology borrowed extensively from *The Sacrifice of the Lord*, but it differed in significant ways.[72] The most obvious difference was the book's size. Much thicker and with a footprint twice as large as *The Sacrifice of the Lord*'s, de Ries's volume was not made to be hidden, thus signifying the more tolerant era in which it was produced. Another visible difference was the artwork on the title page, which, in contrast to the nonillustrated *Sacrifice of the Lord*, depicted a variety of grisly execution scenes. In terms of its content, de Ries's *History of the Martyrs* consisted entirely of prose. The lyrical material that constituted the songbook portion of *The Sacrifice of the Lord* was retained but rendered into prose, no longer to be sung in worship or committed to memory. As with the book's larger size, this literary shift corresponded to the waning of martyrdom in Dutch Anabaptist life. Martyr stories "were no longer

Table 2.1. Dutch Anabaptist Martyrologies, 1562–1660

Date	Abbreviated Title	Primary Editor	Place of Publication
1562	*The Sacrifice of the Lord*	Unknown (1st ed.)	Franeker
1599	*The Sacrifice of the Lord*	Unknown (11th ed.)	Harlingen (or Dordrecht)
1615	*History of the Martyrs*	Hans de Ries	Haarlem
1617	*History of the True Witnesses of Jesus Christ*	Pieter Jans Twisck	Hoorn
1626	*History of the Pious Witnesses of Jesus Christ*	Pieter Jans Twisck	Hoorn
1631	*Martyrs Mirror of the Defenseless Christians*	Hans de Ries	Haarlem
1660	*The Bloody Theater*	Thieleman van Braght	Dordrecht

sung in clandestine gatherings, but rather read by increasingly educated Mennonites in newly secure surroundings."[73]

Another significant difference from *The Sacrifice of the Lord* lay in the scope of de Ries's martyrological vision. The *History of the Martyrs* included more than six hundred Anabaptist martyrs, a number buoyed in part by the addition of material from the Hutterites' *Great Chronicle*. De Ries's work also referred, albeit briefly, to pre-Reformation Christians who had been persecuted for opposing infant baptism. With these references, de Ries pushed the narrative of Christian faithfulness beyond the boundaries of Reformation-era Anabaptism. Although he offered few details about the pre-Reformation martyrs' experiences, de Ries's reference to them was a first step toward closing the historical gap between the New Testament and sixteenth-century Anabaptism. In fact, de Ries's willingness to insert his own voice throughout the book, adding comments as he shaped the martyrs' writings, signaled a new development in Anabaptist martyrological writing. More than just a compilation of martyr writings, de Ries's *History of the Martyrs* was a historically minded minister's attempt to write history, an attempt that appreciably shaped the contours of van Braght's *Bloody Theater* forty-five years later.[74]

Even at this initial stage, it was history writing with a purpose. De Ries lamented the factionalism that marked Dutch Anabaptism, and he devoted himself throughout his ministerial career to healing these rifts.[75] His *History of the Martyrs* was his most ambitious effort in this regard, an effort that entailed two closely related elements. In terms of narrative content, de Ries and his coeditors enlarged the scope of Anabaptist faithfulness by including martyrs from an array of Anabaptist traditions and locales, including some considered suspect by less ecumenically inclined Dutch Anabaptists.[76] Second, de Ries added editorial comments that explained his book's inclusive approach. For instance, he admitted that some observers might wonder "why we have put all their martyrs in one book with the others without making any distinction." His answer was clear: "we want to show ourselves in these [selections] not as sectarian but as nonpartisan Christians."[77] De Ries went on to say that he and his fellow editors had weighed the doctrinal differences between the various martyrs in the book and had found them insignificant. Yes, the martyrs did exhibit doctrinal differences, but none "concerning any article of Christian faith about which anyone might rightly be considered or judged as unbelieving, damned, or not saved."[78] In the final analysis, de Ries employed only two criteria for determining who from the Swiss Brethren tradition, from the Hutterites, and from various Dutch Mennonite factions would be included in his martyr book: adult baptism and the rejection of the sword.[79] Forty-five years later, van Braght invoked these same criteria as he compiled *The Bloody Theater.*

In the meantime, however, de Ries's history drew responses from Dutch Mennonites who maintained narrower definitions of faithfulness. In 1617 Old Frisian leader Pieter Jans Twisck oversaw the publication of a revised version of de Ries's martyrology, one that carried the title *History of the True Witnesses of Jesus Christ.*[80] In addition to retitling de Ries's martyrology, Twisck and his colleague Syvaert Pieters produced a new preface, assuring their readers that all the martyrs in this revised book were "unanimous" in their Anabaptist orthodoxy.[81] They then specified the contours of this orthodoxy by crafting and inserting a thirty-three-article confession of faith that was particularly stringent on some issues.[82] In this Old Frisian rendering of history, the martyrs memorialized were "true witnesses," living and dying for beliefs completely in harmony with the Old Frisian confession.

As Brad Gregory points out, this retrospective claim was dubious, though Twisck and Pieters repeated the claim a decade later in a revised edition of their martyrology, this time titled *History of the Pious Witnesses of Jesus Christ* (1626).[83] The Old Frisians' revised martyrology included yet another new preface. In it, they accused de Ries of playing fast and loose with the historical record in his 1615 work. Specifically, they said de Ries had downplayed the martyrs' commitment to celestial-flesh Christology, a doctrine of supreme importance to the Old Frisians that declared Christ brought his human flesh with him from heaven (as opposed to taking on flesh from Mary).[84] The Old Frisians were half right in their accusation. According to Gregory, de Ries *had* downplayed this distinctive doctrine in some of the martyrs' testimonies. At the same time, for Old Frisians to assert that *all* the Anabaptist martyrs who remained in their revised martyrologies embraced celestial-flesh Christology was claiming too much.[85]

In 1631 de Ries and his Waterlander colleagues answered the Old Frisian accusation by publishing yet another martyrology, this one titled *Martyrs Mirror of the Defenseless Christians.*[86] In this second Waterlander martyrology, de Ries and his friends were more explicit in defining their criteria for including particular martyrs, criteria they called "the essential articles of faith" (*de noodighe Gheloofs-artijckelen*).[87] These essentials included belief in God, the sacrifice of Jesus Christ for the forgiveness of sins, adult baptism, a commitment to discipleship, and the resurrection of the faithful, but there were far fewer items than the Old Frisians asserted in their thirty-three-article confession.[88] In fact, in contrast to the Old Frisians' claim of a fine-tuned theological consensus among the martyrs, de Ries and his coeditors (the primary author of the 1631 preface was likely de Ries's colleague Jan Philipsz Schabaelje)[89] argued that although the martyrs displayed substantial theological diversity, these differences, in their view, did not matter. "The holy crown of the martyrs is not contingent on the variation among such points," they wrote, but rather upon the martyrs' shared commitment to doctrinal fundamentals and their willingness to die for them.[90]

In 1660, when Thieleman van Braght published *The Bloody Theater,* he largely embraced the Waterlanders' more ecumenical view of Anabaptist martyrdom. The 1631 *Martyrs Mirror* set the stage for van Braght's work in two other significant ways. First, even more than in his *History of the Martyrs,* de Ries argued in *Martyrs Mirror* that faithful martyrs could be found in many places from New Testament times to the present, a claim van Braght sought to substantiate by writing an even more expansive martyrology in 1660.[91] Second, de Ries and his coeditors argued, as van Braght did later, that the tolerant environment Dutch Mennonites now occupied was a greater threat to the faith than a context filled with torture chambers and human bonfires. Born in 1553, de Ries had come of age in an era when Dutch Mennonites were still being persecuted, a horrific reality he witnessed firsthand in 1577, when he watched his friend Hans Bret burned at the stake in Antwerp.[92] By the time *Martyrs Mirror* appeared in 1631, however, Dutch Mennonites in the Waterlander region near Amsterdam were more than just tolerated by civic authorities. They were respected, well-to-do members of the community. This newfound prosperity ensured customers for de Ries's relatively expensive book.[93] At the same time, de Ries and his coeditors found this prosperity troubling, for the desire for riches held the potential to compromise Christian commitment. They were almost nostalgic as they described the persecution that, at least in their region of the Anabaptist world, was now past. "In the times of the cross," averred the 1631 preface, "zeal drove

Fig. 2.1. Ornamental title page of Hans de Ries's *Martyrs Mirror* (1631). The page is bordered by biblical scenes (clockwise from top): the stoning of Stephen, Jesus being questioned by the high priest, Cain's murder of Abel, and Joseph's brothers throwing him into a pit.

us in the night . . . into nooks and corners, and into fields and woods" in search of "divine food." Today, however, temporal considerations have replaced spiritual concerns: "Possessions have increased, but in the soul there is leanness. Clothes have become costly, but the inward ornament has perished. Love has waxed cold and has diminished, but contentions have increased."[94]

With this reference to Anabaptist contentiousness, de Ries and his colleagues sought to upbraid their Old Frisian counterparts, cajoling them to relax their doctrinal rigor and to focus instead on commitments that united Anabaptists across time and space. More than that, however, the editors of *Martyrs Mirror* sought to encourage Anabaptists of all stripes, including their fellow Waterlanders, to meditate upon the reflections of godliness contained in this "martyrs mirror" (*Martelaers Spiegel*). De Ries was hardly the first theologian, or even the first Anabaptist church leader, to employ the word *mirror* as a prompt for readers to gaze upon godly exemplars. Menno Simons and other Anabaptist writers referred to Jesus Christ as a mirror, a reflection of God's holiness that Christ's followers could see and emulate.[95] More generally, hundreds of books appeared in the late Middle Ages that used the word "mirror" (*speculum*) in their titles to signal their instructional intent.[96] Even commoners in the sixteenth century knew of this looking-glass metaphor, which was invoked by Anabaptist martyr Lijsken as she moved through a public space before being drowned.[97] "Take an example from me (*eñ een Spieghel aen my nemen*)," advised Lijsken, "all who love the word of the Lord."[98] For de Ries, troubled by the spiritual state of Dutch Mennonitism, martyrs like Lijsken provided a mirror by which his readers could measure their own Christian commitment in an age of comfort.

Thirty years later, in 1660, van Braght reiterated de Ries's concern about temporal comforts in *The Bloody Theater*, incorporating nearly all of *Martyrs Mirror*'s preface into his own work. Of course, by the time van Braght set to work on *The Bloody Theater*, life had grown even richer for many Dutch Mennonites; van Braght considered the material wealth spiritually dangerous, if not deadly. Indeed, like *Martyrs Mirror* before it, *The Bloody Theater* posits something of an inverse relationship between material wealth and spiritual health, between the passing comforts of earth and the eternal comforts of heaven. And who better to validate this reality than those whose earthly consolations were few and far between?

CHAPTER 3

Thieleman van Braght and the Publication

of *The Bloody Theater*

When twenty-first-century readers purchase an English- or German-language edition of *Martyrs Mirror*, they are buying a translation of the Dutch-language martyrology produced by Thieleman van Braght in 1660 and updated by an anonymous editor in 1685. Other Anabaptist martyrologies had been produced prior to 1660, but all of them eventually went out of print, superseded by van Braght's more comprehensive work.[1] A Dutch Mennonite minister, van Braght drew heavily on the martyrologies that preceded his own, particularly the one assembled by Hans de Ries and his Waterlander colleagues in 1631. Still, van Braght's work, the actual title of which begins with the words *The Bloody Theater*, modified and extended these earlier martyrologies in significant ways. In many respects, van Braght's *Bloody Theater* represents the culmination of the Anabaptist martyrological tradition. From this point forward, the most common way to recast the stories of the Anabaptist martyrs was to translate van Braght's work into other languages or to excerpt particular stories from it to create smaller, more readable volumes.[2]

In this chapter we explore the production of *The Bloody Theater*: the Dutch context that nourished it, the author-editor who assembled it, and the printer who prepared it for sale. As this backstory emerges, van Braght's rationale for producing yet another Anabaptist martyrology will quickly become clear. An influential Mennonite leader, van Braght possessed a historical vision that both corresponded to and sought to advance his ecclesiological concerns. In his view, a new and improved martyrology held significant promise for shaping Dutch Mennonitism in the present. Although a more detailed consideration of *The Bloody Theater*'s content will await chapter 4, even now we will begin to see how van Braght recalibrated the Anabaptist martyrological tradition for his own ends. Convinced that the Anabaptist tradition held great riches, but worried that his fellow Dutch Mennonites were spiritually sick unto death, van Braght evoked the memory of the martyrs to breathe new life into the church he loved.

The Mid-Seventeenth-Century Dutch Context

That van Braght could produce a fifteen-hundred-page martyrology and could visualize consumers who could afford to buy it owes to the socioeconomic position of Dutch Mennonites in the mid-seventeenth century. At the time he compiled his martyrology, van Braght lived in the Dutch city of Dordrecht, about fifteen miles southeast of Rotterdam. Anabaptists in Dordrecht had not always fared well. In fact, van Braght's martyrology narrates several executions that took place in the city a century earlier, between 1555 and 1572, including the burning of ten Anabaptists around 1570.[3] A few years after these executions, however, the political climate in and around Dordrecht took a more tolerant turn. In the late 1560s, an alliance of feudal lords, Calvinist freedom fighters, and tax-weary merchants joined forces against Philip II, the Catholic king of Spain, whose possessions included the seventeen provinces of the Netherlands. The Dutch rebellion and Spanish attempts to squelch it continued for decades, from 1568 to 1648—the reason this Dutch war of independence is sometimes called the Eighty Years' War. As early as 1572, however, the city of Dordrecht cast its lot with the rebels and its leader, William of Orange.[4] In 1581 some of the northern Dutch provinces, including the one in which Dordrecht was located, formally seceded from Spanish rule. As time passed, these secessionist provinces increasingly operated as a union of Dutch-ruled states.[5]

The transition in these provinces from Spanish rule to Dutch rule brought with it greater religious toleration. Even before they had formally seceded from Spanish rule, some of the rebellious provinces had entered into an agreement that promised, contrary to Spanish rule, that "every particular person shall remain free in his religion, and that no one will be pursued or investigated because of his religion."[6] This promise was not always fulfilled. As Calvinists sought to assert their newfound authority, they sometimes prohibited competing forms of worship and proselytizing by rival religions. Still, the brutal repression of religious dissent that had characterized the northern provinces under Spanish rule diminished in the last quarter of the sixteenth century. Dutch Anabaptists, who constituted about 10 percent of the population in these regions, continued to suffer ridicule and other forms of harassment well into the seventeenth century, but they no longer needed to fear for their lives.[7]

In time Anabaptists in this new Dutch Republic—in and around cities like Amsterdam, Dordrecht, and Haarlem—participated in the republic's economic vitality. Historians have dubbed the seventeenth century the Dutch Golden Age, for it was an era in which the Dutch Republic enjoyed preeminence as the world's leading power. This preeminence, which manifested itself in military strength and artistic achievement, was built upon a thriving trade-based economy, leading one notable observer, the philosopher René Descartes, to claim that he was the only person in Amsterdam who was "not engaged in trade."[8] Descartes may have exaggerated the extent of Amsterdam's trading enterprise, but with the republic's considerable coastline and plethora of ports, Dutch trading endeavors extended to every part of Europe and beyond. This enterprise was linked to a vibrant financial sector, which facilitated other commercial endeavors, including fishing, shipbuilding, textile production, printing, brewing, and papermaking. The result was a burgeoning urban middle class, the scope and influence of which was previously unseen in Europe.[9] Immigrants flocked to Dutch cities from other regions of Europe, and in their search for economic advancement, they brought additional skills to stoke the Dutch economy. To Calvinist church leaders wary of greed and corruption, the Golden Age represented an "embarrassment of riches," but to most people in the Dutch Republic, the pursuit of wealth was nothing to be embarrassed about.[10]

Dutch Anabaptists rode the wave of their homeland's rising prosperity and were soon participating in many forms of commerce, manufacturing, and trade. By 1645 at least twenty board members of a large Anabaptist congregation in Amsterdam held accounts at the city's Bank of

Exchange, a financial institution that enabled businessmen to transfer large sums of money from one city or country to another.[11] Not every member of this Waterlander congregation was wealthy; in fact, some members were quite poor, including recent immigrants from regions where Anabaptists were still being persecuted. Still, the bulk of Amsterdam's Waterlander congregation came from "the middling class of small businessmen, skilled artisans, and unskilled workers" and "the prosperous class of non-ruling notables, rich merchants, businessmen, shop owners, and intellectuals."[12] The most common enterprise for these prosperous Waterlanders was textiles, both production and retail distribution. Intermarriage between prosperous families in the Waterlander congregation helped to facilitate profit-making, as did business relationships between church members. These "close social and family ties [that] formed within a dissenting church," writes historian Mary Sprunger, "helped the Waterlander *élite* to amass comfortable, not to say large, fortunes."[13]

All of this induced some degree of concern among Mennonites, especially among their leaders. Like their Calvinist counterparts, Mennonite ministers often warned their flocks against the enticements of wealth, and they decried the hold it had on some church members' imaginations. As we saw in chapter 2, this rising tide of prosperity provided incentive for Hans de Ries, a Waterlander living north of Amsterdam, to superintend the publication of a new martyrology in 1631. Twenty years later, Waterlander minister Jacob Cornelisz issued his own admonition against the allure of wealth and social prestige. In a series of sermons he delivered in 1651, Cornelisz cited 1 Timothy 2:9–10 to admonish women against chasing after worldly fashions and to chastise their husbands who allowed them to do so. Cornelisz broadened his invective beyond fashionable attire to include other consumer items. "I have watched with a broken heart," he said, as "[Amsterdam's Mennonites] increase the ostentation of their houses, household goods, weddings, feasts, and clothes." Rather than living lives of deep Christian commitment, these church members "follow on the heels of those who serve the world." All in all, Cornelisz concluded, "one can see little or no difference" between Amsterdam's Mennonite community and the rest of Dutch society.[14]

Although affluence produced something of an identity crisis for Dutch Mennonites, it also meant they were able to buy books, even ones of considerable cost. Living in a region that boasted the highest literacy rate in all of Europe, Dutch Mennonites participated in the flowering of Golden Age literature as writers, printers, booksellers, and book buyers.[15] Many of these printed works were devotional in nature, such as the publications of Jan Philipsz Schabaelje, a Waterlander minister who worked with Hans de Ries to produce the 1631 *Martyrs Mirror*. Schabaelje's most widely read book was *Lusthof des Gemoets* (A pleasure garden of the mind), better known in English by the title *The Wandering Soul*.[16] This was an allegory in which a spiritual seeker named Wandering Soul engages in dialogue with Adam, Noah, and other biblical figures. The inexpensive book, which first appeared in 1635, went through dozens of reprintings and was ultimately read by thousands of Mennonites.[17] Schabaelje died in 1656, just as a new, elaborately illustrated edition of his work was going to press. Schabaelje's allegory, which remains in print today, might have been considered the most important Mennonite publication of the seventeenth century had not another devotional book appeared on the scene a few years later. This latter book, much less allegorical and much more expensive, was none other than *The Bloody Theater*.

Thieleman van Braght and His Ecclesiastical Context

Thieleman van Braght was born in Dordrecht in 1625. His father was a cloth merchant, an occupation that Thieleman likewise assumed as an adult. As sellers of this key Dutch manufacture, the van Braghts were participants in the Dutch middle class, less affluent than aristocrats, shipowners, and directors of trading companies, but more affluent than wage workers, sailors, and mill hands.[18]

Shortly after Thieleman's birth in 1625, his father underwent baptism and joined the Mennonite congregation in Dordrecht, a congregation associated with the Flemish branch of the Anabaptist-Mennonite movement. The Flemish church began as a unique entity in the 1560s, when it divided with the church's Frisian wing (the Waterlanders had gone their own way a decade earlier).[19] Twenty years later, in 1586, the Flemish wing experienced its own division, this time over the issues of church purity and discipline. Driving the division were two interrelated questions: could the earthly church be conceived as distinctly separate from the fallen world ("without spot or wrinkle" was the way some Anabaptists put it), and if so, how was that purity to be maintained?[20] The Old Flemish faction, which proved more committed to maintaining churchly purity than other Flemish churches, took a strict stance on excommunication and shunning, and it opposed marriage to outsiders. The Young Flemish wing took more lenient stances on these two issues.[21] In the decades that followed this intramural Flemish division, various people and congregations made gestures toward reconciliation, but their gestures met with little success. In some places, the divisions actually increased.[22]

When van Braght was born in 1625, the Flemish-Frisian division and subsequent subdivisions still existed, though efforts toward reconciliation soon gained steam. In 1627 four Flemish elders from Amsterdam offered a proposal to unite all the Flemish and Frisian congregations on the basis of their Olive Branch Confession, a statement that delineated key Anabaptist doctrines.[23] "What are the fundamental and unmistakable marks by which the children of God . . . can and must be known?," their confession begins, pointing its readers first to the salvation found in the person and work of Jesus Christ. The confession's first half is largely theological, but the second half turns intensely practical, with detailed sections on nonresistance, baptism, foot-washing, church discipline, marriage, and other issues. With respect to shunning, the Olive Branch Confession advises that Christians "must withdraw from the daily intercourse and communion with impenitent apostates," but it avoids the contentious issue of marital avoidance (i.e., the shunning of one's disciplined spouse).[24] According to the proposal that accompanied the confession, all Flemish and Frisian churches would need to acknowledge other groups that embraced the Olive Branch Confession as representing the true church.[25]

Some, though certainly not all, Flemish and Frisian congregations took hold of the Olive Branch (the hardline Old Frisians, under the leadership of Peter Jans Twisck, were particularly opposed to it), though a more ambitious attempt at reconciliation quickly followed. In 1630 a different group of Flemish, Frisian, and High German Mennonites met to discuss reconciliation, this time based on a confession called the Jan Cents Confession. Unlike the Olive Branch Confession, which was drafted by Flemish Mennonites, the Jan Cents Confession was penned by Young Frisian and High German Mennonites, but the goal was largely the same: to establish a confessional basis by which to unify Dutch Mennonitism. The Jan Cents Confession proved more fruitful in this regard than the Olive Branch Confession, but some issues still needed to be resolved. In particular, the competing Flemish factions (Young and Old) continued to harbor differences with each other that reached back to the initial Flemish division in 1586.[26]

Finally, in 1632, a confession emerged that eventually led to broad reconciliation among Dutch Mennonites, ultimately uniting Flemish factions along with Young Frisians and High German Mennonites. This new confession became known as the Dordrecht Confession, for it was drafted by an elder in Dordrecht's Flemish congregation, the very congregation that Thieleman van Braght, now seven years old, called home.[27] The author-elder, Adriaan Cornelisz, had previously succeeded in uniting Dordrecht's competing Flemish congregations, and he envisioned the Dordrecht Confession as a means to advance his unification initiative beyond his hometown.[28] In it, Cornelisz mapped out a mediating path on divisive issues such as the incarnation and church discipline. More specifically, the Dordrecht Confession "retained the particular Mennonite doctrine of incarnation, albeit in weakened form," writes historian Piet Visser. "It emphasized the ban as the most important means of discipline, but no longer insisted on marital avoidance."[29] Again, not every Dutch Anabaptist group could abide this new confession. For instance, the Old Frisian faction found the Dordrecht Confession too lenient on some issues, and the Waterlanders, who were already marginal to the discussion, would have found Dordrecht's disciplinary strictures too severe. Even in 1632, however, the confession served as a basis for Flemish reconciliation, uniting the long divided Old and Young Flemish groups. Eventually, much of the Dutch Mennonite world found a basis for reconciliation in the confession, which was published in 1633 under the title *Confessie ende Vredehandelinge* (Confession and peace agreement). In 1639 the Flemish, Young Frisian, and High German Mennonites established a formal union, an agreement feted by three thousand people in a five-hour celebration.[30]

In 1639, when this formal union was sealed, Thieleman van Braght was a precocious fourteen-year-old. Twenty years later, he included all three of these Dutch Mennonite confessions—the Olive Branch Confession, the Jan Cents Confession, and the Dordrecht Confession—in *The Bloody Theater*, for reasons we shall explore below. In the meantime,

however, he matured into a leader of some standing in the Dutch Mennonite world. In 1644, at age nineteen, he was baptized into the Dordrecht congregation, and four years later he became a deacon. In the
role of deacon, van Braght assisted the congregation's elders in preaching
and teaching, though his primary work was caring for the congregation's
poor. In 1651 his leadership responsibilities took on added significance
when he became an elder. Van Braght filled this elder role until his death
in 1664 at age thirty-nine. Although his life spanned less than forty years,
van Braght distinguished himself as a regional leader, ready and willing
to tackle issues that plagued the broader Dutch Mennonite world.[31]

The challenges van Braght faced as a church elder were both internal
and external. By this time in the seventeenth century, outright persecution of Dutch Anabaptists had ended, but Calvinist authorities continued to make things difficult for Mennonite congregations and their
members. For instance, because Calvinist congregations were recognized by civic authorities as the only true church, Calvinist ministers
had the authority to enter Mennonite gatherings to correct the theology being espoused. In addition, Calvinist leaders had the authority to
summon Mennonite leaders to debate contentious issues, often on the
Calvinists' own terms. In his elder role, van Braght found himself at the
center of these conflicts, engaging in "disputes on the streets, on ships,
or wherever the occasion offered itself."[32] Perhaps most famously, in 1663
he traveled to Oud-Beijerland to debate the city's Reformed minister
on the subject of infant baptism. It appears that van Braght bested his
Reformed counterpart, at least from a public relations standpoint. The
debate took place at night, continuing until two in the morning. When
van Braght insisted that the debate be opened to the public the next day,
his adversary demurred and broke off the debate. A few months later,
the deflated minister visited van Braght in Dordrecht and requested that
they "no longer dispute quarrelsomely with each other, but debate in
friendly discussion."[33]

While it is conceivable that van Braght relished debating his Reformed
counterparts, it is less likely that he enjoyed navigating the internal disputes among Dutch Mennonites. Although the 1632 Dordrecht Confession had brokered a greater degree of unity among Flemish, Frisian, and
High German factions, the Waterlanders and other Mennonite groups
remained estranged from this newly united group. Indeed, in 1647, when

the Waterlanders proposed a merger with the united Flemish, Frisian, and High German group, their overture was rebuffed; the rejection was based on the Waterlanders' refusal to be bound by the Dordrecht Confession.[34] A decade later, however, two Flemish leaders in Amsterdam came to embrace the Waterlanders' distaste for strict confessional conformity. More specifically, they argued that interchurch unity should be based on the Bible alone, a view that would allow more flexibility on contentious doctrines. For these anticonfessionalists, based in Amsterdam's Church of the Lamb and thus dubbed Lamists, spiritual unity based on generous theological principles was to be prized over doctrinal exactitude.[35] One anticonfessionalist minister went so far as to claim in a sermon that "synods and the like were the work of the Antichrist."[36]

In this debate between confessionalists and anticonfessionalists, van Braght came down firmly on the confessionalist side. In 1660, the same year *The Bloody Theater* was published, van Braght moderated a gathering of Flemish ministers that considered and then condemned the Lamists' minimalist approach to doctrinal uniformity.[37] Van Braght's confessionalist views help explain why he included the three Dutch Mennonite confessions (Olive Branch, Jan Cents, and Dordrecht) in *The Bloody Theater*'s introduction.[38] These three confessions, van Braght wrote in his introduction, "differ in style, but not in faith." Although they were written at slightly different times by slightly different groups, they were adopted, he said, "without contradiction as a unanimous confession" at a gathering of diverse Mennonite leaders in 1649, a gathering that rejected the Waterlanders' proposal requesting a lenient application of the confessions.[39] In contrast to the Waterlander group, and in line with the majority of Flemish-Frisian Mennonites in the mid-seventeenth century, van Braght was a theological rigorist, willing to grant some leeway in belief and practice, but not very much.

In sum, the context in which van Braght produced *The Bloody Theater* entailed several interrelated elements. At this point in Dutch Anabaptist history, many Dutch Mennonites had made their way into a prosperous middle class, achieving a status that raised vexing questions about their relationship to their persecuted forebears. In this post-persecution environment, theological debates with external adversaries continued, but the more time-consuming debates were internal ones. Simply put, Dutch Mennonites could not forge a consensus on what constituted

Christianity's theological essentials. These intramural debates, which often focused on specific issues (the propriety of marrying outsiders and the practice of church discipline, to mention just two), eventually landed on the question of doctrinal uniformity: did Christian unity demand strict agreement on theological matters, or was there some latitude in that? These complicated issues occupied van Braght as an elder. They also occupied him as a martyrologist. Indeed, his *Bloody Theater* sought to raise and answer these questions in ways that would chart a path of faithfulness into the future.

Producing *The Bloody Theater*: Why a New Martyrology?

If van Braght sought to use *The Bloody Theater* to address current issues in the Dutch Mennonites world, the question remains: Why a martyrology? Church leaders have at their disposal a variety of problem-solving methods, almost all of which demand less effort than publishing a fifteen-hundred-page martyrology. Van Braght had already employed many of these less demanding methods—preaching sermons, engaging in public debates, and working behind the scenes—to advance his concerns. Why undertake the monumental task of producing a new martyrology?

One answer to this question lies in van Braght's emerging conviction that the printed word could multiply his ministerial effectiveness. In 1657 van Braght produced a short book entitled *De Schole der zedelijcke Deught* (The school of moral virtue), a catechetical manual on virtuous living aimed primarily at young people. In it, van Braght offered questions and answers regarding the Christian life, supplementing his answers with explanations and images that illustrated difficult theological concepts. Sound doctrine undergirded faithful living, wrote van Braght, but a modest lifestyle was also important, because the flesh "would so love to be beautifully clothed, honored, and greeted."[40] Van Braght's catechetical work sold well enough that a second edition appeared in 1658, one year after its initial publication. It eventually went through eighteen editions.[41]

Not coincidentally, van Braght's rationale for producing *The Bloody Theater* fell precisely in line with the call for modesty he issued in *The School of Moral Virtue*. To van Braght, contemporary Dutch Mennonites inhabited a perilous world, the kind of world that could tempt the eye, destroy the soul, and lead to eternal damnation. "These are sad times in which we live," van Braght wrote in *The Bloody Theater*'s preface, for "there is more danger now than in the time of our fathers, who suffered death for the testimony of the Lord." In earlier times, he said, "Satan came openly . . . as a roaring lion," intent on destroying the body. Now, however, Satan "comes as in the night . . . in a strange but yet pleasing form," and he "lies in wait to destroy the soul." Turning his attention to the Golden Age context, van Braght warned that "the world now reveals itself very beautiful and glorious, more than at any preceding time, in a threefold pleasing form—the lust of the flesh, the lust of the eye, and the pride of life." Van Braght offered specific examples of how lust and pride revealed themselves in his Dutch context: "shameful and vast commerce which extends far beyond the sea into other parts of the world"; "large, expensive, and ornamented houses"; "parks magnificent as a paradise"; and "the giving and attending great dinners, lavish banquets, and wedding feasts." By embracing these things, van Braght warned, seventeenth-century Dutch Mennonites would provide "incontrovertible evidence of a sensual and wanton heart," and they risked not only the "displeasure of God" but "eternal damnation."[42]

Convinced that Dutch Mennonites were rushing headlong into carnality, van Braght offered the martyrs' witness as an antidote. "Come now, ye earthly-minded and ungodly, and learn here to become heavenly and godly-minded," he wrote. Patience, meekness, modesty, humility, contentment, benevolence, piety, and steadfastness—these virtues could be absorbed, he wrote, "not so much by words as by deeds, from those who not only commenced the above virtues, but continued in them unto the end." Going beyond his earlier catechism, which he directed primarily to young people, van Braght promised readers that his *Bloody Theater* offered a "school of practice and virtue" to persons of all ages. Young people "who live after their lusts," the middle-aged who "are deeply engrossed in . . . earthly affairs," and the aged "who have neglected their youth and middle life"—all these people, van Braght advised, would be wise to "enter this school" and thereby be led to godliness "by the living examples of those who went before them." In the final analysis, van Braght thought the martyrs' testimony would be a more effective means for church renewal than any other means he had at his disposal.[43]

Employing an Anabaptist martyrology to curtail advancing worldliness among Dutch Mennonites was not unique to van Braght, of course. Hans de Ries and his coeditors had expressed the same concern thirty years earlier, in 1631, when they worked together to produce *Martyrs Mirror*. But in addition to echoing de Ries's call for faithful nonconformity in an opulent Dutch environment, van Braght issued *The Bloody Theater* for two other reasons. The most obvious reason was to update the Anabaptist martyr record. Thirty years had passed since *Martyrs Mirror* had appeared, three decades that had produced additional Anabaptist martyrs in Switzerland. By including these recent martyr stories in an updated martyrology, van Braght made the Anabaptist martyr record more comprehensive than ever before.[44]

More than simply updating the Anabaptist martyr record, however, van Braght sought to connect this record to the church's pre-Reformation past. In other words, he endeavored to fill in the historical gap between the New Testament saints and the Reformation-era Anabaptists by identifying a succession of faithful, martyred Christians in the intervening centuries. Of course, de Ries and his coeditors had made similar gestures, but their work was relatively limited in this regard. Van Braght, however, devoted hundreds of pages to filling this gap, recounting dozens of martyr stories from the church's first fifteen centuries. In van Braght's rendering, these pre-Reformation martyrs were proto-Anabaptists; in other words, they had been put to death on account of commitments that paralleled the commitments of sixteenth-century Anabaptists. Van Braght acknowledged that some of these earlier martyrs may not have advocated adult baptism explicitly; the historical record, he admitted, was too spotty to claim that with certainty. At the same time, he said, there existed no evidence to the contrary. In van Braght's view, the earlier martyrs were "true witnesses" (*ware getuygen*), for they held views that comported with the views of sixteenth-century Anabaptists, demonstrating a theological affinity that included their commitment to adult baptism.[45]

By including a fifteen-centuries-long line of proto-Anabaptists in his martyr book, van Braght sought to counter charges of theological impropriety that were being leveled by his Calvinist counterparts. Like the Anabaptists' earliest adversaries, van Braght's Calvinist rivals accused Mennonites of holding doctrinal positions that were damning in their originality. If Anabaptist views were theologically sound, they asked, why had no one else in the church's history espoused them? Van Braght's response to this question was simple: Anabaptist theological views, adult baptism in particular, were not original to the sixteenth-century Anabaptists. "For more than a century," he wrote, "people have been made to believe that the Anabaptists . . . have but recently sprung from some erring spirit." To the contrary, van Braght insisted, the Anabaptists' views can be traced to "the source of truth—Christ and His apostles." For anyone who was skeptical of this claim, van Braght invited them to read the first part of his book: not only did his *Bloody Theater* show that Christ's apostles "taught and practiced" adult baptism, but it also offered evidence that this practice continued "through every age, even to the present time."[46]

Van Braght also employed other methods to establish sixteenth-century Anabaptists as the church's measure of authentic Christianity, methods we will consider more fully in chapter 4. For now the important point is this: van Braght believed the future of his beloved church was in peril, threatened both by internal decay and by external attacks. From his vantage point, these dangerous forces went hand in hand, for if Dutch Mennonites were being charmed by social status, they would likely want to flee a church that their refined neighbors considered theologically suspect. For van Braght, a new and improved martyrology could serve the dual purpose of reinvigorating the faith of lukewarm Mennonites and defending their church against its cultured despisers. The outlines of this approach to Anabaptist martyrological writing had already been sketched by Hans de Ries in 1631, but it was left to van Braght to fill in the details for an increasingly sophisticated Dutch Mennonite readership.

Unpacking the Title: The Structure and Scope of van Braght's Argument

The framework for van Braght's martyrological argument shows forth on the title page, for like many seventeenth-century publications, van Braght's martyrology bore a lengthy title that summarized the book's contents and concerns: *Het Bloedigh Tooneel der Doopsgesinde en Weereloose Christenen. Die om het getuygenisse Jesu hares Salighmaekers geleden hebben en gedoodt zijn, van Christi tijt af, tot dese onse laetste tijden toe. Mitsgaders, Een beschrijvinge des H. Doops, ende andere stucken van den*

Godsdienst, door alle de Selve tijden geoeffent. Begrepen in Twee Boeken. Zijnde een vergrottinge van den voorgaenden Martelaers-Spiegel, uyt vele geloofweerdighe Chronijken/Memorien/Gutuigenissen etc.[47] Translated into English, the title reads: *The bloody theater of the baptism-minded and defenseless Christians, who for the testimony of Jesus their Savior have suffered and were slain, from the time of Christ to these our last times. Along with a description of holy baptism and other elements of worship as practiced by them throughout all ages. Contained in two books. being an enlargement of the earlier "martyrs mirror," from many authentic chronicles, memorials, testimonies, etc.*[48]

If the title's initial adjective—bloody—is an obvious reference to the martyrs' spilled blood, the meaning of the initial noun—theater—is less obvious. To van Braght, who may have appropriated this feature of his title from a Catholic martyrology first published in 1587, there was something theatrical about the martyrs' experiences, and especially their executions.[49] Street theater was commonplace in sixteenth-century Dutch life, with each city enjoying a theater company that performed popular dramas in public places.[50] By alluding to this popular form of entertainment, van Braght reminded his readers that the punishment of Reformation-era heretics was often a spectator event, much as it had been for those who killed early Christians.[51] In fact, the governing authorities wanted it that way. Eager to deter the masses from embracing bad theology, they held executions in public places, enabling onlookers to witness the awful consequences of embracing heretical views. Although it is difficult to measure the effectiveness of this deterrent, we do know that some people in early modern Europe, including some Anabaptists, recanted in order to save their lives.[52]

Still, van Braght knew that many Anabaptist martyrs held fast to the end, transforming their execution sites into evangelistic platforms. This was bloody theater in a different sense: a dramatic confrontation that pitted bloodthirsty stage managers against bloodied actors. Terrible though it was, it was theater at its best, for the actors could rebuke the powerful directors and their minions through their stirring words and deeds.[53] Indeed, the martyrs' testimonies sometimes undermined the very purpose of public executions, inspiring some onlookers to embrace the martyrs' views—and, as a consequence, prompting authorities to employ tongue screws and other vicious means to silence the would-be evangelists.[54] In van Braght's view, the high-stakes drama was still unfolding. Although executions were no longer being enacted, a new round of onlookers— his readers—could still be moved by the actors' courage.

In addition to highlighting the dramatic nature of the martyrs' experiences, van Braght's title also identified the criteria he used to compile his catalog of martyrs. Most fundamentally, the martyrs were those who, "for the testimony of Jesus their Savior, have suffered and were slain." In other words, to be included in van Braght's martyrology, a person needed to have been put to death as a direct consequence of the person's confession of faith. To die as a believing Christian, even in the course of heroic action, was not enough. To be counted a martyr, one needed to be put to death *because* of one's particular confession of Jesus Christ.[55]

Van Braght's title reveals two other criteria he used to determine who belonged in his book. One criterion was that the victim be "baptism-minded" (*Doopsgesinde*), that is, committed to the practice of adult baptism. By 1660 the term *Doopsgesinde* was the most commonly used term in reference to Dutch Mennonites. Initially coined by outsiders, the label was eventually embraced by most Dutch Mennonites, who employed it in reference to themselves and their churches.[56] In his introduction to *The Bloody Theater,* van Braght explains his decision to give priority to the term, though not before he registers some reservations about the way it reduces the Anabaptist faith to one particular practice. A better appellation for the *Doopsgesinde,* he suggests, would be "Christ-minded," and if not that, then "Apostle-minded" or "Gospel-Minded." These terms, he says, capture more fully the essence of the Anabaptist faith, for the most fundamental concern of the Anabaptist movement was to restore Christianity to its apostolic, Christ-centered ways.[57]

Still, van Braght realized that using the term *Doopsgesinde* in his martyrology made sense, given his audience's familiarity with the term.[58] Moreover, he understood that adult baptism, while only one churchly practice among many, carried enormous theological weight. Van Braght therefore moves quickly in his introduction to explain why the Anabaptists held adult baptism "in preference to any other article of the Christian and evangelical religion." His explanation is both theological and historical. Theologically speaking, van Braght echoes the arguments that Anabaptists made from the beginning: not only is adult baptism biblically mandated, it is voluntarily chosen and thus represents a "true foundation" for faith in Jesus Christ. Moreover, he writes, it is "the only sign and proof of incorporation into the visible Christian church" and is thus the only means by which a person "can be recognized as a true member of the Christian church." History confirms the significance of this practice, he argues, for "so-called Christian" rulers have gone to great lengths to suppress it. To be sure, van Braght writes, other Anabaptist practices have been similarly reviled throughout history, and if he had more time and space, he could sketch persecuted histories of those practices. But given space constraints, he felt obliged to pick the practice that was most fundamental to Anabaptist faith and was therefore most likely to provoke persecution: adult baptism.[59]

By using the criterion of baptism-minded to evaluate potential martyrs, van Braght operated by the dictum that other martyrologists, Anabaptist and otherwise, had long used: "Not the punishment, but the cause, makes a martyr." In van Braght's view, adult baptism was a both a rightful and a necessary cause to attain martyr status. But adult baptism was not *sufficient* for attaining that status. In addition to adult baptism van Braght added the criterion of "defenselessness" (*Weereloose*) to distinguish true martyrs from false ones.

Van Braght explains his criterion of defenselessness in a note to his readers about two hundred pages into *The Bloody Theater,* a note that directly precedes his account of the persecution enacted under Diocletian in the early fourth century. During this time, van Braght explains, "many errors began to arise among some of those who were called Christians," including a "resort to carnal weapons." Because these so-called Christians had opted for violence, they were sometimes killed by Roman authorities, and their deaths unfortunately obscured "the glorious martyrdom of the true Christian believers." Van Braght's editorial goal, he says, is to clarify this record by ensuring that no one is included in his book of martyrs "who can be shown to have been guilty of gross errors, much less of the shedding of blood." As he did with baptism, van Braght confesses that the historical record on nonresistance is too spotty to certify the facts in every case. Nonetheless, with respect to all the martyrs included in *The Bloody Theater,* "we have not been able to detect [violence] in any of them, and hence in accordance with the spirit of love, we must judge and believe the best of them."[60] In addition to helping van Braght make judgments about pre-Reformation Christian martyrs, this criterion of defenselessness also helped him distinguish between true Anabaptists and the ones who were slaughtered at Münster. The Münsterites were not true Anabaptists, says van Braght. Much to the contrary, the Münsterites were allies of faux Christians "who sanction war," something that true Anabaptists oppose "with heart, soul, and mind."[61]

One last phrase demands our attention for understanding the scope of van Braght's book. In his title, van Braght promises "a description of holy baptism and other elements of worship as practiced by [the martyrs] throughout all ages." By this van Braght means that *The Bloody Theater* is not simply a martyrology, but also a historical treatise that brings to light certain practices that a faithful minority had practiced since the time of Christ. Much of the first book of van Braght's *Bloody Theater* is devoted to this task, offering a century-by-century account of "holy baptism," by which van Braght means adult baptism. Here again we see van Braght contending with his contemporary theological antagonists who claimed that the Anabaptists' views on baptism had always been considered heretical by orthodox Christians. Van Braght's response to this charge is clear: a careful consideration of history reveals that "true baptism upon faith, with rejection of infant baptism, has always obtained, and been practiced . . . by the true church of God."[62]

Centuries later, van Braght's claim that the rejection of infant baptism had "always obtained [in] the true church of God" produced a sense of disquiet in some North American Mennonites. To embrace this particular van Braghtian assertion meant condemning a host of people who claimed the name of Christ but who nonetheless found infant baptism quite appropriate. In van Braght's telling, however, this difference between adult-baptizing churches and infant-baptizing churches was not a relative difference between a less desirable practice and a more desirable one. It was an absolute difference that marked the divide between faith and unfaith. Van Braght may have been persuaded of that divide, but some future Mennonites have been less so. This ambivalence about van Braght's theological assumptions constitutes a major theme in part 3 of this book.

Printing the Book and Invoking Hans de Ries

Near the end of his protracted title, van Braght notes that his new martyrology is "an enlargement of the earlier *Martyrs Mirror*," a reference to Hans de Ries's martyrology, *Martyrs Mirror of the Defenseless Chris-*

tians, published in 1631. Van Braght drew heavily on de Ries's work, incorporating much of it verbatim into the text of *The Bloody Theater.* For a variety of reasons, however, van Braght sought both to broaden and to deepen de Ries's account, adding a lengthy historical section on proto-Anabaptist martyrs in the book's first part, filling out the record of Reformation-era Anabaptist martyrs in the book's second part, and providing more theological and historical commentary throughout.

Generating this enlargement required the production of a massive book. Even with large, print-filled pages, the 1660 edition of *The Bloody Theater* runs nearly fifteen hundred pages in length. With its binding, the volume stands 4¼×8½×13 inches, larger than de Ries's *Martyrs Mirror* (3¾×9×12) and many times larger than the early editions of *The Sacrifice of the Lord.*[63] The book's hefty size attests to the amount of historical material that van Braght wished to include, but it also points to the social location of Dutch Mennonites in the mid-seventeenth century. Given the volume's size, its cost would have been considerable, and its presence in an owner's home would have been conspicuous.[64]

To produce his massive martyrology, van Braght turned to Jacob Braat, a printer who operated in Dordrecht from the mid-1640s to the mid-1660s and who, in the course of his work, had printed at least one other large martyrology.[65] Van Braght's decision to secure Braat's services had implications for the book's physical and visual attributes, for Braat, like other printers of his day, had a unique set of printing tools at his disposal as well as his own design sensibilities. How much influence van Braght wielded over *The Bloody Theater*'s design is impossible to know, though we can be sure that Braat's craftsmanship and the scope of his printing technologies shaped the book's visual features, including the printer's device he placed on the title page. The central feature of this device, a farmer spading the earth in the shadow of a European village, was not unique to Braat's print shop, let alone to *The Bloody Theater,* but it continued to appear, albeit in modified form, in later editions of the book. In the device, the farmer is encircled by a large laurel wreath and, more significantly, awaits a laurel crown straight from heaven's hand. Clearly the digging man is being rewarded for his labor, and the Latin words on the emblem—"Fac et Spera"—reveal the reason for his reward. The literal meaning of these words is "Do and Hope," though many readers would likely have connected them to Psalm 36 in the Latin Vulgate:

"Trust in the Lord, and do good, and dwell in the land, and thou shalt be fed with its riches."[66] For Braat, and for other European printers who employed that same motto, diligent labor, when combined with trust in God, would beget God's blessings.[67]

Although Braat the printer was ultimately responsible for the digging-man device, the message it conveyed—that diligent work for the king-dom of God would not go unrewarded—would have registered with the book's author-editor. Enlarging and updating de Ries's *Martyrs Mirror* was a herculean task, and van Braght's efforts in this regard were all the more impressive given his poor health. In an invocation that launches *The Bloody Theater,* van Braght thanks God for allowing him to finish the work, "for snares of death had compassed me, keeping me bound

Fig. 3.1. Printer's device of Jacob Braat, printer of *The Bloody Theater* (1660).
The Latin words "Fac et Spera" mean "do and hope."

nearly six months" during the previous year. So severe was his illness, van Braght attests, "that I often thought I could not survive."[68] Even so, van Braght persevered, bolstered by the knowledge that his suffering, however modest compared to the martyrs' anguish, allowed him to participate in their sacrifice. Ignoring his doctors' advice to set the project aside, van Braght completed his work in the summer of 1659. Five years later he died, three months shy of his fortieth birthday.

In the long run, de Ries's title, *Martyrs Mirror,* won the day. By the time the second edition of van Braght's *Bloody Theater* was published in 1685, the words "martyrs mirror" had migrated from near the bottom of his lengthy title to near the top and, as a result, became the de facto title.[69] The words "martyrs mirror" maintain that status today. Although van Braght's chosen title may take precedence in formal contexts, in popular parlance the work almost always goes by the name *Martyrs Mirror* or, in German, *Märtyrer-Spiegel.* Publishers have largely accommodated themselves to this reality. For instance, in the twentieth- and early twenty-first-century English editions published by the Mennonite Publishing House and Herald Press, the words "The Bloody Theater" appear higher on the title page, but the words "Martyrs Mirror" appear in a larger font. Moreover, the book's spine features the words "Martyrs Mirror," not "The Bloody Theater."

Still, if de Ries fashioned the most venerable title, van Braght produced the most enduring text. It was van Braght's text, not de Ries's, that was later translated into German and English, editions that continue in print today. Utilizing "many authentic chronicles, memorials, [and] testimonies" (the final phrase on van Braght's title page), van Braght assembled a martyrology that has stood the test of time. These chronicles, memorials, and testimonies are the focus of the next chapter.

CHAPTER 4

The Bloody Theater

Martyr Stories and More

In line with its gruesome title, van Braght's *Bloody Theater* oozes with suffering and death. Consider the story of Hendrick Pruyt, a Dutch Mennonite taken prisoner in Workum in 1574. After separating Pruyt from his wife, Pruyt's inquisitors pressed him on his Anabaptist convictions. His views confirmed, they slathered him with tar, bound him to a boat, and set the boat afire in a nearby harbor. As the flames mounted, Pruyt worked his hands free, but his hopes for freedom were short-lived. Worried their quarry might escape, Pruyt's captors "thrust him through" and thus ended his life. Their contempt for Pruyt was equaled only by their disdain for his wife, who had somehow escaped their grasp. "If I had her here," said the group's leader, "she would have to go the same route."[1]

The account of Pruyt's martyrdom, unique in some of its details, follows a narrative structure—capture, separation, inquisition, torture, and death—that is replicated hundreds of times in *The Bloody Theater*. Still, if van Braght's book is first and foremost a compilation of martyr accounts, it cannot be reduced to one, for along with narrating these stories, *The Bloody Theater* provides a much more comprehensive account of Christian faithfulness. In van Braght's estimation, the martyrs' resolve in the face of danger held great potential to inspire contemporary readers, but inspiration counted for nothing unless it served a particular end. For that reason van Braght needed to do more than recite stories of suffering and death, with victims on one side and tormentors on the other. He needed to sketch a trans-historical picture of what it meant to be authentically Christian. Convinced that his church's future hung in the balance, he needed to offer a moral assessment of Christian history, identifying those who had rightly and wrongly claimed the mantle of Jesus Christ.

Van Braght's assessment takes a variety of forms in *The Bloody Theater*. Most fundamentally, it comes through van Braght's definition of true martyrdom, which he limited to baptism-minded, defenseless Christians who died on account of their faith. But van Braght's assessment of Christian faithfulness shows through in many other ways: through the book's ornamental title page, through van Braght's overview of the true church and its false counterpart, through detailed interrogation accounts, and through the letters that flowed between imperiled Anabaptists and their families and friends. These diverse components of *The Bloody Theater* illumine the martyr narratives, highlighting the convictions for which the martyrs died and, correspondingly, telling readers what convictions they should value. Taken together, they provide a window into van Braght's methods as a Mennonite minister who found history to be both dramatic and useful.

Seeing the Book as Whole

The text of *The Bloody Theater* is complex, comprising an array of literary genres spread among multiple sections. For all its complexity, however, *The Bloody Theater* is unswervingly purposeful. It may appear that van Braght incorporated items that were not directly relevant to his martyrological objectives, but a closer examination reveals how each of the book's components contributes to his overarching goals.

Generally speaking, the 1660 edition of *The Bloody Theater* consists of two main parts (see table 4.1). Part 1 includes editorial front matter and book 1, pre-Reformation historical material compiled by van Braght that, in light of its belated compilation, is sometimes called the New Book. Part 2 also begins with editorial front matter, though it mostly consists of book 2, Reformation-era accounts that van Braght transcribed from Hans de Ries's earlier work, *Martyrs Mirror*. Because book 2 relies so heavily on de Ries's work, it is sometimes called the Old Book.

The front matter to part 1 sets the stage for the nearly fifteen-hundred-page tome, revealing van Braght's purposes most explicitly. Spanning

Table 4.1. Organization of *The Bloody Theater* (1660)

Part 1

Title pages for *The Bloody Theater* (2 printed pages)

Front matter to part 1 (116 printed pages)

    Editor's invocation*

    Editor's preface, in two parts

    Editor's introduction

    Editor's accounts of the true church and the false church

    Poems

    Registers

Title page for book 1 (1 printed page)

Book 1, compiled by van Braght (417 printed pages)

    Baptism/persecution in the first century

    Baptism/persecution in the second century

    Baptism/persecution in the third century

    . . . .

    Baptism/persecution in the fifteenth century

Part 2

Title page for part 2 (1 printed page)

Front matter to part 2 (20 printed pages)

    Editor's preface

    Preface to 1631 *Martyrs Mirror*

Book 2 (892 printed pages)

    Sixteenth-century summary: baptism and martyrdom

    Hans de Ries's Old Book (*Martyrs Mirror*)

    Seventeenth-century persecution

Back matter (28 printed pages)

    Registers

    Disputations

Note: This organizational summary pertains to the 1660 edition. All later editions were formatted and paginated differently. In some cases, new material was added and original material was deleted or presented in a different order.

*Attribution to the editor means it was written by Thieleman van Braght.

more than a hundred pages, the front matter has six subsections: van Braght's invocation, his two-part preface, his introduction, his accounts of the true church and the false church, three poems,[2] and nine different registers or indexes.[3] In his preface, van Braght addresses both Anabaptist readers ("my beloved friends and companions in Christ Jesus our Savior") and non-Anabaptist readers ("good friends and fellow citizens"), inviting both audiences to consider the heroic sacrifices of the Anabaptist martyrs.[4] The preface leads straightaway into the introduction, where van Braght defends his editorial decisions and provides instructions on how to read the book. Here van Braght explains the work's title, elucidates the word *Doopsgesinde,* makes a case for choosing adult baptism as a useful marker of true Christianity, and briefly defends his inclusion of pre-Reformation Christian martyrs in a publication about baptism-minded Christians. The largest subsections of the front matter, and ones we will consider in more detail below, are his accounts of the true church and the false church, which together consume over half of the front matter's 116 pages.

In book 1 (the New Book), van Braght begins to tell stories, pre-Reformation historical accounts that, for the most part, did not appear in de Ries's work. Van Braght divides this narrative material century by century, beginning with the first century and proceeding chronologically through the fifteenth century. He further divides each century into two distinct parts: accounts of believers' baptism in that century, followed by accounts of martyrdom in that same century. Often persons who appear in the baptism segment of a given century make a repeat appearance in the century's martyrdom segment, enabling van Braght to establish a link between martyrdom and baptism-mindedness.

If van Braght did not draw the baptism and martyr accounts in book 1 from de Ries's *Martyrs Mirror,* from where did he derive them? Van Braght answers that question by including four lists of sources among his part 1 registers, and he further addresses this question by directly citing his sources in the text.[5] Of paramount importance to van Braght was the work of Old Frisian minister Pieter van Twisck, in particular Twisck's two-volume *Chroniik van den Ondergangh der Tyrannen* (Chronicle of the downfall of tyrants), published in 1617 and 1620.[6] Twisck himself borrowed from Sebastian Franck's *Chronica, Zeitbuch, und Geschichtsbibel* (1531), a work that had long been popular among Anabaptists and which provided van Braght with additional examples of persecuted faithfulness.[7] In contrast to Twisck's *Downfall of Tyrants,* some of van Braght's key sources for book 1 were not internal to the Anabaptist tradition; in fact, in some cases, van Braght drew on sources that were opposed to it. In the early parts of book 1, which cover the centuries when Christians were being martyred by non-Christians, van Braght draws upon Eusebius's *Ecclesiastical History,* produced in the fourth century. He also draws on the work of two Reformed ministers, Abraham Philippus Mellin's *Groot Rechtgevoelende Christen Martelaers-Boeck* (Great justice-minded Christian martyr book), published in 1619, and Johannes Gysius's *Historie der Martelaren* (History of the martyrs), published in 1657.[8] In book 1's later centuries, those in which the Catholic Church hounded people it deemed heretical, van Braght continues to utilize Mellin's *Christian Martyr Book,* but he also cites the martyrological work of the English Calvinist John Foxe. As van Braght makes assertions about authentic baptismal practices, he often cites Jakob Mehrning's *Heilige Tuaff-Historia* (History of holy baptism), published in 1646–47, to buttress his case.[9]

A second title page signals the beginning of part 2, which, like part 1, begins with editorial front matter. The front matter to part 2 is shorter and simpler than that of part 1, including just two subsections: an editor's preface, written by van Braght, and Jan Philipsz Schabaelje's preface to Hans de Ries's *Martyrs Mirror.* In his editor's preface, van Braght sets the stage for part 2, noting that part 1 accounted for only half of the story of Christian martyrdom. Compared to the effort required for producing the first part, "our labor will be greatly lessened here," he writes, for "previous accounts" compiled by de Ries and earlier martyrologists provide most of the content. "We do not propose to make any essential change" to these earlier accounts, van Braght continues, though he does aim to complement some portions with material obtained "from the hands of magistrates, criminal authorities, criminal clerks and other sources."[10] Following this address, van Braght presents his readers with Schabaelje's preface to de Ries's martyrology.[11] In it Schabaelje identifies the objective for producing *Martyrs Mirror,* namely, to increase the spiritual fervor of Dutch Mennonites whose priorities had become misplaced. Schabaelje also outlines a nascent argument about the succession of the true church through time, an argument that van Braght develops in *The Bloody Theater* much more fully than de Ries did in his *Martyrs Mirror* (see "The True Church and the False Church: Van Braght's Accounts" below).

Book 2 (the Old Book) is the largest section of *The Bloody Theater,* constituting 892 of its nearly fifteen hundred pages. Drawing largely from de Ries's work, van Braght nonetheless reframes de Ries's content with new material: a summary of baptism and martyrdom in the sixteenth century (at the outset of book 2) and some new materials pertaining to the seventeenth century (at the close of book 2). The baptism-martyrdom summary at the beginning of book 2 parallels the bipartite organizational scheme in book 1. In it, van Braght argues that adult baptism "was at this time also correctly taught, practiced and maintained, by those who may be called orthodox believers."[12] To establish his case, van Braght includes testimony from sixteenth-century theological debates that captured the Anabaptists' rationale for adult baptism. Van Braght also includes in this section two confessions: a confession from a second-generation German Anabaptist, Thomas van Imbrœck, and an Old Frisian confession of faith (sometimes called "The Thirty-Three Articles") that had appeared in the Old Frisian martyrology produced by Peter Jans Twisck in 1617.[13] Van Imbrœck's confession, which was written in prison in 1558, makes an extended case for adult baptism and thus fits well in this section devoted to baptism in the sixteenth century.[14] And while the Old Frisian confession covers many topics at length, it too makes an extended case for adult baptism, much more so than the three Mennonite confessions in the front matter to book 1. Taken together, van Imbrœck's confession and the Old Frisian confession advance van Braght's goal of making *The Bloody Theater* an interconfessional, as well as a pan-European, Anabaptist martyrology.

Van Braght follows his sixteenth-century baptism section with information about early-sixteenth-century persecution (that is, persecution that preceded the emergence of Anabaptism in Zurich in 1525), then launches into de Ries's *Martyrs Mirror* material. Of course, de Ries himself had taken much of his material from earlier Anabaptist martyrologies, which means that book 2 includes a lot of material from older Anabaptist sources. Indeed, a modest core of the Old Book's contents can be traced to the first edition of *The Sacrifice of the Lord,* published in 1562.[15] This is not to suggest that van Braght's editorial hand is not present in this part of *The Bloody Theater,* for he reordered some of de Ries's martyr accounts and supplemented others with documents he discovered in his research. For the most part, however, van Braght follows de Ries's lead in book 2 until he gets to the seventeenth century. From this point on in book 2, van Braght once again becomes the primary author-editor. For instance, as he reiterates the well-traveled story of Hans Landis, he adds an entirely new account of Landis's execution that had only recently come to light.[16] He also adds recent edicts against Anabaptists, stories of unjust imprisonments, and letters from influential persons in defense of the Anabaptists, some of which were written in early 1660.[17] Nearly all of this new seventeenth-century material pertains to the Swiss Brethren experience, signaling that van Braght, like de Ries before him, was committed to making his work a pan-European Anabaptist martyrology. As he moves to the conclusion of book 2, van Braght offers a prayer on behalf of secular powers, asking God to forgive rulers who had persecuted the faithful and asking God to bless rulers who had granted them tolerance.[18]

The back matter to part 2 brings *The Bloody Theater* to its conclusion. It begins with two registers that point readers to specific pages and columns in book 2; the first register indexes specific incidents of persecution, and the second register indexes Anabaptist martyrs by name. The second section of the back matter, an unpaged appendix, consists of two disputations that took place in 1569, the first between a Franciscan monk named Cornelis and Anabaptist Jacob de Roore, and the second between Cornelis and Anabaptist Herman Vleckwijk. The disputation with de Roore, also known as Jacob Keersgieter, appeared in the main text of de Ries's *Martyrs Mirror*, but van Braght moved it to the end of *The Bloody Theater*.[19] The Vleckwijk disputation did not appear in de Ries's book.

The editor who revised van Braght's *Bloody Theater* in 1685 took the liberty to add a few items and rearrange some of van Braght's material. Later translators and publishers took similar liberties, the upshot being that no subsequent edition of *The Bloody Theater* presented the same material in the same order as van Braght's edition. Even the ornamental title page changed in subsequent editions, depriving subsequent generations of the chance to see the artwork that launched van Braght's 1660 edition. For that reason, we begin our consideration of *The Bloody Theater*'s content by examining this richly symbolic work of art.

Worth a Thousand Words: The Ornamental Title Page

Despite the iconoclastic impulses of sixteenth-century Protestantism, the practice of ornamenting devotional works, including the Bible, was common in the Dutch Republic.[20] Seventeenth-century Mennonite martyrologies reflected this trend; unlike their sixteenth-century precursors, all seventeenth-century Mennonite martyrologies included ornamental title pages, the production of which was likely a collaboration between the author-editor, the printer, and a hired artist.[21] In the case of *The Bloody Theater*'s ornamental title page, the artist's identity has been lost to history, as has van Braght's role in the page's design. Clearly, however, the artwork exhibits a keen familiarity with the book's central theme: that throughout the church's history, authentic Christians have experienced suffering in the manner of Jesus Christ. Hounded by authorities who feigned allegiance to God, suggests the detailed imagery, Christ's followers chose the path of faithfulness, incensing their foes and prompting their own deaths but culminating in eternal life.

The ornamental page abounds with persecution scenes, but more than merely presaging the book's martyrological message, the images serve to connect Reformation-era martyrs to Jesus and his disciples. The largest persecution scene, on the middle left, shows the biblical figure Stephen being stoned by a helmeted soldier and a bearded Jewish leader. Opposite Stephen's stoning is a picture of a man being crucified upside down, most likely the apostle Peter, who, according to Christian tradition, was crucified in this way at his own request. Other portraits of martyrdom, most of them showing people in early modern garb, ring the page: a body being dropped into a river, a man lashed to a stake while another is beheaded nearby, two corpses hanging limply from the gallows, a man in stocks, a body being devoured by a lion, and two men being hurled over a cliff. Together these images of martyrdom envelop the book's lengthy title, which appears on a white cloth held aloft by two cherubs. At the bottom of the page sit two more cherubs, one in each corner. The bottom-left cherub holds a picture of a priest holding a cross over the burial of a martyr, an example of bogus religiosity that makes the cherub gag. At the bottom right the other cherub weeps as he holds an image of a man and a woman who will soon be flogged.

The cherubs' presence on the page conveys the close connection between the martyrs and their heavenly reward, though another image makes the connection even clearer. At the top of the ornamental page, directly above the title, stands the crucified Christ, bearing his cross and displaying stigmata from the nails that pierced his hands. The crucified Christ gazes upward at a heavenly scene, where he is himself clothed

Fig. 4.1. Ornamental title page of *The Bloody Theater* (1660). The abundant martyr imagery associates Reformation-era martyrs with Jesus and his disciples.

in a white robe. Gathered around the heavenly Christ is a great throng of people, some of them kneeling with their hands piously folded. Arrayed in white, they together worship their Lord, thus depicting Revelation 7:9–17, which describes a great multitude bowing down to worship the Lamb of God. In this apocalyptic vision, John the Revelator asks about the worshippers' identity and is told that they are people "who have come out of the great ordeal." With their suffering now past, God will provide them with the "water of life" and "wipe away every tear from their eyes."[22]

In sum, the ornamental title page provides a visual summary of *The Bloody Theater's* content, trajectory, and argument. By standing with Stephen and Peter, the Anabaptist martyrs inhabit a line of faithful witnesses that stretches back to the New Testament. Like the early Christian martyrs, their only crimes are following Jesus and preaching his pure gospel. Innocent as the cherubs who populate the page, they must nonetheless carry Jesus's cross, enduring the wrath of both government officials and religious authorities. They can rest assured, however, that a just and powerful God rules the universe. In the end their reward will transcend anything they suffer on earth.

The True Church and the False Church: Van Braght's Accounts

Van Braght's accounts of the true church and the false church, which follow directly on the heels of his part 1 introduction, decode the conflict on the ornamental title page. Having explained to his readers the term *baptism-minded,* and having made a case for including proto-Anabaptists in his martyrology, van Braght turns his attention to the conundrum that runs through his text: the reality that most of the martyrs' killers were people who themselves claimed the name of Christ. Who were these faux Christians, and where did they go wrong? What led them to kill the very people whose faith they should have embraced? And why should his readers sympathize with the Anabaptists and not their religious foes? To answer these questions, van Braght offers an expansive appraisal of Christian history, demarcating key distinctions between "the true church of God" and "the ungodly and false church."[23]

Van Braght begins his consideration of the true church with the question of origins, but in contrast to Catholic accounts of the church's origins, van Braght pays little attention to the apostles, much less to Simon Peter. Instead, van Braght asserts that the "divine and heavenly church . . . originated upon earth at the beginning of the world," that is, with Adam and Eve. According to van Braght, the godly church has always shared two attributes. First, it has always provided "divine service" that presents Christ, sometimes typologically, as the means of salvation.[24] Second, God "has always ordained teachers in His church" to proclaim his will.[25] Again, this process of ordaining leaders did not begin with Peter or his fellow disciples; rather, it began in Genesis, when men such as Enoch were ordained by God to preach God's judgment and grace.[26] This preaching office has never stood empty, says van Braght, and he defends his claim with an inventory of leading biblical lights, from Abraham and Moses to the prophets and ultimately to the New Testament apostles.

Van Braght's goal in this is to establish that the church of God has been both durable and visible through time. The godly church was not here one day and gone the next, disappearing in times when ungodly people achieved numerical and political dominance. To prove this assertion, van Braght recites a litany of divine promises in which God guarantees his enduring presence with his people.[27] He takes particular delight in Jesus's postresurrection words: "And, lo, I am with you all the days, even unto the consummation of the ages." In light of this promise, van Braght says, no one can doubt that "the visible church . . . shall exist through all time," even to the present.[28] To be sure, just as the moon is sometimes invisible to particular people, the church has sometimes disappeared from some regions in certain times. Still, "when we speak of the obscuration, concealment, or the becoming invisible, of the church of God, we do not mean the church in general, or in all places, for the church in general has never been obscured and hidden in all places at the same time."[29]

The key to understanding van Braght's argument, then, is to understand what he means by the "general church" (*algemeyne Kercke*). This cannot mean "all the churches which bear the Christian name," he says, "but only those who express the Christian name by their upright faith and pure observance of the Christian and Evangelical commandments."[30] To establish the identity of this upright church, van Braght posits a line of ecclesiastical succession that runs from apostolic times to the seventeenth century. This succession occurred on two levels, he says, through a "succession of persons" who propagated the gospel one to another, and through the "succession of doctrine," which he defines as doctrinal claims that comport with apostolic writings.[31] Citing Tertullian, van Braght argues that the succession of persons is not sufficient for securing the true church, for some successors corrupted the gospel as they passed it along.[32] Nonetheless, he says, a succession of doctrine has been manifest through the ages, for various postapostolic churches preserved and propagated doctrine that corresponded to apostolic teaching. Van Braght offers little evidence in this regard, but he does identify four historic statements that, in his view, demonstrate kinship with the apostles' teaching. Significantly, only one of these four statements, the Apostles Creed, may be considered a broadly ecumenical creed. The other three statements—the Olive Branch Confession (1627), the Jan Cents Confession (1630), and the Dordrecht Confession of Faith (1632)—were all produced by seventeenth-century Dutch Mennonites.[33] Rendering the Nicene Creed invisible and implicitly rejecting all Catholic, Lutheran, and Calvinist confessions as theologically deficient, van Braght effectually identifies the true church with Christians on the margins.

This bold stroke does not conclude van Braght's consideration of church history, however, for alongside the true church there has always existed an ungodly church. Like the true church, this false church had a distinct origin, and it too has a line of succession that can be traced through time. Van Braght locates the false church's origin in Cain's murder of Abel, an act whereby Cain became "a leader of the children of Satan" and Abel became the world's first "martyr."[34] From there van Braght traces a line of unfaithfulness through the biblical text and then into postbiblical history, when the "Roman church" came to power, deceitfully claiming that it stood in the line of true ecclesiastical succession. Van Braght admits that the papists (*Papisten*) could appeal to ancient origins; even so, the biblical record proves that "evil is as ancient as the good."[35] In other words, the proof of Christian authenticity lies not in antique origins but in faithful doctrine and practice, a faithfulness that, in van Braght's view, is sorely lacking in Roman Catholic history.

Van Braght elaborates his critique of Catholicism along two tracks, the first of which addresses Catholic claims about Peter and Rome. With respect to Peter's alleged status as the first pope, van Braght argues that

Catholics have made a mountain out of a molehill of biblical evidence. Yes, a few gospel passages indicate that Jesus called Peter to church leadership, but the responsibilities Jesus assigned to Peter were duties that Jesus assigned to the other apostles as well.[36] Van Braght also accuses Catholics of exaggerating Peter's connection to the city of Rome, which later became the site of the papacy. Peter may have spent some time in Rome, van Braght allows, but not nearly as much time as Paul. Moreover, the Bible never says that Peter headed the Roman church, and the patristic authors who make that claim often contradict one another. In sum, "it cannot be shown that Peter was ever at Rome . . . except at the close of his life, and then he was not received as pope, but was put to death as a martyr."[37] In other words, should the name of Peter be invoked when considering the church's history, he should be placed squarely on the side of the martyrs, not on the side of the persecutors.

Having dealt with the problem of Peter and Rome, van Braght embarks on a second line of critique with respect to the Catholic Church: the papacy's tawdry history. It is one thing to quibble over Peter and his line of succession; it is quite another to examine the century-by-century reality of the papacy. To this end, van Braght draws on numerous published histories, including some by Catholic authors, to show how abject that history has been.[38] In some instances, the seat of the papacy sat empty for years; in other instances, two or three or even four people claimed to be pope simultaneously. Sometimes the papal seat was usurped by power-hungry clerics; at other times politicians installed popes who would do their bidding. The moral behavior of the popes was as scandalous as the selection processes. In fact, the popes' behavior was such that it frequently triggered divine and deadly judgment ("Hadrian IV was choked to death by a fly, which flew into his mouth," and "Leo X died while laughing and frolicking at his cups").[39] In sum, anyone who takes an honest look at the papacy's history would have to conclude that God's purposes were being worked out elsewhere.

With this conclusion van Braght brings his readers full circle, readying them for the hundreds of martyr accounts that lie ahead. His point is simple and starkly dualistic: forsaken in the halls of power, God has nonetheless been present in the faithful, suffering church. Moreover, God's affection for the faithful portends eternal consequences for all involved, for not only will the faithful receive their blessed reward, but their tormentors will receive their just deserts. "He that toucheth you," says van Braght, quoting the prophet Zechariah, "toucheth the apple of God's eye," and touching the apple of God's eye means risking God's wrath.[40] For van Braght the past is important, but it is no more important than the present or the future. And because he considers the future to be every bit as dualistic as the past, with heaven and hell as the only options, van Braght views the present as the most important time of all: the ever-vanishing time to escape the judgment of God. As van Braght approaches history with a preacher's penchant, the martyrs offer him an unparalleled service, forcing his privileged readers to decide exactly where they stand.

Interrogations and the Anabaptist Witness

Much of *The Bloody Theater* consists of narrative material that concludes with a resolute Christian's death. Still, like the Anabaptist martyrologies that preceded it, *The Bloody Theater* does more than recount the who, when, where, and how of death. To be sure, Anabaptist martyrologists wanted to record such details before they were forgotten, but they also wanted to produce manuals that tutored readers in their beliefs and convictions. Toward that end, van Braght's *Bloody Theater* includes a host of interrogation accounts that outline Anabaptist beliefs in memorable fashion. The work's interrogative material takes two primary forms. In some instances, the material derives from official court transcripts that a martyrologist secured and reprinted. In other instances, the interrogative material derives from literary artifacts the martyrs produced, such as letters that recounted jailhouse interrogations. In contrast to the detailed Dutch Mennonite confessions of faith, the interrogation accounts reduce the Anabaptist faith to its bare essentials. For potential readers who may have been daunted or unconvinced by the finer points of Dutch Mennonite theology, these accounts set forth the essential convictions that, in van Braght's view, were worth dying for at all times and places.[41]

The content of these interrogations revolves largely around the doctrinal differences between Anabaptism and Roman Catholicism. In nearly every instance, adult baptism figures prominently, as interrogators ask their subjects whether they were rebaptized, whether they had baptized their infants, and whether they had promoted Anabaptist views on baptism. Baptism questions rarely stand alone, however, for they are frequently accompanied by questions about transubstantiation, the authority of the Catholic Church, the role of Mary, or the unwillingness of Anabaptists to swear oaths. Also common are questions regarding the confession of sins, the status of the Apocrypha, and the existence of purgatory. In all these cases, the interrogators ask questions in a pointed manner, leaving little room for misunderstanding. "Why did you not have your children baptized?" asks one inquisitor, addressing Claesken, a mother of three, before proceeding to question her about Communion ("Do you believe that Christ consecrates himself, and is present in the bread?") and the authority of church tradition ("Are you wiser than the holy church?").[42] The Anabaptists on trial are sometimes ambiguous (in response to what she "think[s] of the holy church," Claesken replies, "I think much of it"), but they are more often forthright in ways that reveal their Anabaptist convictions. For instance, to the question "Why did you not have your children baptized?" Claesken replies, "I cannot find in the Scriptures that this ought to be," an answer the reveals not only the mother's commitment to adult baptism, but also her willingness to reject the pope's authority when her understanding of scripture demanded it.[43]

This latter conviction, that a plain reading of scripture trumps church tradition, finds its way into nearly every interrogation account, informing Anabaptist responses to nearly every other theological question they face. If *The Bloody Theater* is any reflection of reality, Anabaptists knew the Bible well, and they cited it frequently to defend their views. For instance, in response to a bailiff's string of questions, Adrian Corneliss quotes verses from six different New Testament books.[44] In other instances Anabaptist detainees make broader biblical references to support their views, for example, Jacob de Roore's reply to a question about the church's authority to absolve sin, which references seven chapters in the letter to the Hebrews.[45] Even when they were not quoting directly from the Bible or citing chapter and verse, they were often recounting biblical stories and lessons that van Braght cited, chapter and verse, in the margins. Van Braght's use of his book's margins to include scriptural citations was not unique to him (earlier Anabaptist martyrologists had done the same thing), but it did represent a choice on how to use the white space that surrounded the text. Unlike John Foxe, the English martyrologist who used his margins to condemn the persecutors' actions, van Braght chose to include scripture references, a choice that, like *The Bloody Theater*'s ornamental title page, served to link the Anabaptist martyrs to biblical history. More than that, observes historian Sarah Covington, van Braght's inclusion of marginal scripture references bathed his book "in a holy glow, turning [the] text sacred."[46]

Significantly, however, many Anabaptists who are placed on stage in *The Bloody Theater* do more than mechanically cite biblical texts to make their points. They advance clever and sometimes sophisticated arguments to counter the claims made by their opponents. Taken as a whole, these arguments suggest that the Anabaptists were actually more thoughtful than their inquisitors, who, despite their advanced theological training, are shown to demonstrate a limited ability to substantiate their church-approved views. For instance, in the course of being questioned about infant baptism, the Anabaptist Adrian Corneliss asks whether the scriptures were intended for the edification of infants. When his inquisitor-priest answers "no," Adrian quickly replies, "If no Scripture belongs to infants, neither does baptism," a response that baffles the priest, who at that point "had nothing more to say about his infant baptism."[47] This shrewdness was not the exclusive preserve of the Anabaptist men. Anabaptist women also display a keen ability to defend their views, sometimes in haughty tones. For instance, when Maeyken Boosers fends off her inquisitors' initial questions, they warn her that they will soon send "learned men" her way, to which Maeyken replies, "You ought to be wise enough to talk with me."[48] Another woman, Weynken, is even more audacious. When asked, "What do you hold concerning the holy oil?" she responds, "Oil is good for salad, or to oil your shoes with."[49] As one would expect, the inquisitors do not take kindly to these brazen women, and in one case they accuse their female detainee, Elisabeth, of "a spirit of pride." Surely aware of the submissiveness expected from her, Elisabeth rejects her judges' accusation with her own words of censure. "No, my lords," she replies, "I speak with frankness."[50]

In addition to demonstrating the Anabaptists' intellectual prowess, *The Bloody Theater*'s interrogations mark the Anabaptists as more composed and confident in their possession of the truth than their interrogators. Unlike those who question them, the accused rarely become unsettled, let alone unhinged. Nowhere is this contrast more apparent than in the lengthy disputations between Friar Cornelis, a Franciscan

monk, and two Anabaptist men, Jacob de Roore and Herman Vleckwijck, which van Braght placed at the end of *The Bloody Theater*.[51]
Throughout the disputations, de Roore and Vleckwijck answer Cornelis's queries directly and serenely, even as the friar becomes exasperated
and hostile. Almost from the start, Cornelis resorts to coarse language,
so coarse in fact that some later editions omitted the offensive words,
replaced them with hatch marks or asterisks, or rendered them into in-
nocuous phrases.[52] Even in English, however, Cornelis's exasperation
shows through his dismissive utterances, his puerile name-calling, and
his overall demeanor. In response to de Roore's claim that all of God's
people are priests, the friar explodes, "Tush, tush! Now you begin to
preach again, do you?"[53] Later, after de Roore says that "confirmation is
a bugbear about which I know nothing," Cornelis dismisses his Anabaptist foe as an ignoramus.[54] The insults keep coming, picking up steam as
the disputations run their course. At one point during his disputation
with the Anabaptist Vleckwijck, Cornelis becomes so overwrought that
other court officials feel compelled to calm him down. "Ah, father Cornelis, do be modest and keep your temper," says the clerk. "Yes," agrees
the recorder, "converse together with kind, calm words; for it seems that
you . . . quarrel and bicker here like harlots."[55]

The authenticity of these disputations with Friar Cornelis has long
been considered suspect, but the ostensible serenity of de Roore and
Vleckwijck bears a larger point that Anabaptist martyrologists wanted
to convey: the strength of the martyrs' convictions in the face of death.[56]
Anabaptists undergoing questioning know that their convictions, if confessed and reaffirmed, will almost certainly result in torture or death.
Those who are married realize that they may never see their spouses
again, and those with children know that their young ones might be
taken from them. Despite this knowledge, and despite the encouragement of their interrogators to recant their views, the Anabaptists whose
stories fill *The Bloody Theater* maintain their convictions. The inquisitors
sometimes remind their captives of what they have to gain: the chance to
avoid suffering, the chance to go free, and the prospect of living a longer,
more comfortable life. In some cases, the interrogators seem genuinely
troubled about the punishment they will soon be meting out. "My dear
child," the Lady of Friesland tells Jacques Dosie, "come over to our side,
and repent, and you shall get out of this trouble." When Dosie demurs,

she begs him once again, asking now that *he* take pity on *her*. "If you, so young a child, should die for this cause, it would be a heavy cross for my heart." In the end, however, the lady's supplications go for naught. Dosie, according to the narrator, "valiantly repelled all the subtle devices of Satan," which included "severe threats" as well as "fair promises." Since "nothing could move him to forsake Christ, he was condemned to death by the rulers of the darkness of this world."[57]

Undergirding the Anabaptists' willingness to die was a bedrock belief that they shared with many of their theological rivals, and especially with other early modern martyrs: the conviction that Christian faithfulness led to eternal life and, conversely, unfaithfulness led to a fate far worse than death. In Brad Gregory's words, early modern martyrs "measured temporal pain against eternal gain and drew the logical conclusion," namely, that temporary agony was preferable to the horrors of hell.[58] This conviction sometimes surfaced in the martyrs' exchanges with their inquisitors, as it did in the interrogation of Anabaptist Hans Knevel. When Knevel's inquisitor promised him "mercy" if only he would recant, Knevel countered that such a show of mercy would demonstrate love for his mortal body but hatred for his soul. In fact, said Knevel, the real mercy would be "that I shall have my head cut off."[59] With these words, Knevel reveals a common assumption among Anabaptist martyrs: that earthly suffering served as a mark of God's favor. Of course, some Anabaptists in similar circumstances lost their nerve, but Knevel and many others did not, some going so far as to forgo opportunities to escape from imprisonment.[60] The narrator picks up the story after Knevel's inquisition, noting that "he was in no wise to be moved, since he was firmly built upon the cornerstone of Christ Jesus." Though he was burned at the stake in 1572, Knevel's death was not the end of him, concludes the narrator, for he "obtained the crown of eternal glory through the grace of God."[61]

Compared to some interrogations in *The Bloody Theater*, Knevel's interrogation is relatively short. According to the redactors, the original source was a long prison letter in which Knevel recounted his inquisition and "communicate[d] at length the firm foundation of his faith" to two friends. In an attempt to keep the narrative moving, however, the redactors elected to exclude Knevel's letter, "even as we have also done with a large number of similar writings" from other martyrs.[62] Significantly, however, many of these martyrs' letters did make their way into print, providing further insight into the lives of the Anabaptist martyrs and their martyrologist's intentions.

Prison Letters as Vehicles of Spiritual Support

Letters from imprisoned Anabaptists to their friends and family members are a significant component of book 2 of *The Bloody Theater*. One Reformation scholar has counted 246 such letters, more than 70 of them from spouse to spouse.[63] Other letters that appear in book 2 flow from imprisoned parents to their children, from children to parents, from siblings to fellow siblings, and from captive Anabaptists to their congregations or particular members of those congregations.[64] Taken together, these letters reiterate the theological convictions that appear in interrogation materials. What is more distinctive, however, is the way the letters reveal the prisoners' sense of responsibility to serve as spiritual mentors to those on the outside. In the vast majority of cases, this guidance is offered to fellow Anabaptists, though in some cases the addressees are family members who have not joined the Anabaptist cause.[65] Suspecting that their time on earth is short, the letter-writers take it upon themselves to counsel those who will survive them, both persons they know intimately and people they know not at all.

In that regard, it is important to recognize that these writers, while addressing their letters to particular persons, assumed that their missives would circulate among much larger audiences. Most letters contain information that pertains to the direct recipients—practical considerations accompanied by personal expressions of care and concern—but they simultaneously assume the rhetorical structure of public homilies.[66] Some letters record the particulars of interrogations and debates that took place in the past, with the likely intent of instructing future captives on ways to respond to their inquisitors. Other letters, such as the one Jacob van den Wege wrote to his wife and other members of his Anabaptist community, contain confessional statements that provide theological content to distinctive Anabaptist beliefs, including views on adult baptism, the Lord's Supper, and the ban.[67] Although few letters include lengthy, formal confessions such as van den Wege's, a confession he claimed was written for his children's instruction, the letters almost always address some element of Anabaptist belief for which the martyrs were willing to die. In some cases, the letter-writers take pains to narrate the soteriological meaning of their impending deaths, seeming to intend such narrations for audiences beyond their families and friends. Adriaenken Jans's letter to her husband is representative of this approach. In it, she interprets the tribulations that she and another Anabaptist have suffered as "a token of [God's] grace," confirms their ongoing resolve, and assures her would-be readers that their present suffering is not in vain, "for we know and believe that the crown of eternal life is prepared for us."[68]

As with Adriaenken's letter, the most customary form of counsel contained in these prison letters was the encouragement to readers to remain steadfast.[69] The martyrs-to-be whose letters found their way into *The Bloody Theater* had determined for themselves that their eternal reward was worth the cost of suffering, and they wanted their readers to embrace that perspective as well. Captives acknowledged the difficulties that lay ahead for their surviving family members ("you will after my departure be severely assailed," wrote Maerten van der Straten to his wife),[70] but they urged them on nonetheless. Some prisoners expressed reservations about assuming this exhortatory role, for they realized it could be seen as claiming a place of spiritual superiority to their recipients, most of whom were also committed Anabaptists. To counter that possible interpretation, prisoners frequently conceded that they were unworthy to be giving such guidance or, in some cases, proceeded to assure their readers of their confidence in their readers' spiritual state.[71] In one instance, the prisoner justified his admonitions by citing the biblical command to "exhort one another daily." In other cases, the prisoners justified their exhortations by citing a deep Christian love for their readers' souls.[72]

Such expressions were particularly pronounced in letters that flowed between husbands and wives, letters that closely associated marital love and spiritual love. For instance, when an imprisoned husband addressed a letter to his wife, the writer often saluted his recipient as both his "wife" and his "sister" in the Lord, and referred to himself as both her "husband" and her "brother in the Lord."[73] Indeed, as Gerald Mast has noted, these Anabaptist letter-writers "responded to one another first of all as sisters and brothers in Christ and secondarily as husbands and wives."[74] This is not to suggest that human emotion was lacking. Many letters included expressions of longing for the absent spouse, replete with tender forms of address, such as "my beloved," "my chosen," and "my lamb." Some writers even acknowledged the struggle to remain faithful, knowing that abandoning one's convictions would quickly lead to a reunion with loved ones on the outside.[75] Still, the volume of such heartfelt expressions pales in comparison to the letters' more spiritually oriented references, which invariably point to the ability of God to comfort the afflicted. In many cases the emotional longing, once expressed, is reframed as a tolerable loss in light of the eternal rewards that await those who remain steadfast, rewards that include a nuptial reunion in the hereafter.

Such rewards also awaited the prisoners' children, if only they followed in the footsteps of their Anabaptist fathers and mothers. Prisoners sometimes mentioned their children in letters to their spouses, who are encouraged to raise them in a proper Christian fashion. In some instances, however, imprisoned parents wrote directly to their children, including children who were still very young. Joris Wippe, who wrote to his children in mulberry juice after guards had confiscated his ink supply, addressed only his older children, instructing them to care for his surviving widow and his minor children. Such practical details, however, constituted a small portion of Wippe's missive, which gave more attention to the principles of godly living ("fear God," "be diligent in every good work," and "have not fellowship with the children of this world").[76] For his part, Lenaert Plovier wrote a letter to his much younger children, hoping that when they arrived at "the years of understanding," they would read his letter and "seek [their] salvation." In Plovier's case, he first instructed his children to honor and obey their mother, to resist quarrelsomeness, and to be kind. He then proceeded to address more advanced spiritual concerns: read the Bible, follow its instructions, repent, and believe the gospel. Before concluding, Plovier landed on the theme that permeates almost all the Anabaptist prison letters: yes, suffering may come, but "these sufferings are not worthy to be compared with the glory which shall be revealed in us."[77]

Despite the spiritual responsibility the prisoners felt for people outside the prison walls, they did not assume that spiritual support flowed only one way. Prisoners often reassured their recipients that they had remained steadfast, but they nonetheless confessed the need for prayer in light of their tenuous situations. One female prisoner, citing the emotional anguish of being separated from her family, asked her husband to "pray heartily in my behalf, to remove the conflict from me." In her case, the heartsickness she felt led her to wonder about her own steadfastness, hoping only that "the Lord will also help me through even as He has helped many."[78] Imprisoned husbands made the same appeal to their wives. Some asked very specifically for prayer support, including one who noted that "the prayer of the righteous avails much."[79] Other male prisoners begged their wives for letters that would bring spiritual comfort or simply news from home. In one case, a male prisoner cried upon receipt of a letter from his wife.[80] In another case, a prisoner wrote that a letter from his wife meant more "than all the riches on the face of the earth." Comparing his wife's letter to food, the prisoner declared that "a little morsel that comes from without strengthens me ten times more than what I have with me."[81]

Letters such as these were not necessary for establishing the Anabaptist martyrological record. For van Braght, however, prison letters fleshed out the lives of the Anabaptist martyrs in ways that execution scenes rarely did, providing information about the martyrs that he wanted his readers to know. The martyrs' steadfastness was impressive, to be sure, but the letters dug beneath their steely resolve to reveal their delicate humanity. Saints they may have been, but cardboard saints they were not, for their lives were fully embedded in the messy soil of human existence. More than execution scenes, more than lengthy doctrinal statements, and more than interrogation accounts, the prison letters enabled readers to understand the martyrs as human beings who missed their family members, worried about their futures, and wondered about their own ability to remain steadfast. Whether or not the prisoners wrote their letters as public homilies, van Braght made sure they served that function for his Dutch Mennonite readers, a function they continue to serve today.[82]

PART II

Van Braght's Martyrology through the Years

CHAPTER 5

The Bloody Theater Illustrated

The 1685 Martyrs Mirror

When Thieleman van Braght published *The Bloody Theater* in 1660, it is unlikely he thought his contribution to the Anabaptist martyrological tradition would represent its apogee. True, the brutal treatment of the *Doopsgesinde* in Dordrecht was now long past, but persecution remained a bitter reality for many of van Braght's spiritual kin. Indeed, even as van Braght put the finishing touches on his martyrological classic, Anabaptists in and around Bern, Switzerland, were suffering imprisonment, banishment, and worse.[1] Even if van Braght was unable to imagine additional Anabaptist martyrs, he could certainly imagine more Anabaptist martyrologies, especially in a Dutch Mennonite world that was both fractured and fractious. If van Braght stood on the literary shoulders of Hans de Ries and Pieter Jans Twisck, who would perch on his shoulders to produce the next great Anabaptist martyr book?

As it turned out, van Braght set a standard in Anabaptist martyrological writing that stood the test of time, though even his work was not immune to refinement. Twenty-five years after *The Bloody Theater*'s appearance, an unidentified editor joined forces with new publishers, this time in the city of Amsterdam, to revise and reissue the work. Compared to van Braght's efforts in 1660, the new revisions were minor. Still, some modifications were made, none more striking than the addition of 104 copper etchings that illustrated specific accounts in the text. Created by the renowned artist Jan Luyken, these etchings did not always make their way into later editions of the book. Nonetheless, the addition of these illustrations in 1685 must be counted as the most significant post–van Braght revision of *The Bloody Theater,* a revision that even today shapes many people's encounter with the book.

The Bloody Theater: Reception and Republication

The Dutch context that witnessed the publication of *The Bloody Theater* in 1660 may have been tolerant of Anabaptists, but it was still super-intended by Calvinist elites. Calvinist clergy kept a close eye on their Mennonite counterparts, and those who caught wind of van Braght's work were no doubt chagrined by the thought of a new book extolling Anabaptist virtues. Even before *The Bloody Theater* went to press, some of van Braght's Reformed adversaries sought to prevent its publication.[2] When their attempts at censorship failed, a Reformed synod solicited a response to the book from Christianus Schotanus, a Calvinist theologian who taught at the University of Franeker. Schotanus published his critique in 1671, eleven years after *The Bloody Theater* appeared.[3] In it he disputed van Braght's claim that the Anabaptists had no connection to the Münsterite revolt. To the contrary, Schotanus wrote, the origin of the Dutch Mennonite church could be traced directly to Münster's insurgents. Citing the rebels as prototypical Anabaptists, the Reformed theologian argued that Dutch Mennonites should not be tolerated in the present, a clear directive to Dutch authorities who had shown increasing forbearance over the years.[4]

Schotanus's attack on *The Bloody Theater* may have scared off some readers, but it did not eliminate customer demand. Although the number of first-edition copies sold in the decades following 1660 was likely only a few hundred, a group of Amsterdam businessmen visualized sufficient demand in the 1680s to underwrite a second edition of van Braght's work.[5] In contrast to the Mennonite van Braght and his fellow Mennonite printer, these new sponsors were Calvinist businessmen, who, in 1683, established an entrepreneurial group with the aim of producing a new edition of van Braght's work.[6] From an ecclesial standpoint these Reformed church members had nothing to gain from memorializing Anabaptist martyrs. What they did have to gain was money, a clear-eyed goal in light of the success of two new editions of Adriaen

van Haemstede's sixteenth-century Calvinist martyrology, richly illustrated works that were printed in Dordrecht in 1657 and 1659.[7] With an
eye toward securing a customer base, the group developed literature to
interest potential buyers. Just as importantly, they sought the government's protection of their investment by securing an exclusive privilege
to sell the book for fifteen years. By cornering the market in this way, the
publishers could charge a high price for their work, and they did. In the
book's publication prospectus, the publishers offered potential buyers
two choices: a "common" edition at eight and a half guilders, and a "fine"
edition with better paper at thirteen guilders.[8] In an age when many
people's wages were less than fifty guilders per month, even the cheaper
edition was aimed at affluent buyers who likely would have showcased
their purchase with some degree of pride.[9]

Unlike van Braght's *Bloody Theater,* which borrowed from de Ries's
Martyrs Mirror but was considered a new book, the 1685 edition was
considered (and continues to be considered) a revision of van Braght's
classic work. This judgment owes to three factors. First, whereas van
Braght's name appears prominently in the 1685 edition, the new editor's
name goes entirely unmentioned. Clearly there was a new editor—van
Braght had died in 1664, twenty-one years before the 1685 edition was
issued—but his identity remains a mystery. Second, the new editor, whoever he was, did not provide a new preface to the volume, an editorial
lacuna that enabled van Braght to retain the role of narrator in chief.
Third, the material that had appeared in the 1660 edition remained
largely the same in the 1685 edition (though in some cases it appeared in
different locations or in slightly revised formats).[10] For all these reasons,
historians have long agreed that the 1660 edition, not the 1685 edition,
represents the culmination of the Anabaptists' seventeenth-century
martyrological tradition.

This is not to suggest, however, that the 1685 edition lacked substan-
tive changes. Although the production of a new edition was largely a
repackaging endeavor in search of new buyers, some of the revisions
introduced were significant. Moreover, many of these revisions carried
through to later editions of the work, including the Mennonite Publishing House's English edition that has long been the North American
standard—a standard that, at least in popular parlance, carries the name
Martyrs Mirror.[11]

From *The Bloody Theater* to *Martyrs Mirror*

Of all the revisions to the 1660 edition, the most predictable one was the addition of new materials pertaining to Anabaptist martyrdom. These additions, which were relatively modest in scope, appear at various places throughout the text and include additional martyr accounts, documents that illumine previously published martyr accounts, and a few post-1660 documents. One particularly significant addition to the 1685 edition was the story of Hans Haslibacher, an Anabaptist executed in Bern, Switzerland, in 1571.[12] The account tells of Haslibacher's arrest and torture, his steadfast refusal to recant, and the divine visions he received while awaiting his death. The account concludes with a veiled reference to "three special signs" (*drie besondere teykenen*) that, after Haslibacher's death, would demonstrate his innocence for everyone to see.[13] Interestingly, the signs are not disclosed in the 1685 edition, perhaps indicating that they would have been unbelievable to sophisticated Mennonites, or at least ridiculed by their non-Mennonite neighbors. In any case, the three signs are divulged in a Swiss-German hymn that eventually made its way into the *Ausbund:* the sun turned red, the town's well sweated blood, and Haslibacher's severed head broke forth in laughter. Although the hymn does not appear in the 1685 edition, many later editions of the martyrology included the hymn right after the account of Haslibacher's imprisonment.[14]

The anonymous editor of the 1685 edition reached even further into the past for a new conclusion to the work. Van Braght had concluded his 1660 edition with a set of letters written by Dutch civic leaders in 1660, letters that implored Swiss officials to treat Swiss Anabaptists more kindly.[15] The 1685 edition also includes these letters, but it ends with a much older document, a nearly fifteen-hundred-year-old letter from church father Tertullian to imprisoned Christians. In his letter of consolation, penned around 200 CE, Tertullian acknowledges that no one enjoys suffering, but he reminds the letter's recipients that their present afflictions pale in comparison to the glory that awaits them.[16] The incorporation of Tertullian's letter, which remains the conclusion to the English and German translations in print today, extended a theme that van Braght had developed twenty-five years earlier and which continued to be important to Dutch Mennonites in 1685: the Anabaptists were not the children of Münster, but were rather the descendants of the early Christians who suffered on account of their faith.

Another conspicuous addition to the 1685 edition was a ten-stanza poem that appeared at the end of the front matter.[17] The poem, entitled "Crown of Martyrdom for Jesus Christ the Savior, and for the Defenseless Throng That Follows in His Way," was written by Cornelis van Braght, a relative of Thieleman's who later served as an elder in Dordrecht's Mennonite congregation.[18] In it, Cornelis commends Thieleman's martyrology to a new set of readers. "Now for a second time the bloody spectacle is published," the poem begins, "scattered with the testimonies and remains of the faithful." The remainder of Cornelis's poem is predictable in both its gruesomeness and its theology: references to "steaming blood" and "smashed limbs," followed by assurances that "all is made new in glory."[19] Interestingly, about halfway through his poem, Cornelis asserts that "the precious seed" of Christian martyrs will "bring forth a splendid harvest," a clear allusion to Tertullian's dictum that "the blood of martyrs is seed." Might this reference to Tertullian provide a clue to the anonymous editor's identity—as Cornelis van Braght? Or is it only a coincidence that the additions that bookended the 1685 edition—Cornelis's poem of commendation in the front matter and the volume's concluding letter—both draw from Tertullian? Some historians have dismissed the possibility of Cornelis's involvement on the grounds that some Dutch Mennonites held him in low esteem.[20] It is not implausible, however, that the volume's publishers would have contracted Cornelis's services to revise his relative's work, perhaps on the condition that his identity remain concealed. In the final analysis, the 1685 editor's identity cannot be established with certainty. We can only know that he was familiar with Tertullian's views and believed they aligned with the Anabaptists' cause.

From the standpoint of later history, the editor's identity is less important than a modification he or his publishers made to the work's title.[21] Whereas Thieleman van Braght had relegated the words *Martelaers Spiegel* (Martyrs mirror) to the end of his title, where they appear in relatively small letters, the 1685 edition placed the words near the beginning of the title. The 1685 title still begins with the words *Het Bloedig Tooneel* (The bloody theater), but these words lead directly into the phrase "*of Martelaers Spiegel.*" Moreover, the words *Martelaers Spiegel* appear in large capital letters, with the word *Spiegel* printed in the largest font on the entire page. This prioritization of the words *Martelaers Spiegel* over *Het Bloedig Tooneel* is apparent at other points in the 1685 edition, most conspicuously on the book's ornamental title page and also in the headings to the century-by-century martyr chapters in book 1.[22] Thus, even though the words *Het Bloedig Tooneel* appear at the top of the title page, it is quite likely that, even in its day, this new edition was referred to as *Martelaers Spiegel*.

Recalibrating the title of van Braght's work signaled the availability of a new edition, though the specific way it was recalibrated may have been meant to appeal to a certain class of customers. In 1685 the prioritization of *Martelaers Spiegel* over *Het Bloedig Tooneel* may have conjured memories of Hans de Ries, who, in 1631, had titled his Anabaptist martyr book *Martelaers Spiegel*. A Waterlander from north of Amsterdam, de Ries would have been closely aligned, both geographically and theologically, with the customers the publishers wished to interest in their book. It is possible, then, that giving priority to the words *Martelaers Spiegel* was a way for the publishers to remind wealthy Waterlanders that this revised edition continued to be their book, largely compiled by one of their own.

Of course, the decision to emphasize *Martelaers Spiegel* may have had less to do with conjuring the memory of de Ries than with the desire to use the best words possible to engage potential readers. The word *Tooneel* (theater) connoted watching the martyrs perform, and while that was a worthwhile endeavor, the word *Spiegel* (mirror), especially as it was used in early modern Europe, brought the viewers' response to the forefront. Yes, the martyrs had performed heroically on the stage of Christian history, but the real question was how their heroism affected those who looked in history's mirror. Similarly, the word *Martelaers* (martyrs) offered potential buyers a more precise description of the book's topic than the adjective *Bloedig* (bloody), a vivid word, to be sure, but one that could imply a variety of subjects.

In subsequent centuries, as publishers reissued the work and as readers encountered and discussed it, the title most commonly cited was *Martyrs Mirror*. Even today the English and German translations begin their official titles with the words *The Bloody Theater* (in German, *Der blutige Schauplatz*), but the words *Martyrs Mirror* (in German, "*Märtyrer-Spiegel*") are the only words that appear on the books' spines.

Het Bloedig Tooneel,

OF

MARTELAERS

SPIEGEL

DER

DOOPS-GESINDE

OF

Weereloose Christenen,

Die/ om 't getuygenis van JESUS haren Salighmaker/ geleden hebben/ ende gedood zijn/ van CHRISTI tijd af/ tot desen tijd toe.

Versamelt uyt verscheyde geloofweerdige Chronijken, Memorien, en Getuygenissen.

Door T. J. V. BRAGHT.

Den Tweeden Druk.

Bysonder vermeerdert met veele Autentijke Stucken, en over de hondert curieuse Konstplaten.

FAC ET SPERA.

t AMSTERDAM,

By J. vander DEYSTER, H. vanden BERG, JAN BLOM, Wed. S. SWART,
S. WYBRANDS, en A. OSSAAN. En Compagnie. 1685.
Met Privilegie.

Fig. 5.1. Title page of *Martyrs Mirror* (1685), the updated and illustrated
edition of Thieleman van Braght's *Bloody Theater*. The words
Martelaers Spiegel have now taken center stage.

Similarly, those who care about van Braght's martyrology typically refer to it as *Martyrs Mirror* or *Märtyrer-Spiegel*. In that sense, the recalibration of the title in 1685 has had an enduring impact on the book's reception and the conversations the book has spawned.

Illustrating *Martyrs Mirror:* The Work of Jan Luyken

Additional stories, a new conclusion, and a refashioned title—all of these revisions of van Braght's *Bloody Theater* pale in comparison to the addition of 104 images printed from copper etchings. The images, each of which illustrates an event narrated in the text, appear in close proximity to the stories they illustrate and are thus dispersed throughout the book. Typically sized 5½×4⅜ inches, the images take up one-third of their respective pages, effectively focusing the reader's gaze on the pages on which they appear.

Printing images from copper etchings was a common technique in the seventeenth century, but the work was difficult and time-consuming and was thus reserved for high-end publications. To make a copper etching, an artist began with a copper plate slightly larger than the size of the finished illustration. After coating the plate with a thin, waxy resin, the artist would undertake the design work, using etching needles to cut the desired image in reverse into the wax coating. The cuts, which included lines of various widths and dots to produce shading, were often very fine, though they needed to be deep enough to expose the copper surface beneath the wax. Once a particular image was cut, the plate was washed in acid, thus converting the exposed parts of the copper plate into hollow lines. Finally, in the actual printing process, the entire copper face was inked and then wiped, which removed all of the ink except for that which remained behind in the hollows. The remaining ink was then transferred to the paper when it was pressed atop the plate.[23]

The artist responsible for the images in *Martyrs Mirror* was Jan Luyken, born in Amsterdam in 1649.[24] Luyken began his artistic career as a painter and poet. In 1671, at age twenty-one, he published a book of verse entitled *Duytse Lier* (Dutch lyre), a celebration of sensual love that one scholar has compared to the work of John Donne and that Luyken came to regret for its erotic content.[25] After Luyken's conversion in 1673, his poetry, like Donne's, took a spiritual turn, beginning in 1678 with

Jesus en de Ziel (Jesus and the soul), a collection of thirty-nine poems describing the soul's companionship with Christ.[26] At about the same time, Luyken gave up the painter's brush in favor of the etching needle, a decision that also appears to have been spiritually informed.[27] Over the next thirty years, Luyken published ten more books of religious verse. Increasingly, however, his efforts went into producing emblem books that contained meditations he illustrated with detailed etchings. Done in a realistic style, and ranging in content from biblical stories to everyday Dutch life, Luyken's engravings and etchings—more than three thousand in all—soon surpassed his poetry in public acclaim.[28] Numerous Dutch publishers sought his services, which resulted in works such as a pictorial history of the Bible and an illustrated Dutch edition of John Bunyan's *Pilgrim's Progress*.[29]

For the publishers of *Martyrs Mirror*, Luyken was an obvious choice as an illustrator, for he was not only a well-regarded artist, but he was also a Mennonite. Although Luyken's father died five years before Luyken was baptized, Jan's parents were likely influential in their son's becoming a Mennonite; as participants in the pietistic, interchurch Collegiant movement, they had numerous Mennonite acquaintances, including some liberal Mennonite ministers.[30] Shortly after his conversion in 1673, Luyken underwent baptism in the Mennonite church in Beverwijk, about twenty miles from Amsterdam. One month later he transferred his membership to the Church at the Tower in Amsterdam, a Waterlander congregation that had recently united with Amsterdam's Church of the Lamb.[31]

By transferring his membership to the Church at the Tower, Luyken joined a Mennonite congregation overseen by one of his father's Collegiant friends, Galenus Abrahamsz. Ironically, Abrahamsz was an influential Lamist who, a dozen years earlier, had been censured by Thieleman van Braght for his lenient approach to doctrine. Abrahamsz had not modified his views since that time. In fact, he continued to be the leading voice of the anticonfessional Lamist faction. Among other things, Abrahamsz argued for the priority of good works over theological precision. Correspondingly, he believed that his church members' fitness to participate in the Lord's Supper should be determined by their moral bearing, not by their assent to particular doctrines.[32] Given Luyken's choice to join Abrahamsz's congregation, it is fair to assume that Luyken's theological sympathies lay with the Lamists, or at least that his sensibilities tended in a moralistic, spiritualist direction.[33] In any case, by the time he began his work on *Martyrs Mirror,* Luyken was deeply immersed in Amsterdam's Mennonite world. He was also known among his family and friends as a man of compassion, taking in his brother's orphaned children, visiting the poor, and giving generously to those in need.[34]

Luyken's moralism is apparent in both his writing and his etching work. In his emblem books, he repeatedly instructed readers on ethical living. His posthumously published Bible history epitomizes Luyken's ethical concern, devoting six plates to Matthew 25, a passage in which Jesus identifies compassionate action—feeding the hungry, visiting the sick, and so on—as the key to inheriting the kingdom of God.[35] Some twenty-first-century art critics might object to Luyken's approach, for it was unabashedly didactic, but his contemporaries, who lived in an age that "exulted in moral precept freely given," were likely drawn to his artistry and its overt messages.[36] This, of course, was the hope of the publishers who engaged Luyken to illustrate their revision of *The Bloody Theater,* a book filled with moral precepts in a distinctly Anabaptist key. Already didactic in its rendering of history, van Braght's martyrology became even more so with the addition of Luyken's visual portrayals of Christian commitment in the midst of suffering.

Luyken's Images: Location, Prevalence, and Types

Luyken's etchings appear throughout the 1685 edition of *Martyrs Mirror,* beginning with the first page of book 1. Others follow quickly: twenty etchings appear in book 1's first forty pages, and fifteen more appear in the next one hundred pages. In other words, one-third of Luyken's 104 images are located in the first 10 percent of the work's narrative sections. From then on the images appear at a slower pace, though they continue to come into view at relatively regular intervals. All in all, the etchings span 1,278 pages of text, meaning they appear, on average, about every twelve pages.

From the standpoint of images per page, Luyken's images are more prevalent in book 1, the section that runs from the early church to 1500, than they are in book 2, the section that recounts the travails of sixteenth-century Anabaptists.[37] This prevalence hinges on the first forty pages of book 1, which cover the first hundred years of church history and include twenty images. The first image that appears in the book portrays Jesus being nailed to the cross. Two more executions recorded in the New Testament—the beheading of John the Baptist and the stoning of Stephen—follow in quick succession, as do other images of New Testament figures suffering martyrdom.[38] At first glance it seems as if Luyken set out to illustrate every notorious execution recorded in van Braght's text, then changed his mind when he realized the enormity of that task. It is more likely, however, that the plethora of early images was designed to set the tone for the text, communicating two important themes right from the start: that suffering and faithfulness often went hand in hand and that the Anabaptists who suffered in the sixteenth century were in good company with the church's most revered saints.[39]

Most of Luyken's images in *Martyrs Mirror* (74 of 104) depict or immediately foreshadow executions of some sort.[40] Of those 74 images, 49 images portray a particular individual being executed or prepared for execution, 17 focus on a pair of persons or an otherwise small group of people being killed, and 8 depict mass executions, for instance, the burning of a village or mass beheadings. The most common form of execution depicted in *Martyrs Mirror* is burning, which appears in 31 of the 74 execution scenes. Beheadings are also common (9), as are crucifixions (6). Other forms of execution portrayed more than once include drowning (5), attacks by vicious animals (4), stoning (3), and live burial (2). Crucifixion and beheading scenes predominate in the early part of book 1, though burning becomes more prevalent as early church history gives way to medieval history. In book 2, which details sixteenth-century martyrdoms, burning is by far the most common execution method depicted, with drowning, beheading, and a few other methods making occasional appearances. One of the more bizarre and therefore captivating execution images in the volume shows Anabaptist Jan de Smit suspended from the gallows by one leg, a ruthless punishment that continued, reports the text, "till death ensued."[41]

In addition to execution images, five other image types appear that depict the suffering of faithful Christians. The most common type among the remaining five types is torture, which appears nine times.[42] In these scenes, Luyken artfully represents the creativity of the torturers, who use whips and swords to lacerate their victims, hot iron bars to sizzle their

Fig. 5.2. The execution of Jan de Smit, as depicted by Jan Luyken.

hands, sharp metal rods to pierce their bodies, ropes to suspend them from prison rafters, and screws to mangle their tongues. In at least one case, the abandonment of the apostle John on the island of Patmos, the torture appears to be mostly psychological, though even then the accompanying text reports that John's punishment meant contending with the island's fearsome animals.[43]

The martyrs' mental anguish takes center stage in the other four image types: capture, separation, imprisonment, and inquisition, which together offer a visual prelude to the more prevalent scenes of torture and execution. Five of the 104 images give attention to the moment of capture, as the authorities move in to arrest their Anabaptist prey. Closely related to, and sometimes together with, the capture images are scenes of Christians being physically separated from friends and family, including their children. In one particularly riveting scene, the parent-child separation is shown to be irreversible: two children, one of them a toddler, visit the site of their mother's execution, searching among the ashes for the screw that pierced her tongue.[44] A few images portray imprisoned persons awaiting their fate—not being tortured per se, but enduring the isolation of captivity. More often, however, the confined victims are not alone, but are rather accompanied by inquisitors who seek to correct their views. In one scene, the inquisitor dangles from his hand a key ring, suggesting to his prisoner that her freedom is close at hand, if only she recants.[45]

Four other images in *Martyrs Mirror* are arguably one of a kind, failing to fit into any larger type. In an image accompanying an account from the fifth century, King Honoricus is shown lying in bed, suffering horribly from worms and lice. The text makes clear the reason for Honoricus's suffering: after persecuting a countless number of Christians, God saw fit to enact vengeance upon him. The text's retributive theology is matched only by its graphic description of God's wrath: "Worms and lice so gnawed upon [Honoricus's] flesh that his whole body became putrified, one member dropping off after another, so that he was buried piecemeal."[46] In a second unique image, a market vender is portrayed standing tall in the street, refusing to kneel as a Communion procession passes by. Despite the pleas of those who kneel, the shopkeeper stoutly refuses to "give divine honor to this idol made by human hands," an act of protest that ultimately costs him his life.[47] In still another unique im-

Fig. 5.3. The sons of Maeyken Wens search through her ashes for a tongue screw.

Fig. 5.4. Simon the Shopkeeper refuses to bow down to a passing
Communion procession.

age, an Anabaptist leader sits in a boat, Bible in hand, surrounded by a
group of eager listeners. According to the man's sentencing document,
which is reprinted in the text, the preacher was holding illegal meetings
and thus deserved to die.[48]

The fourth one-of-a-kind image in the 1685 edition of *Martyrs Mirror* demands our more sustained attention, for in time it became the
most recognizable of all the volume's etchings. The image, which appears about halfway through book 2, portrays a bearded man standing
on a frozen pond, extending his hands toward a man who had broken
through the ice. The man with his hands extended is Dirk Willems,
an Anabaptist from near Asperen, Holland. The text reports that Willems, being pursued by an Anabaptist-catcher, had fled across a frozen
expanse. Willems made it across, but his pursuer did not. "Perceiving
that [his pursuer] was in danger of his life," the text continues, Willems

Fig. 5.5. Dirk Willems rescues his pursuer, who had broken through the ice.

"quickly returned and aided him in getting out, and thus saved his life." Willems's reward for his compassionate action was no reward at all: he was recaptured, tortured, and then burned at the stake.[49]

In chapter 11 we will consider the historical impact of this particular image. For now, its significance lies in its uniqueness: it is the only image in *Martyrs Mirror* that depicts the faithful Christian in a position of earthly power over the tormentor. Significantly, in his newfound position of authority, Willems prioritizes his enemy's well-being over his own, and his decision leads directly to his death. Although some readers at the time, and certainly many since then, have viewed Willems's choice as foolish, the text urges a different conclusion: Willems's sacrificial actions should be considered an "instructive example to all pious Christians."[50]

Of course, Luyken intended all of his *Martyrs Mirror* images to instruct viewers in the school of pious living. By illustrating the history of the Christian church—from the crucifixion of Christ and the experiences of his earliest followers, through the spiritual wilderness of the medieval church, to the rise of the Anabaptist movement in the sixteenth century—Luyken provided those who encountered *Martyrs Mirror* with a worthy addition to van Braght's text. Luyken's images summarized key written accounts, to be sure, but they also supplemented them by adding contextual specificity, narrative detail, and emotional nuance. In many times and places, Luyken's visual contributions exceeded van Braght's written ones in their emotional power, thus pointing beyond the inherent power of images to the artistry of the person who produced them.

Luyken's Images: Their Emotional and Didactic Power

Although some of its Mennonite martyrological precursors included illustrated title pages, the 1685 edition of *Martyrs Mirror* was the first Mennonite martyrology to illustrate accounts throughout the text. It was not, however, the first post-Reformation martyr book to do so. More than a hundred years earlier, in 1563, the English Protestant John Foxe and his publisher John Day had included fifty-three images in the first edition of *Acts and Monuments of these Latter and Perillous Dayes*, an eighteen-hundred-page martyrology that eventually became known as *Foxe's Book of Martyrs*.[51] The second edition of *Acts and Monuments*, published seven years later, tripled the original number of images, making it one of the most illustrated books published in sixteenth-century England. Some of the *Acts and Monuments* images were assimilated from previous works, though their inclusion in Foxe's martyrology increased their visibility and their staying power. In the future these images gained "an influence all their own," write two historians of print culture, communicating Foxe's message to later generations with a "power that independently fortified the vast verbal arsenal."[52]

The same sort of influence can be claimed for the images in *Martyrs Mirror*, though the two books' respective corpuses of illustrations differed from each other in significant ways. The illustrations in *Acts and Monuments* were printed not from copper etchings but rather from woodcuts, an older illustrating technique that was easier to use but produced cruder images.[53] Second, unlike Luyken, Foxe and Day had their typesetters insert words directly into the scenes, often adding a martyr's

Fig. 5.6. The execution of John Hooper, in John Foxe's *Acts and Monuments* (1563).

last words, a practice built on the assumption that "individuals on the verge of death almost invariably speak the truth."[54] Third, *Acts and Monuments* included generic illustrations that did not portray the specific accounts with which they appeared.[55] These generic illustrations were typically smaller than the ones that depicted specific events, and they were sometimes repeated in the text, leaving *Acts and Monuments* with a less consistent illustrative tableau than the one that appeared in *Martyrs Mirror.*

In addition to being account-specific, Luyken's renderings were far more realistic than those in *Acts and Monuments,* and that realism correlates with Luyken's cultivated and culturally situated artistic sensibilities. As a seventeenth-century artist, Luyken would have been well versed in images of torture and execution, including the work of Lucas Cranach the Elder (1472–1553), whose crucifixion images parlayed "the grotesque realism of late Gothic art into an uncompromising vision of human death stripped of any transcendence."[56] Artists like Cranach, writes

Mitchell B. Merback, depicted Christ's death not as a glorious event but as "an instance of capital punishment," a ferocious penal action that prefigured those of late medieval Europe.[57] Sixteenth- and seventeenth-century artists were well aware of the spectacle associated with medieval punishments, not least the punishments meted out for heresy, and some sought to expand the gallery of spectators through their artwork. This was certainly the case with two mid-seventeenth-century editions of van Haemstede's Calvinist martyrology, now titled *Historie der Martelaren* (History of the martyrs) and featuring 177 illustrations from an unknown artist, some of which bear a striking resemblance to Luyken's illustrations.[58] Indeed, the parallels between Luyken's martyrological images and those that appeared in van Haemstede's earlier work suggest that Luyken was familiar with the Calvinist martyrology, which was printed by the same Dordrecht printer who had published *The Bloody Theater* in 1660.[59]

Luyken's predisposition to realistic portrayal does not mean he was wholly opposed to including symbolic elements in his etchings, elements that a photographer, had one been present at the events themselves, would not have captured on film. The most interesting symbolic referent in this regard is a three-pronged pole, six feet in length, that appears in twenty-nine of Luyken's images, mostly in book 2.[60] Held by a well-dressed man who is often perched atop a horse, the pole appears roughhewn, as if fashioned from a knobby branch.[61] Seventeenth-century Dutch readers would have been familiar with this visual referent, writes James W. Lowry: it was "the rod of justice" (*Roede Justitie*), a pole that was used in early modern Holland to represent the authority of the sheriff's office.[62] In addition to recognizing the pole, which was often brought out at executions, contemporary Dutch readers would have detected Luyken's ironic allusion to the perverse justice that marked the fallen world, where pious Anabaptists were put to death by "servants of justice."[63] This perversion was common, Luyken suggested, not only in sixteenth-century Holland but in other times and places, a reality he underscored by placing the rod anachronistically (or figuratively) in book 1 as well as in book 2.[64]

Luyken offered other symbolic referents in his visual tableau (the tonsured monk, who makes frequent appearances, is the most obvious one), thus highlighting key themes in van Braght's text. Still, the power

Fig. 5.7. *Left*: Pieter van Rosseau as portrayed in Adriaen van Haemstede's *History of the Martyrs* (1659); *right*: Anneken Heyndricks as portrayed by Jan Luyken in *Martyrs Mirror* (1685).

Fig. 5.8. The civic authority carries the rod of justice at the execution of Leonhard Keyser.

of Luyken's artistry has less to do with his inclusion of symbolic objects and figures than with his unflinching portrayal of the human condition. As he portrays the martyrs themselves, Luyken draws a delicate line between their trust in God and the horror of their experience. Luyken's execution scenes often portray martyrs gazing heavenward, their hands folded in prayer, sometimes appearing unmoved by the brutality they suffer (see Anneken Heyndricks in figure 5.7).[65] The martyr's prayerful stoicism is also apparent in some of Luyken's torture scenes, most notably in the torture of Joost Joosten, who watches calmly as his legs are impaled with metal rods from his knees to his ankles.[66] The martyrs' stoicism does not tell the whole story, however, for Luyken complements these images with ones that portray the physical and psychological pain the martyrs endured. As Hendrick Pruyt sits in a burning boat and as Matthias Mair is drowned in a lake, their faces display fear, even horror, as they await their fate.[67] Even more pronounced in Luyken's imagery is the grotesque nature of torture, execution, and death, a theme he launches with Jesus's crucifixion, the book's first image. As the pages turn we see bodies contorted in monstrous ways, severed heads pitching aimlessly in the dirt, skin blackened by searing flames, blood spurting from necks and torsos, and flesh being devoured by ravenous dogs. Some of the martyrs look heavenward with placid acceptance, but others look up in desperation, begging God to release them from their agony. Compared to the martyrs in Foxe's *Acts and Monuments* (see figure 5.6), who are figured as spiritual giants unmoved by their experiences, the martyrs in *Martyrs Mirror* are depicted as heroic yet fully human, enduring the world's brutality as they suffer its agonizing effects.

With Luyken holding the etching needle, the martyrs' adversaries likewise receive humanizing treatment. To be sure, many of these adversaries appear coldhearted as they deal with their Anabaptist prey, displaying a callousness most poignantly illustrated in Luyken's etching of Geleyn Corneliss, whose jailers play cards within feet of his tortured body.[68] Moreover, most of the authorities who superintend the execution sites, including tonsured monks and the rod-holding official, display precious little sympathy for their Anabaptist victims. In these respects Luyken's work advances van Braght's dualistic view of the world, wherein defenseless innocents are slaughtered by evil authorities. This is not the whole story, however, for Luyken's artwork ultimately relays a

Fig. 5.9. The gruesome execution of Wolfgang Pinder. According to the text, the executioner bungled the process and had to behead Pinder "as best he could."

Fig. 5.10. The torture of Geleyn Corneliss, as his jailers play cards nearby.

Fig. 5.11. A soldier weeps as Anabaptist fathers in Austria are separated
from their families.

complex relationship between the martyrs and their adversaries. Many
inquisitors appear less as ravenous wolves than as conversation partners, offering what appear to be heartfelt invitations to recant, replete
with outstretched hands and pained expressions. In one case, the executioner who has just drowned an Anabaptist man—and must soon
drown a second one—appears to regret his brutal deed, pleading with
the second man to avoid his friend's fate.[69] In another case, a soldier dabs
his eyes with a handkerchief as two Anabaptist men are led away from
their grief-stricken families.[70] Luyken's most humanizing portrait of all
the martyrs' adversaries is his rendering of Dirk Willems's pursuer (see
figure 5.5). As the man struggles in the water, he looks Willems in the
eye and extends his arms toward him. Readers who encounter this image
cannot miss the point that Willems is the story's hero. At the same time,
Luyken depicts Willems's adversary as authentically human, desperate
to live another day and unashamed to ask for help.[71]

Fig. 5.12. A bystander in the distance grieves at the drowning of
Anabaptist Jacob Mandel.

Along with portraying Anabaptist victims and their various foes,
Luyken filled many of his plates with spectators, thereby pushing readers
to identify also with those who witnessed the martyrs' suffering. In his
crowd scenes Luyken includes mostly negative character options—military personnel who enforce the status quo, merchants who go about their
business, gawkers who relish the bloody theater, and people who bow to
idols that priests carry through the streets. But Luyken also includes
positive character options. In one scene a woman stands in the distance,
wiping her tears with a towel as she grieves the death of a drowned Anabaptist.[72] Another scene shows a bystander weeping in sympathy for a
pregnant woman about to be separated from her husband.[73] Still other
scenes show onlookers spreading their arms or lifting them above their
heads, unsettled by the events before them or, in perhaps a few instances,
giving praise to God for the martyrs' witness.[74]

Of all the observers he portrayed, Luyken reserved his most sensitive treatment for the martyrs' family members, particularly their spouses and children. Luyken's artwork in such portrayals was facilitated in two ways. First, van Braght's text included numerous family-centered resources. These resources, which included tender family letters and heart-wrenching descriptions of families being torn apart, placed Anabaptists martyrs within a web of family relationships that was ripe for an artist to depict. Second, Luyken lived in a seventeenth-century context that esteemed realistic yet spiritually conscious depictions of domesticity and childhood. Like other artists of his day, Luyken "treated children as moralistic emblems of innocence, and as vulnerable entities best captured in a state of peril."[75] One of Luyken's poems, which he included in a volume that detailed the seasons of life, refers to children as "innocent lambkins" who should do all they can to avoid "the bad ways of [their] elders."[76]

The evils superintended by adults, and their awful effects on innocent children, create a potent theme in Luyken's *Martyrs Mirror* etchings. In one scene, a mother en route to her execution hands her one-year-old son to a bystander who, according to van Braght's narrative, agrees to care for the soon-to-be orphaned boy.[77] In another scene, a young boy scrambles for one last hug as his father is shuttled along to his execution.[78] One particularly riveting image transports readers to the aftermath of an execution: Maeyken Wens's sons, fifteen-year-old Adriaen and three-year-old Hans, sift through their mother's ashes to find the screw that had clamped her tongue (see figure 5.3).[79] The volume's final image may be the most heartrending of all: as a distraught mother is led from her home, her frantic children follow close behind. A small girl, no more than six years old, clings to her mother's skirt, while the girl's older brother clutches his head in despair.[80]

Less prominent, but equally poignant, are Luyken's depictions of spousal separation. In one image, two men are removed from their homes and families; as their arrest unfolds, one of the wives buries her head in her husband's shoulder while the other sobs into a towel.[81] Another illustration depicts a man awaiting his death, bidding goodbye to his tearful wife, who holds a child; according to van Braght's text, the woman "could scarcely hold [the child] because of her great grief."[82] In a similar image, Jacques d'Auchy's wife stands before her chained husband, dab-

Fig. 5.13. Jacob Dircks's son hugs him as he is led to his execution.

bing her eyes with a cloth. That d'Auchy's wife is visibly pregnant makes this image particularly effective, for it alludes to an unborn child who will never know its father. Although some readers might consider the commentary cold comfort, the text softens the heartache by mentioning the parents' ultimate reward. "And thus these two dear lambs were separated," he writes, "but [they] hope to meet again at the resurrection of the just, where wailing and parting will be heard no more."[83]

The pious hope that marks so much of van Braght's text is less explicit in Luyken's imagery, however, and in many of his images it is absent altogether. In that respect Luyken's visual repertoire offers a more austere interpretation of martyrdom than van Braght's text supplies. To be sure, van Braght narrates many horrific accounts of separation, torture, and death, but he (or a source he employed) often accompanies these accounts with assertions about the afterlife or biblical references that sanctify suffering. For his part, Luyken could have inserted into his plates

Fig. 5.14. Two young children display desperation as their mother is arrested in seventeenth-century Switzerland.

more evidence of Christian triumph and more symbols of eternal hope, but he chose not to do so. Similarly, he could have inserted pious words into the martyrs' mouths, providing the sort of admonition that Foxe and Day foregrounded in their *Acts and Monuments* images. For Luyken, however, the martyrs' lessons lay less in the words they spoke than in the company they kept and in the actions they refused to take, that is, in their defenseless approach to the world's brutality. Interestingly, we learn nothing from Luyken's images about the appropriate form of baptism. In all these ways, Luyken's moralism sits front and center in *Martyrs Mirror*, an approach to the spiritual life that, like Jesus's discourse in Matthew 25, places more weight on how people act than on words they speak or the doctrines they espouse. In the Dutch Mennonite context, where doctrinal disputes often hinged on the value of the written word (including creedal precision) vis-à-vis the living word, Luyken's artwork

Fig. 5.15. Jacques D'Auchy's wife weeps as she talks with her imprisoned husband.

underscored the Waterlanders' preference for the latter, reminding viewers that the life of a faithful Christian is the most effective epistle of all.[84]

The Non-Luyken Artwork: Printer's Device and Ornamental Title Page

In addition to Luyken's visuals, two other images appear in the 1685 edition: an emblematic device on the main title page and an ornamental
title page that visually ushers readers into the text. Both of these features
had appeared in the 1660 edition, albeit in different forms. With respect
to the printer's device, the publishers of the 1685 edition largely retained
the one that appeared in 1660, though instead of including the device
in its entirety, they focused on its central figure, the peasant farmer. In
this new edition, the farmer continues to be surrounded by a large laurel
wreath, but the two figures that held the wreath in 1660 are nowhere to

be seen. Similarly, the farmer continues to till the soil under the same Latin words, "Fac et Spera" (work and hope), only now he is accompanied by a bird, perhaps alluding to the Holy Spirit. The village that looms behind the farmer has become more explicitly Christian, with a cross now crowning the church's spire. Why the 1685 publishers reemployed the 1660 printer's device is unclear, though its continued use suggests they wanted to highlight the 1685 edition's connection to its precursor.[85] At the same time, they sought to make the device their own, accentuating the Christian purpose of their publishing endeavor.

More evocative than the device, however, is the ornamental title page, which is entirely refashioned in the 1685 edition. In 1660 the ornamental title page was dominated by execution and torture scenes, at least nine filling the page. In the 1685 edition the ornamental page still contains execution scenes, including beheadings, hangings, and burnings, but

Fig. 5.16. Title-page device for *Martyrs Mirror* (1685), a similar but less elaborate version of the emblem that appeared in *The Bloody Theater* (1660).

the execution scenes are fewer in number and smaller in size. Surpassing them in prominence are images of symbolic significance, including four winged cherubs, three naked children, two women clothed in white, a figure draped in animal skins, a stern-looking bishop, a suppliant monk, and a dove descending from the heavens. This new, more allegorical ornamental page was the work of two artists, Vincent Laurensz van der Vinne, a Dutch Mennonite painter from Haarlem who sketched the piece, and D. Penning, a printmaker who engraved van der Vinne's sketch for printing.[86]

The stylistic differences between Luyken's etchings and van der Vinne's artwork are vast, but from an ideological standpoint they are also complementary: whereas Luyken's illustrations highlight the gritty reality of the martyrs' experiences, the ornamental title page emphasizes the transcendent significance of their struggle.[87] Not wanting viewers to misconstrue van der Vinne's artwork, the editor and his publishers included on the facing page an explanatory key, poetically rendered by L. van de Roer, that decoded the various images. "Here the bloody theater is opened," the key begins, a drama depicting hell's attempt to crush the martyrs' faith "through bloodlust, papal deceit, and deathly violence." The key proceeds to identify the scene's central female figure as the church of the martyrs. With blood streaming from her bosom, she holds God's law and gospel in her lap, experiences the Holy Spirit's "rays of grace," and rests beneath "God's palm tree [that] shadows her with His salvation," all the while resisting the world's allures, represented by the deceitful flatterer dressed in animal skins. At the woman's right hand sits another woman. This second woman represents truth, "hold[ing] school . . . in order to baptize her children with fire and spirit." And "over there," off in the distance, readers can see "the defenseless throng" who, having experienced martyrdom, now enter "the portal of the cross" on their way to the "palace of salvation." Having faithfully endured the abuse of the world and resisted its allures, these "victors" are "kissed, welcomed, and loved" as God's dear children.[88]

Subsequent editors and publishers have thus had two ornamental page designs from which to choose: van der Vinne's allegorical design from 1685 and the execution-heavy image that appeared in 1660. Significantly, some future editions of Martyrs Mirror displayed new ornamental pages, and others included none whatsoever. Still other editions

Fig. 5.17. Ornamental title page of *Martyrs Mirror* (1685). Bleeding from her chest, but with her eyes fixed on heaven, the central woman represents the church of the martyrs.

dispensed with all of Luyken's illustrations, thus confining the story of the Anabaptist martyrs once again to the printed word. The publishing decisions that were made in these respects—decisions made by editors and publishers who held particular views about visual images, or who sought to align their books with their consumers' desires—meant that van Braght's *Bloody Theater* continued to evolve beyond the form it took in 1685. Before long, the literary journey of van Braght's book took it across the Atlantic Ocean to the Pennsylvania frontier, where it was translated into a different Old World language for a New World audience. Because many Anabaptists who inhabited mid-eighteenth-century America had little or no facility in Dutch, they soon had reason for a German translation of their esteemed martyrology.[89]

CHAPTER 6

A North American Edition

The 1748–49 *Ephrata* Martyrs Mirror

The 1685 *Martyrs Mirror* was not only an Anabaptist martyrology; it was also a Dutch martyrology. Like the volume's 1660 precursor, its language was Dutch, its editor was Dutch, and it was printed in a Dutch city, marketed by Dutch publishers, and purchased by Dutch consumers. Even though it included Anabaptist martyr accounts from many regions of Europe, martyrs in the Low Countries received a disproportionate amount of ink. The formal Anabaptist-Mennonite confessions of faith that supplemented the martyr accounts were developed in Dutch contexts, and the etchings that illustrated the book were crafted by a Dutch artist.[1]

That Dutch Anabaptists produced the most comprehensive Anabaptist martyrology is no more surprising than is their predilection toward their own martyrs. By the mid-seventeenth century, the Dutch Republic had become Europe's leading economic power, and its preeminence was buttressed by consumers with the means to acquire nonessential items, including books. Dutch Mennonites participated in this cultural ascendance. Unlike their Anabaptist counterparts in other regions of Europe, mid-seventeenth-century Dutch Mennonites lived in a society that, to a great degree, had lost interest in suppressing the Anabaptist faith. In this context, some Mennonites had the resources to buy and read a substantial book like *Martyrs Mirror*. The number of copies sold was always modest, but the fact remains that the book's center of gravity was firmly fixed in the Netherlands.

In time, however, Dutch editions of the book were joined, and eventually superseded, by editions in other languages. As early as 1696, just eleven years after the illustrated edition of *Martyrs Mirror* appeared in Amsterdam, a picture album containing the 104 Luyken etchings surfaced in Italy with the title *Il Teatro Della Crudelta* (The theater of cruelty).[2] The brainchild of an Italian publisher who hoped Luyken's artwork would tempt collectors' pocketbooks, *Il Teatro Della Crudelta* contained no text whatsoever, thus omitting the martyrs' and their memorialists' theological views, perspectives that would not have been welcomed in Italy's Catholic context. In general, however, the revised editions of *Martyrs Mirror* that appeared in the coming centuries were the result of Anabaptist desires for inspiration in the vernacular, and in that sense they emerged more from religious motivations than from entrepreneurial ambitions. This was certainly the case for the first edition of *Martyrs Mirror* published in North America, a German-language edition that is commonly called the Ephrata *Martyrs Mirror*. Published in 1748–49 on the Pennsylvania frontier, this new edition aimed to serve German-speaking Anabaptists who found life in the New World threatening to their faith.[3] In this perilous environment, a new edition of *Martyrs Mirror* was considered a bulwark against the erosion of Anabaptist commitments, particularly the commitment to defenselessness that van Braght had made central to his definition of martyrdom.

Swiss-German Anabaptists and the Amish-Mennonite Division

In 1659–60, as Thieleman van Braght battled through illness to complete his *Bloody Theater*, Anabaptists four hundred miles to the south were facing a different sort of challenge: an attempt by officials in Bern, Switzerland, to eradicate Anabaptists from their jurisdiction. Van Braght saw fit to include some of the anti-Anabaptist edicts that were published at the time. One Bernese edict, published in 1659, noted that persons discovered to be Anabaptists would "be conducted to the boundary [of Bern's jurisdiction] . . . and be utterly banished from our country and dominion, until their apparent conversion." It further warned that if these banished Anabaptists returned to Bern, they would be "publicly scourged with rods, branded, and again, as before, expelled and banished from the country." The edict concluded with a warning to non-Anabaptists who might be tempted to help their Anabaptist neighbors, making it illegal to give shelter to Anabaptists, attend their church gatherings, or give them money.[4] This mid-seventeenth-century bid to suppress Swiss Anabaptism proved somewhat effective, though not entirely so. In the 1690s, Swiss officials mounted yet another attempt to stamp out the sectarian scourge, revealing that their earlier efforts had not achieved the desired result.[5]

The response of the Swiss Brethren to these rounds of persecution was twofold.[6] Some chose the route of partial compliance with the government's expectations. These compliant Anabaptists participated in worship with their Reformed neighbors and, in some cases, had their infants baptized, even as they maintained their Anabaptist identity by meeting secretly and encouraging one another to hold fast to Anabaptist commitments. Other Swiss Brethren found such compromises unsavory, choosing instead to migrate (or being forcibly removed) to more tolerant regions, a process that led many of them westward to the Alsace or northward to the Palatinate. In both of these regions, migrating Anabaptists found territorial lords who, in the wake of the Thirty Years' War, "were eager to invite newcomers to resettle depopulated villages and to reclaim the fallow farmland."[7] In exchange for the refugees' economic contributions, the lords offered a modicum of religious freedom, thereby enticing other Swiss Brethren to join the exodus. Between 1660 and 1690, more than one thousand Swiss Anabaptists made their way to the Alsace or the Palatinate, where they started new Anabaptist congregations or swelled those that were already there.[8]

One Swiss Anabaptist who moved to the Alsace during this time was an elder named Jakob Ammann, whose actions in the 1690s contributed to a lasting division in the Anabaptist movement. In 1693 a few Alsatian congregations commissioned Ammann to visit some sister Anabaptist churches in the Emmental (east of Bern) to discuss a variety of church-related issues. The visit did not go well. From Ammann's perspective, the Emmental churches had grown lax in their spiritual practices and, moreover, did not seem concerned about their depleted spiritual state. For their part, the leaders whom Ammann visited took offense at Ammann's intrusiveness. The points of contention varied, ranging from the practice of foot-washing and the frequency of Communion to the attitudes church members should hold toward the Truehearted (*Treuher-zige*), those non-Anabaptist neighbors who had assisted Anabaptists in times of peril.[9] The issue that proved most divisive, however, was shunning. What did the Apostle Paul mean in 1 Corinthians 5 when he wrote that Christians should not eat with a wayward member? For Ammann and his supporters, this was a clear call for social avoidance, a practice affirmed by various Dutch Mennonite confessional statements, including the 1632 Dordrecht Confession. By this time the Dordrecht Confession was known in Swiss Anabaptist circles and had even been formally affirmed by some Alsatian Anabaptists.[10] For those who opposed Ammann, however, Dordrecht's stance on shunning seemed overly harsh. In their view, banning a wayward member from the Communion table was discipline enough. To do more would be to violate the spirit of Christ, who, at great risk to his reputation, associated with Gentiles and tax collectors.

In the course of this debate, some participants cited the Anabaptist martyrs in support of their cause. For instance, in a letter to an Alsatian congregation in 1694, Jakob Gut reiterated cautions regarding shunning expressed by Matthias Servaes, an Anabaptist preacher who was executed in Cologne in 1565. As Servaes sat in prison awaiting his death, he wrote family members and fellow believers a series of letters, ten of which made their way into *Martyrs Mirror*.[11] In one of his letters, Servaes warned his fellow Anabaptists to "be on your guard in shunning so that it does not cause you to stumble." While admitting that "shunning is indeed good if one does not misuse it," Servaes suggested that many people had misused it by ignoring the law of love. "I would wish that people would be careful and not hold to one passage so strictly that another would be thereby broken," Servaes wrote, "for people have sometimes come down so hard with shunning without any moderation and pity."[12] As later commentators have pointed out, Gut could just as easily have cited martyr testimonials in support of avoidance, but given Gut's objectives, he was not inclined to provide the complete picture.[13] Like many who invoked *Martyrs Mirror* in the coming centuries, Gut knew that the martyrs' blood-soaked voices carried special authority by virtue of the price they had paid for keeping their commitments.[14]

As it turned out, the differences of opinion between Ammann and his adversaries could not be overcome, thus resulting in what came to be known as the Amish division.[15] From this point forward, the followers of Jacob Ammann, now called the *Amish*, were known for enacting more rigorous disciplinary practices than their Swiss Brethren counterparts, who in time assumed the name *Mennonites*. In subsequent centuries, Amish and Mennonites continued to debate one another, and argue among themselves, over the proper approach to church discipline. At times these disagreements led to further divisions and, in some cases, to new alliances. Generally speaking, however, Anabaptists who assumed the name Amish insisted on more disciplinary rigor than their Mennonite counterparts, both in terms of lifestyle issues to be enforced and the disciplinary actions to be taken when members fell out of line. Of course, these differences of opinion pointed to a more fundamental difference regarding the church's relationship to the larger world. Those who carried the name Amish typically drew sharper lines between the church and the world, and they therefore insisted on a more separatist approach to the Christian life. Correspondingly, their attitude toward the surrounding world, even in contexts where persecution was nonexistent, resonated more fully with the experience of the martyrs than did the attitudes of their more worldly counterparts.

In the meantime, however, it was German-speaking Mennonites, not Amish, who led the way in arranging for a new translation of *Martyrs Mirror*, a translation they hoped would be easier for them to navigate than the Dutch editions already in print.

The Call for a German Translation

In the decades following the Amish-Mennonite division, Swiss-German Anabaptists continued to face the challenge of hostile governments. Immigration to other European realms was sometimes possible, but fragile economic conditions and ethnic tensions often proved forbidding. Increasingly, the most alluring destination was America, where European immigrants were invited to pursue William Penn's promise of economic opportunity in a religiously tolerant environment. German-speaking Mennonites began trekking to Penn's Woods in earnest in the first decade of the eighteenth century, initially arriving in small numbers and settling in Germantown, not far from Philadelphia.[16] Their numbers swelled significantly in subsequent decades, with an additional two thousand

German-speaking Mennonite immigrants arriving in America by 1754.[17] By 1736, and perhaps even earlier, a few Amish families began making their way to Pennsylvania, to be followed by five hundred more Amish immigrants before 1770. Practically all eighteenth-century Amish and Mennonite immigrants to the New World made entry through the port of Philadelphia. Except for the few who settled in Germantown, most moved further inland, making their homes in areas now known as Pennsylvania's Chester, Berks, and Lancaster counties, as well other regions to the north, west, and south.[18]

Although early American Anabaptists were largely rural and therefore socially isolated, their ability to maintain their unique theological character was sometimes tested. In Pennsylvania's teeming religious marketplace, Mennonite leaders needed to work hard to convince their members that the Anabaptist-Mennonite way constituted the most faithful course. Some of their challenges in this regard came from close theological neighbors.[19] For instance, the German Baptist Brethren (Dunkers) sought to win converts from the Mennonite ranks by promoting baptism by immersion and, conversely, by maligning the Mennonite practice of pouring, an argument that Mennonite bishop Heinrich Funck countered in 1744 with his treatise *Ein Spiegel der Tauffe mit Geist, mit Wasser, und mit Blut* (A mirror of baptism: with the Spirit, with water, and with blood).[20] In contrast to the Dunkers' proselytizing efforts, ecumenically minded Christians sought to downplay the theological differences that existed in the Pennsylvania German ethnic community, which consisted of Moravians, Lutherans, Dunkers, and German Reformed, as well as Mennonites and Amish. Most famously, the German Moravian Nikolaus von Zinzendorf visited America in the early 1740s in an effort to create an ecumenical Congregation of God in the Spirit. Some of Zinzendorf's unity conferences took place in southeastern Pennsylvania, and some of the conferences included Mennonite participants. Although Zinzendorf failed in his unifying endeavors—Mennonites were particularly resistant to them—his presence alerted Mennonite leaders to the possibility that people might be wooed away from particular Anabaptist commitments in favor of a more pietistic, common-denominator faith.[21]

Mennonite church leaders faced yet another problem, this one more serious, in their efforts to preserve Anabaptist theological commitments: the bellicose nature of Britain's colonial experiment. England's grasp on its American colonies was firm, but it was never without opposition from competing entities. Native Americans offered some resistance to British colonialism, but fellow European nations posed an even greater challenge. In the early 1740s, Spain and England engaged in what became known as the War of Jenkins' Ear, a naval war in which these two powers vied for control of trade in the Atlantic basin. In time this conflict was subsumed into a larger war, the War of Austrian Succession (1740–48), which pitted allies Spain and France against King George's England. The war's North American theater, sometimes called King George's War, was largely confined to Canada, though significant battles also took place on New York's frontier. In the midst of these conflicts, English authorities urged the colonies to contribute money and sometimes men to the war effort. In Pennsylvania, where Quakers controlled the colony's legislature, conscription laws were slow in coming, but Governor George Thomas and others politicked for war taxes and compulsory military service.[22] For their part, Pennsylvania's Mennonite and Amish residents found themselves unsettled by their government's push for war support. With memories of state-sponsored persecution fresh in their minds, different Anabaptist communities drew the lines in different places. Church leaders worried that the long-standing Anabaptist commitment to nonresistance was flagging and would perhaps be lost altogether.[23]

In the shadow of this threefold threat to Anabaptist integrity—aggressive evangelism on one side, affable ecumenism on another, belligerent colonialism on yet a third—a small group of Pennsylvania Mennonites fixed their hopes on the power of a text: *Martyrs Mirror*. The stout martyrology, now eighty years old, afforded numerous resources to counter the threats they faced. Against the proselytizers from other Christian traditions, and also against those who downplayed the differences between Protestant sects, *Martyrs Mirror* demonstrated the superiority of Anabaptist theological commitments. Not only did *Martyrs Mirror* trace a line from the New Testament straight to the Anabaptists, but it also proved the Christlikeness of the Anabaptist martyrs who, like Jesus himself, were willing to suffer for a righteous cause. Indeed, one of the fundamental commitments that distinguished the Anabaptists from their sixteenth-century adversaries was their Jesus-like pledge to defenselessness, the very commitment that, in the saber-rattling context of mid-eighteenth-century America, Mennonites were most tempted to forsake. Against their Anglo-American detractors, some of whom considered Pennsylvania Germans treasonous, *Martyrs Mirror* offered clear answers: Christ's commands took priority over imperial edicts, and Christ's kingdom transcended national boundaries. Exemplified by the martyrs' willingness to defy the law, and reinforced by the book's pan-European hall of Anabaptist martyrs, these twin truths were hard to miss. Similarly, against those who accused nonresistant Mennonites of cowardice, *Martyrs Mirror* offered a mountain of evidence that defenselessness required great courage.

The problem, of course, was that *Martyrs Mirror* was a Dutch book, and the majority of Mennonite and Amish in colonial America neither spoke nor read Dutch. The solution, then, was to render the text into German. In 1742 Pennsylvania Mennonite church leaders wrote to the Committee for Foreign Needs of the Dutch Mennonite Church, asking for its assistance in producing a German edition of *Martyrs Mirror.* Appealing to this particular committee made sense. In the latter half of the seventeenth century, and again following its reestablishment in 1710, the Dutch committee had frequently assisted Anabaptists in other regions of Europe who faced poverty or persecution, in some cases financing migration to less hostile lands.[24] When the 1742 letter received no response from the Dutch committee, Mennonite ministers from Pennsylvania's Skippack congregation drafted a second appeal, this time in 1745. The second letter stated that, although the colonial American environment had been largely congenial to Mennonites, the situation was growing perilous. In particular, "the flames of war seem to be mounting higher and higher," so high that "cross and tribulation may . . . [soon] fall to the lot of the nonresistant Christian." For that reason, the letter continued, it was important for Pennsylvania Mennonites to "make every preparation for the steadfast constancy in our faith." The letter-writers then proceeded to make their request: that Dutch Mennonites develop a cost estimate for translating and printing a thousand German-language copies of *Martyrs Mirror.*[25]

The Skippack ministers' hopes for a German *Martyrs Mirror* went beyond their desire to promote nonresistance in general, however. Their more particular concern focused on Mennonite youth who had grown up in North America and who, in the future, might be tempted to abandon their Anabaptist commitments. These young people had come of age in an environment that was largely tolerant of Mennonites and their ways. As it was to Thieleman van Braght, this comfort was worrisome to some North American Mennonites, not least to Skippack bishop Heinrich Funck, who one year earlier had published his anti-immersionist treatise in response to the insistent Dunkers. In what was likely an effort to link his baptismal arguments to the martyrological classic, Funck had titled his treatise *Ein Spiegel der Tauffe* (*A Mirror of Baptism*). In it Funck posited a close connection between water baptism and baptism in blood, in other words, between true Christian commitment and earthly persecution.[26] By making this point, Funck extended his baptism-related argument to address a different challenge to Mennonite identity, namely, the notion that faithful Christians could live lives free from suffering. From Funck's perspective, this assumption violated the spirit of true Christianity, for God-honoring Christians had always constituted an offense to their neighbors. Of course, Funck's perspective on the inevitability of suffering comported nicely with the content of *Martyrs Mirror,* which outlined in gory detail the consequences of faithful living in an unfriendly world. Having a German translation of the martyrological classic, wrote Funck and his Skippack brethren, would enable Mennonite youth to see "the traces of those loyal witnesses of the truth, who walked in the way of truth and have given their lives for it."[27]

The transatlantic request for a new *Martyrs Mirror* was to no avail; for reasons that are not entirely clear, the Dutch recipients failed to respond in a timely fashion.[28] In the meantime, Pennsylvania Mennonites looked for a solution closer to home. In their 1745 letter to the Dutch committee, the Skippack ministers noted that they had initially hoped a local entity could produce a new translation, but these hopes had been dashed by a series of problems: the lack of suitable paper, a dearth of expert translators, and the fear that certain people who had offered to translate the martyrology would deliver an unsuitable product. Nonetheless, as they waited for a Dutch response, one local prospect began to look increasingly attractive: a printing press on the Pennsylvania frontier recently established by a community of Pennsylvania-German monastics. This outpost, commonly known as the Ephrata Community, soon provided both the expertise and the labor to render *Martyrs Mirror* into German for an American readership.

The Ephrata Community

Located some fifty miles northwest of Philadelphia, the Ephrata Community came into existence in 1732. The community's founder was Conrad Beissel, an immigrant from the Palatinate and a one-time German Baptist Brethren (Dunker) minister. Like Pennsylvania's Mennonite and Amish residents, the German Baptist Brethren were Pennsylvania-German sectarians with Anabaptist leanings, but they were also heirs of German pietism, which emphasized personal conversion and heartfelt love toward God and neighbor. Beissel first encountered pietism in Germany and embraced a radical, even mystical, strain of the religion. In 1720 Beissel migrated to Pennsylvania, perhaps to join a community of pietist hermits located near Philadelphia.[29] By the time he arrived in America, however, the hermitage had disbanded, and Beissel instead apprenticed himself to Peter Becker, a Germantown weaver and German Baptist Brethren leader. A few years later, Becker baptized Beissel, who had since moved to the Conestoga Creek, about ten miles north of Lancaster. A small community of fellow converts chose Beissel to be the leader of their new German Baptist Brethren congregation.[30]

Beissel's leadership among the German Baptist Brethren was short-lived, however. Within four years of his 1724 baptism, Beissel had distanced his Conestoga congregation from the Dunker movement, and in 1732 he renounced his congregational leadership role altogether. At that point Beissel moved a few miles north, searching for solitude along the banks of the Cocalico Creek. When some of his former church members followed him north, Beissel's solitude gave way to a small but vibrant monastic community that incarnated some of his unorthodox ideas. Even as a Dunker minister, Beissel had advocated Sabbath-day observance and the superiority of celibacy over marriage.[31] Now, in the spiritually unfettered environment of the Pennsylvania frontier, Beissel established a community that embodied those convictions. In addition to advocating celibacy and Sabbatarianism, Beissel preached a mystical gospel that "redefined Christ as a man . . . with a female aspect, Sophia." In accord with this gospel, spiritual seekers could aspire to a "mystical union with Christ or Sophia, who would . . . unify the soul in balanced androgyny, reflecting God's divine nature."[32] Some observers found Beissel's ideas scandalous, but others, including a handful of Mennonites, found his vision compelling. By 1750 nearly three hundred people had joined Beissel's Ephrata Community, which they called the Camp of the Solitaries. Those committed to celibacy lived in large, gender-specific buildings; noncelibate members lived as families in farmhouses near the celibate residences. Other practices unique to the community's members included dressing in hooded garments, sleeping on wooden benches with wood-block pillows, and assembling regularly for midnight worship.[33]

Despite its frontier location, the Ephrata Community soon started a print shop, which specialized in German-language publications. Established in 1745, the Ephrata press was colonial America's second German-language press, preceded only by Christopher Sauer's printing business in Germantown.[34] The Ephrata Community boasted an impressive array of services related to book production: it made paper and ink, it typeset and printed pages, and it bound the printed pages into books.[35] Placing radical pietist writings into print was the press's highest priority, but because of its full-service operation, it attracted outside business as well. Some of the print shop's earliest customers were Pennsylvania Mennonites, who contracted with the press to reprint two German-language devotional books, *Güldene Aepffel in Silbern Schalen* (Golden apples in silver vessels) and *Die Ernsthafte Christenpflict* (The earnest Christian duty), both of which appeared in 1745.[36] Within two years the press had begun the more formidable task of translating and printing *Martyrs Mirror.*

That Mennonites would entrust this important work of translation to the Ephrata Community is worthy of note, for the relationship between Beissel and Mennonite church leaders held potential for conflict. To be sure, many members in the Ephrata Community resonated with key Anabaptist tenets, including believers' baptism and defenselessness. Indeed, the German Baptist Brethren movement that birthed the Ephrata Community was something of an amalgamation of pietist and Anabaptist convictions.[37] Despite these shared convictions, however, points of friction remained. First, the Ephrata Community had demonstrated a willingness to recruit Mennonites away from their Mennonite churches.[38] Second, Mennonite leaders would surely have considered some of Beissel's theology beyond orthodoxy's pale. Some Mennonite leaders may have cringed at the notion of having Beissel's communitarians translate their treasured martyrology, a process that, unlike reprinting previously published works, entailed numerous interpretive judgments.

Discomfort with a would-be translator's theological bent may explain a comment in the Skippack ministers' 1745 letter to the Dutch Committee for Foreign Needs. In their transatlantic appeal, the ministers noted that someone had volunteered to translate *Martyrs Mirror* for them, but the volunteer, they believed, was not entirely trustworthy. "However much we are concerned to have [*Martyrs Mirror*] translated," the ministers wrote, "we are equally concerned that the truth remain unblemished by the translation."[39] Although the letter fails to identify the volunteer by name, the letter-writers may have been referring to Alexander Mack Jr., a member of the Ephrata Community who had recently translated a small portion of *Martyrs Mirror* into German. Mack's abridgment, which was published at Ephrata in 1745, reveals the esteem that Ephrata's members had for the Anabaptist martyrological tradition.[40] At the same time, the Skippack ministers appeared unwilling at this point (October 1745) to place the entire project in Ephrata's hands.[41]

Before long, however, their reservations had subsided, for a variety of reasons. First, the Dutch Committee was slow to respond, and even when it did, its response was not encouraging.[42] Other European options were equally daunting. Working with printers in Europe was time-consuming, expensive, and left no room for examining a work in progress. Sauer's printing enterprise in Germantown was always a possibility, but unlike the Ephrata Community, it did not provide the range of materials and services needed to bring a massive book to fruition. Ephrata's press was by far the most convenient option. Moreover, it was staffed by people who appreciated the Anabaptist tradition. Mennonite ministers may have been skeptical of some of Beissel's teachings, but given the range of differences in the world of Christianity, taking their business to Ephrata was, by and large, keeping their business in the family.

Two additional factors made Ephrata an attractive option for the project: the presence of translator Peter Miller and a customer-friendly publishing agreement with the Ephrata Community. Miller was no Mennonite, but he was an able translator, and it appears that Ephrata's Mennonite patrons held Miller in higher regard than they did the party who had previously volunteered to translate the work.[43] Moreover, the

Ephrata Community consented to translate and publish the work with no money down from their Mennonite clients and no guarantee of future income, since the Mennonites were not obligated to buy any copies once they were printed.[44] In an age when printers were "unwilling to risk much capital on books of any size," the Ephrata Community accepted the entire financial risk in producing a fifteen-hundred-page volume, a telltale sign that the production of *Martyrs Mirror* was, to the Ephrata Community, more than a commercial undertaking.[45]

Producing a German Edition: Ephrata Workers and Their Product

Producing a German-language edition of *Martyrs Mirror* was no mean task. Translation expertise was crucial, but in addition to linguistic proficiency, the translator needed time and space to complete his mammoth task. The press faced challenges as well. Without a steady supply of paper, and without a sizable workforce to typeset and print the many pages, the project would go nowhere. In the end, the Ephrata Community proved equal to the task. Beginning in 1746 or 1747, Ephrata's workers labored for three years to produce the Ephrata *Martyrs Mirror,* which, at fifteen hundred pages, was the largest book published in America before 1800.[46] When bound in leather-covered oak board, the final product weighed more than ten pounds.

From a practical standpoint, no one was more important to the project than Miller, a former Reformed minister who joined the Ephrata Community around 1736.[47] Educated in Germany and fluent in multiple languages, Miller had a keen interest in translation theory, particularly as it pertained to rendering spiritual ideas from one language into another.[48] This, of course, was a leading concern of the Mennonites who solicited the work: that "the truth" residing in the Dutch edition "remain unblemished by the translation."[49] Every step in the process hinged on Miller's translation of words, sentences, and paragraphs. Miller later attested that he slept only four hours per night in an effort to keep ahead of the typesetters.[50]

Other Ephrata workers labored hard to produce *Martyrs Mirror.* According to *Chronicon Ephratense,* the community's internal history, fifteen of Ephrata's male members worked steadily on the project for three years, six in the area of paper production, four as compositors, four as pressmen, and one as the translator-corrector.[51] To make the necessary paper, the community's paper millers soaked tons of linen rags, beat the wet rags into pulp, then spread the pulp across mesh frames for drying.[52] Each page of text called for thirty-eight hundred pieces of type, meaning that nearly 6 million pieces of type were set in the course of producing the fifteen-hundred-page book.[53] Thirteen hundred copies of the book were printed in folio style, two pages at a time on large sheets of paper that, after being hung to dry, were printed on the reverse side.[54] These folio sheets were later folded, sewn into signatures, and cut. Binding the signatures between leather-covered oak boards was the last step in the process, though binding took place only when copies were sold.

That the community would devote itself so fully to this task was possible only with the backing of Conrad Beissel, who hoped the production process would contribute to the community's "spiritual martyrdom" (*geistl. Marterthum*).[55] This interest in spiritual martyrdom was not new to Beissel in 1746, but the publication of *Martyrs Mirror* provided an additional ascetic road to travel on the way to heavenly rewards. According to the community's chroniclers, Beissel "never allowed a suspension of work" on the book, but he rather "seized every opportunity to keep all those who were under his control in perpetual motion, so that no one might ever feel at home again in this life, and so forget the consolation from above, which purpose this Book of Martyrs excellently served."[56] Producing *Martyrs Mirror*, then, was not demanding labor for its own sake, or even for economic reward. Rather, it was a means to imitate the martyrs' suffering in view of mortifying the flesh and approximating Christ's likeness. In a new preface to the Ephrata edition, Peter Miller reiterated this theme of *imitatio*. Despite the immensity of the task, wrote Miller, the Ephrata brethren regretted neither the "pains" they suffered nor the "diligence" it required, for the "memorial of the sacrificed confessors . . . always encouraged us to continue, so that we finally completed the work to the greatest enjoyment of others and ourselves."[57]

Working from the 1685 Dutch edition, the Ephrata publishers demonstrated considerable restraint in departing from the original, but they did introduce some changes that went beyond mere translation. Typifying this tension between preservation and innovation was the inclusion of the printer's device that had previously appeared in the 1685 edition.[58] The Ephrata device retained most of the visual features of the

Fig. 6.1. Title-page device for the Ephrata *Martyrs Mirror* (1748–49).
The digging man is now reversed, and the Latin motto "Fac et Spera"
has been translated into German.

1685 device, only now the image was reversed and the caption appeared
in German ("Arbeite und hoffe") instead of Latin ("Fac et Spera").[59] This
close connection between earthly *Arbeite* and *Hoffe*, labor and spiritual
hope, was fundamental to Beissel's spiritual vision, and rendering the
device's caption in German would have impressed this connection upon
the book's German-speaking readership.[60] These new readers received
more explicit counsel in Miller's preface, which appears three pages after
the device. After listing the spiritual benefits the Ephrata workers reaped
from their publishing efforts, Miller urges those who read his preface
to continue reading, for by reading stories of the martyrs, they would
themselves become more committed Christ-followers. "Thus receive
this work," urges Miller, "and perceive in reading this book the same
taste and awakening by the blessed blood witnesses which others have

enjoyed in the translating and printing thereof; then will your life and death serve discipleship, which had been the aim of this [work]."[61]

The notion of a person's "life and death serving discipleship" appears in visual form in the work's frontispiece, which filled in for the ornamental title pages of the earlier Dutch editions. Fashioned by an anonymous artist, the Ephrata frontispiece follows the precedent of the Dutch editions by including scenes of martyrdom: an upside-down crucifixion, a beheading, and an execution in boiling water. Significantly, however, these martyrdom scenes constitute minor features in Ephrata's frontispiece. Much more prominent is a series of images that, taken together, represent a life of discipleship. At the bottom of the page, potential Christian converts proceed upward along a narrow path, tempted by worldly seductions on their right, but drawn toward conversion by the gentle Lamb of God. As they walk toward the Lamb, they hear words of exhortation, both from heaven and from Moses: "Den solt ihr hören" ("Him you shall hear"). Those who choose Jesus's narrow way proceed to baptism, which is depicted in the middle of the page by an image of John baptizing Jesus. As the converts move beyond baptism, they carry crosses, an allusion to Jesus's admonition that his followers must deny themselves and take up their crosses as they follow him. The cross-bearing Christians gaze upon the martyrs, thereby realizing that the Christian life entails self-denial, suffering, and death. When death finally comes, the Christians fly through the sky, where they are met once again by the Lamb of God and ushered into a heavenly paradise.[62]

Had the Ephrata Community been able to access the frontispiece etching used in the 1685 edition, it may have forgone this new frontispiece design. Still, it is instructive to note how the Ephrata frontispiece departs from its Dutch precursors. No longer are physical torture and martyrdom most prominent, and no longer is the Roman church the primary enemy of Christian faithfulness. In the more tolerant context of eighteenth-century America, bloodletting is largely replaced by the more routine but nonetheless serious theme of Christian discipleship, which includes resisting the temptations of the unchristian world. Traveling this narrow way means bearing one's cross, and perhaps even suffering for one's faith—suffering that is very likely to entail self-denial, but not torture or execution. Ephrata's communitarians, whose experiments in self-denial were legendary, would have resonated with this theme, and

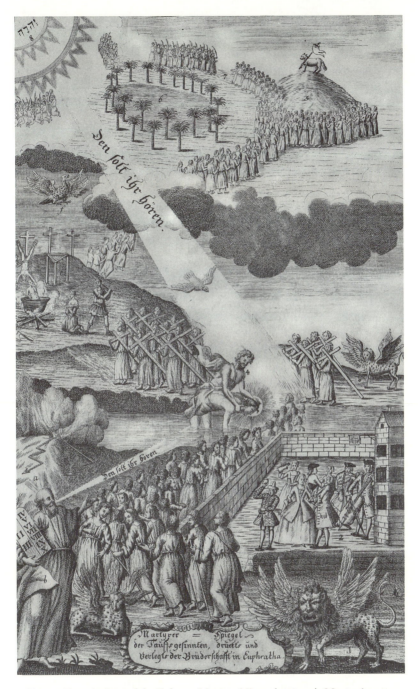

Fig. 6.2. Frontispiece of the Ephrata *Martyrs Mirror* (1748–49). Martyr imagery remains, but the emphasis has shifted to discipleship in a more general sense.

their Mennonite customers would also have found it compelling. Indeed, New World Mennonites interpreted the act of baptism as the ritual entrance into a life of self-denial and, moreover, as the entrance into a community that refused to conform to the world, including the world's reliance on warfare.

As much as Mennonites resonated with the theme of discipleship, some Mennonites would have found one specific feature of the Ephrata frontispiece objectionable. The central component of the frontispiece, both geometrically and thematically, was John's baptism of Jesus, which the engraver portrayed as baptism by immersion. This mode of baptism, practiced by the German Baptist Brethren and their Sabbatarian offspring in Ephrata, was anathema to Mennonite church leaders, who advocated baptism by pouring.[63] Heinrich Funck, the Skippack Mennonite leader who made the publishing arrangements with the Ephrata Community, and who was keeping tabs on the project as it progressed, could not have been pleased with this immersionist image. Of course, Funck and others who objected to this image were quite able to forgo its inclusion in their copies of *Martyrs Mirror*, for as was the case with many eighteenth-century books, copies of Ephrata's *Martyrs Mirror* were not bound until they were purchased. This arrangement allowed buyers to determine which parts of the book were included in their copies, and which parts were not. In the end, many of the copies that were purchased from the Ephrata Community were bound without the frontispiece. At the same time, many copies contained the frontispiece, including some copies that were purchased by Mennonites.[64] In these cases, the Mennonite buyers appear to have been undisturbed by this visual detail or were at least willing to overlook it in light of the artwork's overall message of Christian discipleship.[65]

Receiving a German Edition: Mennonite Customers and Their Martyr Book

During the three years it took for the Ephrata Community to produce *Martyrs Mirror*, the reasons that compelled Pennsylvania Mennonites to solicit a new translation had not disappeared. Although King George's War ended in 1748, the political thrust to create a more militarized Pennsylvania citizenry continued. If anything, circumstances in the 1750s only magnified the pressure on Mennonites to abandon their commitment to nonresistance, as events prefiguring the Seven Years' War alarmed Pennsylvania residents and provoked new calls for men to take up arms.[66]

By this time, of course, the Ephrata Community had completed its work on *Martyrs Mirror*, and the work received a hearty endorsement from those who requested it. In an afterword to the volume, Heinrich Funck and Dielman Kolb, both of whom had signed the 1745 letter to the Dutch Committee for Foreign Needs, deemed Miller's translation to be a faithful rendering of the Dutch original. Having reviewed each page, Funck and Kolb attested that they had failed to find "in the whole book one line which does not give the same grounds of belief and sense as is contained in the Dutch."[67] Given the worthiness of Miller's translation, the two men expressed hope that a new round of readers would "read in it earnestly with thought, so that they may see and learn in what way they should be grounded in belief in Christ, and how they should arrange their lives and walk in order to follow the defenseless lamb." The two Mennonite leaders also expressed optimism with respect to sales, predicting that "the Lord through his Holy Spirit will so kindle the hearts of men with an eager desire for it that they will not regard a little money but buy it."[68]

Funck and Kolb may have overstated the book's affordability—five hundred copies remained unsold five years later—but sales of the book were nonetheless solid.[69] According to the *Chronicon Ephratense*, the price for an unbound copy of *Martyrs Mirror* was twenty shillings, a relative bargain in light of the paper and labor needed to produce it.[70] Still, twenty shillings was a considerable price for most mid-eighteenth-century consumers, and even more so if the buyers had their books bound, as most *Martyrs Mirror* buyers probably did. Laborers working in Philadelphia at the time earned about twenty shillings a week, and, according to historians David Hall and Elizabeth Carroll Reilly, even people of middling wealth could rarely afford large books.[71] With these realities in mind, the sale of eight hundred copies of *Martyrs Mirror* is impressive, especially in light of the book's limited market. While *Martyrs Mirror* would have appealed to some who were neither Mennonite nor Amish (to other Pennsylvania-German sectarians, for instance), Mennonites and Amish constituted the primary customer base. Assuming that half of the eight hundred copies sold by 1753 were purchased by

Pennsylvania Mennonite or Amish customers, about one-third of Pennsylvania's Mennonite and Amish households would have acquired an Ephrata *Martyrs Mirror* within five years of its publication.[72]

Purchasing a book does not equate to reading it, of course, but the chances that *Martyrs Mirror* went unread by the people who secured copies are slim. Personal libraries in colonial America were small, especially in rural or frontier regions.[73] Most of these libraries consisted of fewer than a dozen books, which means the books they contained were often read repeatedly and, in some instances, in the manner Funck and Kolb prescribed: patiently, earnestly, and thoughtfully. In one case, in 1761, a Mennonite lad of less than fifteen years purchased his own copy of the Ephrata *Martyrs Mirror,* then wrote on the inside cover, "This martyr book belongs to me, Christian Burkholder, and I have bought it for my use and my soul's salvation."[74] The young Burkholder went on to become an influential Mennonite minister and bishop who, at the onset of the Revolutionary War, registered his nonparticipation in local military associations that were being formed for military training purposes.[75]

Other evidence indicates that the Ephrata *Martyrs Mirror* was highly valued by those who owned copies. For instance, when family members of a Mennonite farmer inventoried the man's two-dozen book library after his death in 1771, they listed "the Marthers book" fourth on the list, trailing only two Bibles and an unidentified book by Heinrich Funck.[76] Similarly, when another Pennsylvania Mennonite's library was inventoried in 1802, "Book called Martyrology" appeared second on the book list, just behind "Family Bible."[77] Owners often personalized their copies with family information, Fraktur inscriptions, and sometimes even drawings. By adding the names and birthdates of their children to the pages of *Martyrs Mirror,* readers placed their own family histories within the larger narrative of Anabaptist-Christian history.[78] Much like the genealogical information recorded in family Bibles, these mundane details took on sacred significance when recorded in close proximity to the stories of the martyrs.[79] Moreover, the indelible presence of this information on the book's flyleaves indicates that the owner considered the *Martyrs Mirror* a prized possession, one that, because it would never be discarded, would perpetuate ancestral memories in the minds of its inheritors.[80] In all these ways, a book saturated with death became a book filled with life, that is, the lives of those who owned the book and passed it along to others.

In the final analysis, we do not know much about the reading practices of eighteenth-century Mennonites with respect to *Martyrs Mirror*—how often it was read, in what contexts it was used, and what parts its readers found most compelling. What we do know is that Pennsylvania Mennonite concerns about the flames of war continued through much of the eighteenth century until they reached their zenith at the time of the American Revolution. We also know that, despite wartime pressure from their patriotic neighbors, few of Pennsylvania's Mennonite and Amish residents took up arms in America's war for independence.[81] This ongoing Mennonite commitment to nonresistance was likely buttressed by the stories in *Martyrs Mirror*, though quantifying the book's effect in this regard is impossible. At the very least, the book's role in sustaining nonresistance during the American Revolution was *presumed* by future generations of North American Anabaptists, who cited the Skippack Mennonites' foresight as an example to be emulated. "It was in the year 1742 that the Mennonites of eastern Pennsylvania wrote to their brethren in the Netherlands," begins the preface to the 1950 English edition of *Martyrs Mirror*. That preface, written by John C. Wenger, provides a few details about the production of the Ephrata edition before concluding with the comment, "The story of the eventual publication of a German *Martyrs' Mirror* at Ephrata . . . is too well known to require rehearsal here."[82] With this statement, Wenger and his fellow Mennonite publishers laid bare what had become true over the centuries: not just the martyrs, but also the book that told the martyrs' stories, had gained mythic status. The book's experience during and after the Revolutionary War only bolstered its renown.

The Ephrata *Martyrs Mirror* in the Revolutionary War

A landmark and eventually legendary event in the history of *Martyrs Mirror* took place in 1776, one year after the Revolutionary War began. At that time the Ephrata community still held in its inventory several hundred copies of the book, which remained unsold and were therefore unbound. These copies accounted for as much as two tons of paper, a valuable commodity in an age when paper was used for musket cartridges and cannon wadding. When parties aligned with the Continental Army learned of this paper supply, six Continental soldiers arrived with wagons to confiscate the material. Brushing aside the protests of the Ephrata owners, who considered the use of a religious text for military purposes sacrilegious, the Continental soldiers loaded the paper into their wagons and spirited it to Philadelphia. According to one source, 150 copies of the book were eventually fashioned into cartridges and used against the British.[83]

The confiscation of *Martyrs Mirror* for war purposes fueled the imaginations of eighteenth-century storytellers, who sympathized with the book's wartime plight. The Ephrata chroniclers recorded the story shortly after the war's conclusion, personifying the book and granting it nothing less than persecuted status. Conjuring Jesus's experience in Gethsemane, the chroniclers wrote that the paper's existence was "betrayed" (*verrathen*) by an informant. Once its existence was betrayed, soldiers arrived to make an "arrest" (*Arrest*) of the remaining copies, an action that led the chroniclers to conclude that "the testimonies of the holy martyrs had been quite maltreated." The chroniclers filled out their account by noting that those who witnessed the confiscation believed that the war "would not end favorably" for the patriots' side, a belief that had already been proved false by the time the chroniclers wrote their account, but which nonetheless spoke to the book's spiritual eminence.[84]

Even as the Ephrata chroniclers were writing their account of the book's confiscation, an Amish or Mennonite man named Joseph von Gundy was recording his own account on the flyleaf of his *Martyrs Mirror*.[85] Like the Ephrata chroniclers, von Gundy wrote that the book was "seized" (*genomen*) by the authorities and was then transported to Philadelphia. There, he said, the martyr book was turned into a "murder book" (*mordbuch*). In other words, in its captivity it suffered the fate that Mennonite ministers feared for their churches' members in the 1740s: it was forced into military service. In contrast to the Ephrata confiscation account, however, von Gundy devoted more attention to the book's postwar redemption than to its wartime captivity.[86] According to von Gundy, the book's captors finally came to their senses when "their own conscience told them it had not been printed for such a purpose." At this point the new American government informed "the lovers of this volume" (*die lieb haber dieses buchs*) that they could buy back the unused copies at a modest price. In the end, von Gundy wrote, 175 copies of the book were repurchased by people who treasured the book.[87] The confiscation and redemption of the Ephrata *Martyrs Mirror* continued to be invoked by Mennonite and Amish historians and storytellers in subsequent centuries.[88] Among these many accounts was a piece published in 1986 in two different venues: in *Family Life*, a monthly magazine read by a largely Amish readership, and in *Pennsylvania Mennonite Heritage*, a quarterly periodical produced by the Lancaster Mennonite Historical Society.[89] Written by an Amish historian and carrying the vivid title "The Ephrata Martyrs' Mirror: Shot from Patriots' Muskets," the piece details the full eighteenth-century history of the Ephrata *Martyrs Mirror:* its publication, its confiscation, and its redemption. Of particular interest is the article's concluding paragraph, in which the author observes that 1986 marked the two-hundredth anniversary of the book's return "from its Philadelphia captivity," a phrase that rhetorically aligned the book's experience with a key biblical event, the Jews' Babylonian captivity, which ended when Yahweh "stirred up the spirit" of King Cyrus to release the captive Jews.[90] Although the Amish writer did not make that explicit connection, his readers could have easily inferred that, in the case of the Ephrata *Martyrs Mirror,* God had once again intervened on behalf of his people, stirring the consciences of the governing officials to free their precious book.

Fascinating in its own right, the captivity story reveals an important reality with respect to *Martyrs Mirror* as an artifact of Amish-Mennonite history. When the Skippack ministers solicited a German translation of *Martyrs Mirror,* they wanted a text that could be *read.* In their words, they wanted their Pennsylvania church members to learn about those who had remained defenseless in times of trial, and they were pleased when the Ephrata community produced a German edition that mediated these martyr accounts. Future generations continued to find both comfort and challenge in the book's narrative details, whether they were conveyed in German, English, or some other language. Nevertheless, in certain times and places, and increasingly over time, these details took a backseat to the book's imposing, symbolic presence. The reasons for this were many, though one stands out: even when translated into the vernacular, *Martyr Mirror* was a difficult text to navigate. In some households, at least, it was rarely if ever read. Nevertheless, even in households where the weighty tome rarely left its perch, it signified something important to those who owned it, recalling for them a time when their theological ancestors were faithful unto death. A history book, an instructional manual, an heirloom, an icon—*Martyrs Mirror* came to be all these things on the North American landscape.

CHAPTER 7

Martyrs Mirror in
Nineteenth-Century America

The publication of the Ephrata *Martyrs Mirror* signaled the emerging self-sufficiency of Anabaptism in North America. Determined to have an edition in their own language, and unable to rely on Dutch Mennonites for assistance, Pennsylvania's German-speaking Mennonites took it upon themselves to find a translator and a printer for van Braght's martyrology. Although few could have imagined it at the time, this mid-eighteenth-century publication of *Martyrs Mirror* prefigured the book's trajectory for the next two centuries. From that point forward, as the center of Anabaptist gravity moved steadily from Europe to North America, new European editions of *Martyrs Mirror* proved to be exceptions to the prevalence of North American editions.

Even in 1780, when Amish leaders in the Palatinate published the next edition of *Martyrs Mirror,* North Americans played a major role in its production. The Pirmasens edition, named for the town in which it was produced, materialized for the same reason as the Ephrata edition: the desire of German-speaking Anabaptists to have an edition in their primary language.[1] This desire dates to at least 1710, when Swiss Anabaptist leader Benedikt Brechbill asked Dutch Mennonites for a German-language copy of *Martyrs Mirror.*[2] By the time this edition appeared in the Old World—seventy years after Brechbill first made his request—the Ephrata Community had issued its own German-language edition and, rather than producing a new translation, the Pirmasens publishers borrowed heavily from the Ephrata edition. To be sure, the Pirmasens publishers put their own stamp on the volume, making minor textual changes, reincorporating Jan Luyken's etchings, and adding new ornamentation. Even so, they followed Peter Miller's translation and his organizational scheme from beginning to end; this degree of textual appropriation led one historian to conclude that the Pirmasens edition was "for all practical purposes" a reprint of the Ephrata edition.[3] It was noteworthy, if not ironic: European Anabaptists were now indebted to New World translators for their Old World martyr book.[4]

In the nineteenth century, no fewer than six new editions of *Martyrs Mirror* appeared, all but one of them taking shape in North America.[5] That North American Anabaptists could support the production of five different editions of *Martyrs Mirror* in the nineteenth century speaks to the staying power of the Anabaptist martyrological tradition. At the same time, these different editions reveal another reality of Anabaptist life in nineteenth-century America: its expanding cultural and theological diversity. The most telling development in this regard was the translation of *Martyrs Mirror* into English, first in 1837 and again in 1886. Of course, the diversity of nineteenth-century Anabaptism extended far beyond the realm of language to theological priorities, differences that were also refracted through the prism of *Martyrs Mirror*. This is not to say that *Martyrs Mirror* was responsible for the fractured nature of North American Anabaptism. In fact, in some times and places the book helped divergent Anabaptist groups locate a common identity. In other places, however, *Martyrs Mirror* served its publishers and its readers in a different way: as a resource to advance their theological perspectives. In these latter cases, Mennonite and Amish church leaders, much like Dutch Mennonite leaders in the sixteenth and seventeenth centuries, sought to marshal the power in the martyrs' blood to promote particular visions of authentic Anabaptism. In that sense, *Martyrs Mirror* once again served the Anabaptist community as a measure of faithfulness, albeit a measure that yielded different results in the hands of different people.

Mennonites and Amish in North America: Growth, Division, Assimilation

The nineteenth century reshaped North American Anabaptism in profound ways.[6] As the century dawned, nearly all of North America's Anabaptists could trace their roots to German-speaking regions of Europe and, after that, to the colony of Pennsylvania, where their immigrant ancestors had helped to create a Pennsylvania-German (Pennsylvania Dutch) ethnic culture.[7] Beginning around 1730, some Mennonites began migrating to other locales, pushing first into Virginia and Maryland and later into Ontario, New York, and Ohio. As the eighteenth century gave way to the nineteenth, their numbers increased and their geographical footprint widened, so that by 1860, about forty thousand baptized Mennonites and Amish inhabited at least eleven states and provinces.[8] In the second half of the nineteenth century, Pennsylvania-German Anabaptists were joined by Anabaptist immigrants from other parts of Europe, who, like their Pennsylvania-German predecessors, were fleeing hostile lands for the more welcoming environs of North America. These newer immigrants, many of whom came from Russia, but whose roots reached back to Flanders and Friesland in the Netherlands, created a bipartite Anabaptist mosaic in late-nineteenth-century America: Swiss-German Anabaptists, both Amish and Mennonites, on the one side, Dutch-Russian Mennonites on the other.[9]

Ethnic differences contributed some diversity to North American Anabaptism, but ecclesial divisions were more numerous, taking shape long before the late-nineteenth-century Russian migration. In 1693 Swiss-German Anabaptists had divided into Amish and Mennonite factions, and they carried that division with them from Europe to the New World. In time this two-party division gave way to a multitude of Amish and Mennonite groups, each with its own particular vision of Christian faithfulness. Because Anabaptist churches were largely congregational in structure, and also because they developed exacting standards for faithful living, theological and lifestyle differences frequently led to congregational division. Sometimes congregational alliances would emerge, and sometimes these alliances would shatter, creating a shifting mélange of Anabaptist conferences, affiliations, and denominations. The distinctions between different Anabaptist groups were not always apparent to those who observed them from afar, but inside the fold most Anabaptist church members were well aware of the things that distinguished their group from other Anabaptist options.

Even in the eighteenth century, theological differences drove wedges between people who were previously in close fellowship. Like many other colonial churches, Mennonites experienced conflict over revivalist preaching and the theological assumptions that undergirded it.[10] On a different front, colonial Mennonites sometimes disagreed on what should be rendered to Caesar in times of war. Even though Mennonites almost universally opposed bearing arms, they could not always find consensus on the more complicated questions of supporting war efforts through tax payments or the hiring of substitute soldiers.[11] In one well-documented case, a Mennonite bishop north of Philadelphia—the son of Heinrich Funck, one of the men who had proofread the Ephrata *Martyrs Mirror*—was censured in 1778 for countenancing the payment of taxes to the revolutionary cause in lieu of military service. When Christian Funk's fellow ministers could not abide his level of patriotism, they stripped him of his preaching role. Funk responded by meeting separately with those who supported his views, a group that became known as the Funkites.[12]

Although these two eighteenth-century conflicts, one centered on revivalist preaching and the other focused on a Christian's patriotic duties, seem to have little in common, they both had roots in the more fundamental issue of separation from the world. In the former case, the world took the form of revivalist preachers who sought to downplay theological convictions that distinguished one set of Christians from another. In the latter case, the world took the form of civil authorities who sought to order the world through military means. In both cases some Mennonites believed that a closer association with the world would not compromise the principles of authentic Christianity but would in fact increase the long-term viability of Anabaptism, whereas other Mennonites believed that a closer association with the world would violate key biblical principles and should therefore be avoided.

As the North American Anabaptist community grew in size, the prevalence of conflict likewise grew. During the nineteenth century, North America's Anabaptists "struggled for unity but often did not succeed," writes historian Albert Keim; as a result "an important part of their story [was] the fraying of their churches' fabrics." Personality conflicts contributed to some of these divisions, but as Keim points out, the splintering of Mennonite and Amish groups into multiple factions cannot be separated from their attempts to achieve "spiritual vitality and renewal."[13] Revivalist preaching, Sunday school instruction, the adoption of Protestant hymnody, the use of English in worship—these are just a few means of spiritual renewal that appealed to some nineteenth-century Anabaptist groups and that other Anabaptists interpreted as spiritual decline. No part of the nineteenth century was free from these conflicts, though the century's third quarter witnessed the most significant "sorting out" processes.[14] Some of the groups that emerged during this time, the ones that resisted change most vigorously, became known as *Old Orders*.[15] By the close of the nineteenth century, trajectories had been set that even today characterize the world of North American Anabaptism, with world-rejecting Old Orders on the one end of the spectrum, world-embracing progressives on the other end, and a teeming variety of options in between.[16]

Despite these divergent approaches to Christian living, nearly all Anabaptist groups continued to hale the sixteenth-century martyrs as embodiments of godliness who offered lessons for contemporary living. The unresolved question, of course, concerned the content of the martyrs' lessons. By 1800 nearly two centuries had passed since the last Swiss Anabaptist died at the hands of an executioner. Not only had time passed, but times had also changed, with religious freedom now the norm in North America. Anabaptists were genuinely grateful for the opportunity to worship freely, but this freedom made it difficult for them to conceive of themselves as suffering people. Of course, Thieleman van Braght had faced a similar challenge in the 1650s, as he prepared *The Bloody Theater* for a comfortable Dutch readership. Like van Braght before them, the nineteenth-century publishers of *Martyrs Mirror* proved to be creative as they framed the martyrs' stories for use in a more charitable context.

A *Martyrs Mirror* for Americans: The 1814 Ehrenfried Edition

The first nineteenth-century edition of *Martyrs Mirror* was published in Lancaster, Pennsylvania, in 1814.[17] Sixty-five years had passed since the Ephrata edition was printed, and few if any of the copies remained for sale. Convinced that a new generation of Amish and Mennonites would benefit from *Martyrs Mirror*, Pennsylvania Mennonites worked with Lancaster-based printer Joseph Ehrenfried to produce a new German-language edition of the work.[18] Much like the Pirmasens edition, the text of the 1814 Ehrenfried edition closely followed the Ephrata edition, modifying Peter Miller's German translation only in minor details.[19] Because Jan Luyken's copper plates remained in Europe, the Ehrenfried edition, like the Ephrata edition, lacked Luyken's illustrations.

Although the Ehrenfried edition replicated the Ephrata edition on some levels, it was distinctly more American than its eighteenth-century predecessor. Nowhere did this contrast appear more sharply than in the device on the title page. Like the digging-man device in the Ephrata edition, the Ehrenfried device featured a farmer laboring under the banner "Arbeite und hoffe," but instead of digging within view of a European village, the farmer turns the soil with only his homestead in view. Clad in colonial garb, the shaggy-haired man does his work before a rough-hewn building with a thatched roof and a fenced-in herd of sheep. Compared to the stubby men who appeared in the Dutch and Ephrata devices, the Ehrenfried farmer is lanky and muscular, a testament to the strength needed to tame the American frontier. No longer laboring in the shadow of a village, the frontiersman works his own plot of ground in relative isolation.

An American accent also characterized the work's introduction, which extols the blessings of American-style government.[20] True to Anabaptist form, the anonymous piece defends political separatism in general ("Christ teaches us how we are to be submissive, but not that we are to rule") and defenselessness in particular ("the Gospel in no way allows us to take revenge"), but the writer also gives thanks for non-Anabaptists who are "willing, loyal, gifted, and withal called by God" to manage governmental affairs. Moreover, the writer thanks God that Mennonites now inhabit a land where every person is allowed to "serve the Lord according to his own understanding." In America, the writer continues, God has "shed his Holy and true light" upon both rulers and their subjects, enabling them to see that "tyrannical force" is not a tool of God but one of the Devil, a statement that might well have been uttered by a patriot-preacher during the Revolutionary War.[21]

Introducing *Martyrs Mirror* with a tribute to American liberal democracy correlates with the Americanization of the Mennonite sponsors, but it may have also been a strategic ploy. Written shortly after the conclusion of the War of 1812, the introduction would have functioned as a plea for continued toleration. Indeed, some historians have identified the War of 1812 as the catalyzing event for the production of this

Fig. 7.1. Title-page device for the Ehrenfried *Martyrs Mirror* (1814). The digging man and his homestead have moved to the American frontier.

new edition of *Martyrs Mirror,* much as the bellicose environment of the 1740s had spawned the Ephrata edition.²² Although no explicit evidence exists in that regard—the introduction does not discuss current events, and no documents exist that explain the genesis of the new edition—the introduction's emphasis on religious toleration suggests that those who oversaw the book's production were closely attuned to the public relations challenge of nonparticipation in war. Religious freedom, they knew, was always a tenuous ideal, one that was easily compromised when religious groups were deemed threatening to the status quo.²³ In that sense, the introduction was much more than a tribute to American liberty. It was also an appeal to governing authorities to live according to the light that God had granted America's founders, wisdom that included the benevolent treatment of religious outsiders.

Equally striking in its American tone is the introduction's emphasis on theological forbearance between Protestant groups. The introduction admits that Anabaptist teachings frequently diverge from other Christian views, but it nonetheless softens the lines between Amish-Mennonite views and those of other Protestant groups. "The gap between us [Anabaptists] and them [other Protestant groups] is not all that big, like some would like to imagine," avers the introduction. In fact, there is "only one faith, one Lord, one baptism, one God and Father," which means that everyone "is approved of God who fears Him and lives justly." To be sure, Anabaptists and their Protestant adversaries vilified each other during the Reformation, "but everything has its reason and its time." Because the reformers were operating under "the dark cloud of Papal power," they should be excused for their impertinence and instead be viewed as divine "implements" that undermined Roman Catholicism. God works through many kinds of people, and therefore the better part of wisdom is to consider all points of view and "sip the honey out of all kinds of flowers." If contemporary Mennonites would only take this advice, "our Christians could serve others, and other Christians could help us (as they actually do)."[24]

That *Martyrs Mirror* would be contextualized by a distinctly ecumenical plea is both ironic and telling. It is ironic because *Martyrs Mirror* is a strikingly anti-ecumenical text, repeatedly drawing sharp lines between what its producers considered authentic Christianity and Christianity in its many other forms. The Ehrenfried introduction recasts those lines. Although Anabaptists continue to be regarded as the epitome of faithfulness, the truly significant line now falls between Protestant expressions of the faith and Roman Catholicism. In this way, the introduction to the 1814 Ehrenfried edition outlines an assimilationist path that some Mennonites were going to follow toward the Protestant mainstream of North American life. In other words, even as the introduction to the Ehrenfried edition praises the Anabaptist martyrs for their strong convictions, it offers a rationale for Mennonites to moderate their theological angularity and forsake their sectarian ways. Perhaps more than any other edition of *Martyrs Mirror,* the Ehrenfried edition is a have-your-cake-and-eat-it-too edition: lauding the martyrs, contrasting their resolute lives to the "dangerous pleasure walk" of mainstream American living, but downplaying the differences between the martyrs' convictions and the rest of Protestant Christianity.[25]

This complex nature of the Ehrenfried introduction raises questions about its authorship. The piece frequently employs the first-person plural in reference to Anabaptists, and it concludes with the comment that many Mennonite leaders had deemed the prefatory comments necessary. It is therefore likely that a Mennonite minister, or perhaps a handful of Mennonite ministers, took the lead in crafting the piece, which they ran by other Mennonite ministers prior to publication. Even so, printer Joseph Ehrenfried may have also played a part in shaping the introduction, for it not only plugs a book that Ehrenfried had printed a few years earlier (*Enchiridion: Oder Handbüchlein, von der christlichen Lehre und Religion,* a work by sixteenth-century Dutch Mennonite leader Dirk Philips), but it also speaks in tones befitting Ehrenfried's Swedenborgian faith.[26] In particular, the introduction's references to divine enlightenment that leads to godly living, which in turn leads to God's approval, comports well with the Swedenborgian emphasis on benevolent living.[27] The introduction's ecumenical tone could also have derived from Ehrenfried's desire to expand his book's market beyond Amish-Mennonite buyers to the broader customer base identified in the introduction's opening line: "For the interested and devout (God seeking) reader, whoever he may be."[28]

If expanding his customer base was indeed Ehrenfried's hope, it appears to have been misplaced. Ehrenfried optimistically printed a few thousand copies of his *Martyrs Mirror,* a risky undertaking that likely contributed to his bankruptcy a few years later.[29] The Ehrenfried introduction may have softened the theological lines that separated Anabaptists from other Protestants, but its gesture toward theological détente did not make the book itself appealing to non-Anabaptists. *Martyrs Mirror* had always been a book about the Anabaptist faith for an Anabaptist readership, and even in the comparatively irenic environment of nineteenth-century America, *Martyrs Mirror* remained a book that few outsiders would wish to purchase.

Over the long term, however, the Ehrenfried *Martyrs Mirror* did contribute to softening the lines between Anabaptists and other Protestants, a least in a literary sense. Seventeen years later, in 1831, word-for-word chunks of the Ehrenfried edition were incorporated into another German-language martyrology, *Allgemeine Geschichte des Christlichen Marterthums* (Universal history of Christian martyrdom).[30] Published in Philadelphia by George Mentz, *Allgemeine Geschichte* combined excerpts from John Foxe's *Book of Martyrs* with Amish and Mennonite history, including martyr accounts that Mentz lifted directly from Ehrenfried's *Martyrs Mirror.* Over the next forty years, Mentz's martyrology was reprinted five times, and during this period it was purchased by some Amish and Mennonite customers.[31] In the meantime, another Philadelphia publisher, the American Baptist Publication Society, produced an English-language martyrology that likewise combined the work of Foxe and van Braght, a literary amalgamation that the society titled *Memorials of Baptist Martyrs*.[32] This latter work, which included accounts of Felix Mantz, Balthasar Hubmaier, and other sixteenth-century Anabaptist martyrs, featured an introductory essay that identified the "distinctive principles of a pure Christianity," which in good Baptist fashion included both "freedom of conscience" and "baptism only on a conscientious confession of faith."[33] In contrast to van Braght, however, the essayist did not identify defenselessness as a mark of true Christian discipleship, an omission that made the martyrology generically Baptist rather than Anabaptist.[34] In other words, even as some nineteenth-century Mennonites were moving toward the Protestant mainstream, certain parties within that mainstream were enveloping the Anabaptist tradition, a rapprochement that entailed the diminishment of the Anabaptist commitment to nonresistance.

Of course, some North American Amish and Mennonite groups found this sort of ecclesial rapprochement problematic. To them the notion of downplaying particulars in favor of a common-denominator faith represented a worldly lure that could lead godly people astray. One of those groups, the Reformed Mennonites, soon facilitated its own American edition of *Martyrs Mirror*.

Reformed Mennonites and the First English Edition

When the persons who authored the Ehrenfried introduction asserted that the gap between Mennonites and other Protestants was relatively modest, they controverted the sectarian impulse that ran deep in the Anabaptist tradition. More than that, they gainsaid unnamed parties who insisted on a sharp divide between faithful Anabaptism and the mass of Protestant Christianity. Given the sectarian inclinations of the Amish, the introduction's writers may have had their Amish neighbors in mind when they crafted these remarks, but the book's 1814 publication date suggests a more likely target: an upstart Mennonite faction that came to be known as the Reformed Mennonites. Never a large contingent among Lancaster County Mennonites, but nonetheless irksome to the Mennonite mainstream, Reformed Mennonites proved central to the publication of the next edition of *Martyrs Mirror,* an English edition produced in Lancaster in 1836 or 1837.[35]

Much like the Amish before them, the Reformed Mennonites were born from the desire for a purer church. The seeds of this desire were planted by Francis Herr, a Lancaster County Mennonite who had grown disenchanted with what he perceived as spiritual laxity, including advancing materialism and political involvement, among his fellow Mennonites.[36] In Herr's estimation, North American Mennonites had departed from Menno Simons's teachings, most significantly in the area of church discipline. As early as 1798, Herr and a handful of sympathizers began worshipping together, but not until 1812 did their new church become a formal entity. By this time Francis Herr had died, and his son John had assumed his leadership mantle. In an act that replicated the Anabaptists' first baptisms in 1525, John Herr and another disgruntled Mennonite baptized each other, reestablishing what they considered to be the true Mennonite Church. Those who witnessed these unfolding events called Herr's group *New Mennonites,* in contrast to the *Old Mennonite* majority, though they later became known as the *Reformed Mennonites.*[37] It was, writes historian John Landis Ruth, the first schism among Lancaster County Mennonites "in which the departing body retained the name Mennonite and claimed to be the true Mennonite body."[38]

Like his father before him, John Herr drew a sharp line between true Christianity and apostasy masquerading as Christianity. In a work published in 1815, the younger Herr roundly condemned other Protestant groups, calling them "captives in Babylon." "You esteem yourselves enlightened and regenerated Christians, whilst your fruits testify to the contrary," he wrote, adding "ye have not received the nature of Christ," and you refuse to "help him bear the cross."[39] A few years later, Herr was even more scathing in his critique of nominal Christianity. "Is the life of the present nominal Christian much better than the lives of men were in the times of Sodom and Gomorrah?" he asked rhetorically, then proceeded to list their spiritual failings: "They lie and deceive; they curse and swear; they dance and carouse; they commit fornication and adultery, they strive and dispute," and so on.[40] Herr's pointed language was hardly novel in Anabaptist history. In fact, the way Herr described the surrounding world paralleled van Braght's assessment of nominal Christianity in his preface to *The Bloody Theater*. It is not the "open enemies of God" who are most dangerous, van Braght had warned his readers, but those who "fain be saved," that is, people who "praise God and His Word with their mouths" but who demonstrate with their lives that "the world is their dear friend."[41]

Herr likewise inhabited a world in which God's openly avowed enemies were few and far between, a world in which Satan's attacks were, in his view, less noxious than they were alluring.[42] Still, like van Braght before him, he believed the experiences of the Anabaptist martyrs were relevant to all who wished to follow Christ. These suffering men and women, Herr wrote, "presented to us a glorious church," for they "bore testimony to the truth" and "sealed it with their blood."[43] More than simply citing the martyrs' faithfulness, Herr used the martyrs against his Old Mennonite adversaries, who, in his estimation, had abandoned the doctrines for which the martyrs had died. "The holy way of the cross, which was so gloriously trodden several hundred years ago by the holy martyr-witnesses of the truth," has now been "overgrown with the bushes of vanity and the thorns of perverseness," Herr asserted.[44] For that reason, he continued, contemporary Christians who wish to discern the truth would be wise join with the Reformed Mennonites in embracing "the doctrine which Menno Simons and the holy martyrs confessed and practiced," the same doctrine that Old Mennonite ministers regarded "very lightly."[45]

Herr's son-in law Daniel Musser was even more explicit in holding up the Reformed Mennonites as the true heirs of the sixteenth-century martyrs. In his combative history of the group, Musser went to great lengths to delineate the succession of the true church through the ages. Van Braght had himself advanced a theory of apostolic succession in *The Bloody Theater*, a theory that gave priority to the perpetuation of correct doctrine over time. Musser's history of the Reformed Mennonite Church assumed van Braght's successional theory, and he repeatedly referenced *Martyrs Mirror* as he made his case. Of course, the ultimate purpose of Musser's history was to show how the Reformed Mennonite Church fit snugly in van Braght's line of doctrinal succession, more snugly than other churches that made that claim. Francis Herr, wrote Musser, was "a firm believer in the doctrine of the gospel as set forth in the writings of Menno Simons," and he launched out on his own because he "knew of no church, or organization, which held and carried out these views."[46] For his part, John Herr "advocated the principles which his father held," convictions that forced him and his Reformed Mennonite followers to experience a taste of martyrdom. Joining the Reformed Mennonites was not for the fainthearted, Musser conceded, for those who joined "knew they were taking a position which would bring upon them reproach and contempt." Thankfully, even in this bloodless persecution, there was seed, for despite opposition from other churches, the Reformed Mennonite movement "continued to grow and increase."[47]

The Reformed Mennonites' desire to claim the martyrs' mantle galvanized their interest in *Martyrs Mirror* and made it an indispensable resource to them. Early on in their history, however, this presented a problem, for copies of the Ephrata edition were scarce, and the 1814 Ehrenfried edition was accompanied by an introduction that maligned those who perceived a large gap between strict Anabaptists and other Protestant groups. Whether or not these prefatory comments were directed at the Reformed Mennonites, people like John Herr would have considered the introduction precisely the wrong thing to place in the hands of lay people. The solution to that problem was clear if also quite daunting: the production of a new edition of *Martyrs Mirror*. In 1837 that new edition appeared, published in Lancaster County by David Miller.[48]

No contemporaneous evidence has been located to prove Reformed Mennonite involvement in the production of the 1837 *Martyrs Mirror*, but circumstantial evidence points strongly in that direction. First, one of the David Millers living in Lancaster's Lampeter Township in 1837 was a prominent Reformed Mennonite with financial means to underwrite the book's publication.[49] Second, John Herr was well acquainted with the man who translated the 1837 edition, I. Daniel Rupp, having recently worked with Rupp to publish an English translation of Menno Simons's *Dat Fundament des Christelycken Leers* (Foundation of Christian doctrine).[50] Third, the 1837 edition of *Martyrs Mirror* was an English-language edition, not a German-language edition. Even as the Reformed Mennonites clung to the old-time religion of Menno Simons and the sixteenth-century martyrs, they embraced the English language more fully than did their Old Mennonite counterparts, sometimes preaching in English and, in time, translating all of John Herr's German-language publications into English.[51] Eager to broadcast their message far and wide, Reformed Mennonites were willing to cast it in a language that reached beyond the Pennsylvania-German subculture, and the production of an English edition of *Martyrs Mirror* would only help in that regard.

Despite its linguistic assimilation to Anglophone America, however, the 1837 edition of *Martyrs Mirror* was in many ways the plainest edition of *Martyrs Mirror* ever produced. No illustrations appear in the book at any point. There is no frontispiece, there are no ornamental markings, and all that remains from the digging-man device are the words "Arbeite und Hoffe." The 1837 edition is also distinct from earlier translations of *Martyrs Mirror* in its refusal to add a new preface. Without fanfare or commentary, the volume simply begins with van Braght's prayer of invocation. It is as if the 1837 publishers had supreme confidence in the work's perspicuity, a transparency that would allow readers to grasp the text's meaning without their editorial help. Of course, the omission of a publisher's preface may also be read as a critique of the 1814 Ehrenfried edition. Unlike the Ehrenfried publishers, who felt constrained to soften the judgmental statements in van Braght's original, the publishers of the 1837 edition felt no such need. In their view, *Martyrs Mirror* stood on its own, much like the Bible itself, transcending time, place, and culture. Those who historicized its contents, excusing its searing messages by attributing them to an alien context, missed the point: in both sixteenth-century Europe and nineteenth-century America, the gap between true Christians and the rest of the world was enormous, and to think otherwise was spiritually naive.

For fifty years, until 1886, the 1837 edition was the only complete edition of *Martyrs Mirror* in the English language.[52] Reformed Mennonites purchased this unadorned edition, though other English readers, including other Mennonites, did as well.[53] Still, demand for an English translation was limited. Only twenty-five hundred copies of the 1837 edition were printed, a relatively small print run considering the total population of Amish and Mennonites in nineteenth-century America.[54] That twenty-five hundred copies could satisfy the market for fifty years before another English translation appeared reminds us that, through much of the nineteenth century, North American Anabaptists still preferred their books to be in German. The next North American edition of *Martyrs Mirror,* this one published by an Amish man, attests to that ongoing preference.

Sorting Out the Amish: Shem Zook's 1849 Edition

In broad strokes, the story of the Amish in eighteenth-century America reads much like the Mennonite story: immigration in search of religious toleration and economic opportunity; scattered agrarian communities, initially in Pennsylvania, then expanding geographically; and encounters with revivalism, militarism, and materialism. But not everything was the same. Mennonites were generally wealthier than their Amish counterparts, and in many contexts they were more changed-minded. The Amish "hold very fast to the outward and ancient institutions," Philadelphia Mennonites observed in a letter to Dutch Mennonites in 1773. In the twentieth century, Amish traditionalism bolstered the retention of young people and stimulated church growth. In the eighteenth century, however, Amish communities were small and widely scattered, and maintaining members was difficult. Although five hundred Amish immigrated to America in the eighteenth century, and most of the immigrants produced large families, fewer than a thousand Amish people lived in North America in 1800.[55]

The nineteenth century brought additional Amish immigrants to America, but it also brought increased division. Again, the broad strokes parallel the Mennonite experience. During these years, the Amish "struggled to decide how they were to relate to the American society in which they found themselves."[56] The question of conforming to, or resisting, broader social trends was never fully answered, for as soon as one issue was settled, another issue presented itself. In the midst of these struggles, Lancaster County Amish bishop David Beiler distinguished himself as a leading traditionalist. When the elderly Beiler recorded his memoirs in 1862, he looked back wistfully at the days of his youth, when "Christian simplicity was practiced, and much more submission was shown toward the ministers, especially toward the old bishops." In those days, he said, Amish people walked to church barefooted, and everyone was satisfied with home-made goods. Girls learned how to work the spinning wheel, and boys worked hard every day, as opposed to "wasting the precious time of grace in telling jokes and in unprofitable conversation." Beiler placed some of the blame on formal education, but in good Amish fashion, he ultimately traced the problem to a lack of church discipline. If anyone sixty years ago "would have dressed and conducted himself in the high fashion as is too much the case today," Beiler wrote, "he would have had to be put out of the church as a disobedient person."[57] With statements such as these, Beiler set himself against more progressive Amish church leaders who, in the mid-nineteenth century, placed some Amish congregations on a path that eventually led them into the Old Mennonite Church.[58]

In the midst of these debates, the Anabaptists' book of martyrs was often employed to buttress arguments. In the late 1850s, for instance, a disagreement erupted over the appropriateness of having deacons preach in Sunday services. From the traditionalists' point of view, preaching had always been the preserve of bishops and ministers; it was not within the purview of deacons, who were ordained to oversee material aid and alms distribution. Progressives took a more expansive view of deacons' responsibilities, and they appealed to *Martyrs Mirror* in two distinct ways. First, they pointed to specific martyrs who, in their view, embodied or affirmed the practice of deaconate preaching.[59] Second, they cited a broader principle, underscored by one of the martyrs' adversaries, that supported their cause. The principle, lifted from the lips of Friar Cornelis in his inquisition of Herman van Vleckwijck, was this: Anabaptists, unlike their Catholic adversaries, operated according to biblical precepts, not according to "the teachings of their forebears."[60] Friar Cornelis had intended this to be a critique of the Anabaptists' contempt for Catholic tradition, but Anabaptists had always considered it a compliment. In the debate over deacon preaching, Amish progressives were happy to use Friar Cornelis's words to cast aspersions on the traditionalists' point of view. Because the practice of denying deacons the pulpit had no basis in scripture, they said, it should be discarded.

Martyrs Mirror played an even more significant role in a second nineteenth-century Amish conflict, this one focused on baptismal practices. Unlike the Dunker-Mennonite baptism debate, in which Dunkers advocated immersion against the Mennonite practice of pouring, the internal Amish debate focused on *where* baptism by pouring should take place: should it take place in an indoor worship service, or could it take place in a stream or river, as some progressives were suggesting? Conflict over this issue erupted in many mid-nineteenth-century Amish communities, but nowhere did the debates run hotter than in Mifflin County, Pennsylvania, where the issue remained unsettled for decades.[61] As the Mifflin County conflict gathered steam, the traditionalist David Beiler made his views known from Lancaster County. In one attempt to bolster the traditionalists' view, Beiler cited the example of martyr Faes Dircks, who, according to *Martyrs Mirror*, was baptized in a house along with eight or nine other persons.[62] Dircks was not an exception, wrote Beiler. In fact, hundreds and perhaps thousands of the Anabaptist martyrs had been baptized in houses, establishing a precedent that should not be broken.[63]

Progressives could not deny the prevalence of house baptism in *Martyrs Mirror*, so they often appealed to a different authority: the Bible. One Mifflin County progressive who took this approach was Shem Zook, a layman who was deeply involved in the affairs of the larger world, including business, public education, and politics.[64] As a strong supporter of stream baptism, Zook made repeated arguments for the practice, contrasting "the example of the Holy Scripture," most notably Jesus's baptism, to the "traditional way" of house baptism. In one instance Zook called out the esteemed Beiler for turning a blind eye to his own reading of scripture. "Even David Beiler writes that the old form of baptism is without precedent [in the Bible], while there is evidence for baptism in the water," charged Zook.[65] Zook shied away from demanding the wholesale abandonment of house baptism. He simply wanted traditionalists to accept stream baptism as valid. At the same time, Zook's writings left no doubt that he considered stream baptism the more biblical practice and therefore the worthier choice in the present.

Zook's argument may have relied more on the Bible's testimony than it did on the martyrs' examples, but he was unwilling to relinquish *Martyrs Mirror* entirely to the traditionalists. Almost simultaneously with the controversy's eruption, in 1849, Zook published a new German edition of *Martyrs Mirror* that lent graphic support to the stream-baptizing view.[66] On the title page of book 2, Zook included an image that was original to his edition, an image that would have delighted stream-baptizing proponents. The image depicts Jesus's baptism as described in the first chapter of Mark's gospel.[67] In it, both Jesus and John the Baptist

Fig. 7.2. Illustration that appeared in Shem Zook's *Martyrs Mirror* (1849),
depicting the baptism of Jesus in the Jordan River.

stand in the Jordan River, water up to their waists. Unlike the Ephrata
edition's frontispiece, which portrayed John baptizing Jesus by immersion, Zook's edition includes no hint of immersion. Clearly, however, the
baptismal rite is being performed in a river.[68] Of course, traditionalists
like David Beiler admitted as much, knowing that Mark 1:9–10 was un-
ambiguous on the site of Jesus's baptism. Even so, it must have rankled
Beiler and his allies to know that their esteemed martyr book was now
making that point for all to see. The ploy of a shrewd Amish operator,
Zook's baptism image promoted his progressive view in a way that could
hardly be disputed, let alone condemned. One can almost hear Zook
chuckling as his *Martyrs Mirror* went to print.

Zook may have laughed all the way to the bank. A successful businessman, Zook was never averse to making money, but he was certainly
averse to losing it.[69] At the very least he knew that publishing a massive
book was a serious financial undertaking that posed risks but could also
yield rewards. For that reason, Zook took pains to secure fifteen hundred
subscribers before having the book printed, a job he commissioned to a
Philadelphia firm, to save five hundred dollars.[70] Moreover, the preface

to his new edition, more than the prefaces in earlier editions of *Martyrs Mirror*, reads like a modern advertisement. This new edition, the preface avows, is "noticeably improved" in "language and style" relative to earlier German editions, a promise that Zook hoped would persuade people to buy his book even if they already owned a German-language edition.[71] Zook's attentiveness to the market is also apparent in his admission that, early on, he had considered abridging the volume, presumably to make it more readable and perhaps to make it more affordable. Before the book went to print, however, potential buyers had convinced Zook that abridging *Martyrs Mirror* was a bad idea.[72] Modifying the book's language was one thing, but eliminating large sections of the text would be considered unseemly, if not sacrilegious. In that way, the tradition-minded market that Zook sought to tap forced the progressive publisher to pull back from his abridgment plan.

Throughout the 1850s and 1860s, *Martyrs Mirror* continued to be cited in the course of the Amish baptism controversy, and it would sometimes make its way into discussions and debates on other divisive issues. According to historian James W. Lowry, the ease with which nineteenth-century Amish leaders located evidence within *Martyrs Mirror* to advance their respective arguments reveals that many of these leaders had a "habitual familiarity" with the volume's contents.[73] Like the Bible itself, however, the text of *Martyrs Mirror* was multivocal and therefore open to interpretation. Although the martyrs were universally held in high regard, even they could not keep the nineteenth-century Amish church from drifting inexorably into two camps: a tradition-minded Old Order camp and a change-minded Amish Mennonite camp. By 1870, and perhaps even earlier, the die had been cast for the emergence of an Old Order Amish contingent that, in time, would become the most renowned Anabaptist entity on the North American landscape.[74] In the 1860s, no one could have imagined the breadth of the sociological divide that eventually emerged between the tradition-minded Old Orders and their progressive counterparts. Most conspicuous today in the realms of language usage, dress styles, and transportation choices, this divide is also apparent in contrasting approaches to nurturing a martyrological memory (see chapters 9 and 10).

An English Edition for the Ages: John F. Funk and the
1886 Elkhart Edition

North American Mennonites underwent their own sorting-out processes in the second half of the nineteenth century. The question that
factionalized Old Mennonites during the century's second half was
largely the same one that spawned the Reformed Mennonite Church
in the 1810s and the Old Order Amish in the 1860s: how fully should
Jesus's followers embrace the values and practices of the larger world?
Although Old Mennonites were more world-embracing than their
Amish counterparts, their nineteenth-century churches retained many
conservative elements long after the Reformed Mennonites had left the
fold. In the century's third and fourth quarters, some of these conservatives resisted changes afoot and produced Old Order Mennonite groups
that paralleled the Old Order Amish. At the other extreme, progressive
Mennonites warmly embraced the customs of the larger society, including higher education, middle-class professions, and a variety of Protestant evangelical practices. One progress-minded Mennonite was John F.
Funk, whose writing and publishing endeavors included two new editions of *Martyrs Mirror*, one in German and the other in English. For
Funk, producing new editions of *Martyrs Mirror* was both a moneymak-
ing endeavor and a way to remind his fellow Mennonites of their godly
heritage. Furthermore, it was a means to identify the martyrs' legacy
with the Old Mennonite Church, an effort Funk undertook to counter
Reformed Mennonite assertions to the contrary.

Funk's biography lays bare some of the forces that pressed upon
mid-nineteenth-century Mennonites.[75] The great-great-grandson of
Skippack bishop Heinrich Funck, Funk was born in 1835 on an eastern
Pennsylvania farm in a largely Mennonite community.[76] His immediate
family attended the Line Lexington Mennonite Church, though Funk
later recalled that some of his most formative childhood religious experiences had occurred in a Baptist Sunday school, an educational fo-
rum that most Mennonites at the time considered worldly. In 1857, when
Funk was twenty-two years old, his brother-in-law persuaded him to
move to Chicago to join his lumber business. Funk rose quickly within
the company, and with his brother-in-law's family he attended Sunday
services at Chicago's Third Presbyterian Church. This was the era of

the businessmen's revival, and like other urban businessmen in the late 1850s, Funk attended noonday prayer meetings on a regular basis.[77] He also participated in church-sponsored Sunday school initiatives, where he worked alongside a shoe salesman named Dwight L. Moody. Moody was only twenty years old at the time and was not yet a famous revivalist, but revivalist Christianity was definitely in the air. In January 1858, less than a year after he landed in Chicago, Funk attended revival services at Third Presbyterian, where he was said to have "made a deep and complete surrender to God."[78] Funk considered leaving the Old Mennonites at this point, but one year later, on a visit home to Pennsylvania, he was baptized and taken into membership at his family's church. Although he continued to associate with a broad range of Christians in Chicago, his trajectory as a Mennonite had been reconfirmed. By the time he left Chicago for Elkhart, Indiana, in 1867, he had already established himself as one of the Old Mennonites' leading young voices.

Funk established his leadership primarily through religious publishing, a realm he entered in 1863 while still living in Chicago. With the Civil War at full boil, Funk wrote a manuscript in support of nonresistance and had a thousand copies printed for distribution.[79] Encouraged by his book's reception, and troubled by the dearth of contemporary Mennonite literature, Funk soon launched the *Herald of Truth*, a monthly periodical aimed at a Mennonite readership.[80] At the time of its launch, Funk's *Herald of Truth* (and its German-language correlate, *Herold der Wahrheit*) encountered considerable opposition from conservatives within the Mennonite fold, but it eventually became standard fare in many Old Mennonite communities.[81] After moving to Elkhart in 1867, Funk redoubled his publishing efforts, first as a sole proprietor, then through a business partnership with his brother Abraham, and finally as the founder of the joint-stock Mennonite Publishing Company. Established in 1875, the publishing company eventually fell on hard times, and by 1908 it had sold off its periodical rights and printing equipment.[82] In the meantime, however, Funk's company served as the chief producer of Mennonite literature in North America. All told, Funk published nearly 120 titles, half of them in German and the other half in English. Although most of the books he produced were original works, 20 percent were republications of earlier Anabaptist-Mennonite sources.[83]

Two of the republications Funk undertook were new editions of *Mar-*

tyrs Mirror. In 1870 Funk and his brother issued a German-language edition of *Martyrs Mirror,* the third and final German-language edition published in the nineteenth century.[84] Based closely on Shem Zook's 1849 edition, Funk's *Märtyrer Spiegel* sought to tap the Mennonite market that he had captured with his periodicals, *Herald of Truth* and *Herold der Wahrheit.*[85] Even before the book was finished, the two periodicals included regular publication updates and instructions on how to secure copies in advance of the book's release. Funk wanted his readers to *buy* copies of *Märtyrer Spiegel,* but he also wanted his readers to *sell* copies. For that reason, his updates promised readers that, if they ordered twelve copies of *Märtyrer Spiegel,* they would receive an additional copy free of charge. "We want agents in every neighborhood, to go to work in earnest, and sell all the books they can," wrote Funk in his update, "as we have gone to great expense in getting up the book, and wish to sell them off as rapidly as possible."[86]

Before long the sales of Funk's *Märtyrer Spiegel* gained a small but welcome bump from across the Atlantic. In 1872, an elder in the Kleine Gemeinde, a small band of German-speaking Mennonites in Russia, contacted Funk about buying copies of *Märtyrer Spiegel* for distribution to his community.[87] By this time the Kleine Gemeinde had existed as a distinct ecclesial entity for sixty years; even so, the martyrological passions of its now deceased founder, Klaas Reimer, remained. For Reimer, who had migrated from Prussia to Russia in 1804, the people he encountered in *Martyrs Mirror* embodied a disciplined form of the Mennonite faith that, in his view, was missing among his new Russian Mennonite neighbors. Inspired by what he read in *Martyrs Mirror,* Reimer distanced himself from other Russian Mennonites and started his own "small church" (*kleine Gemeinde*) in 1812.[88] Sixty years later, as the Kleine Gemeinde faced challenges both internal and external, elder Peter Toews wrote to Funk expressing interest in Funk's new edition of van Braght's work. Toews's plea for the book echoed that of the Skippack ministers in 1745, citing as it did the tenuousness of the Kleine Gemeinde's nonresistant commitment, especially among the youth.[89] Although Funk's sales to the Kleine Gemeinde paled in comparison to his North American tallies, the transatlantic nature of the interaction underscores the continuing, if also shifting, relationship between Old World and New World Mennonites, the latter of whom had assumed principal stewardship of the martyrs' stories.

A decade and a half later, in 1886, Funk's Mennonite Publishing Company published another edition of *Martyrs Mirror*, this one in English.[90] More than four decades had passed since Rupp's English translation had appeared in 1837, and in Funk's view the market, which he hoped might extend beyond the Amish-Mennonite world, was ripe for another English edition. Funk surely knew of the 1833 martyr book *Allgemeine Geschichte*, which supplemented John Foxe's martyr stories with Anabaptist martyr accounts, and which, by the 1870s, had been reprinted numerous times.[91] He may also have been aware of two Baptist-sponsored endeavors: *Memorials of Baptist Martyrs*, the 1854 martyrology published in Philadelphia that paired nearly a dozen Anabaptist martyr accounts with other martyr accounts; and the more ambitious work produced by the London-based Hanserd Knolleys Society, titled *A Martyrology of the Churches of Christ*.[92] The latter work, sponsored by English Baptists at midcentury, was not intended to be a new martyrology but was rather an updated translation of van Braght's classic.[93] Appearing in two volumes in 1850 and 1853, the Hanserd Knolleys edition of *Martyrs Mirror* was never completed, but along with *Allgemeine Geschichte* and *Memorials of Baptist Martyrs*, it attested to a broader Protestant interest in Anabaptist martyr stories, certainly in Baptist circles but perhaps among other Protestants as well. Although Funk may have proceeded with a new English translation without envisioning this broader market, his sense that it existed soon informed his preface to the work.

Funk's decision to produce a German-language edition first, and only later publish an English-language edition, owes in part to the language preferences of nineteenth-century Mennonites: whereas most North American Mennonites in 1870 were still fluent in German, the shift toward English gained considerable steam as the century hastened to its end.[94] Of course, the sixteen-year lag time between the German and English editions also owes to the magnitude of preparing the English translation. Unlike Funk's German edition, which relied heavily on the German-language edition that preceded it, Funk's English edition was a start-from-scratch translation based on the 1660 and 1685 Dutch editions. Had Funk based his new edition on the text of the 1837 English edition, on the Hanserd Knolleys edition, or even on one of the German editions, chances are good that his *Martyrs Mirror* would have been ready sooner. Instead, Funk chose the more time-consuming course of producing a fundamentally new translation, a process that took six years

Fig. 7.3. Employees at the Mennonite Publishing Company in Elkhart, Indiana, circa 1886. John F. Funk Photographs, 1860-1952, Mennonite Church USA Archives, Goshen, IN.

to complete from the time he announced his intention in late 1880 to publish a new English edition.[95]

The task of producing this new translation fell to Joseph F. Sohm, a young Austrian immigrant who worked for Funk as a compositor.[96] Shortly after immigrating to the United States in 1873, the teenaged Sohm converted from Roman Catholicism to Methodism, a change of allegiances that set him in good stead with the evangelical Funk. Shortly after starting his translation of *Martyrs Mirror,* Sohm traveled back to his native Austria for health reasons, prompting Funk to ask his *Herald of Truth* readers to pray for the "pious conscientious Christian," that his translating endeavors "under the very shadow of papal churches . . . may leave a blessing even there."[97] Not unlike Thieleman van Braght, whose work on *The Bloody Theater* compromised his health, and not unlike the Ephrata communitarians, whose painstaking efforts came at a cost, Sohm suffered in the course of translating the massive text. Indeed, because of his painstaking work, Funk wrote, Sohm's health became "somewhat impaired," so much so that, in 1885, upon completion of his translating work, he needed to take yet another European respite.[98] In Funk's retrospective view, however, the sacrifice Sohm made on behalf of the project brought him great blessings, for his encounters with the martyrs made him "a more enthusiastic and devoted Christian than ever before." Sohm never became a tried-and-true Anabaptist, and years after he left Funk's employment, Funk heard a rumor that Sohm had returned to the Catholic Church.[99] His contribution to the Anabaptist tradition, however, is impossible to deny: more copies of Sohm's translation have been printed than all other translations combined, and even today it continues to outsell any other comprehensive translation of van Braght's text.[100]

As a shareholder in the Mennonite Publishing Company, Funk had a clear financial incentive to produce an English edition of *Martyrs Mirror*—and to proclaim it as far superior to Rupp's translation.[101] As he had with his German-language edition, Funk once again used his periodicals to galvanize consumer interest and secure his readers' services as selling agents. "We especially ask every minister to present the matter before his congregation and encourage their people to lend their aid in this publication," Funk enjoined his *Herald of Truth* readers in a brief editorial. "All our people should have it as a family book," he continued, "for

it is the testimony of those who for the faith we profess have offered possessions, comfort, life and all."[102] Other Mennonite leaders voiced their
support, which Funk sometimes amplified in the *Herald of Truth*.[103] In
a further attempt to entice customers, Funk reintroduced Jan Luyken's
illustrations, images that had not appeared in any of the previous North
American editions. Printed from newly fashioned engravings, thirty-six
Luyken-like illustrations made their way into Funk's 1886 edition. Although the new engravings lacked the precision of Luyken's originals,
and in some cases included rather cartoonish facial expressions, they
nonetheless provided the kind of visual enhancement that Luyken had
added to the text two hundred years earlier.[104] In a further reiteration of
the 1685 edition, Funk reintroduced the 1685 ornamental title page (see
figure 5.17), and he even added a full-page engraving of Thieleman van
Braght.[105] In sum, in contrast to the 1837 English edition, which contained no illustrations whatsoever, Funk's 1886 edition was a visually
rich book, offering readers something to ponder beyond the words that
dominated the pages.

Funk knew that his primary market for the 1886 edition would be
Americanized Mennonites, but he also hoped the book would appeal
to a larger Christian audience. His preface therefore splits the difference
between *Martyrs Mirror* as a book for Mennonites and *Martyrs Mirror*
as a book for all Protestants to read. In the latter respect, Funk wrote that
the martyrs' endurance under test provided a powerful incentive for contemporary Christians to live faithfully.[106] Even more significantly, Funk
invoked the popular evangelical notion of consecration, noting that the
martyrs' witness should inspire "sincere souls to live a more consecrated
life."[107] Expanding his scope to Americans at large, Funk observed that
a book like *Martyrs Mirror* would "help us to appreciate more highly
the privileges with which God has blessed us," namely, "the privileges of
citizenship" in a nation that guarantees religious freedom.[108] Perhaps in a
further attempt to attract non-Anabaptist buyers, or perhaps in an effort
to emphasize the Anabaptists' orthodox Christian foundations, Funk's
1886 edition invested most of its visual capital in martyrs that all Christians could claim: Jesus, John the Baptist, the apostles, and other heroes
of the early church.[109] In contrast to the 1685 edition of *Martyrs Mirror*,
in which more than 50 percent of the 104 illustrations portrayed the travails of the Anabaptists, only six of the thirty-six images that appear in
the Funk edition depict sixteenth- and seventeenth-century martyrs.[110]

Fig. 7.4. Portrait of Thieleman van Braght that appeared as the frontispiece in the Mennonite Publishing Company's *Martyrs Mirror* (1886).

Still, despite casting his book as a spiritual resource for Protestant Christians of all stripes, Funk sought first and foremost to claim the martyrs' legacy for his Mennonite buyers. The stories contained in *Martyrs Mirror*, he wrote, "are especially precious to us, as Mennonites," because through the martyrs God provided "the living exemplification of the peculiar tenets and doctrines which we hold and practice at the present day."[111] By asserting that the martyrs exemplified the faith that Old Mennonites were presently practicing, Funk contested the Reformed Mennonites' claim that Reformed Mennonites were, in fact, the authentic inheritors of the martyrs' mantle. Fifty years had passed since the Reformed Mennonites had sponsored the first English-language edition of *Martyrs Mirror* in 1837, but the Reformed Mennonites' allegation in this regard still rankled Old Mennonites, and especially so in the wake of Daniel Musser's history of the Reformed Mennonite Church, which he published in 1873.[112] Musser's account so aggravated Funk that, five years after Musser's history appeared (and eight years before he published *Martyrs Mirror*), Funk replied with his own book, *The Mennonite Church and Her Accusers: A Vindication of the Character of the Mennonite Church of America from Her First Organization in This Country to the Present Time*.[113] Funk's book took direct aim at Musser's accusation that, "as soon as the bloody persecutions" had passed, Old Mennonites "began to forget God, departed from his pure doctrines . . . , and gradually became corrupt."[114] In response to this charge, Funk recounted the words and deeds of various Old Mennonite leaders that demonstrated their fidelity to the martyrs' commitments. For instance, he asks, why would Heinrich Funck and his Old Mennonite colleagues have invested so much time and energy in producing the Ephrata *Martyrs Mirror* if they were not committed to the doctrines for which the martyrs had died? And why would so many Old Mennonite families have owned a copy of *Martyrs Mirror* if they did not apply its contents to their spiritual lives?[115] Funk acknowledges that the Old Mennonites had sometimes erred in their ways, but so too had the Reformed Mennonites. In fact, Funk implies that the Reformed Mennonites' eagerness to criticize others placed them on the same side of the spiritual ledger as the Scribes and the Pharisees, who "esteemed themselves righteous above others," including God's own Son.[116]

In this literary wrangling between Funk and Musser, and in the dueling decisions of the Reformed Mennonites and the Old Mennonites to publish new editions of *Martyrs Mirror*, we see most clearly the desire of nineteenth-century North American Anabaptists to claim the martyrs' legacy as spiritual leverage in an ecclesial conflict. For Musser and his Reformed Mennonite friends, their small and spiritually rigorous community extended the martyrs' legacy more authentically than any other group. Like the sixteenth-century Anabaptists, they stood steadfastly on the side of truth, a stance that, in Musser's words, brought them "much enmity and hatred."[117] From Musser's perspective, his church's existence as a marginalized, ridiculed sect only underscored what he already knew was true, namely, that the Reformed Mennonites were chosen by God to defend and advance the truth.

The Old Mennonites were not convinced, however, and through Funk's writings they sought to turn the tables on the Reformed Mennonites' arguments. In Funk's construal of church history, the Reformed Mennonites were not the true inheritors of the martyrs' mantle; they were rather the spiritual descendants of the martyrs' adversaries. In earlier times, Funk asserted, "when men fell into the delusion that they alone were right," they killed those who they considered heretics. In nineteenth-century America, however, this "spirit of self-righteousness" had assumed the form of "multiplying sects, each claiming that they are the only true church of God."[118] Few present-day sects exhibited this self-righteous spirit more clearly than the Reformed Mennonite Church, continued Funk; it was, he said, a spirit they inherited from their founder, John Herr, a spirit they ultimately shared with the martyrs' tormentors.[119] Fortunately, "our Church has stood the storm of persecution for centuries," Funk assured his Old Mennonite readers. "She has been slandered, maligned, abused, and misrepresented, but never destroyed"—not by the Roman Catholics in the sixteenth century, and certainly not by those who "heap their severest vituperations upon her" in the present. For that reason, Old Mennonites should accept their accusers' criticism as "a mark of acceptability with God," and in the spirit of Christ, they should forgive their theological foes, "'for they know not what they do.'"[120]

No historical analogy is perfect, but by equating the horrors of sixteenth-century persecution with the problem of nineteenth-century sectarianism, Funk stretched Anabaptist history to its breaking point.

On the one hand, Funk was right: the Reformed Mennonites *were* judgmental, and Musser's insider history of the Reformed Mennonite Church was not an impartial assessment of the past. Still, the Reformed Mennonite approach to the Christian life had much more in common with the martyrs' experience than did the progressive wing of the Old Mennonite Church. In their unbending commitments to adult baptism, nonresistance, and church discipline; in their pointed condemnation of the larger world; in their zeal to draw sharp lines between other churches and their own; and in their refusal to compromise with those they believed were wrong—in all these ways the Reformed Mennonite experience paralleled the experiences of many sixteenth-century Anabaptists, and especially those whose names filled the pages of *Martyrs Mirror*. Although Funk rightly perceived some continuity between the Old Mennonites and the Anabaptist martyrs, he and people like him inhabited a context much more akin to the Dutch Golden Age, a context in which Mennonites, much to van Braght's chagrin, had made peace with the larger world. To be sure, many Old Mennonites in the late nineteenth century continued to think of themselves as a separate people, and in some respects they were. Nonetheless, the nineteenth century had set many of them on a trajectory that significantly softened the lines between Mennonite life and the American way. These lines continued to soften in the twentieth century, a softening that would compel some twentieth-century Mennonite Church leaders to plead for renewed attention to *Martyrs Mirror*. At the same time, it was the conservative Mennonite and Amish groups, the North American Anabaptists who could most readily imagine themselves inhabiting the world of the martyrs, who would give *Martyrs Mirror* its most sustained attention in the next century.

CHAPTER 8

Martyrs Mirror in
Twentieth-Century America

I f measured only by the production of new translations of *Martyrs Mirror,* twentieth-century Anabaptists in North America fell far short of their nineteenth-century counterparts. Should we broaden our scope, however, to consider new editions and reprints of the work, the story changes considerably. With books, even hefty ones, becoming ever more affordable, twentieth-century Mennonite and Amish publishers produced a burgeoning array of reprints and editorially enhanced editions of van Braght's work, both in German and in English. In some cases, these new editions offered nothing new but a revised publication date. In other cases, the publisher reset the type, altered the frontispiece, reinserted Jan Luyken's images, or added editorial features, such as indexes or historical notes. Many of these new editions sold in the thousands, meaning that more copies of *Martyrs Mirror* made their way into buyers' hands during the twentieth century than during the previous three centuries combined. Additionally, a multitude of *Martyrs Mirror* excerpts and paraphrases found their way into grade-school texts, Sunday school literature, church periodicals, and various other print media.[1] In all these ways, the content of *Martyrs Mirror* became available to the Anabaptist masses in the twentieth century to a degree previously unknown.

Production is not synonymous with influence, and consumption fluctuates for many reasons. In the case of the twentieth-century (Old) Mennonite Church, which took the lead in producing new editions of

Martyrs Mirror, the connection between the production and influence of *Martyrs Mirror* must always be read in two ways: the wide distribution of *Martyrs Mirror*-related literature may have sustained the book's influence, but the drive to produce it almost always stemmed from fears that important convictions were on the wane.[2] During these years, Mennonite Church leaders, many of whom paved the way for assimilation into mainstream American life, worried that their fellow church members were exchanging their Anabaptist birthright for a mess of spiritual pottage. For these latter-day inheritors of van Braght's fears, *Martyrs Mirror* offered the same benefits that van Braght had envisioned: the blood of the sixteenth-century martyrs, they hoped, would be seed for the renewal of a spiritually lukewarm church.

More specifically, the Mennonite impetus for producing new editions of *Martyrs Mirror* derived from a complex of twentieth-century factors. First, the prevalence of war in the twentieth century alerted Mennonite Church leaders to the tenuous state of the church's nonresistant stance. Second, the presence of influential historians in the seats of Mennonite Church leadership meant that history itself was awarded a key role in securing Mennonite faithfulness. Third, resourceful agents at the denomination's publishing house advanced the view that Anabaptist convictions could be safeguarded by producing quality literature, including texts rich in Anabaptist-Mennonite history. *Martyrs Mirror* was one of those texts.

The Mennonite Publishing House may have taken the lead in producing *Martyrs Mirror,* but if we shift our attention to consumption, a different picture emerges. For as the twentieth century ran its course, consumer demand for these new editions came less from change-minded Mennonite customers and more from Old Order Amish and other traditional Anabaptist groups. Not only did the book's primary themes—resistance unto death, to name one—feel out of sync with the experiences of change-minded Mennonites, but the book was also harder to navigate than were other devotional books available to them. Among traditional Anabaptists, however, the twentieth-century reception of *Martyrs Mirror* traced a different arc. In these groups, all of which retained robust views of nonconformity to the world, van Braght's martyrological themes continued to resonate. For them the barriers to consumption had less to do with the book itself—its content and its medium—than with access to it: the book was relatively scarce and, in some people's eyes, quite expensive. In time, however, a new distributor of *Martyrs Mirror* emerged on the scene, an Old Order Amish publisher that combined a spiritually ambitious mission with a business model that met the needs of frugal customers. Founded by a Canadian Amish community in the mid-1960s, Pathway Publishers sought to undergird Old Order Amish life by producing affordable literature, a corpus that eventually included an economical German-language edition of *Martyrs Mirror.* Although the Mennonite Publishing House remained the exclusive publisher of the English edition, it came to rely more and more on Pathway and its sales agents to actually sell the book. In sum, as the twentieth century ran its course, *Martyrs Mirror* increasingly found both its distribution hub and its customer base in the Old Order realms of the North American Anabaptist world.

Change-Minded Mennonites and the Use of History

By the dawn of the twentieth century, the North American Anabaptist world had become hodgepodge of congregations, informal affiliations, and formal associations. Even though all claimed and drew from a common theological heritage, various factors had led to a fragmented Anabaptist world in which chariness between groups often exceeded cooperation. In some ways, the most prominent divide derived from European soil. Mennonite and Amish immigrants who migrated to the New World in the eighteenth and early nineteenth centuries came almost exclusively from Switzerland and southern Germany. Later in the nineteenth century, the Swiss-German Anabaptists were joined in North America by Dutch-Russian Mennonites, who differed from their Swiss-German counterparts in both ethnic customs and theological emphases. According to James C. Juhnke, the Swiss-German contingent "made a virtue of their marginality" and incarnated an ethos of "humility, non-resistance, and separation," whereas the Dutch-Russian immigrants were more assertive and more engaged in the larger society.[3] In time, as these respective ethnic communities breathed the modernizing air of nineteenth-century America, they sorted themselves into various associations and denominational families. For instance, the (Old) Mennonite Church, the largest Mennonite denomination in the United States in 1900, consisted almost entirely of ethnic Swiss-Germans. Dutch-Russian Mennonites, whose migration to America began in earnest in the 1870s, made their ecclesial homes in the General Conference Mennonite Church, a previously small federation of Swiss-German congregations that, as early as the 1840s, had pursued a more progressive path than other North American Mennonites, and also in the Mennonite Brethren Church.[4]

Ethnicity may have been one fault line in the North American Anabaptist world, but it was not the only one. Swiss-German Anabaptists had long been divided into Amish and Mennonite contingents, and as the nineteenth century passed, these contingents multiplied and, in turn, occupied a widening spectrum of theology and practice. On one end of the spectrum were Old Order groups that displayed cultural markers distinguishing them from the larger society, markers such as the Pennsylvania Dutch language, plain dress, and the rejection of common technologies. On the other end of the spectrum was the General Conference Mennonite Church, which forswore dress regulations, launched a seminary, and undertook missionary activities.[5] A contingent of late-nineteenth-century Old Mennonites—people like John F. Funk—shared some of these liberalizing tendencies with their General Conference counterparts, promoting revivalism, Sunday school, and higher education in Mennonite Church circles. In between the Old Orders and people like Funk lay a multitude of points on the spectrum, Anabaptist groups that were more tradition-minded than Funk but less so than the Old Orders.

Yet another factor contributed to the fraying of Anabaptist life in the first third of the twentieth century: the roiling debate between Protestant modernists and Protestant fundamentalists. Issues including the plenary inspiration of the Bible, Jesus's virgin birth, and substitutionary atonement found ready debate in some Anabaptist circles, with some participants deeming them essential affirmations of the Christian faith. Old Order Anabaptists, devoted as they were to church tradition, were scarcely involved in this wrangling, but on the change-minded end of the Anabaptist spectrum—that is, in both the (Old) Mennonite Church and the General Conference Mennonite Church—the disputes that beset many Protestant denominations during this time made their presence known. Mennonite educational institutions, including the Mennonite Church's

Goshen College and the General Conference Mennonite Church's Bluff-ton College, became centers of controversy. Although full-bore theolog-ical modernists were few and far between, some Mennonites lauded the Social Gospel movement and embraced historical-critical approaches to the Bible. Compared to some Protestant denominations at the time, the General Conference Mennonite Church showed considerable tol-erance for members who leaned in a modernist direction. In contrast, the Mennonite Church's *Gospel Herald,* under the editorial leadership of Daniel Kauffman, became a megaphone for antimodernist viewpoints, carrying articles with titles such as "The Protestant Apostasy" and "The Consequences of Higher Criticism."[6]

In this theologically unsettled environment, change-minded Menno-nites worked overtime to marshal Anabaptist history as their ally. Cor-nelius H. Wedel, the first and longtime president of Bethel College, a General Conference Mennonite college in central Kansas, took the lead in this work, writing a four-volume history of Mennonites in support of his idea of *Gemeindechristentum* (congregation Christendom).[7] For Wedel, *Gemeindechristentum* was a genuine, apostolic Christianity that had continued in some form since the first century, typically showing itself on the margins. According to J. Denny Weaver, Wedel's notion of *Gemeindechristentum* was "a norm against which to interpret all of Christian history," and in particular a way to critique state-church Chris-tendom.[8] Drawing on *Martyrs Mirror,* Wedel contended that medieval sectarians had preserved *Gemeindechristentum* through the ages and that it was later assumed by the Waldensians and eventually by the six-teenth-century Anabaptists. Significantly, two defining features of We-del's *Gemeindechristentum* were congregational autonomy and freedom in religious doctrine, ecclesial characteristics that, from the beginning of the General Conference Mennonite Church in the mid-nineteenth century, distinguished it from Old Mennonite groups.[9]

Wedel's work was influential in its day, but using history as an identity-defining resource climbed to new heights among General Conference Mennonites in subsequent decades.[10] No one was more important in this regard than C. Henry Smith, who, after receiving his PhD from the Uni-versity of Chicago in 1907, accepted a teaching post at Goshen College. A member of the (Old) Mennonite Church, Smith appeared to be a good fit for Goshen, but his tenure there was short-lived. In 1913, with institutional tensions on the rise, he left Goshen for a faculty position at Bluff-ton College, a General Conference school that more readily abided his theologically progressive views.[11] Smith's historical arguments fell in line with his progressivism. In an address he gave while in graduate school, Smith claimed that, contra many people's views, Mennonites were actu-ally "the most liberal of all denominations," for they dismissed human tradition and allowed each person "to decide for himself" how to inter-pret the Bible.[12] Three years later, in his dissertation-turned-book *The Mennonites of America*, Smith argued that the early Anabaptists were "radicals" in their insistence upon the individual's freedom of conscience against both state and church coercion.[13] Smith's historical vision, which aligned the early Anabaptists with broader American values, remained influential in General Conference Mennonite circles through much of the twentieth century. In contrast to the Old Order Amish, and also in contrast to many (Old) Mennonites, General Conference Mennonites pursued a path that was both more engaged with the larger world and more inclusive of dissent, two values that, as we will see below, shaped their reception of *Martyrs Mirror*.

On the (Old) Mennonite Church side, Harold S. Bender proved Smith's equal in using history as a spiritual resource. In 1924, at age twenty-seven, Bender assumed a faculty position at the newly reopened Goshen College, which the Mennonite Board of Education had closed the year before after years of theological unrest.[14] Bender took the new post at the behest of his father-in-law, John Horsch, a key leader among Mennonite fundamentalists and a founding member of the Mennonite Church's Historical Committee.[15] A historian himself, Horsch sought to counter Smith's perspectives, leveraging sixteenth-century Anabaptist history to bend contemporary Mennonites away from modernism's in-fluence. According to Horsch, not only did the early Anabaptists share far more theology in common with twentieth-century fundamentalists than they did with modernists, but they also set the bar for standing firm on doctrinal truth, a resoluteness most evident in those who suffered martyrdom.[16] Horsch encouraged Bender to cast his lot with Goshen, hoping that his son-in-law's presence would help him stanch the mod-ernist threat there and elsewhere in the Mennonite Church. It is arguable that Bender helped in that regard. At the same time, he never became the fundamentalist that his father-in-law was. Bender may have "tilted to the antimodernist side of the equation," wrote his biographer Albert Keim, but he "instinctively reached for the middle," eschewing the polemicism of his father-in-law in favor of institution-building.[17] For the next three decades, Bender's fingerprints could be found on nearly every institutional initiative of the Mennonite Church.

For our purposes, Bender's significance lies in his success at bringing Anabaptist history to bear on discussions about Mennonite identity in the twentieth century's middle third, and especially in the Mennonite Church, whose publishing house produced a new edition of *Martyrs Mirror* during this time. More than simply producing his own scholarship, Bender created venues that enabled others to research and write about Anabaptist-Mennonite history, none more important than the *Mennonite Quarterly Review,* an academic journal devoted to Anabaptist-Mennonite history and theology. In addition to launching the journal, Bender encouraged his fellow Mennonite Church members to support the denomination's publishing house in its history-related endeavors. Founded in 1908 in Scottdale, Pennsylvania (and often called *Scottdale* by its Mennonite constituents), the Mennonite Publishing House assumed many of the publishing ventures that John Funk had launched nearly fifty years earlier.[18] Writing in the *Gospel Herald* in 1927, Bender praised a recent denominational directive that instructed the publishing house to reserve a portion of its profits for history-related projects, but he also called for more generous grassroots support. In particular, Bender sought to raise money for the "the authoritative history of the [Mennonite] Church" and other related publications. "From this activity," he wrote, Mennonites could expect greater "appreciation for the Church" and heightened "loyalty to her principles . . . , especially among the younger people."[19]

Of course, young people were the cohort that most worried Mennonite Church leaders in the 1920s and 1930s. During these decades *Youth's Christian Companion,* a Scottdale-produced periodical aimed at Mennonite Church youth, ran dozens of articles on the theme of nonconformity, particularly in the areas of dress, entertainment, and secular learning. As the 1920s gave way to the 1930s, and especially as tensions rose in Europe, other *Youth's Christian Companion* articles appeared that focused more specifically on the doctrine of nonresistance. In September 1938, for instance, Bender's Goshen College colleague Guy Hershberger published a piece that pointed youthful readers to the hymn "Faith of Our Fathers," specifically its poetic pledge to "be true to [our fathers' faith] till death." Hershberger proceeded to recall the martyrs' courage, noting that nearly all of the early Anabaptist leaders "died young," many of them "before they were thirty years old." These same Anabaptist martyrs refused to defend themselves, wrote Hershberger, and if they lived today, they would reject the sword again, even to the point of refusing noncombatant roles in the military. Hershberger concluded by challenging his young readers to stand firm in their convictions, quoting once again from the popular hymn:

How sweet would be their children's fate
If they, like them, could die for thee![20]

Just months after Hershberger published this tribute to youthful martyrdom, the Mennonite Publishing House released its first English edition of *Martyrs Mirror*. This new edition, urged into production by the Mennonite Church's Historical Committee, drew heavily from the edition that John Funk had produced in 1886 (employing, for instance, Joseph Sohm's translation), which may explain why no new publisher's preface appears. Instead, the 1938 edition simply repeats the preface that appeared in Funk's 1886 edition. The fifty-two-year-old preface was outdated at points, but given the anxieties of the church's leadership, the publication board would have found much in it to like, particularly this line: "It is the duty of the church to maintain and teach the pure Gospel of Jesus Christ and to transmit the same to coming generations."[21] This "grand record of [the martyrs'] sufferings" has ably performed this function in the past, the preface continued, and it therefore promises to "perpetuate the pure doctrines of the Gospel" to new generations of Mennonites.[22]

The 1938 English edition may have lacked originality with respect to its preface, but it did offer something that no North American edition had offered before: the artwork of Jan Luyken. Up to this time, Luyken's martyrological images had appeared in only two editions of the work: the 1685 Dutch edition and, nearly a full a century later, the 1780 Pirmasens edition (Funk's 1886 edition had included knockoffs of Luyken's images, but not his actual images). Now, for the first time in 158 years, the original images were once again included in the text of *Martyrs Mirror*, this time printed from photoengraved zinc plates. Perhaps because of cost, the Mennonite Publishing House chose to include only 55 of the 104 original images. About half of the 55 images appear in book 1, the proto-Anabaptist section of *Martyrs Mirror;* the other half appear in book 2, which picks up the story of martyrdom in the sixteenth-century. Whatever the reason was for including certain images and excluding others, the distribution of images across sixteen centuries of church history meant that readers of the 1938 edition encountered pictures that linked Jesus's crucifixion and the persecution of his disciples to the suffering of the sixteenth-century Anabaptists.[23] The 1938 edition thereby underscored a point that Mennonite Church leaders wanted their young people to embrace, namely, that Anabaptism represented Christianity at its finest. And because all of Scottdale's subsequent editions of *Martyrs Mirror,* even those printed today, were essentially reprints of the 1938 edition—only the publisher's front and back matter later changed, not the text, the layout, or the pagination—this imagistic association of Jesus and his disciples with the Anabaptists remained.

The 1938 English edition added another feature that remained in print for years, a feature that was eventually granted special meaning by many who encountered the book. This feature, which bookbinders call a *sprinkled edge,* was achieved by spattering drops of red dye on the edges of the pages. Issuing books with sprinkled edges was not unique to the Mennonite Publishing House, let alone to the 1938 production of *Martyrs Mirror.* Indeed, decorating book edges began as early as the fourth century and became common in early modern Europe, when it took a variety of forms. According to book historian Mirjam M. Foot, the most common way to decorate book edges in early modern Europe was sprinkling, with red serving as the most common sprinkling color; that may explain why the publishing house chose it for the edges of *Martyrs Mirror.*[24] Scottdale itself did not grant the red sprinkles any special significance, but many *Martyrs Mirror* devotees came to associate the crimson splotches with the martyrs' blood, as if the heavy book were squeezing out their bloody witness drop by drop. Although the Mennonite Publishing House discontinued this decorative practice in 1998, some readers were still making this connection years later when discussing copies of *Martyrs Mirror* that they owned or had seen.[25]

The publishing house may not have made this connection to the martyrs' blood, but it nonetheless thought the decorative flourish would increase the book's appeal. In fact, advertisements for 1938 edition cited no less than four distinct features that had nothing to do with the book's actual content: a "sprinkled edge," "easily read type," an "imitation leather" cover, and a "substantial binding."[26] Narrative content was one thing, but Scottdale realized that the martyrological content was housed in a marketable commodity. In an increasingly competitive marketplace, particularly in the realm of religious literature, selling copies of *Martyrs Mirror* was every bit as important as printing them. This reality became even clearer in 1950, when the Mennonite Publishing House issued its next edition of *Martyrs Mirror*.

Marketing *Martyrs Mirror* at Midcentury

No twentieth-century edition of *Martyrs Mirror* appeared to more fanfare than Scottdale's 1950 English edition. Scottdale's 1938 edition may have included some new features, but twelve years later the stakes were higher and, correspondingly, the marketing thrust was more aggressive.[27] The stakes were higher because of war, not one that loomed on the horizon, but the war just past. To the dismay of many Mennonite Church leaders, the church's commitment to nonresistance had proved fragile during World War II. Of the three thousand men from the Mennonite Church who were drafted during the war, only 60 percent chose conscientious objector status. The fact that 40 percent chose military service signaled failure to many Mennonite Church leaders.[28] Writing in 1946, Harold Bender observed that although the church had a "fairly strong program of peace teaching" before World War II, that teaching had disappeared during the war. "Some of our brethren were afraid to speak over the pulpit and give advice," lamented Bender. Thus, when young Mennonite men were drafted, many of them were influenced more by "the war spirit" than by the spirit of God. "The record shows," said Bender, that the church had failed its youth with respect to teaching this fundamental doctrine.[29]

The willingness of Mennonite Church youth to take up arms during World War II likely had as much to do with the church's advancing assimilation as it did with lax teaching on nonresistance. Simply put, the "war spirit" gained sway among Mennonite youth as their churches became less separatist in general. In response, Bender and other Mennonite leaders looked for ways to shore up the church's nonresistant stance, fixing on *Martyrs Mirror* as their most promising literary ally. In his preface to the new 1950 edition, Bender's friend John C. Wenger, secretary of the Mennonite Church's Historical Committee, began by lauding the foresight of the eighteenth-century Skippack Mennonites who sponsored the Ephrata edition. Now, precisely two centuries later, "we again find the Mennonite brotherhood laboring to strengthen its young people in the nonresistant faith of the fathers." Two world wars had tested the church's peace position more severely than any events since the sixteenth century, wrote Wenger, and the pressures to abandon nonresistance were strong. For that reason, "vigorous efforts must be made to capture the loyalty of our youth," efforts that included the production of yet another edition of *Martyrs Mirror*.[30]

The Mennonite Publishing House poured considerable resources into producing and marketing this new edition. It was not a new translation—like the publishing house's 1938 edition, the 1950 edition used Sohm's 1886 translation—but it did include new front and back matter, including a paginated listing of Luyken illustrations and a five-page index of Anabaptist martyrs. Optimistic that buyers could be found, the publishing house produced a first run of twenty-five hundred copies, an expensive undertaking, though, in the view of one employee, not a particularly risky one. "*Martyrs' Mirror* will probably sell as long as there are Mennonites on earth," conjectured salesman Ford Berg in a letter to his publishing house superiors. The question, Berg said, is not *whether* the 2500 copies would sell, but rather *how quickly* they would sell.[31]

Wishing to move copies quickly, Scottdale launched an advertising campaign that surpassed all of its previous campaigns. In addition to producing a glossy brochure, the publishing house placed numerous advertisements, sometimes masquerading as editorials, in the periodical literature it produced on behalf of the Mennonite Church.[32] One *Gospel Herald* editorial, titled "A Publishing Event," outlined the edition's new and improved features and then made a case for the volume's indispensability. Because it "is a spiritual tonic to read of these fathers of ours who so gladly gave up their lives for the principles which they had espoused," *Martyrs Mirror* "is a must for every home library." In fact, "no Mennonite has completed his education in Mennonite materials until he has at least scanned *Martyrs' Mirror.*" The anonymous writer then paused to authenticate his claim about the book's indispensability with a bold business assertion. All publishers try to sell their books, he conceded, "because sales mean profits." In the case of *Martyrs Mirror,* however, "we would try to sell this book [even] if every sale meant a loss."[33]

Scottdale's claim that, given the spiritual value of *Martyrs Mirror,* the publishing house was willing to lose money on it, begs deeper consideration, for the evidence cuts both ways. It is clear that the Mennonite Church leadership saw the production of *Martyrs Mirror* as an important spiritual investment, particularly in the lives of Mennonite young men, who, even in the 1950s, continued to face the choice of conscientious objection or military service.[34] Nothing revealed this youth-oriented spiritual concern more clearly than an article that appeared in 1950 in *Youth's Christian Companion.* Gerald Studer, in an attempt to rouse the periodical's youthful readership, summarized three different *Martyrs Mirror* accounts in which teenagers were put to death, including one in which a sixteen-year-old girl was drowned in a horse trough.[35] Referencing the denomination's youth program, Studer noted, "It would seem that Mennonite Youth Fellowship is no new thing, for these Mennonite youth knew Jesus 'and the power of his resurrection, and the fellowship of his sufferings.'"[36] Studer became more pointed as he drew his piece to a close, reminding his young adult readers that the doctrine of nonresistance was not a peculiar Mennonite add-on but rather stood at the heart of the Christian faith. Reading *Martyrs Mirror* would not only prove this to be the case; it would also "help us to stop pitying ourselves for any of the treatment we may have suffered . . . during the World Wars." Sounding much like van Braght, Studer suggested that *Martyrs Mirror* would enable young Mennonite readers "to live as though we really believed we were strangers and pilgrims in the earth instead of wealthy, complacent citizens of a smug North American community."[37]

Still, even as Studer and others touted the book's spiritual benefits, the Mennonite Publishing House could not ignore the economic reality of packaging these benefits in a costly book. Indeed, the very title of Studer's article based the book's blessings on the willingness to buy it, cajoling readers with the assertion, "You Can Afford a *Martyrs Mirror.*" Moreover, no evidence exists that Scottdale sought to increase sales of

Martyrs Mirror by selling copies below cost, despite its public claim that it would be willing to do so. In fact, in a letter to an Iowa bookseller who was encountering resistance to the book's price, a Mennonite Publishing House sales manager noted that the $9.75 retail price was necessary "for a proper margin" for both the publishing house and its dealers. The sales manager admitted that a ten-dollar book might seem expensive to potential buyers. Nonetheless, he wrote, if people "can pay over $20.00 for a Bible, they can certainly pay $9.75 for *Martyrs' Mirror*."[38]

Significantly, the bookseller who complained to Scottdale about the book's high price had spent her previous week canvassing an Iowa Amish community. She had been pleasantly surprised to find that some Amish people showed interest in Scottdale's new English edition. At the same time, she said, their interest often flagged when they encountered the book's price tag. Complicating the situation was the fact that another North American publisher was making plans to enter the *Martyrs Mirror* market, in this case with a new German edition that would cost much less than the Mennonite Publishing House edition. With the Old Order segment in the Anabaptist world growing, and with its relatively stronger interest in the Anabaptist martyrological heritage, the question of how to tap the Amish market for *Martyrs Mirrors* occupied Scottdale for the rest of the twentieth century.

Tapping the Amish Market: Mennonite Publishers and Amish Buyers

From the time of their midcentury decision to produce a new *Martyrs Mirror,* Mennonite Publishing House executives sought to build an Amish market for their work. Along with placing advertisements in at least four Mennonite Church periodicals, Scottdale's marketing staff purchased advertisements in the *Budget,* an Ohio-based correspondence newspaper that circulated in Amish communities well beyond Ohio's borders.[39] "Mennonites and Amish have carried copies [of *Martyrs Mirror*] with them for generations," noted one of the ads, for they believed that reading the book would strengthen their faith "come what may."[40] A few months later, the *Budget* carried a glowing review of the new edition that made various connections to Amish life, including the martyrology's inclusion of the confession used by Amish ministers in baptismal classes. "I wonder how many have read [the Dordrecht Confession] in the past 20 years," pondered John A. Hostetler, a rising Mennonite Church leader who was soon to become the world's leading authority on Amish life. "Or must you confess you haven't read it for some 30 years, as did one brother who was hailed to court in defense of his stand on the school conflict?" With this reference to the Amish community's closest equivalent to religious persecution—the ongoing conflict with government officials over mandatory educational requirements—Hostetler underscored the book's continuing relevance for Amish life. The book's ten-dollar price "may seem rather high," he acknowledged, "but it is not too high to pay for keeping youth supplied with good sound reading."[41]

The most formidable obstacle to this marketing strategy, of course, was the historic Amish preference for reading *Martyrs Mirror* in German. In addition to being the language of their ancestors, German continued to be used in Old Order Amish worship services for both Bible reading and hymn singing. In the eighteenth and nineteenth centuries, German-language editions of *Martyrs Mirror* appeared in North America more frequently than English-language editions, with Mennonites superintending most of those editions. By the mid-twentieth century, however, few change-minded Mennonites continued to read German. Because the Mennonite Publishing House saw its primary mission as serving the Anglophone Mennonite Church—it was, after all, a denominational publisher—it focused its attention on other things, including the production of new English editions of van Braght's work.

This Anglophone turn by the Mennonite Publishing House forced early- and mid-twentieth-century Amish leaders to take the lead in producing *Märtyrer Spiegel*. Lacking the requisite technologies to print the actual books, these Amish leaders secured the assistance of non-Amish printing establishments, including the Mennonite Publishing House, to do the printing. For instance, in 1915, an Illinois Amish man contracted with the Mennonite Publishing House to print and bind *Märtyrer Spiegel* (essentially a reprint of John Funk's 1870 edition) on the condition that he could ensure sales of at least a thousand copies.[42] The Amish underwriter, L. A. Miller, was himself a bookseller, though given his willingness to sell advance copies of the book at the wholesale price, Miller's interest in spiritual benefits clearly outweighed his desire for financial gain.[43] With Miller financing the project, another Amish man worked

Binding 2,500 Martyrs' Mirrors

Mary Harshberger, Anna Stull, Glen King, and Betty Brenneman are shown above binding copies of Martyrs' Mirror. To the front on the left are copies which are to have covers placed upon them, while in the center rear are many copies under tremendous pressure so that they will have proper shape. Each book is checked carefully before it is released for sale.

Martyrs' Mirror is one of the most unique books in all history. It lists 1141 pages of helpful material, describing the faith and testimony of the truth of martyrs since the time of Christ until 1660. The book has been reprinted many times, always for those people who believe in the nonresistant faith.

Martyrs' Mirror has been compiled from various authentic sources, including chronicles, memorials, and testimonies. Order your copies today!

Ea., $9.75; 3 to 5, $9.25; 6 to 9, $8.75; 10 or more, $8.25

Fig. 8.1. Advertisement for *Martyrs Mirror* that appeared in the *Budget,* an Ohio-based newspaper with a wide Amish readership.

to drum up orders. In a letter in *Herold der Warheit*, minister Hans E. Bornträger urged his fellow Amish ministers to appoint people in their churches to obtain subscriptions for the book and then forward those subscriptions to Miller. The need was urgent, he wrote, for many Amish youth wished to read the book, but the 1870 edition was no longer available.[44] Two months later, Miller reported in the same periodical that 514 copies had already been ordered, an impressive start that enabled the book to be printed within the year.[45]

Thirty-five years later, in 1950, Amish leaders used a similar strategy to produce the next German-language edition of *Martyrs Mirror*, only this time they bypassed the Mennonite Publishing House altogether.[46] Why these later Amish financiers took their business to an Indiana-based print shop is not entirely clear, though in doing so they disrupted Scottdale's plans to produce its own German edition. Scottdale's plan to print a new German edition in 1950 appears to have been an after-thought, occurring only after it had devoted considerable resources to producing its new English edition. Before the German edition could become a reality, however, word trickled back to Scottdale that a group of Amish men had decided to publish a German edition and, moreover, was planning to sell copies for five dollars apiece.[47] Shortly thereafter, small classified ads began to appear in the *Budget* offering individual copies of the book for five dollars plus postage. In retrospect, Amish customers who purchased this inexpensive 1950 German edition may have experienced buyer's remorse, for the printing was uneven and some sections were difficult to read. At the time, however, the price seemed right. At five dollars, this German edition was half the retail price of the Mennonite Publishing House's English edition—a bargain made possible by financiers who made less than a dollar on each copy they sold.[48]

In the words of one Mennonite Publishing House official, the market presence of a five-dollar German edition of *Martyrs Mirror* was a "complication" that he was "not sure how to meet."[49] Not only did this complication spell an end to Scottdale's midcentury attempt to publish its own German-language edition, but the book's low price also served to alienate Amish people who expressed interest in Scottdale's English edition but could not fathom why it would cost twice as much as the new German edition. This problem, which underscored the gulf between Scottdale and the book's most enthusiastic customer base, was soon exacerbated with the founding of Pathway Publishers, an Old Order Amish publishing house in Aylmer, Ontario.

Pathway Publishers and *Martyrs Mirror*

The founding of Pathway Publishers marked a new era in the world of Amish-sponsored publishing.[50] Long before Pathway's establishment in 1964, a variety of Amish people had utilized publishing as a means to nurture the Amish faith, though in most cases enterprising Amish persons contracted with outside presses to produce their literature. With Pathway, however, religious publishing became a full-fledged Amish enterprise replete with Amish editors, Amish writers, and Amish workers to run presses, distribute literature, and handle accounts. Through its production of books, school curriculum, and periodicals, Pathway exerted considerable influence on North American Old Order life in the last quarter of the twentieth century. It continues to do so today.[51]

From its earliest days, Pathway demonstrated a keen interest in the edification of Amish youth, commending to them the faith of their Anabaptist forebears.[52] Among other things, this meant disseminating the content of *Martyrs Mirror*, sometimes in revised forms. Of particular use in this regard were the Pathway Readers, reading anthologies that the publisher produced for grade-school children in Amish schools. Pathway's sixth-grade reader, first published in 1968, included a short historical essay entitled "What's a *Martyrs' Mirror*?"[53] In a slightly more advanced reader, also published in 1968, eighth-graders encountered Elmo Stoll's "Dirk Willems and the Thief Catcher," a fictional embellishment of the Dirk Willems story that appears in *Martyrs Mirror*.[54] Later that year, Pathway published *The Drummer's Wife and Other Stories from "Martyrs' Mirror*," an anthology that placed Stoll's "Thief Catcher" story alongside eleven other paraphrased martyr accounts. According to Joseph Stoll, the Pathway cofounder who crafted most of the stories in *The Drummer's Wife*, these enhanced martyr accounts were neither "a mere product of my imagination," nor were they history for history's sake. "If these stories could awaken a new interest and a deeper faith among our Amish and Mennonite people of today," he allowed, "my prayers and hopes for this book would be realized."[55]

Nowhere did Pathway's martyrological interests show themselves more clearly than in the publisher's flagship periodical, *Family Life*. In the periodical's first year (1968), no fewer than six of its articles fixed upon the content of *Martyrs Mirror*. In "Half-Way Baptism," which appeared in the inaugural issue, Pathway's David Luthy introduced a consideration of Anabaptist baptismal views by recounting an exchange between an Anabaptist prisoner and his inquisitor that appears in *Martyrs Mirror*.[56] In the next issue, Joseph Stoll began a series entitled "Chats about the Anabaptists," which summarized various *Martyrs Mirror* accounts of well-known Anabaptist leaders.[57] Yet another *Family Life* issue included "The Death of a Church," in which Luthy traced the history of the Dutch Mennonite Church from martyrdom to toleration to "the road downhill." Along the way Luthy detailed the marks of a declining church, including the loss of nonresistant convictions, the embrace of theological modernism, and the ordination of women. "Let the death of the Dutch [Mennonite] Church be a lesson to every congregation, Amish and Mennonite," Luthy concluded. "Let us seriously ask ourselves, 'How many compromises has our congregation made with the world, and how many steps has it taken from its Bible-based Anabaptist heritage?'"[58]

Committed to helping Old Order Anabaptist churches avoid the fate of Dutch Mennonitism, Pathway undertook to republish the entire *Märtyrer Spiegel*. By the time Pathway published its first edition in 1967, three twentieth-century editions of *Märtyrer Spiegel* had already appeared (in 1915, 1950, and 1962), all of them financed by Amish persons and produced by non-Amish presses.[59] Together, these three German-language editions amounted to about three thousand copies, a relatively modest number, though not insignificant in view of the Old Order Amish population at the time. Indeed, it is likely that, in the mid-1960s, nearly half of the Old Order Amish households in North America owned at least one German-language copy of *Martyrs Mirror*. Still, with the Old Order Amish population doubling every twenty years, and with other German-speaking Anabaptists (for instance, Low German–speaking Mennonites in both North and South America) wanting copies, the market was not exhausted. Pathway stepped in to meet that demand.[60]

Two details pertaining to Pathway's 1967 edition of *Märtyrer Spiegel* carry particular significance. First, the press run of nearly two thousand copies doubled that of any previous twentieth-century printing of

Märtyrer Spiegel, a testament both to the numerical growth of tradition-minded Anabaptist communities and to the optimistic sales outlook of the Pathway leadership. Pathway's optimism was not misplaced. The two thousand copies sold out in six years, an achievement that correlated with the edition's second noteworthy detail: its preproduction price of $6.50. This bargain-basement price was three dollars *less* than the list price of the 1962 edition of *Märtyrer Spiegel* and about half the retail price of the 1968 English edition produced concurrently by the Mennonite Publishing House.[61] Pathway's ability to offer *Märtyrer Spiegel* at a low price owed to several factors, including the company's low overhead, its modest wage structure, and its profitability in other areas. Unlike the Mennonite Publishing House in 1950, Pathway never claimed it would sell copies of the martyrology below cost, and it never did. Pathway's pricing did, however, help to sustain a market for *Märtyrer Spiegel* that continues to this day in some of North America's most conservative Amish communities, as well as among Low German Mennonites in Mexico, Belize, Bolivia, and other Latin American countries.[62]

In many tradition-minded North American households, however, the prospect of owning an illustrated English edition grew increasingly attractive during the century's last third.[63] In response Pathway once again stepped to the fore, reframing the market that Scottdale had previously cornered. Although Pathway stopped short of publishing its own English edition, its sales catalog, which carried non-Pathway items, began advertising the Mennonite Publishing House's English edition as early as 1964.[64] Pathway was glad to sell copies of *Martyrs Mirror* below Scottdale's suggested retail price, though even then it knew that its customers were finding the price prohibitive.[65] By 1995, when Scottdale's suggested retail price topped fifty dollars, Pathway's leaders had had enough. They first approached the Mennonite Publishing House about assuming publication of Scottdale's English edition, and when Scottdale nixed that idea, they proceeded to explore the prospect of producing their own English edition by reissuing I. Daniel Rupp's 1837 translation.[66] Pathway eventually abandoned that plan, but only when the Mennonite Publishing House secured an outside establishment to print the book more cheaply. In addition, Scottdale agreed to give Pathway a 50 percent discount, much of which Pathway passed along to its customers. As a result Pathway's customers could buy an English edition of *Martyrs Mir-*

ror for just a few dollars more than Pathway's *Märtyrer Spiegel*, that is, for about half the price of buying the English edition directly from the Mennonite Publishing House.[67]

In sum, during the last third of the twentieth century, the distribution matrix for *Martyrs Mirror* moved decidedly in the conservative direction, toward tradition-minded Anabaptist groups. Between 1965 and 1999, North American Anabaptists of all stripes continued to buy *Martyrs Mirror*, and they did so at unprecedented levels: 42,000 copies of the English edition, produced by the Mennonite Publishing House, and 10,000 copies of *Märtyrer Spiegel*, produced by Pathway Publishers. Ascertaining the destination of these copies is more difficult than identifying their publishers, but it is likely that most of the 52,000 copies were purchased by tradition-minded Anabaptists for whom van Braght's martyrological themes continued to resonate.[68] Still, to say that change-minded Mennonites had lost interest in *Martyrs Mirror* would be an overstatement. Even as their assimilationist practices introduced them to new authorities and new concerns, some change-minded Mennonite leaders concluded that *Martyrs Mirror* contained resources that could help twentieth-century Mennonites live faithfully as culturally engaged citizens. The challenge was to translate the book's content into messages that were pertinent to assimilated Mennonites and, moreover, into vehicles that could sustain their attention. In an era of sensory-rich media, when change-minded Mennonites were fast embracing radio, television, and other entertainment technologies, some *Martyrs Mirror* devotees worried that van Braght's demanding medium was stifling his message. The key to unlocking this quandary was finding consumer-friendlier ways to promote the martyrs' witness.

Engaging Change-Minded Mennonites in Unsettled Times

In the decades following World War II, the assimilative trajectory of change-minded Mennonites rose to new heights. Assimilation was nothing new, of course. Change-minded Mennonites' acceptance of mainstream cultural habits—in language, educational pursuits, vocational choices, and church practices—had traced a steady line through much of the nineteenth and twentieth centuries, this despite efforts by some leaders, especially in the (Old) Mennonite world, to safeguard the notion of Christian nonconformity. By the 1960s, however, the tide that ran between social engagement and a strict separation from the world had shifted inexorably toward engagement. During these decades, writes historian Paul Toews, Mennonite identity among change-minded Mennonites had less and less to do with "nonconformity visually defined," that is, with rurality and unconventional social practices, and more and more to do with abstract commitments such as social activism and volunteerism.[69]

Mennonite experiences surrounding World War II provided impetus to this ideological shift. Even before World War II, some North American Mennonites had determined that a Christian's commitment to nonresistance was best demonstrated through service to persons outside one's local church community. These voluntary service endeavors took a variety of forms, though in some cases they entailed overseas relief work, including work performed under the auspices of the Mennonite Central Committee (MCC), an inter-Mennonite relief agency founded shortly after World War I.[70] Later, during World War II, many U.S. and Canadian Mennonites, rather than serving in their nations' militaries, participated in Civilian Public Service in the United States and Alternate Service in Canada, once again displaying the conviction that an Anabaptist peace ethic meant participation in the social order, not withdrawal from it. In response, leaders in both the General Conference Mennonite Church and the (Old) Mennonite Church spoke increasingly of the Christian's responsibility to the larger world. This concern took center stage in 1950 at an inter-Mennonite peace conference sponsored by MCC.[71] The conference's summary statement took an activist tone, invoking the words *love* and *service* a combined twenty-six times, in contrast to *nonresistance,* which it used only twice—and which, in coming years, would be nudged aside in many change-minded churches by terms like *pacifism, peacemaking,* and *justice.*[72]

In the 1950s and 1960s, a host of Mennonite intellectuals, from Guy Hershberger to Gordon Kaufman, from John Howard Yoder to J. Lawrence Burkholder, offered their own visions of what a socially engaged Anabaptist faith should look like. To be sure, consensus on this issue was always elusive. Even Mennonites who agreed that their people should be more attentive to the world disagreed with one another on the theological rationale for social engagement and, as importantly, on the specifics of a social agenda. Still, various endeavors among change-minded Mennonites showed how far they had traveled since the decades before World War II. As early as 1957, an article appeared in the Mennonite Church's *Gospel Herald* that spoke positively of civil rights protests and asked if there might be a role in the movement "for Christians in the nonresistant tradition?"[73] Correspondingly, some Mennonite leaders and students began to head south to participate in strategy meetings and protests, an option that became more appealing to some after Martin Luther King Jr. visited Goshen College in 1960.[74] Goshen College professor Guy Hershberger was one Mennonite leader who commended King's work, writing in *Gospel Herald* that King was engaged in "a heroic effort" to bring about change "by peaceful means." In answer to the question of Mennonite involvement in the civil rights movement, Hershberger advised Mennonites, especially those who lived in the South, that they should not confuse the doctrine of nonresistance with facile obedience to civil laws. "The Mennonite Church has always been a martyr church," Hershberger reminded his readers. "This is no time to run away from trouble.[75]

In addition to supporting the civil rights movement, some change-minded Mennonites lent their voices and their bodies to protesting the Vietnam War. Antiwar activists were always a small minority, even among change-minded Mennonites, but their "witness to the state" set the stage for broader, more institutionally situated responses.[76] In 1972 MCC's Peace Section presented to congressional representatives a "Declaration of Conscience" with respect to the Vietnam War. Unlike Mennonite visits to Washington preceding World War II, which focused on securing alternative service options for conscientious objectors, the 1972 declaration called on Congress to terminate war funding and pay reparations to war victims. The declaration concluded with a prophetic appeal: "Repent! Turn about, make a fresh start."[77]

As change-minded Mennonites assumed this prophetic stance, some found a venerable ally in *Martyrs Mirror*. In 1967, for instance, the General Conference Mennonite publication *Mennonite Life* devoted an entire issue to van Braght's martyrology.[78] Assembled by Bethel College historian Cornelius Krahn, the issue led off with Krahn's editorial, which he titled "Toward a Restitution of the Witness."[79] In it Krahn highlighted the assertiveness of the early Anabaptists, who would interrupt state-

Fig. 8.2. Martin Luther King Jr., who visited Goshen College in 1960, talks with Goshen College professors Willard Smith (*left*) and Guy F. Hershberger (*center*). Courtesy of the *Elkhart Truth*.

sponsored church services and "ask to be heard as the prophets of old had done." These Anabaptist prophets advocated for their own concerns, he conceded, but they would also "ask for fairness and justice for others by giving an oral or written witness, by participating in secret meetings and public marches, and [by] any other means which they considered fair and effective." Unfortunately, Krahn continued, the heirs of this witnessing tradition had forsaken their ancestors' ways. In fact, "as withdrawn tillers of the soil the descendants of these aggressive witnesses often settled down in quietness." Mennonite quietism may have been justified in some times and places, but not now. In the present context, wrote Krahn, Mennonites should provide a full-throated witness by being "the first to call attention to injustices in their communities and in their country," a clear reference to the civil rights struggle that, in his view, too many Mennonites were ignoring.[80]

Krahn was not alone in invoking early Anabaptist radicalism to validate Mennonite political activism during the 1960s and 1970s. Vincent Harding, an African American Mennonite pastor who urged his fellow Mennonites to join the civil rights cause, found inspiration in the martyrs' willingness "to accept death rather than inflict suffering."[81] For their part, some Mennonite college students concluded that the Anabaptists' "prophetic lifestyle" was a useful template for Vietnam-era antiwar activism, since the early Anabaptists demonstrated a commitment to God's kingdom that, translated into today's context, challenged the idol of the nation-state.[82] In 1969, at a session of the Mennonite Church's national conference in Turner, Oregon, one draft-aged delegate pushed this view to its logical conclusion. In an attempt to secure the conference's blessing for draft resistance, Doug Baker cited stories in *Martyrs Mirror* as historically applicable examples of civil disobedience.[83] It is hard to know whether Baker's invocation of *Martyrs Mirror* helped or hindered his appeal—Baker and his youthful allies met their own kind of resistance from the conference's more conservative delegates—but in the end the conference affirmed their draft-resisting cause, recognizing noncooperation with the draft as "a legitimate witness."[84]

The significance of Krahn's contribution to rekindling the martyrs' witness extended beyond his message to the vehicle in which he placed it. The forty-eight-page *Mennonite Life* issue that Krahn assembled included some text, including excerpts from *Martyrs Mirror*, but it also featured thirty Jan Luyken images, two maps, and at least ten other martyr-related illustrations. It was, for all practical purposes, a martyrological picture album.[85] Krahn's consumer-friendly vehicle anticipated other endeavors by change-minded Mennonites to place martyrological material into media that were easier to consume than *Martyrs Mirror* itself. Most determined in this regard were John L. Ruth, Alice Parker, and Jan Gleysteen, who in the late 1960s developed a multifaceted plan for translating "our rich Anabaptist history into the contemporary media, with the *Martyrs' Mirror* as the keystone."[86] Although some elements of their plan never came to fruition, many of them did. For instance, in 1969 Gleysteen and Ruth toured Europe taking pictures of martyr-related sites. The photographs were then used for church bulletins and narrated slide shows.[87] In 1971 Parker and Ruth collaborated to produce a *Martyrs Mirror* oratorio that was performed at numerous sites throughout North America.[88] Four years later, in 1975, Gleysteen and a handful of other artists released *The Drama of the Martyrs,* a picture album that photographically reproduced all of Jan Luyken's etchings that had appeared in the 1685 Dutch edition.[89] These sensory approaches to expanding the martyrs' witness were well suited for the second half of the twentieth century, but the creators' fundamental goal fell precisely in line with that of the Skippack ministers in the 1740s. Devising their plan at the height of the Vietnam War, Gleysteen and Ruth lamented that Mennonite youth were leaving the church "without really knowing what they are turning their backs to," a particularly sad state of affairs when "our own history may hold exactly what they are looking for."[90]

The new *Martyrs Mirror* media that emerged in the 1960s and 1970s were not uniform in carrying politically progressive messages, to be sure.[91] They did, however, correlate with the fact that change-minded Mennonites, whatever their political persuasions, were more receptive to new media than their grandparents had been. Despite their assimilation to North American life, and perhaps because of it, Mennonite opinion makers continued to see the martyrs as relevant, but only to the degree that the martyrs' witness could capture the attention of contemporary audiences. This concern undergirded another attempt to mediate the martyrs in the late 1980s, an attempt that made the most of a new and important discovery.

Taking the Martyrs on Tour

Of all the consumer-friendly media produced during the twentieth century's last third, none matched the creativity or the staying power of a traveling exhibit called *Mirror of the Martyrs.* The brainchild of General Conference Mennonite historian Robert Kreider and his Mennonite Church colleague John Oyer, the display drew together various strands in the martyrology's twentieth-century history that we have already encountered. Once again historians took the promotional lead, and once again the promotional efforts meant giving renewed priority to the book's visual elements, that is, to the Luyken prints. In this particular case, however, the impact of the prints was magnified, for the images now took the form of life-sized reproductions displayed in public settings. Even more significantly, these large images were accompanied by copper plates that Luyken himself had etched nearly three centuries earlier. Ironically, North American Mennonites, who had long spurned the Catholic notion of martyrological relics, now had their own relics to treasure. Although they were never deemed to possess miraculous power, the metallic remains did offer formative power, all the more so in light of their own beleaguered past.[92]

Initially fashioned for the 1685 *Martyrs Mirror*, Luyken's plates had led quiet lives for much of their three hundred years. In the century following their production, they were occasionally put to use, beginning with the production of the Albrizzi picture album in 1696 and concluding with the Pirmasens *Martyrs Mirror*, published in Germany in 1780.[93] From that point forward, however, they fell into disuse, and only occasionally did they merit mention in historical records. Valued enough to be retained, but never enough to be exhibited, the plates had various owners over the years, including Munich businessman Hans Weber Sr., who purchased ninety of them around 1925.[94] According to some accounts, Weber offered the plates to Harold S. Bender when the Mennonite dynamo visited Germany in 1932, but Bender was unable to produce the two thousand dollars that Weber asked for the set.[95] Shortly thereafter, as Europe devolved into war, the plates disappeared, or so it seemed to European and North American Anabaptists who later tried to find them. The prevailing view among Mennonite scholars was that the plates either had been confiscated by the Nazis or had been destroyed during the Allied bombing of Munich. In fact, the plates had been spirited out of Munich in 1939 when Weber resettled his family in Grünstadt, nearly 250 miles to Munich's northwest. In an effort to safeguard the plates from confiscation, Weber wrapped them in newspaper, placed them in boxes, and covered them with building materials, before hiding the boxes in his house or the nearby outbuilding. As the war reached its climax, the Weber family left Grünstadt for safer environs, and when they returned, only one box of thirty plates remained. In time the Webers largely forgot about the plates, until 1975, when they were rediscovered by two of Weber's grandchildren.[96]

The rediscovery of thirty Luyken plates sparked the immediate interest of Mennonite collectors, whose interest was in part religiously inspired. Amos Hoover, an Old Order Mennonite who had collected an impressive array of Anabaptist materials, observed in a letter to a friend that the plates' rediscovery was "providential," and he moved quickly to purchase all thirty.[97] To Hoover's dismay, a non-Anabaptist art collector had also expressed interest, and in the ensuing competition to secure the plates, Hoover ended up with only seven.[98] As Robert Kreider later wrote, the twenty-three Luyken plates had once again been "lost" to their rightful Anabaptist heirs, this time "slipp[ing] into the hands of a non-communicative art collector."[99] When the art collector died in 1988, Hoover prevailed upon Kreider to take the lead in the plates' procurement, and before long Kreider had mobilized a group of Mennonite patrons who, in 1989, purchased the remaining twenty-three plates for approximately fifty thousand dollars.[100] In an article he published the next year, Kreider recounted in reverential tones the experience of examining the plates for the first time in a German bakery. "Each of the copper plates—300-year-old artistic treasure—was carefully unwrapped and laid before us on the white linen cloth," he wrote. "The aroma of coffee and freshly baked pastry enveloped this ritual of the unveiling," and "a sense of awe" pervaded the room.[101] To Kreider, and perhaps to others who accompanied him that morning, the entire experience—a solemn unveiling replete with treasures, aromas, and wonderment—was nothing short of sacred. The martyrs may have been dead, but their images, etched in resilient copper plates, lived on to embody their witness. Kreider found it perfectly appropriate to personify these chunks of copper, calling them "straggling survivors of a 300-year odyssey."[102]

The dramatic rescue of the lost plates provided the impetus to take the martyrs on tour. Within eighteen months Kreider and Oyer had overseen the creation of a gallery exhibit designed to travel from one Amish-Mennonite population center to another.[103] The *Mirror of the Martyrs* exhibit, displayed in one location for a few weeks before proceeding to the next, featured life-sized illustrations based on eight of the recently secured plates. The original copper plates were also part of the exhibit, providing visitors with material links to the age of Anabaptist martyrdom. According to the group that had acquired them, the plates were intended to function as "carriers of collective memory" and were not to be viewed merely as "aging artifacts."[104] Therefore, in an effort to forge the right collective memory—that is, to tell gallery visitors what they were seeing, what messages they should imbibe from the exhibit, and what lessons they should carry into the future—the exhibit's design team provided textual commentary that interpreted the plates and the illustrations. For those who wanted more information about Anabaptist martyrdom, Kreider and Oyer published a ninety-six-page catalog book that reprinted the images and recounted the faithful witness of the Anabaptist martyrs. While admitting that *Martyrs Mirror* eludes "conventional analysis," Kreider and Oyer did not refrain from identifying the benefits of encountering van Braght's text. Titling the first section of their catalog's introduction "We Are in Awe," Kreider and Oyer asserted that an encounter with *Martyrs Mirror* takes one into "the midst of a people who had child-like faith and yet were biblically wise." A few pages later they concluded their introduction with words of hope for their Mennonite contemporaries: that by recovering a martyr memory, "a weary and uncertain people can renew their strength and vision."[105]

We will explore the response of one late-twentieth-century Mennonite to the *Mirror of the Martyrs* exhibit in chapter 10. For now it is sufficient to note that, as much as Oyer and Kreider wished to affirm the martyrs' witness, they nonetheless found themselves questioning some of the assumptions that informed van Braght's work. This tension was apparent even in their catalog book, which, in the course of affirming the martyrs' steadfastness, paused long enough to acknowledge that "one cannot read the *Martyrs Mirror* without being haunted by difficult contemporary questions." One of these questions, "What beliefs are worth dying for?" alluded to the fact that many early Anabaptists had been put to death because they promoted adult baptism over infant baptism.[106] That Christians would kill other Christians on this account might have struck some exhibit visitors as strange, but almost as vexing to some contemporary Mennonites was that their theological ancestors had considered this conviction a commitment worth dying for. Indeed, by this time in the twentieth century, some change-minded Mennonite congregations no longer required membership candidates who had been baptized as infants to undergo rebaptism.[107] In these change-minded communities, a goodly number of people would not have deemed adult baptism an essential marker of Christian faithfulness, let alone a practice worth dying for.

Another question in Oyer and Kreider's catalog book—"Why do good people torture and kill good people?"—revealed even more plainly the gap between their historical vision and van Braght's.[108] To Oyer and Kreider, university-trained scholars with ecumenical inclinations, identifying the Anabaptists' tormentors as "good people" accomplished two ends. First, it acknowledged that the Anabaptists' tormentors operated from standard medieval assumptions about civic responsibility. In that sense, the magistrates who persecuted the Anabaptists could be seen as good people who were simply carrying out what they believed to be their God-given duties.[109] Oyer and Kreider's use of "good people" did more than contextualize the actors, however. It also served as an olive branch to the persecutors' theological descendants, which included Catholics, Lutherans, and other mainstream Protestants. In contrast to van Braght's view of Christian history—good versus evil, or at least uncompromising Christians versus apostate ones—Oyer and Kreider set forth a more complicated view. Although they were deeply committed to the Anabaptist cause, they nonetheless recognized that van Braght's history writing was far from objective. Worse yet, van Braght's rendering of history, if taken at face value, threatened to impair ecumenical relations in the present.

Significantly, it was the *Mirror of the Martyrs* description of the persecutors as "good people" that drew the strongest criticism from more tradition-minded Anabaptists. Tradition-minded Anabaptist leaders were not opposed to the traveling exhibit, and some had even been key players in its development. Still, the use of "good people" in reference to the Anabaptists' persecutors struck at least a few tradition-minded Anabaptists as folly. "Persecutors are not good people," wrote James Lowry, a conservative Mennonite historian who was himself one of North America's leading authorities on *Martyrs Mirror*.[110] Pathway's David Luthy agreed with Lowry, noting in a letter to Kreider that "it would be difficult for a Jew in Germany to read about the Gestapo as 'good people.'" Luthy continued with his critique, essentially charging Kreider and Oyer with being seduced by the siren call of late-twentieth-century tolerance. "We are living in an era of 'I'm o.k.—you're o.k.,'" Luthy concluded, "which fits the use of 'good people' for the persecutors."[111]

In Kreider and Oyer's use of the phrase "good people," and in Lowry and Luthy's responses to it, we see evidence of the social chasm that had developed between change-minded Anabaptists and tradition-minded Anabaptists in the course of the twentieth century. This divide was not new, of course, but it had only widened as the twentieth century progressed, and it could not help but contribute to a significant interpretive divide with respect to *Martyrs Mirror*. North American Anabaptists from across the social spectrum continued to value *Martyrs Mirror*, though how much they valued it and, more importantly, how they read it, diverged ever more sharply. It was one thing to place *Martyrs Mirrors* into the hands of readers or persuade Anabaptist church members to spend an evening at an exhibit. It was another thing entirely to make them think about the book's contents in a particular way. To these issues of reception and interpretation we now turn.

PART III

Contemporary Approaches to Martyrs Mirror

CHAPTER 9

Tradition-Minded Anabaptists and the Use of *Martyrs Mirror*

F ord Berg's assertion in 1950 that *Martyrs Mirror* would sell as long as Mennonites endured can never be finally proved, but decades later his claim still holds true. Although the Mennonite Publishing House no longer exists—it was absorbed into the Mennonite Publishing Network in 2004, and its Scottdale publishing facility closed in 2011—its surviving book division, Herald Press, reprints the English edition every few years.[1] Similarly, Pathway Publishers continues to produce copies of *Märtyrer Spiegel* on a regular basis. All told, more than thirty-five thousand copies of van Braght's classic have made their way into print since the turn of the twenty-first century, with more printings planned for the future.[2]

While Berg may have foreseen unending sales, he could not have imagined what we easily see in retrospect: the long-term sales prospects of *Martyrs Mirror* had much less to do with change-minded Mennonites than with tradition-minded Anabaptists, who became the primary market for the book. This twentieth-century market transformation owes to many factors, but above all to numerical shifts in North American Anabaptism. In 1936, the two primary change-minded denominations, the Mennonite Church and the General Conference Mennonite Church, had a combined U.S. membership five times the combined membership of the leading tradition-minded groups, the Old Order Amish, the Old Order Mennonites, and the Beachy Amish.[3] By 2000, however, the combined membership numbers of these more tradition-minded groups had come to rival and perhaps surpass those of the Mennonite Church and the General Conference Mennonite Church.[4] Since 2000 this transformation has continued apace, extending the trend identified by historian Steven Nolt a decade earlier. "Each year the shift is the same," wrote Nolt. "Self-consciously conservative and Old Order Mennonites, along with Amish groups of various sorts and Hutterites, make up a larger and larger share of the American Anabaptist pie."[5]

More adult members mean more customers, of course, but it is equally significant that this numerical growth occurred in the realms of the Anabaptist world that most valued the book. As the twentieth century ran its course, change-minded Mennonites embraced non-Anabaptist spiritual resources to a much greater degree than did tradition-minded Anabaptists, and this trend continues in force today. Although tradition-minded Anabaptist groups have never lived in a spiritual cocoon, they continue to give high priority to time-honored resources that reflect a traditional Anabaptist worldview. These resources include *Martyrs Mirror*, and it is therefore not unusual to find tradition-minded ministers encouraging their members to heed both the martyrs' example and van Braght's warnings about lukewarm Christianity. How these martyrological messages are communicated by tradition-minded leaders in the late twentieth and early twenty-first centuries, and how they are received by tradition-minded lay people, constitute the orienting questions of this chapter.

The Varieties of North American Anabaptism

The spectrum of belief and practice among contemporary North American Anabaptists is wide. Whereas some present-day Anabaptists drive horse-drawn carriages, others work as airline pilots; whereas some conclude their formal educations after eight grades, others hold doctorates from top-flight research universities; and whereas some groups ordain only males who are chosen by lot, others ordain men and women who are credentialed through intricate denominational processes. These examples could be multiplied many times over to illustrate the variety that exists among people who even today consider the Anabaptist martyrs their theological ancestors.

In a recent book on North American Anabaptist life, Donald B. Kraybill offers a useful typology to help make sense of this social reality. According to Kraybill, North American Anabaptist groups stretch across a traditional-to-assimilated continuum that correlates with two fundamental factors: "the locus of moral authority" and "how sharply the community separates itself from the larger society."[6] On the one end of the continuum, traditional (or tradition-minded) groups "accent the authority of the church community over the individual" and "reject many of the prevailing practices of the larger society."[7] On the continuum's other end, assimilated groups "grant greater freedom to individual choice, mingle more freely with the outside world, and seek to engage the larger social order."[8] These orienting values in turn affect the amount of diversity that exists within the respective groups. In tradition-minded groups, the church's expectations of remaining separate from the world exert a strong influence on individuals and, in many cases, limit the range of practices deemed acceptable. In assimilated groups, where individuals assume more authority in making their own decisions, the variety of beliefs and practices within a denomination or a congregation is wider. Ultimately, says Kraybill, the traditional-to-assimilated continuum "reflects the degree to which a group rejects or accepts the values, features, and structures of modern society that emerged in North America in the late 19th and 20th centuries."[9]

In addition to sketching this continuum, Kraybill notes that substantial differences exist on the traditional side with respect to technology choices, religious expression, and language use. Accordingly, he identifies two traditional subtypes: *Old Order* groups, which more strictly retain inherited traditions, and *conservative* groups, whose devotion to tradition is strong but, at least in some areas of life, not as strict as it is in Old Order groups. For instance, Old Order groups typically travel by horse and buggy, speak a non-English dialect such as Pennsylvania Dutch, and preserve time-honored forms of worship. In contrast, conservative groups allow their members to own and drive cars, they use English at home and in worship settings, and they embrace most modern technologies, except perhaps television and the Internet. To be sure, some Anabaptist groups do not fit neatly into any of the three types, mixing and matching the social characteristics identified in table 9.1.[10] Moreover, some assimilated Anabaptist groups engage in practices—a cappella singing during Sunday worship, for example—that many of their non-Anabaptist neighbors would consider old-fashioned. Nonetheless, Kraybill's tripartite typology arranges social reality more neatly

Table 9.1. Typical Traits of Old Order, Conservative, and Assimilated Anabaptists

Old Order Groups

Accept the collective authority of the church
Use horse-drawn transportation
Downplay individual religious experience
Rely upon oral tradition in religious matters
Speak a special dialect
Selectively use technology
Preserve older forms of religious ritual
Forbid divorce
Limit formal education to high school or less
Ordain lay ministers, males only
Practice nonresistance
Resist or reject formal denominational structures
Wear plain clothing

Conservative Groups

Accept the collective authority of the church
Own and drive cars with modest features
Encourage individual religious experience
Emphasize rational, written doctrine
Use technology except television and/or Internet
Forbid divorce
Discourage higher education
Ordain lay ministers, males only
Engage in evangelism
Practice nonresistance
Operate denominations with limited bureaucracy
Wear plain clothing

Assimilated Groups

Permit greater range of individual choices
Own and drive cars of choice
Encourage individual religious experience
Emphasize rational, written doctrine
Pursue higher education
Hold professional jobs
Hire salaried ministers, including women
Employ technologies according to individual choice
Adapt or adjust worship rituals
Tolerate divorce and remarriage

Table 9.1. (*continued*)

Engage in evangelism
Engage in peacemaking and social justice work
Operate bureaucratic church organizations
Wear clothing of choice
Participate in most mainstream cultural activities
Participate in local, state, and national politics

Source: This table is adapted from Donald B. Kraybill and C. Nelson Hostetter, *Anabaptist World USA* (Scottdale, PA: Herald Press, 2001), 56. Used by permission of MennoMedia.

Note: A specific group may not exhibit all the features of a particular type; in addition, a specific group may combine features of two adjacent types.

than, for instance, a label like *Mennonite,* since groups that carry the Mennonite label may fall into any one of the three social types.

In this chapter, which explores the use of *Martyrs Mirror* in traditional Anabaptist groups, we will consider both Old Order and conservative groups, sometimes together and sometimes separately. Van Braght's martyrology is, of course, a traditional Anabaptist resource with a lengthy history and an equally long track record of being recommended from one generation to the next. It is not surprising, then, that tradition-minded Anabaptists have generally held the book in higher regard than have assimilated Anabaptists. Still, a closer look is required to see how the book has been used in these tradition-minded communities and for what end. We begin by examining its use in the home.

Reading for Inspiration: *Martyrs Mirror* in Tradition-Minded Homes

Unlike earlier eras, when copies of *Martyrs Mirror* were expensive and therefore rare, most tradition-minded Anabaptists today can easily afford their own copies. Some people do indeed purchase copies for themselves, but there are two reasons why a potential tradition-minded buyer would think twice before buying one. First, copies of *Martyrs Mirror* are often passed down to family members, typically from parents to one of their children. Second, *Martyrs Mirror*s are often given as gifts, most commonly to a child coming of age or to a couple entering into marriage.[11]

Table 9.2. Representative Anabaptist Groups by Type

Old Order Groups*
    Hutterites (various subgroups)
    Old Order Amish (various subgroups)
    Old Order Mennonites (various subgroups)
Conservative Groups
    Beachy Amish
    Church of God in Christ, Mennonite
    Eastern Pennsylvania Mennonite Church
    Nationwide Fellowship Churches
    Washington-Franklin Mennonite Conference
Assimilated Groups
    Church of the Brethren
    General Conference Mennonite Church (through 2001)
    Mennonite Church (through 2001)
    Mennonite Church Canada (beginning 2001)
    Mennonite Church USA (beginning 2002)
    Mennonite Brethren Church

---

*Some Mennonite groups that consider themselves Old Order permit their members to own and drive cars. Similarly, the Hutterites' employment of technology runs counter to their placement in the Old Order category.

The practice of giving *Martyrs Mirror* to emerging adults, signifying the recipient's status as one who can both embrace and transmit the Anabaptist faith, tracks a long history in Anabaptist circles, though it is more common today in tradition-minded groups than in assimilated groups. If there is any irony involved in giving a book filled with torture and death as a wedding gift, it is wholly lost on tradition-minded givers and receivers. "I gave two of my special friends one for a wedding gift," reported a thirty-year-old Hutterite woman who treasured the book's impact on her own life.[12] In a similar vein, an Old Order Amish woman recalled the exact date her uncle's wedding gift arrived, "a package in the mail [containing] *Martyrs Mirror*!" To this woman, receiving a copy of *Martyrs Mirror* ensured that her marriage would begin on the right track, and in a letter describing her devotion to the book, she moved quickly from describing her delight with the gift to describing the way it aided her husband in the instruction of their children. "In the evening," she recalled, "we'd gather 'round for devotions with the children and he would read aloud the interesting parts he'd come across."[13]

Indeed, while some tradition-minded Anabaptists read *Martyrs Mirror* in private, it may be that the most common way for *Martyrs Mirror* to be used in the home is in family devotions. This is especially true of families with grade-school children. One Old Order Amish woman, now a young mother, recalled her family's custom on off-Sundays (the alternating Sundays when Amish congregations do not meet for worship), when she and her siblings would crowd onto her father's lap as he sat in a rocking chair. "Together we would look at all the pictures," she wrote, "and Dad would tell the story to each picture . . . even if we knew them by heart."[14] A conservative Mennonite father takes a similar pedagogical approach with his own children (ages 14, 11, 8, and 3), in his case reading from *Martyrs Mirror* one evening each week during family worship. "We wanted our children to understand that it is something normal to suffer for the faith," he explained. Initially fearful that his youngsters might find the age-old stories boring ("I was prepared to hear a lot of groans"), he was pleasantly surprised to discover otherwise. In fact, they "sat there spellbound," and if he failed to read from *Martyrs Mirror* on the designated evening, they quickly reminded him, "Tonight is the night."[15] These tradition-minded fathers found the Luyken images particularly effective for engaging their children's attention. In fact, references to the power of the Luyken images is widespread in the family reading accounts of tradition-minded Anabaptists, offering evidence that the English edition is warmly embraced in many such communities.[16]

Reading martyr narratives and showing gruesome pictures to grade-school children may strike some people as questionable parenting practices, but tradition-minded Anabaptists are much less likely to possess this sentiment than assimilated Anabaptists.[17] In fact, some tradition-minded Anabaptists connect the more unsettling aspects of the book with their gratitude for it. The Amish mother who as a young child perused *Martyrs Mirror* while sitting on her father's lap remembered that the martyr accounts did indeed trouble her, especially during quiet moments. "I remember many times sitting in church wondering how it would be if the house was set on fire," she recalled, "thinking how the babies and little children would suffer so innocently." Despite these troubling thoughts, this same woman proceeded to give thanks for the "sweet, lingering, golden memories" of gathering around *Martyrs Mirror* with her family. Moreover, she hoped that "maybe someday our children will also have sweet memories of sitting on [their] Dad's lap and hearing stories from the *Martyrs Mirror*," a sentence she concluded with an exclamation point and a smiley face.[18]

Few waxed as sentimental as this Amish mother, but others were similarly grateful—and not at all chagrined—that they were exposed to *Martyrs Mirror* as children. A young father whose Beachy Amish grandfather read *Martyrs Mirror* to him at bedtime admitted that he was disturbed by what he heard, but less by fear than by sadness. "I don't recall ever being afraid," he said, but "I [do] remember being sad," particularly in response to the story of an Anabaptist woman being buried alive ("I remember crying that night," he recalled). Sadness did not have the last word, however, for although these stories taught him that faithfulness could lead to death, they also taught him that a faithful death "rewards us with living with Jesus." In other words, encountering stories of persecution as a child was "not a bad thing," because in van Braght's rendering persecution was always accompanied by hope: "Live or die, Jesus can never be taken from us." In this man's recollection, his childhood encounters with *Martyrs Mirror* were above all opportunities to ponder the rewards that lay beyond death for those who are faithful.[19]

Even in tradition-minded families that do not use *Martyrs Mirror* for family devotions, children sometimes pull the book off the shelf and explore it on their own, often furtively. "I remember as a 14–15-year-old spending many hours lying on the floor in our upstairs hall . . . reading the *Martyrs Mirror*," wrote one conservative Mennonite man, an activity he connected to his burgeoning adolescent search "for a real relationship with God."[20] A young Hutterite woman recalled her first encounter with *Martyrs Mirror* as a sixteen-year-old, which occurred after she begged to borrow her grandfather's copy. "The more I read, the more I wanted to read," she wrote. "I was right with them [the martyrs]," she continued, particularly "with the mothers who had to leave their children behind." Later, when some of this woman's friends cautioned that the content might be too disturbing to her, she responded logically, if also rhetorically, contrasting the agony of the martyrs' experience with the modest discomfort of reading about it. "How would I face it [persecution] to go through with it," she asked them, "if I shouldn't be able to read it?"[21]

Reflection on this question, "What would I do if I faced persecution on account of my faith?" constitutes the most common response of tradition-minded Anabaptists who study *Martyrs Mirror*. Devotional readers and listeners regularly place themselves in the martyrs' shoes, an imaginative practice that enables them to consider and theoretically test their own levels of faithfulness. "[One of the] two points I'd ponder upon the most," wrote one Amish woman, was "if ever we will be required to suffer for our faith, will we be able to endure?"[22] "If these people could suffer, why can't I?" asked another woman.[23] Yet another tradition-minded reader was even more specific in delineating this sort of response to *Martyrs Mirror*. As a young man, the more martyr accounts he read, "the more I realized that they all ran the same theme: they suffered for Christ and stayed true to him NO MATTER WHAT." In this man's case, reflecting upon the martyrs' steadfastness led to his conversion, for it "made me realize that they had the kingdom of God within them which I did not."[24]

Few tradition-minded readers connect actual conversion experiences to their reading of *Martyrs Mirror*, but many attest to reflecting on the more common challenge of facing life's difficulties in God-pleasing ways. For these readers, the persecution experienced by the sixteenth-century martyrs stands in for the multitude of challenges that afflict their own lives, from physical illness to financial hardship to workaday drudgery. Similarly, the martyrs represent for them the possibility of meeting these challenges with a brave face, in part because the readers perceive their own tribulations as trivial compared to the martyrs' ordeals. "Each time I read [*Martyrs Mirror*], my heart feels like jelly and becomes all mellow," relates one woman, "because I see my own earthly trials as nothing compared to theirs."[25] A middle-aged Amish mother offered a more concrete example of the effect *Martyrs Mirror* has had on her, noting that when she finishes reading in it, she "feels more contented with the plenty we have." As she looks around her house, it no longer matters "that my floor is worn. My kitchen doesn't need paint after all. The children's limited wardrobe is enough after all."[26] For this woman and others like her, the stories in *Martyrs Mirror* prove that contentment with one's earthly lot is indeed within reach.[27] Moreover, contentment is more easily achieved when one considers that life could be much worse.

The continuing effect of *Martyrs Mirror* on tradition-minded Anabaptists raises questions about its level of use in these communities.

What shall we make of a recent assertion by an influential Amish historian that, even among conservative Anabaptists, *Martyrs Mirror* has "mostly become 'shelf book,' rarely read or quoted from"?[28] Although it is impossible to know how much the book was actually read in the past, two observations are in order. First, the theme of spiritual declension is omnipresent in Anabaptist history, with older generations almost universally lamenting the loss of spiritual fervor among younger generations. Given both the persistence of this lament in Anabaptist history and the fact that *Martyrs Mirror* sells more briskly today than it ever has, one must resist embracing too quickly the claim that *Martyrs Mirror* is read less frequently now than in the past, an assertion that may be rooted less in reality than in the nostalgic imagination.

That said, there are some indications that the use of *Martyrs Mirror* among tradition-minded Anabaptists has declined in the past few decades. The evidence is largely anecdotal, but it nonetheless carries weight, for it comes from people who esteem the book highly but who also recognize its diminishing role in their own lives. For instance, one Old Order Amish woman recalled that years ago she read *Martyrs Mirror* regularly as she recovered from childbirth. Van Braght's martyrology was more important to her at that time, she said, because "in those days we did not have the magazines and many books published by those of Anabaptist background, so we read and reread oftener the books we then had."[29] In other words, *Martyrs Mirror* had declined in importance for her, not because of spiritual declension, but because it had been displaced by competing devotional options. Other tradition-minded informants spoke of the book's lack of readability—an outdated translation on large, crowded pages—particularly when compared with other information sources they could easily access.[30] In the same vein, some tradition-minded respondents, when asked about their use of *Martyrs Mirror*, referred to abridgments of the work, such as Pathway's compilation of embellished martyr stories, *The Drummer's Wife*.[31]

References to *The Drummer's Wife* are significant, for they remind us that the medium for these sixteenth-century martyr accounts has never been static. They also remind us that the influence of *Martyrs Mirror* in Anabaptist communities cannot be reduced to the act of reading the hefty tome with one's own eyes. The messages of *Martyrs Mirror* are mediated in other ways, not least through references to the work in corporate settings.

Martyrs Mirror in Corporate Life: The Old Order Amish

The Old Order Amish are the largest segment of the tradition-minded Anabaptist world, constituting approximately 75 percent of Old Order Anabaptists in the United States and Canada. Unlike assimilated Anabaptists, whose congregational sizes vary widely and occasionally exceed a thousand members, Old Order Amish life revolves around congregations made up of about thirty families, or approximately 150 people. These congregations, which divide if they grow much larger than that, are geographically circumscribed; that is, Amish people attend worship services with other Amish families who live near them in the same bounded church district. In fact, attending Sunday worship within one's district is mandatory. An Amish person may have closer friends in a neighboring church district, or prefer the preacher in a nearby district, but such preferences are immaterial. When an Amish congregation gathers for worship—a gathering that occurs every other Sunday in the home, barn, or shop of one of the church's members—all of the members of that congregation are expected to be there.

These every-other-Sunday gatherings are, for all practical purposes, the sole gathering in Amish life devoted to religious instruction. There are other community gatherings, but they do not focus on religious training per se, and they rarely involve all of the district's members. Modes of religious instruction common in other Protestant churches, including most assimilated and conservative Anabaptist churches—Sunday school classes, vacation Bible schools, revival meetings, and spiritual life conferences—do not exist in Old Order Amish life. This Sunday morning monopoly on religious education ensures that the district's ordained leaders provide the instruction that occurs, thus militating against the introduction of novel ideas and controversial opinions. It also ensures that everyone, from the youngest child to the most elderly member, shares in the same educational process.

The longest and most defining feature of Amish worship is the sermon. In fact, Amish worship services typically have two sermons, an opening sermon that runs fifteen to twenty minutes and a main sermon that lasts closer to an hour. Each sermon is delivered by one of the district's ordained ministers in Pennsylvania Dutch, an everyday dialect that Amish listeners comprehend more easily than they do High German.[32] The ministers who preach these sermons do so extemporaneously, forgoing all written notes. Although the ministers study the lectionary scriptures in advance and contemplate ideas to include in a sermon, even they do not know whether they are going to preach on a given Sunday, since that determination is made only after the worship service has begun. After the main sermon, the ministers who did not preach the main sermon have the opportunity to offer *Zeugniss* (testimony) in order to affirm, clarify, or even correct the sermon's content. *Zeugniss,* notes one Ohio Amish leader, ensures that "one man cannot run away with his pet theories."[33]

References to the martyrs—both references to the martyrs in general, and references to specific martyrs—are commonplace in Old Order Amish sermons. Amish people view innovation warily, and nowhere is it less welcome than in Amish worship gatherings, where four-hundred-year-old hymns are sung to age-old melodies.[34] Amish ministers are particularly beholden to tradition, and although they draw sermon illustrations from other realms of life, many continue to give priority to the martyrs. "We hear about the martyrs almost every time we have church," said one Pennsylvania Amish woman in the aftermath of the 2006 Nickel Mines School shooting, quickly clarifying that these biweekly references long predated the school shooting.[35] "We refer to *Martyrs Mirror* regularly in our sermons," concurred an Indiana Amish minister, because we "feel it's important for future generations to know about the sacrifices of their ancestors."[36] Even as tradition-minded Anabaptists sense a dwindling use of *Martyrs Mirror* in their personal lives, Amish ministers believe the book's sermonic use has declined, possibly owing to the proliferation of other information sources. Still, few Old Order Amish people cannot recall a sermon reference to the martyrs. "I had to think about you on Sunday," wrote one Lancaster County Amish man, who knew I would be interested in his minister's mention of a *Martyrs Mirror* account.[37]

The specific martyr accounts cited in Old Order Amish sermons span the corpus of van Braght's martyrology. References to the persecution of New Testament figures, including Peter, James, John, and Andrew, are perhaps most common, but other proto-Anabaptist figures receive attention. The story of Polycarp, a second-century bishop who was put to death for refusing to worship the emperor, is a common sermon illustration, as is the story of Irenaeus, a third-century Christian who, because of his leadership role, was pursued more aggressively and tortured more brutally than his fellow believers.[38] As for the Anabaptist martyrs themselves, the martyr accounts of the founders—people like Michael Sattler, Felix Mantz, and George Blaurock—receive the most play, but like preachers in other traditions, Amish ministers often choose illustrations for their dramatic effect. This criterion leads Amish ministers to stories that have extraordinary and sometimes supernatural elements, including the story of Leonhard Keyser ("the guy who was chopped up but didn't burn," summarized one Amish minister) and the story of Hans Haslibacher, whose decapitated head fell into his hat and laughed, just as an angel had promised.[39]

The frequent use of stories with supernatural twists, and the absence of skepticism about these details, exposes a fundamental theological assumption of the Old Order Amish: the God of the Bible possesses extraordinary power that even today can work miracles. At the same time, the unblinking acceptance that these supernatural elements accompany stories of human suffering reveals another key Amish assumption: God rarely uses the power at his disposal to spare the faithful from dire situations. In fact, the invocation of martyr accounts in Amish sermons, and the approbation of these stories by Amish listeners, correlates with the widespread Amish view that faithfulness is less a safeguard against suffering than it is a path to suffering. Yes, God will ultimately rescue his people from death ("there's hope in the hereafter," said one Amish minister, citing his favorite takeaway message from *Martyrs Mirror*), but not before they suffer and die.[40]

Contemporary Amish ministers know full well that present-day Amish people do not suffer as their Anabaptist ancestors did, a recognition that puts them in good company with Thieleman van Braght. Like van Braght, contemporary Amish ministers often warn their listeners that persecution will someday return. Furthermore, they warn them that easy times are more spiritually perilous than difficult times. "Down through history prosperity has been shown to bring people down," said one Amish minister when asked to summarize van Braght's central message. "We need persecution to make us stronger."[41] Indeed, of all the *Martyrs Mirror*-related messages that punctuate Amish worship services, few outpace the warning that Satan is a more formidable enemy now than he was during times of persecution. "Elmer the preacher commented that the devil came in those times as a roaring lion," recalled one Amish lay person, "whereas today he comes in more subtle and cunning ways, . . . as an angel of light, but still seeking whom he can devour."[42] Another Amish leader echoed this sentiment, noting that that Amish people "are on a dangerous pedestal now," more dangerous than even a few decades ago. Unlike earlier eras in American life, when Amish people were often ridiculed by their non-Amish neighbors, they are now esteemed by the larger world, he said, and that is "dangerous."[43]

To be sure, few if any Amish people are eager for persecution to befall their communities. In fact, Amish leaders work regularly with non-Amish allies to make sure their religious liberties are respected.[44] Still, the notion is widespread among the Amish that the world's esteem portends spiritual danger.[45] This notion is also common among conservative Anabaptists, some of whom find resources in *Martyrs Mirror* to reinforce their marginal status and their countercultural practices.

Martyrs Mirror in Community Life: Conservative Anabaptists

In Kraybill's typology, the mediating conservative Anabaptist type comprises many different Mennonite groups as well as the Beachy Amish. Although not as numerous as Old Order or assimilated Anabaptists, conservative Anabaptists, with nearly 100,000 adult members, nonetheless constitute nearly 15 percent of the North American Anabaptist pie.[46] Most Americans would consider these conservative groups peculiar, for they display clear marks of social nonconformity. The most conspicuous marker in this regard is dress, which is modest and plain (though not as plain as Old Order Amish dress). Women in particular dress modestly, wearing mid-calf-length dresses and head coverings, and forgo makeup and jewelry. Although not as wary of new technology as the Old Order Amish, most conservative groups forbid television and sometimes other digital technologies. Car ownership in these communities is commonplace but regulated; flashy cars are forbidden, and in some groups the members' cars must be black or dark blue. Ministers are generally ordained by lot, and they are invariably male. Divorce is forbidden, as is marriage to previously divorced persons. Some conservative Anabaptist children complete twelve years of education, but higher education is generally discouraged.[47]

Despite these socially nonconformist practices, conservative Anabaptist communities display culturally assimilative tendencies that Old Order Anabaptist communities have effectively resisted. Unlike the Old Order Amish, most conservative Anabaptist congregations do not circumscribe their geographical reach or their congregational size. Typically gathering for worship in church buildings as opposed to homes and barns, conservative Anabaptists participate in congregations of various sizes, from a few dozen members to a few hundred. Worship services in these communities are conducted in English, with hymnody drawn primarily from the eighteenth and nineteenth centuries and reproduced in English-language hymnals replete with musical notation. Unlike Old Order Amish ministers, who preach extemporaneously without any notes, conservative Anabaptist preachers prepare their sermons in advance and preach from notes or even manuscripts. For that reason, sermons in conservative churches have a more rational edge than Old Order Amish sermons. Similarly, conservative Anabaptist groups are more likely than Old Order groups to develop and publish formal theological statements outlining their beliefs and practices.

Reflecting this more rational approach to religious life, conservative Anabaptists employ a variety of educational modes that the Old Order Amish have forsworn. Sunday school classes, evening meetings, and extended Bible classes are common in these communities. Some groups hold protracted meetings in tents or other facilities, with the twin goals of renewing their own members and converting the unconverted, including their own children. In some conservative Anabaptist groups, emerging adults attend regional Bible schools that offer short-term courses on a variety of spiritually oriented topics. These Bible schools, usually held in the winter, bring together post–high school youth from like-minded communities for the expressed purpose of spiritual formation and the unexpressed purpose of matchmaking for the young adults. Some of the course offerings are explicitly biblical ("Life of Peter"), some are theological ("Doctrine of the Church"), and some are practical ("Building Christian Homes"). Still others focus on Reformation or Anabaptist history ("History of Mennonite Missions").[48] In any case, the ultimate goal of the schools is the same: to provide spiritual instruction to emerging adults in an environment that is both theologically safe and abounding with potential spouses.

Like their Old Order counterparts, ministers in conservative Anabaptist churches find *Martyrs Mirror* a rich resource for Sunday sermon illustrations. In some conservative settings, however, *Martyrs Mirror* sheds its supporting role and assumes center stage as a principal resource for edification. In these settings *Martyrs Mirror* is carefully parsed, with full assurance that its content, like scripture itself, is "profitable for doctrine, for reproof, for correction, for instruction in righteousness: that the man of God may be perfect, thoroughly furnished unto all good works."[49] To be sure, no conservative Anabaptist minister would suggest that *Martyrs Mirror* is the inspired Word of God, and the ministers do not return to its pages week after week as they do to the Old and New Testaments. In fact, thoroughgoing considerations of van Braght's text may be very occasional. From a strictly functional standpoint, however, the use of *Martyrs Mirror* in these conservative settings closely parallels the use of the Bible as a resource for faithful living.

A Sunday afternoon "Bible meeting" at an Eastern Pennsylvania Mennonite Church (EPMC) congregation illustrates this exegetical approach to *Martyrs Mirror*.[50] This gathering, held in the congregation's unadorned brick meetinghouse, included the children and adults from a half dozen EPMC congregations in central Pennsylvania.[51] As is customary on Sunday mornings in EPMC churches, the men and boys sat on one side of the sanctuary and the women and girls on the other, though at this particular meeting the teenaged children sat with their peers in front of the main seating area, boys on the left and girls on the right. The entire focus of the two-hour gathering was *Martyrs Mirror*, with spoken prayers, congregational hymns, and two sermons all aimed at helping people encounter the martyrology's messages. For instance, before the first sermon, the congregation sang the W. P. Rivers hymn "The Righteous Marching Home," which speaks of "battle wounds and scars" that will disappear once Christians "dwell with God beyond the stars."[52] Later in the service, the congregation sang the first two verses of "Faith of Our Fathers," entirely from memory. The focal points of the service, however, were two sermons, one titled "The Account of Holy Baptism," which delineated the risks of Christian baptism through the centuries, and the other titled "The Testimony of Those Who Suffered," which revolved around a nine-letter acrostic, "T-E-S-T-I-M-O-N-Y."[53] Both sermons, delivered by visiting preachers with expert knowledge of *Martyrs Mirror*, offered example after example from the book, providing listeners with names and narrative details to illustrate the commitment of Christians through the ages.[54]

Three particular elements of the afternoon presentations signal the conservative Anabaptists' approach to *Martyrs Mirror*.[55] First, from a rhetorical standpoint, the textual use of *Martyrs Mirror* paralleled the use of scripture itself, with both texts functioning as unquestioned spiritual authorities. In both sermons, the preachers moved seamlessly between the Bible and *Martyrs Mirror,* quoting liberally from both to make their points. "Psalm 56:4 says, 'In God I have put my trust. I will not fear what flesh can do unto me,'" recited preacher Darvin Martin, grounding the first letter of his T-E-S-T-I-M-O-N-Y acrostic in the fact that the psalmist "Trusted in God" in perilous situations. So too, Martin continued, did the Cappadocian shepherd Mamus, whose martyr account appears in book 1 of *Martyrs Mirror* and whose "faith in God . . . enabled him to endure to the end."[56] For the majority of his nine points, Martin began with a biblical text and only then moved to an account or quotation from *Martyrs Mirror.* In addition, Martin concluded his sermon by noting that the martyrs could quote the Bible at length, reminding his listeners that the martyrs' words and actions were always subject to a higher textual authority. In these ways Martin acknowledged that *Martyrs Mirror*'s authority does not equal the Bible's, let alone supersede it. *Martyrs Mirror* does, however, function as an indisputable authority in conservative Anabaptist communities. Like the Bible itself, its content can be confidently employed for instruction in righteousness.

A second significant element of the afternoon presentations was the instructional priority given to adolescents in attendance. Again, the teenagers sat together in a strategic location; they were not only close to the preacher's lectern but were also in full view of the rest of the congregation. In the course of the afternoon's sermons, the preachers returned time and again to stories of teenaged martyrs, sometimes mentioning them generally but more often talking about specific adolescents, such as "Eulalia, not more than twelve or thirteen years old, who was filled with such desire and ardor of the spirit to die in the name of Christ."[57] In one case, preacher Clifford Martin told of a fourteen-year-old boy who was favored by the Roman emperor until he refused to pay homage to the Roman gods, at which point the young man was threatened with decapitation. Turning straightaway to his youthful listeners, Martin asked, "Youth here this afternoon . . . would you be able to so defend your faith as this youth did?"[58] Martin quickly acceded that everyone in attendance, regardless of age, "should ponder this question," though by the choice of his and his fellow preacher's examples—they invoked the words "young," "youth," and "youthful" twenty-seven times and mentioned specific ages of teenagers eleven more times—the focus of the afternoon was clearly on the youth.

Translating the martyrs' witness to the present constituted the third noteworthy element of the afternoon's presentations. As would be expected, the preachers frequently touched upon the theme of holding fast to the faith in adverse circumstances. In some cases, they even asked hypothetical questions to help their listeners imagine their responses in the face of persecution (e.g., "What would you do in your last hour of freedom?" and "How would you prepare yourself for martyrdom?"). More significantly, however, the conservative ministers identified the temptation to abandon Anabaptist nonconformity as their listeners' chief adversary. "How do you prepare yourself every day to face your enemy who wants to wreck your faith through more gentle means than [martyrdom]?," asked Clifford Martin. "How could we ever stand [martyrdom] if we are faltering . . . on the level of self-denial?" The afternoon's preachers did not leave the application of the principle of self-denial to their listeners' judgment. Carrying cell phones, accumulating material possessions, nursing anger toward hostile neighbors, and, more generally, running after anything that "the church forbids"—all these activities were cited as instances of refusing to deny oneself. Youth in particular were urged to abandon their earthly desires. In *Martyrs Mirror,* they were reminded, adolescents as young as twelve vowed themselves to Christ and "obeyed him with all their heart."

Conservative Anabaptist Bible schools reinforce these same martyrological messages in classrooms filled with emerging adults. One of the three-week courses offered at the Ashland Mennonite Bible School in early 2010 was titled "*Martyrs Mirror.*"[59] For forty-five minutes each morning, instructor Wendell Miller led his students through van Braght's martyrology, proceeding chronologically from the first to the sixteenth century.[60] Each day, however, the learning objective went beyond historical knowledge to spiritual application. In his course outline, Miller identified daily goals such as "to remove our fear of death," "to link us with the faithful of the past," and "to strengthen our convictions for nonresistance." For their part, students completed worksheets that required them to search *Martyrs Mirror* for the answers. Although many

Table 9.3. Course on *Martyrs Mirror*

Ashland (PA) Mennonite Bible School, 2010	
Teacher: Wendell Miller	
Lesson 1	Introduction
Lesson 2	Development and History of *Martyrs Mirror*
Lesson 3	Class Goal: To remove our fear of death
	First Century, pp. 67–104
Lesson 4	Class Goal: To understand the meaning of endurance
	Second to Eighth Centuries, pp. 104–240
Lesson 5	Class Goal: To understand that a life of steadfastness is based on
	sound Bible doctrine
	Confessions of Faith, pp. 27–44, 373–410
Lesson 6	Class Goal: To develop a greater appreciation for religious freedom
	Ninth to Fifteenth Centuries, pp. 240–352
Lesson 7	Class Goal: To link us with the faithful of the past
	The Succession of the Faith, pp. 27–44, 353–410
Lesson 8	Class Goal: To strengthen our convictions for nonresistance
Lesson 9	Class Goal: To help us comprehend the cost and value of
	discipleship
Lesson 10	Class Goal: To help us understand the value of the church and
	church membership
Lesson 11	Class Goal: To see the importance of the assurance of salvation
Lesson 12	Class Goal: To see God's increasing care for His people and the
	final triumph of the faithful

Note: The page numbers cited in the various lessons refer to *Martyrs Mirror* (1938).

of the questions focused on straightforward narrative details, nearly as many questions asked students to identify a lesson pertaining to their spiritual well-being. "On what basis could the martyrs face death fearlessly?" asked one worksheet. "Does being nonresistant hinder Christian joy?" asked another. Still another worksheet asked students to respond to the questions "Why do true Christians place a high value on church membership?" and "In what practical ways do we show that we value the church today?" In all these instances, two pedagogical assumptions reigned: first, the questions were not open-ended but had right and wrong answers; and second, the answers could be found in *Martyrs Mirror*.

At Ashland some of the spiritual lessons that were taught via *Martyrs*

Mirror had a generically Christian ring to them, but many of the lessons had specific Anabaptist overtones, focusing, for instance, on the
importance of adult baptism and nonresistance. More than that, many of
the lessons included tradition-minded Anabaptist emphases that would
be out of place in assimilated Anabaptist congregations. For instance,
the theme of submitting to the church found prominence in lesson 10.
In response to the worksheet question "In what practical ways do we
show that we value the church today?," one student wrote "give offering"
and "loyal attendance," though the student was later helped to see that
valuing the church also meant to "support group decisions."[61] The class
also spent a day on van Braght's preface, during which they considered
the question "What present day luxuries parallel the extremities of van
Braght's era?" To this question one student answered, "splendid architecture" and "strange clothing fashions," phrases that carry special meaning
in Anabaptist churches where modestly attired men and women meet in
simple, functional church buildings.

In sum, leaders in conservative Anabaptist communities use *Martyrs
Mirror* to reinforce their churches' nonconformist location. Given the
liminal position of these communities—participating in the world to a
greater degree than traditional Anabaptist communities but nonetheless resisting a full-armed embrace of North American cultural conven-
tions—these churches face numerous challenges in retaining their youth
and preserving the ecclesiastical status quo. Indeed, the retention rate in
these communities has tended to be lower than it has been among the
Old Order Amish, whose more separatist lifestyle enables them to retain
close to 90 percent of their youth.[62] In the midst of these challenges,
educational modalities such as Bible meetings and Bible schools serve
as means to secure their churches' future, for they bring together mar-
riageable youth to imbibe from a common fountain of theological truth.
Martyrs Mirror is only one wellspring that supplies that fountain, but
it is an important one, for it reminds young people that their churches'
very existence was purchased with blood. Authentic faith that leads to
eternal life carries a cost, these young people are told, often by way of
gory, heart-wrenching examples. Yes, forgoing a cell phone or dressing
modestly may be hard, but such sacrifices pale in comparison to the
sacrifices made by teenagers who inhabit the pages of *Martyrs Mirror*.
By helping contemporary teens imagine themselves in Eulalia's place,

conservative leaders seek to replace their churches' current generation of faithful Christians with a new generation that, like their parents and grandparents before them, effectively resists the world's allures.

Martyrs Mirror and Tradition-Minded Historiography

The use of *Martyrs Mirror* as a spiritual guide hinges on its standing as an authoritative historical resource. From the very beginning, Anabaptist martyrologists recorded what they deemed to be the most significant events in their movement's history: the unjust deaths of faithful witnesses. For these early martyrologists, chronicling the lives of the suffering faithful was the predominant mode of doing church history; for all practical purposes, Anabaptist historiography and Anabaptist martyrological writing were one and the same. By the mid-seventeenth-century, van Braght saw fit to connect these sixteenth-century martyr accounts to larger historical currents that coursed through Christian history. In his telling, the treatment the Anabaptists received was tragically unexceptional, for this is how Christ's followers had always been treated by those who ran the world. In that sense, van Braght's historical writing was inherently teleological, for in addition to telling what happened in the past, it also implied what would happen in the future.

In tradition-minded Anabaptist communities, the historiographical and teleological assumptions that shaped *Martyrs Mirror* continue to hold sway. By and large, historians in these communities are not professionally trained; in fact, many have only eighth-grade educations. Still, tradition-minded Anabaptist communities hold history in high regard, and they look to their historians to fashion usable histories that comport with communal memory and nurture spiritual commitment. Although much of this historical writing is narrow, more expansive histories, including some that survey the entire history of Christianity, receive ready welcome. Particularly in these more expansive histories, themes and arguments that infuse *Martyrs Mirror* provide both narrative structure and teleological thrust.[63]

The most prominent theme in these tradition-minded histories is a soft triumphalism, in which the faithful receive God's blessing and triumph over their foes. These victories are modest, to be sure. Christ's followers will always find themselves on the margins of society, and they will never possess the political power needed to vanquish their foes entirely. At the same time, all efforts at eradicating God's witnesses will fall short. For van Braght, this soft triumphalism meant charting the existence of adult-baptizing Christians through the centuries, a line that culminated in the sixteenth century with the advent of Anabaptism. Tradition-minded Anabaptist historians echo this soft triumphalism, placing the Anabaptist movement at the center of God's providential plan. For instance, Old Order Amish historian Ben Blank, in his three-hundred-page church history, which runs from Jesus's resurrection to the twentieth century, devotes an outsize portion (nearly a hundred pages) to the early Anabaptist movement.[64] According to Blank, efforts at eradicating the Anabaptists were utterly counterproductive. "It has been estimated," Blank writes, "that for every martyr dying for his or her faith at least six other people came to them from the outside." Because outsiders realized that the Anabaptists practiced "the true religion of Jesus Christ," the Anabaptist movement "had power, and was not to be stopped."[65]

The flipside of this soft triumphalism is the assertion that, through much of its history, the Christian church has been a fallen entity, seduced by worldly power and perverted by watered-down conceptions of the faith. This assumption pulses through *Martyrs Mirror* from beginning to end, though it is most obvious in van Braght's summary accounts of the true church and the false church.[66] Tradition-minded historians echo this assessment of Christian history. For instance, Blank devotes a lengthy chapter to the Constantinian shift, noting that under Constantine "it became fashionable to become a Christian." Before long, says Blank, Constantine and his allies had perverted Christianity almost beyond recognition.[67] An EPMC church history text, *The Price of Keeping the Faith,* seconds this van Braghtian view of church history.[68] Lesson 6 of the twelve-lesson textbook, which focuses on the church's first five hundred years, chronicles "the decline of true Christianity" that began in the third century when "nonresistance and nonconformity to the world were lost."[69] The lesson continues by charting other lamentable aspects of the fourth and fifth centuries—the mixing of Christianity with paganism, the rise of the papacy, and Constantine's union of church and state—and concludes with a list of spiritual treasures lost during this time: believers' baptism, nonresistance, nonconformity to the world, and church purity.[70] From that point forward in the textbook, which reaches its culmination with the emergence of the EPMC in the 1960s, the true church is to be found only in faithful remnants that are ridiculed and sometimes persecuted by the larger church.[71]

In these tradition-minded readings of history, as in *Martyrs Mirror,* the Roman Catholic Church comes in for particularly harsh critiques, though the real bugbear is the one van Braght identifies in his *Martyrs Mirror* preface: the quest for worldly respectability and power. According to tradition-minded historians, this sinful pursuit lay at the heart of the Roman Catholic Church's failings. Rather than humbly serving God, the Catholic clergy raced after special privileges and imperial support.[72] But even as the Catholic Church receives considerable censure, so also do Protestants, for they too could not resist the allure of power and prestige. Lesson 8 in *The Price of Keeping the Faith* surveys the Protestant Reformation, and although Luther and Zwingli are lauded for their basic theological sensibilities, their reforming successes are ultimately dismissed in a section entitled "The Failure of Protestantism." This failure, the text notes, results from two compromises that both men made. First, they hitched their reforming wagon to the horsepower of the state; and second, they watered down "Gospel principles" in order to include as many people in their churches as possible.[73] Amish historian Blank agrees that Luther made salvation too easy. "It is unfortunate that Martin Luther's idea of free grace was to lead to a do-as-you-please way of life in many Protestant churches, and later even in some Anabaptist circles."[74]

Blank's final observation, that moral licentiousness can be found even in Anabaptist circles, echoes another van Braghtian theme: the decline of Anabaptism itself. For van Braght, this declension was most notable among Dutch Mennonite elites, who built fancy homes, threw lavish dinner parties, and wore fashionable clothing. For today's tradition-minded historians, the declension shows itself most clearly in world-embracing iterations of North American Anabaptism. *The Price of Keeping the Faith* notes that, even as Dutch Mennonitism fell prey to "worldliness" and "neutrality on doctrinal issues," these "same factors also affected American Mennonites in the last half of the twentieth century."[75] The text goes on to enumerate more specific aspects of this decline: the acceptance of worldly dress, the rejection of male headship, the toleration of divorce and remarriage, the embrace of higher education, the displacement of nonresistance by activist peace initiatives, and the abandonment of the holy kiss.[76] In the midst of these failings, "those who stood for truth" were stigmatized by assimilated Anabaptists and suffered "the rejection of family and friends" when they retained their traditional ways.[77] Old Order historians, further removed from progressive Mennonites than conservative groups, have been less critical of assimilated groups, though they too echo van Braght's critique. Citing Jan Luyken's artwork in *Martyrs Mirror,* Blank observes that Luyken always portrayed the early Anabaptists in "plain garb," a striking contrast to his portrayal of non-Anabaptists with "fancy extras on their clothing."[78] In light of their commitment to modest dress, Blank says, the early Anabaptists would be shocked to find contemporary American Mennonites wearing skin-exposing clothing, including shorts and miniskirts. They would be equally distraught to discover that "the women's prayer veiling would no longer be required in some Mennonite congregations and that some [Mennonites] would even tolerate divorce."[79]

What we see in tradition-minded historians, then, is a common-sense, originalist approach to interpreting *Martyrs Mirror.* Living in a post-persecution era, van Braght did not expect his readers to die for their faith. He could, however, cajole them to pursue spiritual martyrdom, assuring them that they could join hands with actual martyrs by forsaking the worldly practices of the larger culture. For tradition-minded groups, this van Braghtian vision applies to all times and places, which means that Christian history is best read as an endless battle against spiritual declension. The Anabaptist martyrs provide for tradition-minded Anabaptists the positive standard, a measure that reminds them that faithfulness is possible, even when it is painful. Conversely, more worldly varieties of Christianity, including assimilated Anabaptists, provide their negative referents, demonstrating how easy it is for Christians to lose their way. But in addition to serving as warning signs, these assimilated groups serve as sources of comfort, assuring tradition-minded Anabaptists that their own way of life at least approximates the faith of the martyrs. Blank's historical observations are instructive here. Implicit in his claim that the early Anabaptists would be shocked to find North American Mennonites wearing shorts and tolerating divorce is the assumption that they would find themselves quite at home in Blank's Old Order Amish community, where these things are not allowed. Amish humility does not allow Blank to make this assertion explicitly. He even goes out of his way to state that "practically all" Mennonite and Amish groups have forsaken "some of the basics grounded in Scripture which were important to the first Anabaptists."[80] Still, the trajectory of his argument is clear: more than their assimilated counterparts, tradition-minded groups are the rightful inheritors of the martyrs' mantle.

Traditional Anabaptist Values and Martyr Complexity

All Anabaptists, whether traditional or assimilated, encounter the same problem when they read *Martyrs Mirror*. The problem is one of prodigious spiritual standards. If van Braght's account is to be trusted, the founders of Anabaptism were extraordinarily faithful in the most difficult circumstances. Convinced that truth was knowable, that God was on their side, and that eternal rewards outweighed temporal suffering, the Anabaptists portrayed in *Martyrs Mirror* faced death with assurance and sometimes even joy.[81] Although professional historians remind us that hundreds of early Anabaptists recanted under threats of torture or death, *Martyrs Mirror* does not dwell on that reality, let alone sympathize with parents who, fearing the loss of their children (and perhaps their own lives), decided to have them baptized.[82] Some contemporary readers might find this lack of sympathy unseemly. Isn't keeping one's family intact a sufficient warrant for massaging a few details of theology? In tradition-minded Anabaptist communities, however, van Braght's exacting standards of faithfulness continue to rule the day. Although many people in these tradition-minded communities wonder if they could demonstrate the martyrs' steadfastness, few question whether they should.

This consonance with van Braght's perspective correlates with other deeply held convictions in tradition-minded communities. Foremost among these convictions are the ones that shaped and sustained the martyrs themselves: that truth is knowable, that God stands on the side of faithful Christians, and that heavenly rewards are well worth any suffering the faithful might incur. These convictions existed in Anabaptist communities before *Martyrs Mirror* was compiled, and they have traveled down to contemporary tradition-minded communities through a host of sources in addition to *Martyrs Mirror*, including doctrinal statements, sermons, and songs. For instance, when Old Order Amish teen-agers undergo catechetical instruction, their ministers point them to the Dordrecht Confession, which says that the pious shall be "taken up to be with Christ to enter into eternal life," whereas the ungodly shall be condemned to "eternal hellish torment."[83] Every time they gather for worship, these same young people sing the *Loblied,* an *Ausbund* hymn that prays that God's people might remain undeceived.[84] This hymn, like so many that are sung in tradition-minded communities, draws a stark line between truth and untruth, between the faithful and the unfaith-ful. Moreover, it assumes that each individual can discern the difference and thus has a critical choice to make. Parents add their voices to this claim, echoing the dualistic message that their children hear in church. If church membership statistics tell us anything, most young people be-lieve what they hear. In some Old Order Amish communities, over 90 percent of the children join their church of origin. Even in non–Old Order conservative communities, the retention rate is much higher than it is in most North American denominations, where leaving or switching is pervasive.

How do tradition-minded Anabaptists think about other Christians? Do they think those who baptize their infants and participate in military service are bound for everlasting torments? More specifically, what do they think about their assimilated Anabaptist counterparts who con-sider themselves Anabaptists but who nonetheless tolerate divorce and attire themselves in the latest fashions? Few tradition-minded Anabap-tist communities are willing to make explicit judgments about an in-dividual's eternal fate, conceding that such judgments should be left to God.[85] Even so, nearly all tradition-minded Anabaptists operate on the assumption that their own community, in contrast to many Christian churches, stands firm against worldly compromise. Correspondingly, they believe that people who commit themselves to their community's standards are more likely to be judged faithful by God than are those in churches that pooh-pooh those standards. In other words, they believe it is much safer spiritually to commit oneself to the tradition-minded community than it is to launch out on one's own. This assumption is part and parcel of *Rumspringa,* the time in an Amish adolescent's life when the teenager explores the larger world before joining the Amish church. For many Old Order Amish teens on *Rumspringa,* the thought of dying outside the Amish church fosters significant anxiety, which in turn compels them to join.[86] Even in conservative Anabaptist communities, where the boundaries are looser, retention rates are lower, and church switching is more common, the view is largely the same: the safest path to eternal life lies in the context of a tradition-minded Anabaptist community.

This sense of spiritual superiority is not dependent on *Martyrs Mirror*, but references to *Martyrs Mirror* help to sustain it. Like many other Reformation-era martyrologies, *Martyrs Mirror* is an anti-ecumenical document, for it paints other Christians as deficient in their theological and moral rectitude. Of course, when it comes to sketching the history of a particular denomination or sect, nearly all insider accounts of the group's origins assume the group's spiritual superiority. What sets tradition-minded Anabaptists apart from most North American Christians is the reverence they have for the past—reverence for the traditions of their parents and grandparents, for the convictions of their ancestors, and for the martyrs who first stated those convictions. Given that high regard, tradition-minded groups are always wary of declension, always concerned that something or someone will seduce them away from godliness. Although the sources of this deception take various forms, *Martyrs Mirror* reminds them that throughout history many of these sources have carried the name *Christian*. This lesson, brought forward to the present, reinforces an anti-ecumenical outlook among tradition-minded groups that makes cooperation difficult, even with other Anabaptists. In the final chapter of the EPMC text, readers are told that one of the leading threats to authentic faith is ecumenism, which emphasizes collaborative efforts over doctrinal particulars. Because "many denominations of professing Christians no longer hold to the true faith," readers are warned, cooperative service ventures with such groups "will be counterproductive."[87] Some tradition-minded Anabaptist groups are less opposed to cooperative efforts than the EPMC, to be sure. At the same time, the schismatic nature of tradition-minded Anabaptism, which exists today in countless forms, bears out its anti-ecumenical disposition.

Divided though they are, tradition-minded Anabaptists share a devotion to the martyrs and, just as importantly, a sense that they are the martyrs' rightful heirs. They recognize that they do not uphold that legacy perfectly, and they readily admit that the trials they face today are not as deadly as the ones the martyrs faced five hundred years ago. They take comfort, however, in the fact that they live outside the mainstream of North American life, forging a countercultural path through a pagan wilderness. Moreover, they find their faithfulness confirmed by the harassment, ridicule, and slights they perceive that they suffer. EPMC members are reminded that, just as the martyrs paid the price of faithfulness, EPMC members "pay the price of being considered strange" when they forgo worldly entertainments. Similarly, they "pay the price to stand alone" when extended family members belittle their conservatism.[88] For their part, Old Order Amish church members learn that resisting government regulations that impinge on their lifestyle—in areas such as education, health care, zoning, and vehicle use—places them in a long line of Christians who suffered on account of their faith. Most Old Order Amish leaders are not averse to negotiating with government officials; in fact, in some instances, Amish communities have adjusted traditional practices to pass legal muster.[89] Nonetheless, Amish resistance to the state, which tracked a consistent line through the twentieth century, continues today, particularly in the most world-rejecting Amish communities, where smoke alarms and slow-moving-vehicle symbols are considered worldly.[90] "We are taught to mind our own business and obey the government," conceded one Amish man, "but when . . . the government interferes with our way of living, we can balk like a stubborn mule."[91] Or, he might have said, like a steadfast martyr.

It may strike many Christians as strange that Amish people would risk jail time rather than affix safety symbols to their buggies, but the Amish who engage in these forms of civil disobedience take heart in their church's martyrological heritage. More than most Americans, they realize that religious freedom has limits, and by bumping up against those limits, they find confirmation that they have not abandoned the faith of their fathers and mothers. As one Amish writer admonished his readers, the Amish remain "children of martyrs" only to the extent that they refuse to "shrink from hardships, from self-denial, from sacrifice."[92] Assimilated Mennonites, as much as they imagine their faith to be countercultural, have a much harder time claiming the martyrs' legacy. For them, as will become clear in the next chapter, discerning the contemporary relevance of *Martyrs Mirror* is much more difficult.

CHAPTER 10

Assimilated Mennonites and the Dilemma of *Martyrs Mirror*

For many outside observers, the terms *Amish* and *Mennonite* are practically interchangeable, conjuring images of plain-dressed people driving horse-drawn buggies or dark-colored cars. An increasing majority of North American Anabaptists, the ones we have called traditional Anabaptists, fit this description. Among Mennonites alone, however, there continue to be fewer tradition-minded Mennonites in North America than there are culture-embracing assimilated Mennonites. The Mennonite Church USA and the Mennonite Church Canada, two of the largest Mennonite bodies in contemporary North America, both sit squarely in the assimilated camp.[1] These sister denominations, organized in the wake of the 1995 decision to combine the Mennonite Church and the General Conference Mennonite Church, cooperate on many fronts, and together they oversee MennoMedia, which produces Internet content, Sunday school curriculum, and other congregational resources.[2] MennoMedia also includes a book publishing division, Herald Press, the Mennonite Publishing House holdover that produces English-language copies of *Martyrs Mirror,* thirty thousand of them since the turn of the twenty-first century.[3]

Identifying assimilated Mennonite congregations in North America is a relatively easy task, but describing a typical one is not. Most assimilated congregations meet in dedicated church buildings, but some meet in members' homes, whereas others meet in schools or office complexes. In most cases, the people who gather for worship are white, and their services are conducted in English; in other cases, however, the congregants are mostly African Americans, Latinos, or Asians, and in some cases they worship in languages other than English. Lead ministers are typically male, but female clergy are not uncommon. At Sunday worship services, some congregations sing from hymnals produced by Anabaptist publishers.[4] Others opt for contemporary choruses that are beamed onto wall-sized screens.

The diversity among these churches extends also to theology. In regions with many assimilated Mennonite congregations, local Mennonites know which ones have a more liberal theological bent and which ones are more conservative. This divide has little to do with the way people dress or the technologies they use. Instead, it mirrors disagreements that cut across North American Christianity, disagreements that create liberal factions, conservative factions, and a host of moderate options in between. Unlike traditional Anabaptist groups such as the Old Order Amish, who have largely forgone the theological debates that roil other North American churches (over evolution or, more recently, same-sex relationships), assimilated Anabaptist denominations have often been drawn into these debates, both at the congregational level and denominationally.[5]

Assimilated Anabaptist congregations also differ in how much they value their Anabaptist heritage. Most congregations in the Mennonite Church USA and the Mennonite Church Canada include the word *Mennonite* on their church building signage, and the members know they attend a Mennonite church. Even so, some local congregations pay scant attention to Anabaptist history and theology. In some churches neither the Sunday school curriculum nor the hymnal derives from a Mennonite source, and new members learn little about Anabaptist belief and practice. Some ministers, hesitant to offend members with military connections, soft-pedal nonresistance. Of the twenty-some assimilated Anabaptist denominations or associations that appear in Donald B. Kraybill's *Concise Encyclopedia of Amish, Brethren, Hutterites, and Mennonites,* a few have effectively relegated Anabaptist particulars to history's dustbin.[6] Even in assimilated denominations that retain a strong Anabaptist identity, some individual congregations do not.

Given this diversity, it is more difficult to describe the role of *Martyrs Mirror* in assimilated Anabaptist churches than to describe its role in tradition-minded churches. This much is certain: the role of *Martyrs Mirror* in assimilated Anabaptist circles is both more muted and more complicated than in traditional Anabaptist circles. In some assimilated congregations, hardly anyone has heard of the book, let alone pondered its contents. In fact, some who attend assimilated Mennonite congregations have no knowledge whatsoever of their church's martyrological heritage. In other assimilated circles, the story is different. Although *Martyrs Mirror* the book may go unread, cognizance of the martyrs remains strong, in part because of late-twentieth-century efforts to cast the martyrs' stories into more consumer-friendly media. Moreover, assimilated Mennonite scholars continue to engage *Martyrs Mirror* with vigor, often moving beyond historical description to moral prescription, promoting the book as a spiritual resource or, in other cases, questioning its merits.[7] Indeed, unlike their counterparts in traditional Anabaptist circles, who may not often read *Martyrs Mirror* but who uniformly trumpet its benefits, assimilated Mennonites sometimes part ways on the book's value for today. In that sense, *Martyrs Mirror* remains a mirror, reflecting the diversity of viewpoints within the assimilated Mennonite world.[8]

In the following section, we look at Mennonite academics who have engaged *Martyrs Mirror* in recent decades. Although many of these conversations have taken place out of earshot of ordinary Mennonites, their outlines have often been intuited and voiced by people in the pews. In addition, some scholars' perspectives have been refracted through denominational resources intended for congregational use. We will consider these resources in this chapter's final sections, where we explore the role and influence of *Martyrs Mirror* in the homes, schools, and churches of assimilated Mennonites.

Mennonite Malaise and the Promise of History

The fear that emerging generations of Anabaptists will forsake their Anabaptist commitments has been ever-present in Anabaptist history. Rarely, however, has the concern been more deeply felt than in the past thirty years, as assimilated Mennonite leaders in North America watch and wonder about the future of their churches. To be sure, some congregational leaders experience no anxiety in this regard, striding as they are toward a generic form of evangelical Christianity that downplays Anabaptist themes. But the presence of such leaders only exacerbates the anxiety among those who believe that the distinctive elements of the Anabaptist tradition are well worth preserving.

In some ways, these assimilated Mennonite denominations are only experiencing what other North American denominations have experienced in the last half century, namely, the decline of denominational loyalty. In his book *The Restructuring of American Religion,* Robert Wuthnow identifies factors that have conspired against denominational loyalty since the 1950s, including greater geographical mobility, higher rates of intermarriage, and increased interdenominational cooperation.[9] These forces, strongly allayed in traditional Anabaptist communities, have affected assimilated Mennonites in profound ways, and they continue to do so today, softening commitment to Anabaptist distinctives and, in some cases, pulling members away from Mennonite churches altogether.[10] One Mennonite sociologist, Conrad Kanagy, reflecting on the results of a 2006 survey of Mennonite Church USA members, went so far as to characterize twenty-first-century Mennonite congregations as "collections of persons with no identifiable home, lost without a sense of what distinguishes [them] from evangelical and mainline, from right and left, and from the broader society."[11] Not every observer of contemporary Mennonite life would paint such a dreary picture. In fact, some would highlight the esteem for Anabaptist perspectives in other realms of Christianity.[12] Still, the situation is such that some Mennonite leaders describe contemporary North American Mennonitism in much the way van Braght described seventeenth-century Dutch Mennonite life. Kanagy's observations are instructive here, both for their transparency and for the way they echo van Braght. Assimilated Mennonites are both more "comfortable" and more "secure" than ever before, writes Kanagy. Fearful of being scorned by their neighbors, they have "stopped speaking the whole truth about Christ," and when they do speak of faith, they do so in language "that ensures that [they] won't lose [their] skin over the deal."[13] Again, not every assimilated Mennonite leader would concur with Kanagy's jeremiad, but few would dismiss his concerns as entirely unfounded.

Since 1990, when John Oyer and Robert Kreider proposed that a recovered martyr memory might renew a "weary and uncertain people,"

Mennonite historians have continued to take the lead in promoting *Martyrs Mirror* as an antidote to the modern Mennonite malaise.[14] One Mennonite historian who quickly added his voice to this chorus was the missionary-educator Alan Kreider, who, along with his wife Eleanor, helped to launch the Anabaptist Network, an association of churches in Britain and Ireland with an interest in Anabaptism.[15] Faced with the task of communicating Anabaptist values in a largely post-Christian context, Kreider concluded that the martyrs' relevance for contemporary Christianity was abundant, for despite their late-medieval context, they wrestled with issues of timeless significance. In particular, the sixteenth-century martyrs faced the challenge of holding together spiritual realities that Christians throughout history had frequently uncoupled, including "spirituality and social nonconformity" and "renewal and radicalism." By probing the martyrs' witness, said Kreider, contemporary Mennonites could find resources for maintaining a holistic faith.[16]

Had Kreider left these spiritual dyads undefined, it is possible that North American Anabaptists from across the traditional-to-assimilated spectrum could have agreed with his assessment, but as he described them, his argument took a particular turn. Taking aim at assimilated Mennonites, Kreider argued that the martyrs condemned a particular type of social conformity that characterized many late-twentieth-century Mennonites, a conformity that worshipped the twin idols of materialism and militarism. On these two issues, Kreider said, the martyrs' sensibilities were clear: not only did they reject violence, but they also displayed an economic bias that rejected unbridled accumulation in favor of "redistribution towards the poor." Kreider thus found in *Martyrs Mirror* a critique of "the American Way," a way of life exemplified by North American Christians, including many Mennonites, who ran after big houses and hefty investment portfolios.[17]

Countercultural though it was, Kreider's reading of *Martyrs Mirror* did not lead him to the kind of nonconformity embodied in tradition-minded Anabaptist circles. Echoing Cornelius Krahn's argument in the late 1960s, Kreider argued that the sixteenth-century martyrs set a pattern for social engagement that bore little resemblance to the apoliticism of traditional Anabaptist groups. Early Anabaptists may have been nonviolent, Kreider said, but they were not nonresistant in the face of evil. As evidence, Kreider cited an Anabaptist martyr who sang a hymn within earshot of a public official. It was, said Kreider, a hymn of radical resistance, for the lyrics proclaimed that "truth has fallen in the public squares."[18] In Kreider's view, this particular feature of the martyrs' witness—agitating for justice—had gone unheeded in Anabaptist circles for too long. Pushing his argument further, Kreider lauded Christian movements that extended the martyrs' witness in ways that few Anabaptists did, such as African American Christians who took to the streets during the civil rights movement. Through such people, said Kreider, God was pleased to "transform the world."[19]

If Kreider located in *Martyrs Mirror* resources for progressive activism, his fellow Mennonite historian, John D. Roth, fixed on a different set of resources, which he hoped could stem the tide of late-modern skepticism. In Roth's telling, published a year after Kreider's piece appeared, the revitalizing possibilities of *Martyrs Mirror* were to be found primarily in the book's endorsement of orthodox Christian belief.[20] *Martyrs Mirror* affirms "traditional Anabaptist—and, I believe, essential Christian—convictions," wrote Roth, convictions that included the authority of scripture and the preeminence of Christ. More generally, *Martyrs Mirror* upbraids the "wisdom of our culture" by challenging the relativistic view that truth is finally unknowable. According to Roth, the martyrs' actions were possible only because they held fast to three convictions that had fallen out of favor in modern America: "that truth is knowable, that truth compels us to action, and that death in the defense of truth has meaning." Aware of how quarrelsome Anabaptist groups had used *Martyrs Mirror* in the past, Roth warned against employing van Braght's martyrology as a tool to reinforce divisions. Rather, he said, the best way to use *Martyrs Mirror* would be "to read it as a prayer: 'Lord, I believe, help thou my unbelief.' "[21]

Roth's call to read *Martyrs Mirror* as a particular prayer, one drawn from the gospel of Mark, helps to situate Roth's talk at the close of the twentieth century. The prayer, spoken in Jesus's presence by the father of a demon-possessed boy, comes on the heels of Jesus's complaint that he is dealing with a "faithless generation."[22] Roth never calls late-twentieth-century Mennonites a faithless generation. He does, however, imply that, in a pluralistic age, many people find it hard to believe that God would demand the sort of faithfulness demonstrated by the sixteenth-century martyrs. "To leave family, vocation, and future; to voluntarily renounce life itself in obedience to Christ," wrote Roth, "all this flies in the face of common sense." But even though such faithfulness is largely irrational, it comports well with the mystery of the incarnation, wherein God's Son was obedient unto death and, as a result, was exalted by his Father.[23] For Roth, then, the primary message of *Martyrs Mirror* was the connection it drew between faithfulness and reward: exaltation after death depends on the willingness to follow Jesus in life. To read the martyrs' stories as a prayer against unbelief means finding ways to remain faithful in an age when the temptation to renounce Jesus has less to do with torture chambers than with the niggling doubts that plague modern minds.

Kreider's and Roth's readings of *Martyrs Mirror* landed on different themes, but they were not necessarily incompatible. In time, the essence of both readings found their way into educational materials intended for lay audiences, including materials for Mennonite youth. In Mennonite academic circles, however, some people remained unconvinced. In particular, some believed that living confidently in a pluralistic world could yield a new set of problems, particularly in view of building relationships with others. For them, the martyrs' certitude represented a spiritual stance that was best avoided.

Purity, Pride, and Persecution Complexes

The same year that Roth published his endorsement of *Martyrs Mirror,* Melvin Goering, a Mennonite mental health administrator in Kansas, took to the pages of *Mennonite Life* to argue otherwise.[24] Goering's polemic hinged on the fact that assimilated Mennonites occupied a vastly different social terrain from the ones the martyrs occupied. Unlike the martyrs, who defined themselves in opposition to the larger world, many late-twentieth-century Mennonites (like Goering himself) filled roles that assumed worldly responsibility. In these roles, said Goering, the perfectionistic ethic championed by the early Anabaptists did not always make sense. In fact, operating by that ethic was entirely inappropriate in situations where leaders needed to sacrifice purity for the sake of the greater good. Goering acknowledged this loss of purity, but he did not lament it. What he did lament was that Anabaptist ethical theory had been formulated with small Christian communities in mind, an approach that did not account for the complexities of large-scale institutions. Late-twentieth-century Mennonites thus found themselves bound by an ethic that was "not very functional in a world of systematically interrelated institutional settings."[25]

Goering's assessment of contemporary Mennonite realities vis-à-vis sixteenth-century realities set the stage for his critique of *Martyrs Mirror*. First, said Goering, *Martyrs Mirror* offered a simplistic view of human reality. In contrast to real life, where good and evil comingle in each and every person, *Martyrs Mirror* associates evil with people "who care for the civic, social, cultural, and religious welfare of the people," and it associates good with those who forswear those activities. Second, the martyr tradition represented by *Martyrs Mirror* allows "no room for compromise," a moral stance that both nourished and validated Mennonite disengagement from the world's problems. Third, said Goering, the martyrs themselves exhibit an utter disdain for dialogue, for in their minds "they are right and they know it." While readers who share the martyrs' theological convictions may see the martyrs as faithful and courageous, those who do not share the martyrs' convictions cannot help but conclude they are morally arrogant. In any case, said Goering, the martyrs fail to model a search for truth that takes other people and their opinions seriously. Even worse, the primary lesson they offer—the importance of maintaining theological purity—cannot but encourage a self-centeredness that neglects the needs of others.[26]

Setting Goering's critique of *Martyrs Mirror* alongside Roth's commendation sheds light on the tensions within the late-twentieth-century assimilated Mennonite world, in part because of the common ground the two analyses shared. Written almost simultaneously, the two analyses did not reference each other, but they fixed upon the same van Braghtian theme: the resolute certainty of the martyrs' convictions. In Roth's view, the martyrs' resolve was a posture to be valued: the martyrs reminded twentieth-century readers that "truth is knowable," so knowable in fact that it sometimes made sense to die for it.[27] In Goering's analysis, however, this stance was inherently problematic. The martyrs, he observed, "project a clarity of belief" that is epistemologically naive and, in the end, morally conceited.[28] Goering never denied outright that truth is knowable, but he did dispute the notion that the martyrs possessed the truth absolutely and their adversaries not at all. Moreover, Goering knew that many people *think* they know the truth when in fact they are mistaken. To emulate the martyrs' resolve in the present might be psychologically reassuring, he said, but it was hardly the way to live in a complex world. Unlike Roth, whose recommendation in an age of skepticism was to sit at the martyrs' feet, Goering proposed leaving the martyrs behind.

Goering's argument that *Martyrs Mirror* cultivated a sense of moral superiority in the martyrs' Anabaptist descendants had plenty of support. In the same *Mennonite Life* issue that carried Goering's critique, John Sheriff offered a rather incendiary observation: that anyone who has spent any time in a Mennonite community would almost certainly have encountered the Mennonite myth of moral superiority.[29] A faculty member at Bethel College, Sheriff attested to seeing that myth in action, and he feared that a renewed emphasis on the martyrs might reinforce it.[30] Of course, Sheriff's critique begged an important question: is it possible for people to sustain a vibrant religious tradition without *some* sense of that tradition's moral superiority? Indeed, why would people make anything other than a loose commitment to a particular tradition if they thought other religious traditions possessed moral visions that were just as good? Perhaps that was Sheriff's point: that the Anabaptist tradition was merely one of many ethnoreligious traditions bolstered by adherents who assumed their way was best. In any case, Sheriff concluded that contemporary Mennonites would be well served to liberate themselves from their "jail cell of intellectual pride," from their "messianic delusions," and from their "persecution complex," all of which were sustained by celebrating the martyrs.[31]

It is arguable that Goering's and Sheriff's resistance to reinvigorating a martyrological mentality among Mennonites correlated with the fact that both men were General Conference Mennonites. Compared to their Mennonite Church counterparts, General Conference Mennonites had long engaged the larger world more fully and, moreover, had demonstrated a greater willingness to slaughter sacred cows, or at least put them out to pasture. Still, skepticism about the usefulness of *Martyrs Mirror* in the present was not confined to General Conference Mennonites. As the twentieth century gave way to the twenty-first, Mennonite intellectuals of various stripes, including those with roots in the Swiss-German Amish-Mennonite tradition, found *Martyrs Mirror* to be something less than an authoritative resource for moral guidance. Inspiring as it was, at least in the sense of provoking reflection on critical issues, the book was too complex to be facilely embraced as a spiritual roadmap.

Some of the most poignant observations in this regard came from Mennonite writers who, during these years, participated in a literary renaissance in assimilated Mennonite circles.[32] Two poets, both with Amish family roots and Mennonite Church connections, exemplified the depth of this ambivalence, particularly as it pertained to ecumenical relations. In her poem titled "Catholics," first published in 1992, Julia Spicher Kasdorf recounted a playground encounter with Catholic friends who, in her childhood memory, happily displayed their Catholic faith. Kasdorf recalled her martyrologically self-righteous attempt to put the girls in their place ("Your people killed my people"), finally admitting that she was mostly jealous of their religion's material beauty. In hindsight, she now wished her Catholic friends had corrected her puerile imagination, telling her

> those priests were not me,
> those martyrs weren't you,
> and we have our own martyr stories, too.[33]

Similarly, in a poem titled "No Apologies," Esther Yoder Stenson referenced the Anabaptist martyr Jan Gerrits and the letter Gerrits wrote to a Lutheran preacher.[34] Gerrits's missive chastised the preacher's "unreasonable or willful stupidity" on the topic of baptism, a challenge that led to Gerrits's execution.[35] In her poem, Stenson proceeded to name other Anabaptists who,

> speaking Scripture to Power
> . . . refused to sacrifice [their] young
> to the Pope or to Luther.

In the end, however, Stenson returned to her own situation, closing with words—and a surprising revelation—that underscored the distance between her own experience and that of her Anabaptist predecessors:

> My heart bleeds for you
> my brothers and sisters

but only for you.
As for me,
I married a Lutheran![36]

That Stenson titled her poem "No Apologies" provided further commentary on the modern-day dilemma posed by *Martyrs Mirror.* She wrote the poem at a time when Lutheran and Mennonite church leaders were reviewing the history of Lutheran-Anabaptist relations, including the Reformation-era persecution of Anabaptists by some Lutheran leaders. In 2010, the same year Stenson composed her poem, the Eleventh Assembly of the Lutheran World Federation took formal action to apologize for Lutheran actions in the past. The assembly's mea culpa was wide-ranging, covering topics both great and small, but Stenson, the Amish-born poet who married a Lutheran, remained skeptical of its value and its necessity.[37] Yes, the sixteenth-century martyrs deserve our sympathy, and their persecutors deserve our censure, but present-day Mennonites should not feign to stand in as victims. For Stenson, blanket apologies from nonoffenders like her husband, begging forgiveness from nonvictims like herself, served no end, except perhaps to trivialize the suffering of the actual victims.

The effectiveness of Stenson's poem owed in part to its ironic playfulness, but some participants in this conversation were not so lighthearted. Of all the writers who advanced the concern that *Martyrs Mirror* fostered peculiarly Mennonite pathologies, no one hit harder than Ross L. Bender, the son of a respected Mennonite Church leader.[38] Contemporary Mennonites find themselves trapped in a "psychic pretzel," Bender wrote in the iconoclastic Mennonite publication *Mennonot.* On the one hand, modern-day Mennonites revere their martyrs and hang "horrifying caricatures of the Anabaptist heroes in seminary lounges." On the other hand, they live materially prosperous lives. All this prosperity complicates Oyer and Kreider's notion of a "weary and uncertain people" in need of renewal, Bender said. In fact, in Bender's suburban Philadelphia experience, "the only thing uncertain about [Mennonite] life . . . is whether or not we're going to buy the second BMW." Thus, "while it may be true the Mennos need renewal," everyone would be further ahead if North American Mennonites were described as they actually were, not as weary and uncertain but rather as "sleek and wealthy."[39]

In that regard, at least, Bender's assessment of contemporary North American Mennonites was not far removed from van Braght's assessment of seventeenth-century Dutch Mennonites. The difference between Bender and van Braght was not insignificant, however. First, Bender was less certain than van Braght that wealth and social status were moral evils to be deplored. Second, Bender had no illusions that reading martyr stories would impel North American Mennonites to amend their upwardly mobile ways. Mennonites, he said, "have great trouble perceiving the multi-dimensionality of their psychic situation." In fact, North American Mennonites had evolved to the point where they possessed a communal neurosis that enabled them to live comfortably with incompatible commitments and desires. This is how Mennonites could both worship a savior who condemned riches *and* drive BMWs, and how Mennonites could possess both a "profound sense of humility" *and* a "profound sense of pride" in their spiritual heritage.[40] To Bender, this distinctive Mennonite neurosis explained how the sixteenth-century martyrs could still matter, but not really matter at all.

Martyrs Mirror and the Specter of Victimization

Ross Bender's critique was acerbic, but it was mostly benign, fixing on the incongruities between assimilated Mennonite experience and the lives of the martyrs. For one of Bender's contemporaries, however, there was nothing benign about the place of *Martyrs Mirror* in Mennonite life. Building on Melvin Goering's earlier critique, and also on the work of Mennonite creative writers, Stephanie Krehbiel contended that valorizing the Anabaptist martyrs was tantamount to valorizing victimhood, which in turn meant abiding the evils that ran roughshod over vulnerable people.

Krehbiel's essay drew on her experiences, including an emotional breakdown, in the aftermath of the September 11, 2001, terror attacks.[41] By the time of 9/11, Krehbiel was nearly ten years removed from her first sustained encounter with *Martyrs Mirror,* which had occurred in her Mennonite Sunday school class during the run-up to the Gulf War. As a fourteen-year-old, Krehbiel was not sure what to make of the book, but later, in the aftermath of the 9/11 attacks, she experienced something akin to déjà vu. The atmosphere of suspicion that emerged in the wake of 9/11 felt "menacingly familiar," Krehbiel wrote, for this was exactly the air one breathes when reading *Martyrs Mirror*.[42] Only unlike the martyrs, who in van Braght's chronicle demonstrated confidence, courage, and even joy in the face of peril, Krehbiel felt paralyzed by fear. And with the fear came self-loathing. "I wanted to stay silent, to protect myself, and this shamed me," Krehbiel recalled. By 2006 Krehbiel was far enough removed from 9/11 to analyze her shame, which she attributed to the martyrological messages of her Mennonite upbringing. As she recalled the sixteenth-century witness of Maeyken Wens, a young mother who responded with joy to the prospect of her death, it all became clear. "Now looking back," Krehbiel wrote, "I think this is the cruelest use of *Martyrs Mirror* to which I fell prey: the idea that not only do our beliefs invite painful death, but that we should give it a rapturous welcome."[43]

Krehbiel was hardly the first Mennonite to highlight the ability of *Martyrs Mirror* to shame its sensitive readers. In fact, Anabaptists of nearly all stripes attest to feelings of inadequacy as they compare their own spiritual resolve to that of the martyrs. For less alienated readers, this shame is often deemed beneficial—perhaps not pleasant in the moment, but nonetheless useful for edification. For Krehbiel and others like her, however, *Martyrs Mirror* could itself be an instrument of cruelty, producing victims of a sort that van Braght could not have imagined. For instance, Julia Kasdorf, whose poem "Catholics" warned of the book's anti-Catholic bias, has theorized that Mennonite memories of trauma have hindered the production of imaginative literature in Mennonite communities for generations.[44] Taking a slightly different tack, writer Jeff Gundy has suggested that the telling and retelling of martyr stories have conspired to make Mennonites overly paranoid, "wondering who was really on [their] side."[45]

Krehbiel affirmed these two lines of thinking, but she went one step further in criticizing the book's effects, especially upon women. Recalling her graduate adviser's comment that *Martyrs Mirror* struck him as "pornographic," Krehbiel concluded that he was fundamentally correct, for *Martyrs Mirror* not only offered gruesome images of torture and death, but it also encouraged readers to identify with the martyrs' victimhood.[46] Krehbiel found further confirmation of her assessment in Miriam Toews's novel *A Complicated Kindness,* which revolves around a sixteen-year-old Mennonite girl who summarizes the essence of Mennonitism with trenchant sarcasm: "A Mennonite telephone survey might consist of questions like, would you prefer to live or die a cruel death, and if you answer 'live,' the Menno doing the survey hangs up on *you*."[47] In light of these observations, both hers and others', Krehbiel decided that *Martyrs Mirror* was a text to be avoided, not valorized. Fixing upon the popular television series *Buffy the Vampire Slayer,* Krehbiel suggested that Buffy offered a better archetype for meaningful living than did Maeyken Wens, for Buffy was a woman who used the power she possessed to enact change. Sure, death may result from confronting evil, but *Martyrs Mirror* placed far too much emphasis on dying, "as though dying is a thing that makes us great."[48] It was time, Krehbiel concluded, to reject that sort of thinking. For the sake of a vulnerable world, the time had come for privileged North American Mennonites "to claim our power [and] to stop thinking of ourselves as 'defenseless Christians.'"[49]

Krehbiel's call for Mennonites to employ the power at their disposal paralleled Alan Kreider's call, but whereas Kreider found resources in *Martyrs Mirror* to advance that agenda, Krehbiel concluded that *Martyrs Mirror* pushed too strongly in the opposite direction. Aware that many North American Anabaptist communities were resolutely separatist, and drawing from her own adolescent experience with van Braght's book, Krehbiel concluded that *Martyrs Mirror* was more hindrance than help to living responsibly in the world. If van Braght's tribute to defenselessness was indeed a tribute to people who embraced their suffering, then it was better to be a "warrior" than to be a "martyr." To be sure, Krehbiel eventually deconstructed her use of the word *warrior,* noting that although she would "carry the sword" in her efforts to change the world, she would carry it "only in metaphor."[50] Still, because the word *warrior* connoted to her power and agency, whereas the word *martyr* connoted passivity, Krehbiel found the former label more compelling than the latter one.

Krehbiel's appraisal of *Martyrs Mirror* evoked a range of responses, both positive and negative. Of those who disagreed with her, none did so more thoughtfully than Gerald J. Mast, a Mennonite communication scholar who has written extensively on sixteenth-century Anabaptist history.[51] The power of Mast's response rested on three foundations. First, Mast's sociopolitical leanings were not far removed from Krehbiel's; he was sympathetic both to Krehbiel's concern about the victimization of women and to her desire for Mennonites to embrace the power at their disposal. Second, Mast possessed a deep familiarity with van Braght's text, and he was thus able to marshal evidence to suggest that the martyrs were not as passive as Krehbiel assumed them to be. Third, like Krehbiel, Mast could also recall youthful encounters with *Martyrs Mirror*, only his encounters eventually nudged him in a different direction: inspired by the witness of "argumentative Christian disciples," he read the text as sanctioning various forms of nonviolent resistance.

The reasons that Mast located the theme of resistance in *Martyrs Mirror*, whereas Krehbiel saw mostly passivity, are undoubtedly complex, though their respective modes of textual encounter should not be ignored. Mast, who was raised in a conservative Mennonite home, tells of a childhood bereft of television and movies but filled with books. In his search for reading material, he became captivated by *Martyrs Mirror*, pulling it off his grandparents' bookcase and poring over its pages. Reading Mast's account, one gets the sense of a boy who dived deeply into the text and let its narratives shape his emerging worldview. Krehbiel's encounter was less thoroughgoing, more pedagogically directed, and apparently more focused on the book's gruesome imagery: her Sunday school teacher, she recalled, showed images "demonstrating the various functions of Inquisition-era torture instruments, graphic tales of stake-burnings, and heads exploding with mouths full of gunpowder."[52] In light of these memories, it is easy to see how Krehbiel came to the conclusion that, in *Martyrs Mirror*, dying was *the* goal, and all else served that goal.

Of course, Krehbiel's and Mast's divergent readings of *Martyrs Mirror* may also correlate with their gendered locations. With few exceptions the most vigorous critics of *Martyrs Mirror* in the contemporary Mennonite world have been women, some of whom who have underscored the book's potential to sanctify victimization, and particularly the oppression of women. For instance, the Mennonite poet Di Brandt has written that every generation needs its scapegoats, and the "best deaths" are the ones died by mothers

> sacrificing themselves to the world
> denying themselves into goodness
> so the rest of the black sinful clan
> could be saved by their dying.[53]

Another Mennonite poet, Becca J. R. Lachman, wrote that she came from

> a long line of [female] martyrs
> who gave up their lives to be heard.

These women martyrs used to be "burned, baked, stretched and smothered," she said, but more recently they have found a different way to secure their heavenly reward: they

> follow a man
> across the country, raise
> his children, cook his potatoes
> just the way he likes them.

Significantly, Lachman began her poem epigraphically with what she called an Amish proverb: "True humility is neither thinking too highly of one's self nor thinking too little of one's self, but rather not thinking of one's self at all."[54]

Still, even as some feminists have linked the historic subjugation of Mennonite women to the martyrs' legacy, some Mennonite women have continued to find *Martyrs Mirror* useful. Indeed, some have found within its pages resources to advance feminist concerns. These resources received considerable attention in 1995 at the "Quiet in the Land?" conference, an academic and creative arts gathering that explored the experiences of Anabaptist women both past and present.[55] The question mark in the conference's title signaled the organizers' goal: to destabilize the common stereotype of Mennonite and Amish women as quiet, meek, and mild. One of the conference's presentations, by Linda Huebert Hecht, took aim at *Martyrs Mirror* for its hagiographical depictions of Anabaptist women. At the same time, Huebert Hecht suggested that the female martyrs set "an important precedent" for contemporary Anabaptist women, for they made their own religious decisions, defended them ably in male-dominated settings, and were nothing less than "pillars in the Anabaptist movement."[56] One year later, in 1996, Huebert Hecht co-edited a book with C. Arnold Snyder that focused entirely on the experiences of sixteenth-century Anabaptist women, including some whose stories can be found in *Martyrs Mirror*. While dismissing the claim that early Anabaptism was radically egalitarian, Snyder noted that Anabaptist women did find "greater opportunities for participation in the Anabaptist movement than was possible for them in society at large."[57] In fact, Anabaptist women assumed remarkable levels of "informal leadership" in the movement's early years as they undertook the work of teaching, preaching, and hymn writing. It should come as no surprise, observed Snyder, that at least one-third of the Anabaptist martyrs were women.[58]

The influence of these academic analyses on ordinary Mennonites is difficult to measure. At times, however, the line between the two realms has been quite direct. This was certainly the case in a sermon preached in 2011 at Pilgrims Mennonite Church, a progressive Mennonite congregation in Lancaster County, Pennsylvania. In the sermon, Jean Kilheffer Hess employed the stories of Anabaptist women in *Martyrs Mirror*—stories she had earlier explored in an academic paper—to contest

Fig. 10.1. The 1995 "Quiet in the Land?" conference sold tee shirts, designed by Julie Musselman, that replaced *Martyrs Mirror*'s digging man with a digging woman.

the notion that sixteenth-century Anabaptist women were quiet and submissive.[59] Janneken, Claesken, Kalleken, and many more: all these Anabaptist women raised their voices in settings where women were expected to hold their tongues.[60] This courage to speak up was not unique to the movement's female members, conceded Kilheffer Hess, but their courage was arguably more noteworthy than that of their male counterparts, for they operated in a culture "thick with rules designed to keep women silent." In the face of those obstacles, Anabaptist women martyrs "confess[ed] their faith," "provoke[d] their interrogators," and "trick[ed] questioners into answering *their* questions." For Kilheffer Hess, the implication of the martyrs' example was clear: contemporary Anabaptist women should not be afraid to challenge those who believe that women should speak softly and politely, if at all.[61]

By finding these proto-feminist resources in *Martyrs Mirror,* Kilheffer Hess effectively split the difference between feminist readers who criticized *Martyrs Mirror* as an accomplice to oppression, and tradition-minded readers who rejected the assertion that *Martyrs Mirror* had contemporary significance for gender equality. This difference-splitting left one conservative Mennonite unimpressed. "Van Braght was no feminist," said James Lowry, who insisted that advancing women's status was not high on van Braght's agenda.[62] If we consider only van Braght's authorial intent, Lowry was right, but progressive readers like Kilheffer Hess had no interest in restricting their interpretations to van Braght's centuries-old intentions. For Kilheffer Hess and others like her, the venerable text contained messages for today that van Braght could not have imagined. Moreover, the multilayered text allowed for many interpretations that contradicted traditions that traced long arcs through Anabaptist-Mennonite history.

Of course, to see *Martyrs Mirror* and its readers as cocreators of textual meaning is itself a posture that distinguishes assimilated readers from their tradition-minded counterparts, whose esteem for tradition means pledging allegiance to van Braght's worldview. That many assimilated Mennonites cannot pledge such allegiance does not render *Martyrs Mirror* useless to them, however, for the text's multivalence enables them to draw lessons from a book that they might otherwise find problematic. Not just in scholarly circles, but in homes, churches, and Mennonite schools, assimilated Mennonites continue to enter the interpretive arena to make both sense and use of van Braght's martyrology.

Martyrs Mirror in Assimilated Mennonite Life

Even as Herald Press continues to produce English-language copies of *Martyrs* Mirror—twenty-five hundred copies nearly every year—use of the burly book languishes in assimilated Mennonite communities. This is especially true in the home. Indeed, were we to gauge the importance of *Martyrs Mirror* in assimilated Anabaptist circles by measuring its home-based use, we would have to conclude that the book matters little. Few assimilated Mennonites read the book regularly, and many owners admit that they cannot remember the last time they cracked its covers.[63] Assimilated Anabaptists who can recall reading *Martyrs Mirror* at home usually point to experiences in the relatively distant past.[64] Similarly, references to using the book in family devotions are almost never present-tense references.[65] To be sure, the infrequent use of *Martyrs Mirror* in present-day family devotions may say more about the state of family devotions in assimilated Mennonite homes than it does about the importance of *Martyrs Mirror.* Still, the shelf-book lament expressed by an Amish commentator with respect to *Martyrs Mirror* in Amish homes appears even more fitting for the book's station in assimilated Anabaptist homes.[66]

In assimilated Mennonite churches and schools, the book makes more appearances, often in cameo roles to illustrate a particular point, though at times taking center stage for a few weeks at a time. In some places adult teachers introduce the book to junior high or high school–aged students during Sunday school or other weekly youth gatherings. Many assimilated congregations have a library copy for intrepid teachers to employ, as did one junior high teacher in Denver, Colorado, who showed his students Luyken's etchings of early Christian martyrs and then read aloud the stories of Dirk Willems and Anneken Heyndricks.[67] On occasion an assimilated congregation will take a more thoroughgoing approach. For instance, in 2010 Peace Mennonite Church in Dallas "read, sang and prayed selections" from *Martyrs Mirror* in celebration of All Saints Day. In addition to reflecting on Anna of Rotterdam's letter to her soon-to-be-orphaned son, Peace Mennonite sang a martyr hymn adapted for congregational use, discussed other aspects of the book during the Sunday school hour, and sent members home with a compilation of martyr prayers to pray each day for the next month.[68]

Few assimilated congregations appropriate van Braght's text as fully as Peace Mennonite, though some utilize less demanding means to introduce their congregants, and especially their youth, to the book's themes or stories. Some churches stage reenactments of actual martyr stories. In one case, a Lancaster County Mennonite church, during a weekend retreat to Ocean City, New Jersey, reenacted Dirk Willems's rescue of his pursuer, trading the icy pond water in the original for a body-swallowing sand pit along the Jersey shore.[69] One assimilated Mennonite congregation ventured even further to help its young people imagine the cost of discipleship: the youth leaders packed the church's teens into a crowded basement room to help them experience clandestine worship, and then directed them to play Persecution, a game in which a team of Anabaptist-catchers sought to torture their captives by splattering them with eggs and blanketing them with flour. One young woman who participated in the food-slinging activity admitted it was "ludicrous." Nevertheless, she said, "plenty of Mennonite youth in our area played it without question."[70]

Local Mennonite congregations are not left to their own devices, however. Some draw on educational resources developed by outside parties, many of which assume adolescent audiences. In the Philadelphia area, for instance, some Mennonite churches have featured the work of Cruz Codero, a Mennonite hip-hop artist whose "Onward Martyrdom Rap" calls youth to discipleship "in the hood" by referencing a half dozen Anabaptist martyrs.[71] A more widely used resource over the years has been *The Radicals,* a one-hundred-minute feature film that tells the story of martyr Michael Sattler: his decision to leave the Catholic Church, his marriage to a former nun (their pious romance is a central theme in the film), and his torturous death at the stake in 1527.[72] For churches that want their youth to encounter a wider array of martyrs, MennoMedia's *Adventures with the Anabaptists* offers a ten-lesson introduction to sixteenth-century Anabaptist history for use in Sunday schools.[73] The fifth of the ten lessons, "Blessed Are the Picked On," focuses specifically on those who suffered martyrdom, including Felix Mantz, George Blaurock, and Elizabeth Dirks.[74] Still another martyrological teaching resource employed in assimilated circles is the *Journeys with God* school curriculum, developed in the mid-1990s by the Mennonite Board of Education and the Mennonite Publishing House. Unlike the Sunday school–oriented *Adventures* curriculum, the *Journeys with God* curriculum was designed for use in Mennonite parochial schools, with sixteen lessons for seventh- and eighth-graders devoted to Anabaptist history. Two of the sixteen history lessons give sustained attention to martyr-dom, with *Martyrs Mirror* serving as the primary information source.[75] The second of the two lessons, titled "To Die For," introduces students to seven *Martyrs Mirror* martyrs with the goal of helping students discern why these men and women were willing to die "without regret."[76] In addition, the lesson asks students to consider how they would respond when faced with similarly difficult decisions.

The most prominent themes that emerge in these assimilated educa-tional resources parallel the ones that traditional Anabaptist leaders em-phasize in their employment of *Martyrs Mirror*. Students learn first that the founders of the Anabaptist-Mennonite tradition were persecuted for refusing to forsake their biblically based commitments. Second, students are reminded that, even in contemporary North America, Christians of-ten feel pressure to abandon, or at least downplay, certain aspects of the Christian faith. Third, students are asked to consider whether they, like the sixteenth-century martyrs, possess a faith that is strong enough to withstand worldly pressures.[77] Finally, students are assured that, even as God abided with the Anabaptist martyrs, he continues to abide with peo-ple who suffer on account of their faith.[78] By highlighting these various themes, assimilated Anabaptist educators, like their tradition-minded counterparts, seek to inspire a rising generation to resist the siren call of a sinful world and embrace the faith of their fathers and mothers.

There are some points, however, at which the assimilated approach diverges from the traditional approach, both in pedagogical method and content. The most obvious difference lies in the assimilated curriculum's use of open-ended questions that encourage the students to voice their personal opinions, even views that may contradict their teachers' views. For instance, one question in the *Journeys with God* curriculum asks stu-dents to identify the similarities and differences between the Anabaptist martyrs and contemporary suicide bombers, whereas another asks, "Is it healthy to wish for one's own death?"[79] A related pedagogical strategy in the assimilated Anabaptist curriculum is having students empathize with the martyrs' killers. In fact, one of the two *Journeys with God* lessons assumes this approach throughout. In addition to titling the seven *Mar-tyrs Mirror* excerpts "Executioner Stories," it asks students to imagine life from the killers' perspective (e.g. "How do you think the people felt after they executed the martyrs?" "What did taking part in such killing do to them?").[80] Bringing into focus the question that Oyer and Kreider first raised in their *Mirror of the Martyrs* catalog book, the lesson proceeds to ask students whether the executioners were bad people, or whether they were simply fulfilling duties that they understood to be given by God.[81]

The divergence runs deeper than pedagogical strategies, however, to shed light on the social location of assimilated and traditional Anabaptists. In tradition-minded circles the martyrological lessons for young adults point primarily to nonconformity—that is, to the notion that, even today, Christ's followers will find themselves out of step with the North American mainstream on multiple fronts. This theme does at times appear in the assimilated martyr lessons. For instance, the "Blessed Are the Picked On" lesson refers to Christ's "upside-down approach to life," a synonym for nonconformity that became popular in assimilated Mennonite circles in the last quarter of the twentieth century.[82] Still, the Anabaptist emphasis on nonconformity is muted and largely individualized in the assimilated martyr lessons. In the *Journeys with God* curriculum, for instance, students are asked to complete the sentence "I could see myself making difficult choices because of my belief in . . . ," and the exercise allows for a wide range of answers.[83] The very title of the *Adventures* Sunday school lesson, "Blessed Are the Picked On," echoes this more individualized approach by invoking a common phrase that any adolescent, Christian or not, could identify with. The lesson then gives students the opportunity to write their own faith stories with future Anabaptist readers in mind, prompting them with the expansive question "What kind of Anabaptist were you?"[84]

In one important respect, however, *Martyrs Mirror* continues to be used in assimilated Anabaptist circles to promote social nonconformity: as Anabaptists have done for generations, assimilated Mennonites continue to use *Martyrs Mirror* to reinforce the historic Anabaptist commitment to defenselessness. Of course, assimilated Mennonites are more likely to employ the terms *pacifism, nonviolence,* and *peacemaking* than they are to refer to *defenselessness* or *nonresistance,* but the point remains that some assimilated Mennonites regard the martyrs' practice of forgoing violence as a model for contemporary Mennonites to emulate. Even today, some assimilated Mennonites promote the *Martyrs Mirror* a la Heinrich Funck in the 1740s, suggesting that each Mennonite family "needs a copy of this book" in order to sustain "our call of being peacemakers."[85] In recent years, no one has worked harder at peace education via *Martyrs Mirror* than Gerald and Carrie Mast, who, in 2011, produced a booklet titled *Teaching Peace to Children with the "Martyrs Mirror."*[86] Assembled with the Masts' assimilated Mennonite congregation in mind, the booklet begins by acknowledging that some *Martyrs Mirror* readers have found the book's portrayals of the Anabaptists' persecutors troubling. Without denying that literary reality, the Masts assert that young people's commitments to peace can be strengthened when the content of *Martyrs Mirror* is presented "in a way that is consistent with the vision of its editor: to help readers 'rejoice in the salvation of the Lord.'" As with other youth-oriented curricula in assimilated circles, the Mast's *Teaching Peace* booklet includes open-ended questions and role-playing opportunities for students to engage the text more fully than they might otherwise.[87]

Even on this point of developing peace commitments, however, the assimilated Mennonite approach to *Martyrs Mirror* sometimes parts ways with the approach of tradition-minded Anabaptists. For traditional Anabaptists, the martyrs' peace witness in *Martyrs Mirror* points to traditional nonresistance, which forbids social activism in favor of separatism. For at least some assimilated Mennonites, however, *Martyrs Mirror* sanctions a more assertive approach to the world's ills, a view that echoes the arguments fashioned by Cornelius Krahn and Alan Kreider. For instance, when Dallas's Peace Mennonite Church devoted a Sunday morning to *Martyrs Mirror,* one story that the congregation's members considered was the account of Simon the Shopkeeper, the market vender who refused to bow down to a Communion procession. Simon's death-defying act, wrote one member of the congregation, struck the members of Peace Mennonite as a good model of "nonviolent resistance."[88] To be sure, not every assimilated Mennonite church in North America would draw that conclusion from Simon's example, but Peace Mennonite—which, according to its website, is a community "rooted in the principles of peacemaking, loving our enemies, [and] speaking out against injustice"—surely did.[89] In fact, reading Simon's example in this manner aligned with the congregation's prophetic undertaking two weeks later, when it participated in a service of lament at the dedication of the George W. Bush Presidential Library at Southern Methodist University. The goal of the interfaith lament, wrote the congregation's correspon-

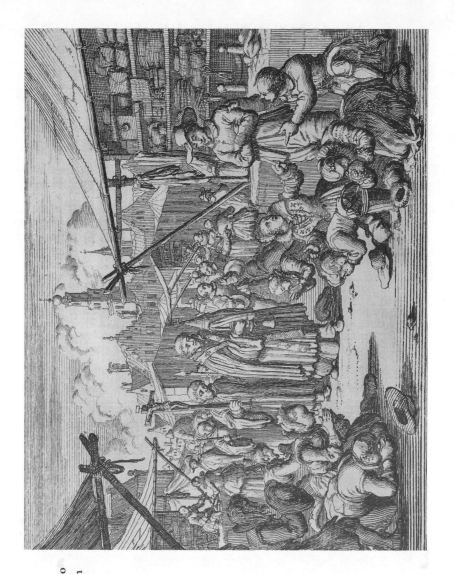

Fig. 10.2. Some assimilated Mennonites have interpreted Simon the Shopkeeper's refusal to bow to a Communion procession as an example of nonviolent resistance.

dent, was to "remember the atrocities of war and violence that took place under the Bush administration . . . which all of us were complicit in allowing."[90]

The correspondent's report, which concedes that a Mennonite congregation committed to peace is complicit in its nation's war-making, endorses the point that Melvin Goering made so forcefully twenty years earlier: that good and evil are not dualistically situated in the world but are rather comingled within each and every person.[91] For Goering, van Braght's fatal flaw as a martyrologist was his tendency to carve up the world too neatly, good on one side and evil on the other. As Peace Mennonite's example suggests, however, many assimilated Mennonites, even those who find the world more morally ambiguous than van Braght ever did, continue to find *Martyrs Mirror* useful to them. Their one-armed embrace is an embrace nonetheless.

Finding Meaning in a Multivalent Text

Exceptions to the shelf-book existence of *Martyrs Mirror* in assimilated Mennonite homes are rare, but they do exist. Some of these exceptions involve emerging adults who devote themselves to reading *Martyrs Mirror,* often in an effort to make sense of the religious tradition into which they were born. Significantly, these emerging adult readers sometimes find themselves reading against the text, questioning van Braght's assumptions about the Christian faith or about Christian history. One young adult reader acknowledged that, during a break from college, she threw herself into "Anabaptist research mode" and read *Martyrs Mirror* from cover to cover. Although she found herself inspired by the martyrs' steadfastness, she couldn't help but wonder if she agreed with van Braght's thesis "that there is a constant, traceable line of 'anabaptist' martyrs from the early church up to the time of the writing of the *Martyrs Mirror.*"[92] Another emerging adult reader wondered if the martyrs' eagerness to die had less to do with martyrs' temperament than with the storytellers' "poetic license." This same reader admitted that he was both surprised and put off by van Braght's inclusion of adult baptism as a criterion for true martyrdom, adding that, in his view, placing such a high priority on baptismal practice was "silly."[93]

Questioning the importance of adult baptism did not render *Martyrs*

Mirror meaningless to this reader, however, for despite his theological disquiet, he found power in the blood of his ethnic ancestors. Even when sitting on the shelf, he said, *Martyrs Mirror* functioned for him as a powerful "Mennonite relic," representing an ethnically rooted faith that, to his chagrin, his parents had forsaken.[94] Few contemporary Mennonites use the word *relic* in reference to *Martyrs Mirror,* but many are pleased to claim genealogical connections to people in the book. "My sixth or seventh great-grandfather is listed in it," wrote one young man. "He was branded on the forehead with a hot iron, . . . imprisoned for two years, [and] banished from the Canton of Bern."[95] An older woman made a similar claim: "My last name was Hess," she wrote, adding that her family lineage traces "a direct line to the Hans Jacob Hess and his wife Anna Egli of *Martyrs Mirror.*"[96] For these ancestry-minded Mennonites, discovering that the martyrs' blood courses through their veins enabled them to participate in a faithfulness that exceeded their own. Few statements reveal this sense of genetic participation more poignantly than the response of a Mennonite mother to her daughter who had inquired about their family's past. "We're mentioned in *Martyrs Mirror,*" the mother told her daughter, plainly implying that *we* meant an entire ancestral line. It was a statement, the daughter said, that her Mennonite father, a first-generation convert to Mennonitism, could not make.[97]

In some assimilated Mennonite families and churches, these genealogical connections to the book exhaust its relevance. As we have seen, however, some assimilated congregations continue to employ the book and its themes to shape people's spiritual imaginations. Recall the young woman whose Mennonite youth leaders organized the food-splattering simulation they called Persecution.[98] That her youth leaders had compelled her to play a ludicrous game—ludicrous in the sense that it turned an awful reality into a fun-filled activity for privileged American teenagers—did not dim this young woman's appreciation for what the leaders were trying to accomplish. While admitting that it was difficult to identify with the kind of suffering the martyrs experienced, the martyr stories she heard along the way shaped her to believe that true faith entailed sacrifice. "Following Jesus . . . has traditionally set Anabaptists and Mennonites at odds with our neighbors," she wrote, and this willingness to "be radical" was something that she wanted to claim for herself. This, of course, was a different lesson from the one Stephanie Krehbiel felt was thrust upon her as a teenager, a lesson that, in Krehbiel's view, pointed mostly toward death. For this other young woman, it was not the martyrs' deaths that made them radical, but the way they lived. "As followers of Jesus we are not called to suffer," she said. Rather, Jesus calls his followers "to live in a way that does not fear suffering," a way that "accepts [suffering] when it comes and rejoices when it does not."[99]

Of course, all human beings suffer, not just Christians and certainly not just Mennonites. Still, as this young woman reflected further on the possibility of suffering in twenty-first-century America, she landed upon a more specific element of her faith that threatened her easy existence, the Anabaptist commitment to nonviolence. "To put away the sword" is often seen as "crazy" in twenty-first-century America, she said, and it often invites scorn. Still, if the martyrs could reject the sword in their circumstances, so could she.[100] In that regard, this twenty-first-century Mennonite teenager—a young woman who played on her high school soccer team, dressed like other American teenagers, and worried about what her non-Mennonite friends thought of her—found in *Martyrs Mirror* exactly what the eighteenth-century Skippack Mennonites hoped their children would find in the book: resources to buttress their countercultural commitment to nonviolence.

The degree to which *Martyrs Mirror* functions in assimilated Mennonite settings as a resource to nourish nonviolence is difficult to determine. On the one hand, many assimilated Mennonites take pride in knowing that, unlike other late-medieval Christians, the Anabaptists refused to persecute their enemies. For them, *Martyrs Mirror* lays bare the reality that killing on behalf of one's religious convictions is both heinous and futile. On the other hand, when it comes to the more specific martyr accounts in the book, some assimilated Mennonites find the martyrs too passive, too otherworldly, in their approach to the evil that fills the world. These skeptics may be impressed by the martyrs' steadfastness, but the martyrs do not strike them as meaningful models for living in the present. In their estimation, the martyrs take this world, and the possibility of making this world a better place, too lightly.

There is, of course, one martyr who represents this-worldly agency in a way that the other martyrs do not: Dirk Willems, the Dutchman who dashed across the ice, the fugitive-turned-rescue worker, the Anabaptist martyr par excellence.

CHAPTER 11

The Most Usable Martyr

Putting Dirk Willems to Work

Just east of Lancaster, Pennsylvania, nestled among the strip malls and fast-food restaurants that dominate Route 30, sits Lancaster Mennonite High School (LMH). Founded in 1942 by Lancaster Mennonite Conference as a way to safeguard Mennonite youth from a "pleasure loving world," the school now boasts 650 students in grades nine through twelve.[1] At the time of its founding, LMH displayed many signs of Mennonite sectarianism, including strict dress requirements, daily chapel with a cappella singing, and a faculty roster filled with ethnic Mennonite names such as Graybill, Lehman, and Wenger. Today many of those signs have disappeared. Two-thirds of the LMH students now come from non-Mennonite homes, including a sizable contingent of international students in search of a college preparatory education. Even so, LMH continues to take its Mennonite heritage seriously. The word *Mennonite* appears often in the school's identity statements, Bible-related courses are a required part of the curriculum, and students learn about Anabaptist and Mennonite history in a variety of ways.[2] Some students may not be very interested in Anabaptism, or even Christianity in general, but none can escape the fact that they attend a Mennonite school.[3]

Since the late 1980s, LMH students have been reminded of the school's Anabaptist identity through a striking visual image located in a student gathering area: a detailed and colorful wood carving based on a Jan Luyken etching from the 1685 edition of *Martyrs Mirror*. This carving, by Amish craftsman Aaron Zook, depicts the Dutch Anabaptist martyr Dirk Willems extending his arms toward a drowning man. According to the account in *Martyrs Mirror*, the drowning man was an Anabaptist-catcher who, in his pursuit of Dirk, chased him across an icy expanse.[4] As the story goes, Dirk made it safely across, but the Anabaptist-catcher did not, breaking through the brittle ice. Rather than let his pursuer drown, Dirk turned back and pulled him to safety.[5] For nearly thirty years, LMH students have seen this image as they change classes, hurry to lunch, and confab before the school day. Although they rarely stop to consider it, the image is familiar to them, and many would know the broad outlines of the story from a chapel talk or a religion class. Some students have found Dirk's example inspiring, or at least worth pondering. Along with photographs of social events, special-interest clubs, and athletic teams, Dirk's image occasionally makes its way onto student social media sites or into the LMH yearbook.[6]

The rise of Dirk as a prominent symbol in North American Anabaptist life is inversely correlated with knowledge of the book as a whole. Although most Anabaptists in contemporary North America have heard of *Martyrs Mirror*, few are intimately acquainted with its contents. When asked to identify names of particular martyrs, some Amish and Mennonite respondents draw complete blanks, and many others can identify only a few. Even in very traditional Amish communities, only a handful of people know more than a smattering of names and stories. To be sure, not everyone who is acquainted with Dirk's experience or Luyken's etching of him can remember his name, nor can everyone recount his story in precise detail. In some cases, people assign him the wrong name or describe him as "the guy who fell through the ice" when, in fact, Dirk remained atop the ice. Still, in contrast to the vast majority of martyrs whose stories fill *Martyrs Mirror*, Dirk and his experiences are well known and frequently cited in many twenty-first-century Anabaptist communities.

This was not always the case. References to Dirk outside of *Martyrs Mirror* are practically nonexistent in nineteenth- and early-twentieth-century Anabaptist sources. In fact, in the nineteenth century, Dirk seems to have captured the fancy of non-Anabaptist Christians more than that of his theological kin. Only as the twentieth century ran its course did Dirk and his iconic image gain ascendance in the Anabaptist world. By 1990 the curators of the *Mirror of the Martyrs* exhibit could claim with confidence that "no story of an Anabaptist martyr has captured the imagination more than the tale of Dirk Willems."[7] This chapter charts that ascendance, probes the reasons for it, and elucidates Dirk's significance in North American Anabaptist life. More than any other martyr—in fact, more than any other facet of *Martyrs Mirror*—Dirk forces contemporary Anabaptists to fathom the essence of their faith.

Memorializing Dirk: The Story and the Illustration

The account of Dirk Willems's martyrdom first appeared in Pieter Jans Twisck's *History of the True Witnesses of Jesus Christ,* published in Hoorn in 1617.[8] Twisck's account, which made its way into *The Bloody Theater* forty-three years later, included two different texts that memorialized Dirk's experience: a sympathetic narrative of Dirk's capture and death, and the transcription of a legal document that summarized Dirk's crimes and sentence.[9] According to the legal document, Dirk committed a variety of offenses: he had been rebaptized, he participated in secret gatherings, and he espoused heretical doctrines, all of which were "contrary to our holy Christian faith, and to the decrees of his royal majesty." As punishment for his crimes, but also as a deterrent to others, the Asperen authorities sentenced Dirk to be burned at the stake. The sympathetic narrative confirms that this sentence was carried out, though according to a second account added later, things did not go according to plan.[10] At Dirk's execution, a strong east wind blew the flames away from his upper body, which caused him to die a lingering death. As he slowly but surely roasted, Dirk cried out "O my Lord, my God" over seventy times, his voice carrying to the nearby town of Leerdam. So intense was Dirk's agony that the official in charge turned away in horror, ordering the executioner to expedite Dirk's death. "How or in what manner the executioner then dealt with this pious witness of Jesus Christ, I have not been able to learn," writes this second narrator, though he did know this much: Dirk "passed through the conflict with great steadfastness, having commended his soul into the hands of God."[11]

Dirk's comportment in his final moments recalls the crucifixion of Christ, who similarly cried out to God before committing his spirit into God's hands.[12] Still, more than Dirk's bearing in death, Dirk's conduct at the time of his capture—compromising his safety to save his pursuer's life—made him an Anabaptist martyr without compare. Grateful that Dirk had saved his life, the Anabaptist-catcher wished to release him, but a town official instructed the rescued man to honor his oath of duty, whereupon he arrested Dirk and handed him over to the authorities. The initial narrative proceeds to its conclusion with an anti-Catholic polemic that contrasts Dirk's faithfulness with the depravity of those responsible for his death: "After severe imprisonment and great trials proceeding from the deceitful papists, [Dirk was] put to death at a lingering fire by these bloodthirsty, ravening wolves, enduring it with great steadfastness, and confirming the genuine faith of the truth with his death and blood, as an instructive example to all pious Christians of this time, and to the everlasting disgrace of the tyrannous papists."[13]

That the narrator identifies an Anabaptist martyr as an example to others is not uncommon in *Martyrs Mirror*. What is uncommon is the way the artist Jan Luyken memorialized Dirk's experience. As we saw in chapter 5, all but four of Luyken's 104 images depicted martyrs in one of the five stages of martyrdom: capture, separation, inquisition, torture, or death. Not only does the image of Dirk depart from that pattern, but it is the only Luyken image that depicts an Anabaptist martyr in a position of bodily power over the person's adversary. While the image depicts human suffering, the suffering person is not the Anabaptist but the Anabaptist's enemy. Although the narrative does not detail the mechanics of the rescue, Luyken portrays Dirk in a forward-leaning crouch, extending his arms downward, with both hands open wide. It is more likely, of course, that Dirk would have lain down to distribute his weight across the ice, perhaps lengthening his reach with a branch or reed. In Luyken's depiction, however, Dirk assumes an upright position above the flailing man, with a posture that condescends in full-bodied love.

Along with the water rescue itself, Luyken's etching included another element of the narrative: the presence of the burgomaster who ordered the rescued man to arrest his Anabaptist helper. In Luyken's depiction, three observers stand along the bank, two engaged in close conversation and a third a short distance away. One man points at the scene, another throws up his hands, and all three appear baffled or disturbed. Are they frustrated with the Anabaptist-catcher? Are they worried that the two men may drown? Or are they unsettled by Dirk's act of Christlike love?

Fig. 11.1. Jan Luyken's image of Dirk Willems, which first appeared in
Martyrs Mirror in 1685.

We do not know what Luyken had in mind in this regard, and different
viewers have interpreted this secondary scene variously.[14] What cannot
be missed in Luyken's etching, however, is his suggestion that Dirk was
willing to do for his enemy what the town officials were unwilling to do
for their friend, namely, put themselves at risk to save his life.

In that way, Luyken gives visual expression to the dualistic conclusion
offered by the story's narrator. In Luyken's depiction of the scene, viewers
see a man of "genuine faith" who was willing to die rather than abandon
his convictions. More than just holding fast to his beliefs, Dirk incarnated a particular set of convictions that corresponded to the self-giving
love of Jesus Christ. Dirk could thus serve as an "instructive example"
to all people who considered themselves Christians, an example that is
all the more impressive when set beside the actions of those who stood
along the bank. Like Dirk, these men held a particular set of theological

convictions, but their convictions compelled them to do nothing when their underling fell into the icy water. These men, who would rather have their lackey drown than risk their lives to save him, are the same men who wanted Dirk dead. By their shameful actions they represent "the everlasting disgrace of the tyrannous papists," who had made life miserable for the early Anabaptists and who, in 1685, continued to get things wrong. Their presence in Luyken's sketch was neither an afterthought nor an accident.[15] It was part and parcel of the pro-Anabaptist, anti–state church story that Luyken wished to illustrate.

Luyken's etchings made their way into some later editions of *Martyrs Mirror*, but not all of them. Except for the Pirmasens edition, published in 1780, no new edition of *Martyrs Mirror* included the Luyken images for two hundred years, until John F. Funk's Mennonite Publishing Company produced an English edition in 1886 that included 36 of Luyken's 104 images in a proximate form. Reengraved by American artists, this set of knockoff images included the Dirk Willems image with all of its primary features.[16] Fifty-two years later, in 1938, the Mennonite Publishing House produced yet another edition of *Martyrs Mirror*. For this edition the Mennonite Publishing House used a photoengraving process to produce precise facsimiles of Luyken's originals, once again including the Dirk Willems image among the fifty-five images it incorporated into the text. Today, more than seventy-five years later, this English edition continues in print in much the same form, with the same text, the same pagination, and the same fifty-five illustrations as the 1938 edition. As he did in 1938, Dirk continues to perform his intrepid act of service on page 741.

By 1990 Luyken's image of Dirk's rescue had also made its way into *Märtyrer-Spiegel*, the German-language edition of *Martyrs Mirror* published by the Old Order Amish–run Pathway Publishers. Before that time no German-language editions, save the 1780 Pirmasens edition, had included any of Luyken's images, in part because of concerns that tradition-minded Anabaptists would not abide them. However, in the process of producing its fourth edition of *Märtyrer-Spiegel*, Pathway editor David Luthy got the idea of replacing the digging-man device on the book's first title page with a minimized version of Luyken's image of Dirk. In a letter to Pathway senior editor Joseph Stoll, Luthy suggested that Dirk "is such a hero of our faith . . . that it would seem proper to

Fig. 11.2. Knockoff etching of Dirk Williams that appeared in the Mennonite
Publishing Company's edition of *Martyrs Mirror* (1886).

honor him this way."[17] Six years later, in 1996, Luthy reverted to using the
digging-man device on the work's first title page because of its historical
significance. At the same time he chose to include a larger reproduction
of the Luyken image on the title page that launches part 2.[18]

Including the Dirk Willems image in *Märtyrer-Spiegel* was not without risks, though Pathway's officials were rightly confident that its inclusion would not compromise sales. Of course, they did not choose just any
Luyken image to add to their title page; they chose a particular image,
one that by 1990 had become well known in North American Anabaptist
communities across the traditional-to-assimilated spectrum. How and
why that particular image gained prominence above all other Luyken
images, a prominence that did not exist before 1940, is the question to
which we now turn.

Resuscitating Dirk: The Seeds of Dirk's Emergence

Dirk's appearance in the 1938 English edition of *Martyrs Mirror* presaged his emergence as the most significant Anabaptist icon of the twentieth century. Granted, Dirk's "noble deed" had not gone unnoticed during the previous two centuries, even among non-Anabaptists.[19] In 1819 Dutch poet Hendrik Tollens elaborated the story of Dirk's rescue with dubious details, praised Dirk for his heroism, and condemned the authorities who killed him.[20] Six decades later, in 1879 and 1885, two British writers, including the Anglican bishop William Boyd Carpenter, likewise feted Dirk's actions in verse.[21] Carpenter first described Dirk's deeds in flowery language:

> He reached out his arms o'er the fatal gulf
> With laboring movement slow
> He hung o'er the crumbling chasm
> And drew forth his drowning foe!

and then followed Dirk to his execution site, where he confirmed Dirk's heavenly reward and assured readers that all who followed Dirk's example would receive the same reward.[22] These poetic tributes, along with an assortment of prose retellings of the story, some in Britain and some in the United States, prove that Dirk's spiritual impact extended far beyond the Anabaptist orbit in the nineteenth century.[23] Nonetheless, it was not until the mid-twentieth century that the story, hitched tightly to Luyken's depiction of it, began to surpass all the other martyr stories in the moral imagination of North American Anabaptists.[24]

Gaining that prominence required the pictorial Dirk to slip outside the covers of *Martyrs Mirror*. Before 1938 only a few visual depictions of Dirk's heroism had appeared in other venues, and mostly in venues intended for non-Anabaptist audiences. For instance, when Tollens's poem appeared in 1819, it was accompanied by an image of Dirk rescuing his pursuer from an icy moat, an image that bears almost no resemblance to Luyken's original. In 1879, when the London publication *The Sunday at Home* published a second poem, it too included a rescue image that bore little resemblance to Luyken's etching.[25] These images would not have been seen by more than a few North American Anabaptists. Moreover,

Fig. 11.3. Depiction of Dirk Willems that appeared in the Dutch publication
Nederlandsche Muzen-Almanak (1819).

most North American Anabaptists who owned copies of *Martyrs Mirror* at this time would have owned copies devoid of Luyken's imagery. In 1886 and again in 1938, when the Mennonite Publishing Company and later the Mennonite Publishing House released new English editions of *Martyrs Mirror,* Luyken's image of Dirk (or a close approximation of it) became more broadly available to North American Anabaptists, but even then only to those who had access to these new editions.

Shortly after 1938, however, Luyken's image of Dirk began to surface in other Mennonite Publishing House media, allowing Mennonite and Amish readers to encounter the noble Dirk without cracking the covers of *Martyrs Mirror*. John C. Wenger's *Glimpses of Mennonite History* launched this trend in 1940, featuring Luyken's image of Dirk in a full-page spread and explaining it with the caption "Dirk Willems, a Dutch Mennonite, Saves His Captor's Life, 1569."[26] Two years later, in 1942, John Horsch's *Mennonites in Europe* included the Luyken image in a small pictorial insert, using the same caption that Wenger had used.[27] The following year Dirk migrated from Scottdale's bookshelf to its periodical rack, appearing on the front page of a weekly Sunday school leaflet; and six years later, in 1949, he appeared on the front page of the publishing house's youth-oriented weekly, *Youth's Christian Companion*.[28] By 1950, the enemy-loving Dirk had been conscripted by Mennonite Publishing House's marketing staff to help sell copies of *Martyrs Mirror*, with his image featured in a *Mennonite Community* advertisement and also in a four-page mailer.[29] The mailer contained four photographs of the hefty book, but Dirk's image was the only Luyken image to appear. In fact, one of the flyer's four pages consisted entirely of page 741 in *Martyrs Mirror*, the page that features Dirk's image above his capture narrative. By 1950, then, the iconic die had been cast. Little known in 1938, Dirk had become by 1950 the Mennonite Church's paradigmatic martyr, the one who stood in for the "more than 4,011 people burned at the stake" who filled the renowned martyr book.[30]

Dirk's iconic ascension was, in part, the result of advancing technology. Photoengraved plates were not difficult to make, nor were they expensive to use. Moreover, they could be reused in multiple contexts, not only in books but in high-volume periodicals and flyers. For instance, the Willems plate that was made for *Martyrs Mirror* in 1938 was used again five years later, in Horsch's *Mennonites in Europe;* and the plate that was made for Wenger's *Glimpses of Mennonite History* was used again in *Words of Cheer* (1943) and then again in the *Mennonite Community* advertisement (1950).[31] Still, the fact that Dirk's plate was the one that was fashioned and reused the most by the Mennonite Publishing House begs the question, Why Dirk? What was it about Dirk, as opposed to another Anabaptist martyr, that captured the imagination of mid-twentieth-century Mennonite Church leaders who oversaw these publications?

The answer to the question, "Why Dirk?" lies in the image's uniqueness. Not only is it the one Luyken image in which the Anabaptist possesses bodily power over the adversary; it is also the one image in which an Anabaptist performs an act of service for the sake of the larger world. Suffering and martyrdom are important aspects of Dirk's story, but in contrast to the vast majority of plates that Luyken etched for *Martyrs Mirror*, Anabaptist suffering is not apparent in his depiction of Dirk, which focuses instead on Dirk's compassionate response to a person in need. In Luyken's portrayal of the Willems account, Dirk is less a martyr than he is a humanitarian, demonstrating Christlike love in a costly way. This, of course, explains how Dirk could be so easily appropriated by non-Anabaptist commentators who may have been cool toward Anabaptist theology but could nonetheless appreciate Dirk's virtuous act. In fact, for some of these non-Anabaptist commentators, Dirk's martyrdom seems to have been quite beside the point: when a contributor to a British Sunday school journal summarized the Dirk story in two paragraphs, he concluded by noting that Dirk and his pursuer "reached a place of safety together," with no mention of what happened next.[32] Mid-twentieth-century Mennonite commentators were less likely to elide Dirk's death, but they too placed the emphasis on what he did, rather than on what was done to him. In Horsch's *Mennonites in Europe,* the main caption under Luyken's image reads, "Dirk Willems, a Dutch Mennonite, Saves His Captor's Life, 1569," with the words "Willems was later burned at the stake" appearing lower on the page, in a much smaller font.[33] In the *Mennonite Community* advertisement, which includes the Luyken image without a caption, Dirk is feted in the accompanying narrative less as a martyr than as a person who demonstrated through his rescue that "the Christian life is one of supreme discipleship."[34] In sum, Dirk's renaissance in mid-twentieth-century Mennonite life had less to do with available print technologies than with the spiritual trope he symbolized so well: discipleship as service to the needy.

The importance of serving others, including persons outside of one's own church community, was not new to North American Mennonites in the 1940s, though it assumed added weight in the context of World War II. Two decades earlier, during World War I, North American Anabaptists had experienced significant adversity as a result of their pacifist convictions, in part because the U.S. and Canadian governments had not made clear provisions for conscientious objection to war. In the United States, for instance, Amish, Mennonite, and Hutterite draftees were assured that their pacifist convictions would be respected if, as required by law, they reported to military camps. Once there, however, some draft-ees were ordered to perform activities their consciences could not abide, such as wearing military uniforms. When they defied these orders, some objectors were beaten, others were given lengthy prison sentences, and still others were threatened with execution. In many ways, the treatment of Anabaptist conscientious objectors (COs) during World War I paral-leled the persecution Anabaptists had faced in early modern Europe. Although only a few COs died in government custody, many feared that they would not return home alive.[35] It is hardly surprising that, dur-ing these years, contributors to the Mennonite periodical *Gospel Herald* compared the plight of contemporary Anabaptists to the experiences of the martyrs. "Most people imagined that the day of religious perse-cutions belongs to the darker ages of the past," wrote one contributor in 1919, but "the past year has witnessed scenes that rival those of the Spanish Inquisition."[36] In the midst of such circumstances, it was easy to conceive of martyrdom, or at least bodily suffering, as the truest sign of Christian discipleship.[37]

By the end of World War II, however, things had changed. As World War II loomed, Mennonite church leaders in both the United States and Canada undertook efforts to advance the authorities' understanding of their nonresistant convictions. In addition to explaining the religious bases of their views, these leaders sought to convince government of-ficials that meaningful accommodations could be made for men who objected to military service. A key pillar of their argument was that COs could perform critical work in the civilian realm. COs did not want to shirk their civic responsibilities, they argued; they simply wished to ful-fill those responsibilities in ways that comported with their pacifist con-victions. In the end, these arguments proved successful. In 1940 the U.S. Congress authorized the creation of the Civilian Public Service (CPS) program, enabling conscientious objectors to perform "work of national importance" in nonmilitary contexts.[38] As the program ran its course, thousands of COs spent time in CPS camps, performing work in soil conservation, forestry maintenance, agricultural research, and health care. The Canadian government made similar provisions for Canadian COs, who also did various kinds of work to advance the public good.[39]

Alternate service assignments were hard on the participants and painful to their families, but they could hardly be construed as martyrdom. In fact, participants often complained that the work they were doing was both tedious and mundane. Over time the U.S. government added riskier endeavors to the CPS docket, including firefighting in national parks and serving as human guinea pigs in medical research. For young Anabaptist males, whose patriotic peers were risking life and limb on far-flung battlefields, engaging in these more hazardous activities assured them that conscientious objection was not a cowardly response to war.[40] Of course, it also connected them to the lives of the Anabaptist martyrs. Nonetheless, even the riskiest CPS assignments fell far short of the risks Anabaptists had faced during World War I, let alone the hazards of the sixteenth century.

In this more tolerant context, Luyken's image of Dirk held great potential, for it underscored a conception of discipleship—service to others— that was more relevant than martyrdom to midcentury North American Mennonites. Like the more venerable martyr motif, this service motif had a sharp edge, for service a la Dirk required both courage and conviction. More than martyrdom, however, service reflected an activist approach that midcentury Mennonites were increasingly wont to take. Dirk may have been a martyr, but the Luyken etching made it abundantly clear that he was not a passive victim, ensconced in a separatist community, waiting for persecution to find him. Like the CPS workers of the 1940s, and like an increasing number of midcentury Mennonites, Dirk put his faith into action, sacrificing his well-being to help a vulnerable person and make the world a better place. That the vulnerable person was also Dirk's enemy made Dirk all the more appealing—and uniquely useful—to North American Anabaptists in the decades ahead.

Canonizing Dirk: The Pan-Anabaptist Symbol

The North American Anabaptists who cultivated Dirk's emergence in the 1940s were members of the (Old) Mennonite Church. At this point in its history, the Mennonite Church was beginning to slough off its separatist past and, in the manner of its General Conference counterpart, was fast becoming a socially assimilated denomination. As we saw in chapter 8, this more engaged orientation correlated with a changing social ethic, one that placed an increasing emphasis on the Christian's responsibility to the larger world. Although the word *responsibility* appeared only once

Fig. 11.4. This group of Civilian Public Service smokejumpers, stationed in Montana in 1945, consisted primarily of Mennonite conscientious objectors.
Courtesy of the National Smokejumper Association.

in the 1950 inter-Mennonite peace conference summary statement (the word was likely seen as too beholden to the nonpacifist ethic of Reinhold Niebuhr),[41] the statement's rhetorical approach, which prioritized *love* and *service* over *nonresistance,* should not be underestimated.[42] In this more socially engaged climate, the loving servant Dirk proved very useful indeed.

In the century's third quarter, assimilated Mennonites of various stripes led the way in putting Dirk's image or his story, or both, into circulation, typically in popular formats intended for children, young adults, or families. Story collections that could be read at home, elementary and Sunday school materials, and family-oriented periodicals were the primary media in which Dirk appeared.[43] In some cases, the story or image was modified for contemporary relevance or to make a clearer point. For instance, in 1954 the Lancaster Mennonite Conference produced a third-grade reader entitled *Happy Life Stories* that summarized the Dirk story under the title, "The Man Who Saved His Enemy." Significantly, a modified image of Dirk accompanied this particular summary: stretched out across the ice, Dirk, now shorn of his beard, would have looked more Mennonite than Amish to the Mennonite children who read the book.[44] In a different sort of modification, the Mennonite Church periodical *Christian Living* elaborated Dirk's life in a story "based on the true account in *Martyrs Mirror*." In this iteration of the story, published in 1971 and illustrated with a detailed approximation of the Luyken image, Dirk is denounced by his neighbors who learn of his Anabaptist commitments. However, when flooding threatens their low-lying town, they welcome Dirk's help in stacking sandbags. In other words, much like CPS workers during World War II and their successors in the Vietnam War, Dirk's convictions made him suspect, but he ultimately proved himself a caring friend and a loyal citizen.[45]

This emphasis on self-sacrificial service was one that tradition-minded Anabaptists could embrace as well. For a variety of reasons, including the absence of Luyken's images in *Märtyrer-Spiegel*, the Old Order Amish were two decades slower than their change-minded counterparts to fix upon Dirk as a martyr of special note. Whereas John C. Wenger's *Glimpses of Mennonite History* had featured the pictorial Dirk as early as 1940, Dirk's first appearance in an Amish-produced text came in 1963, in Noah Zook's ecclesial history *Seeking a Better Country*.[46] Even then, Zook did not tell Dirk's story or underscore his significance. He included only the Luyken image, which he lifted along with other images from John Horsch's *Mennonites in Europe* (1942). In this first Amish use of Dirk, Dirk's appearance seems mostly derivative, a product of mining Horsch's more detailed history for good raw material.[47]

Dirk's ascent in the Amish world began shortly thereafter, however, empowered in the late 1960s by the editorial staff at Pathway Publishers. In the wake of publishing the entire *Märtyrer-Spiegel* in 1967, Pathway began disseminating smaller segments of van Braght's text in popular forms, and in the process Dirk began to gain status among the martyrs. Joseph Stoll's story collection *The Drummer's Wife* (1968) facilitated this rise by using Elmo Stoll's story, "Dirk Willems and the Thief-Catcher," complete with the Luyken image, as its culminating entry.[48] The anthol-

Fig. 11.5. Depiction of Dirk Willems, now shorn of his beard, that appeared in the
Lancaster Mennonite Conference publication *Happy Life Stories* (1954).

ogy sold well, but perhaps more significant for the long haul was the
inclusion of Stoll's thief-catcher story in Pathway's eighth-grade reader
Our Heritage.[49] Compiled with Amish school children in mind, *Our Heritage* has sold nearly fifty thousand copies since its first printing in 1968,
though its readership surely outpaces its sales numbers.[50] In his imaginative retelling, Stoll portrays Dirk as wrestling hard with the decision
to save his pursuer before concluding that saving his foe from damnation was more important than avoiding his own demise. Stoll closes his
story by quoting Jesus—"Greater love hath no man than this, that a man
lay down his life for his friends"[51]—thus bridging the gap between the
divine Jesus and the godly Dirk. To ensure that students would absorb
the right message, Pathway's editors appended questions and a hymn
for further reflection. "Why did Dirk not run away when he saw the

thief-catcher break through the ice?" asks one question, alluding to the story's claim that "something [conscience] held him back."[52] The venerable hymn "Faith of Our Fathers" follows the reflection questions. Stanza three of the hymn declares,

> We will love
> Both friend and foe in all our strife,

a vow that underscores Dirk's love for his enemy. All three stanzas conclude with a hearty pledge:

> Faith of our fathers! Holy faith!
> We will be true to thee till death![53]

In addition to its wide circulation, two things make this particular use of the Dirk narrative significant, especially as it pertains to Amish life in the 1960s. First, the Amish publishers do not shy away from the story's martyrological elements. As in *Martyrs Mirror* itself, the story of Dirk as told in *Our Heritage* is not simply a story about showing compassion toward another human being; it is also a story about the trauma one will suffer when living out the Christian faith. The editors at Pathway believed that eighth-graders were old enough to hear that message, ponder its implications for the present, and begin to embrace their ancestors' faith despite potential hardships. The second noteworthy element of the *Our Heritage* piece is the absence of Luyken's etching. Whereas *The Drummer's Wife* had included the image with Stoll's story, the image did not make its way into *Our Heritage*. Of course, illustrations of all types are few and far between in *Our Heritage*, which, as a reader for older children, was never intended to be a richly illustrated text. Nonetheless, it is clear that Pathway's editors did not feel obliged to include the Luyken etching. At this point in time, it was seen as an optional touch, even when telling the story to grade-school students.

In the course of the next three decades, however, the imagistic Dirk assumed preeminence over the textual Dirk in nearly every realm of North American Anabaptist life. With the increased affordability of photocopying and print-on-demand services, bolstered by the advent of desktop publishing, Dirk's image became easier than ever to reproduce and circulate. Correspondingly, Anabaptist culture-makers realized that their Anabaptist audiences, even Old Order ones, were becoming more and more attuned to visual imagery. This potent combination—the ease of production and perceived audience desires—resulted in a surge of duplicated Dirks across the Anabaptist spectrum.[54] For instance, just sixteen years after Pathway published *Our Heritage* sans the Luyken image, an Ohio Beachy Amish man commissioned an oil painting of Luyken's image, then printed a thousand copies for display in Amish and Mennonite school classrooms.[55] Rod and Staff Publishers, run by an association of conservative Mennonites, assumed publication of John Horsch's *Mennonites in Europe* and in the process transplanted Dirk's image from an internal location to the book's front cover.[56] By 2001 Dirk had become such a recognizable figure in assimilated Mennonite circles that Herald Press could employ him in a waggish way to market its products: on a banner displayed at the Mennonite Church's biennial assembly, the publisher depicted Dirk extending a stack of books to a modern teenager flailing in icy waters.[57]

Dirk's rising renown in North American Anabaptist life owes to the explosion of print sources, but it also owes to the image itself. On one level, Luyken's image of Dirk was appealing to those who employed it because it could speak for itself. Even a child could decode the picture's basic storyline: an able person assisting a helpless person. No Anabaptist, regardless of church affiliation, could find this primary narrative problematic. To the contrary, all could affirm it as a key corollary to the gospel. Moreover, given that Luyken's etching of Dirk does not foreground persecution or martyrdom, it was an image that parents could share with their children without prompting difficult questions, let alone spawning bad dreams. In sum, the Luyken image was usable because it conveyed a clear message in a family-friendly and relatively tame way.

But in addition to speaking for itself, Luyken's image was widely employed because it did not say too much. As with other broadly usable symbols, the original Luyken image retained a degree of ambiguity, thereby allowing its replicators and its viewers to award it more specific meanings as they saw fit. In many instances, and particularly in more tradition-minded segments of Anabaptist life, the image was used as a symbol of nonresistance—the willingness to forgo violence in the face of a bodily threat—as, for instance, on the cover of C. D. Wenger's booklet *Why I Am a Conscientious Objector.*[58] In other cases, the Luyken image stood in for something more than just forgoing violence; it was deemed to represent the more activist and more broadly applicable ethic of demonstrating compassion to one's enemy.[59] Still other Anabaptists broadened the message even more, suggesting that Dirk represented the virtue of showing compassion to anyone whose needs present an opportunity for service. "There is always the choice of going away to safety, of leaving the troubled scene and blending in with the scenery," said one assimilated Mennonite pastor in a sermon to his progressive congregation. "But if we are children of Dirk Willems, we carry with us this reflex for turning back, . . . returning to the broken ice, reaching out as ambassadors of peace to a hurting world."[60]

Dirk as a paradigm of nonresistance, Dirk as an exemplar of enemy-love, Dirk as a willing servant of others—none of these interpretations of Luyken's image required the end of the story as narrated in *Martyrs Mirror,* where Dirk was put to death as a direct consequence of his loving act. Still, many people who encountered Luyken's iconic image were aware that Dirk was captured and later executed because he favored his enemy's life over his own. In some Anabaptist settings, these consequences, however awful, were not considered tragic, let alone senseless. For instance, in Elmo Stoll's "Thief-Catcher" story, readers were assured that, as Dirk sat in prison awaiting death, he experienced "peace in his heart and joy in his soul," for his life-saving venture was a way to express love to Jesus Christ. Moreover, from the time of his capture to the end of his life, Dirk "knew he could not have done differently."[61] These claims—that Dirk's faith gave him no choice in the matter, and that he felt joyful assurance over his decision to turn back—went well beyond what was stated in *Martyrs Mirror,* where Dirk was said to be faithful and steadfast but not necessarily to lack regret. As the twentieth century came to a close, some Anabaptists who encountered the story wondered what Dirk *was* thinking when he turned around, and whether in fact he later regretted that move. Reiterating concerns voiced about van Braght's martyrology as a whole, some even questioned whether Dirk's example of self-sacrificial service was an example worth emulating.

Wrestling with Dirk: A Martyr to Be Emulated?

Little known among North American Anabaptists in the 1940s, Dirk Willems was renowned enough fifty years later to function without explanation. In "How to Write the New Mennonite Poem" (1993), Jeff Gundy informed would-be poets that "dead Mennonites" were a fertile topic for verse, and because "Dirk Willems is hot this year," poets would be particularly well served to employ him.[62] Gundy's poem, playful yet prickly, suggests that by the early 1990s Dirk had become a cliché in Anabaptist circles, an overused and too-often-trite allusion to the piety of early Anabaptists.[63] These repeated references to Dirk bothered Gundy, for they signaled to him a lack of imagination. Other Mennonites, most of them highly educated, raised a second set of concerns about Dirk's growing ubiquity. For these plaintiffs, placing Dirk on anything like a pedestal made it difficult to ask important questions about his legacy and that of his fellow Anabaptist martyrs. Even as Dirk had become a pan-Anabaptist icon—much like a fraternal handshake that, without any words, establishes one's insider status—some Mennonites found his story too tragic, and his example too troubling, to reduce them to platitudes.

No one wrestled harder with this problem than James Juhnke, a historian at Bethel College and the editor of *Mennonite Life*. In the late 1980s, with his faculty colleague Robert Kreider hard at work on the *Mirror of the Martyrs* exhibit, Juhnke entered the interpretive arena himself, training his lens on Dirk with a drama titled *Dirk's Exodus*.[64] As the title suggests, Juhnke compared Dirk's getaway to the Israelites' escape through the Red Sea, trusting that his audience would notice the obvious contrasts: whereas Dirk's pursuer lived to see another day, the Israelites' pursuers perished in the sea; and whereas Dirk rushed back to save his foe, the Israelites celebrated their enemies' demise as a saving act of God. Juhnke could have used these contrasts to underscore the superiority of Dirk's Anabaptist values, but he used them instead to raise questions that the account in *Martyrs Mirror* ignored. For instance, as Juhnke's Dirk sits in prison awaiting his death, a fellow prisoner reminds him that some bystanders had heard the drowning man's shouts and could have pulled him from the water. This same character presses Dirk on the place of his family in his decision-making process: "If you were close to your children," she asks, "why did you return from your escape?" This question, which sets Dirk's love for his children against his religious convictions, is never fully resolved in the play. Clearly, however, in contrast to Elmo Stoll's Dirk, Juhnke's Dirk is plagued by second thoughts. When presented with the opportunity to recant, Dirk imagines asking his children for their opinion on the matter. "Peter and Nelleken . . . , what are you telling me? Are you saying 'Be strong, father, resist the evil tempter,' . . . Or are you saying 'Be prudent, father. Bend a little and survive'?" In Juhnke's account, Dirk never gets an answer to this question, and he thus approaches his end with something less than a tranquil heart.[65]

Juhnke's drama succeeded in making Dirk both more human and more Christlike than he appears in *Martyrs Mirror,* for it added a Garden of Gethsemane experience to his martyrological résumé. Other commentators, focusing only on the canonical account, suggested that Dirk might in fact be a bad example for contemporary Mennonites, for he raised the bar too high—or perhaps set it too low—for ethical behavior. Debra Gingerich, in her poem "Migraines and Other Mennonite Pains," took inventory of the demanding dictates that circulated in Anabaptist churches. Along with prescriptions about whom to marry, what to wear, and how to spend one's time, Gingerich included "Know what it means to be a disciple," adding quickly that "Dirk Willems knew (burned to death after saving his captor)." For Gingerich, who concluded her poem with the ironic assertion "The pain is nothing you can't stand," Dirk's example had become both a sledgehammer and a palliative in the hands of some Anabaptists, who used it to remind others that, whatever hardships they faced, they should take their cues from Dirk's willingness to suffer.[66] Jeff Gundy, in a poem titled "The Martyrs & the Child," likewise suggested that making Dirk a definitive paragon of Christian virtue was a dubious endeavor. Unconvinced that God commanded Dirk to sacrifice his life, Gundy offered his readers a different account of the story, replete with a miracle that Dirk may have mistook. Perhaps, Gundy winked, Jesus laid down a sheet of ice so that Dirk could follow him out of town, beyond his captor's grasp.[67]

That Dirk would sacrifice his life to save his enemy was challenging even to those who held Dirk in high regard, including James Lowry, a conservative Mennonite who considered *Martyrs Mirror* "a worthy sequel to the eleventh chapter of Hebrews."[68] Jesus may have talked about laying down one's life for one's friends, conceded Lowry, but the man who chased Dirk was clearly not his friend. To the contrary, and here Lowry quoted *Martyrs Mirror*, Dirk's pursuer was "a wolf."[69] Had Dirk kept running for his life, not one person in his church would have criticized him for it. In fact, "the story might even [have been] told as a judgment of God on the persecutor."[70] Stories of God's wrath befalling evil people were easy to find in the Bible, said Lowry, who, like Juhnke, referred to God's punishment of the Egyptian army.[71] Lowry also knew that similar stories suffused *Martyrs Mirror*, as for instance when God took vengeance on a bloodthirsty town official, whose "brains were dashed out" in a sleigh accident.[72] In the end, however, Lowry resolved this dilemma by pointing to Jesus's command to love one's enemies, an ethic that Jesus had exemplified by his death on the cross. Lowry admitted that Dirk's enemy-loving actions were unique in *Martyrs Mirror*, but he implied that this uniqueness owed mostly to a dearth of opportunities. "Not many Anabaptists had the opportunity Dirk had—to love the enemy so actively, to do good so strikingly." Fortunately, Dirk performed his loving act "for all of us," representing for future generations the Christlikeness of the sixteenth-century Anabaptists.[73]

Lowry's positive appraisal of Dirk's actions remained the common one as the twentieth century wound down, even in assimilated Mennonite circles. Significantly, however, a few assimilated Mennonites, while continuing to esteem Dirk, took pains to contrast his actions with other motifs in *Martyrs Mirror*, particularly those pertaining to the early Anabaptists' assessments of their foes. Many of these assessments, observed Joseph Liechty, reveal a lack of love on the part of the Anabaptists, who often thought the worst of their enemies and, moreover, wished the worst for them.[74] Liechty, who worked and taught in the area of peacebuilding, highlighted this contrast by giving close attention to the entire Dirk account in *Martyrs Mirror*, not just his act of rescue. In the larger account, the narrator draws a sharp line between Dirk and the "ravening wolves" who persecuted him, a dualism that, in Liechty's words, was "the common mental property" of both the sixteenth-century Anabaptists and the seventeenth-century Mennonites who memorialized them.[75] Because of this black-and-white ordering of the world, wherein all people were deemed either wolves or lambs, the Anabaptists "were inclined to dehumanize their enemies," and this contempt "must have stained their souls." In this context, Dirk did something that was rare among the sixteenth-century Anabaptists: he envisioned his pursuer "as both an agent of the devil *and* a helpless human brother."[76] For Liechty, then, Dirk provided a positive example for contemporary Anabaptists not because he represented sixteenth-century Anabaptism, but precisely because he did not.[77]

Representative or not, Dirk has made appearances in recent ecumenical conversations between Mennonites and the theological descendants of their persecutors. For instance, when the eleventh Lutheran World Federation met in 2010 to formulate an apology on behalf of their Lutheran ancestors, Mennonite World Conference (MWC) representative Larry Miller employed Dirk's image to communicate the long-standing Anabaptist ideal of loving one's enemies. In his presentation to the assembly, Miller conceded that Mennonites have often used their martyr tradition to assert their moral superiority, displaying a smugness that has sometimes "blind[ed] us to the frailties and failures that are also deeply rooted in our tradition." In this setting, however, where Lutherans aspired to apologize, Miller felt that using Dirk's image was appropriate, for Dirk's act of rescue represented something akin to offering forgiveness.[78]

Miller's employment of Dirk at the Lutheran assembly followed a similar presentation of Dirk to Pope Benedict XVI in 2007, when the Pontifical Council for Promoting Christian Unity invited a delegation from the MWC to the Vatican for a week of ecumenical dialogue. Early in the delegates' visit, Pope Benedict received them for a private audience, at which time Nancy Heisey, then president of the MWC, presented Benedict with Dirk's image.[79] In a nod toward Christian unity, the image Heisey presented took the form of an Eastern Orthodox icon, the creator of which used Luyken's image as his model.[80] Heisey later recalled that, as she offered the pope the icon, she "underlined that Dirk's story reflected an important commitment we share as Christians, that of love for enemy." In other words, rather than using Dirk to establish the Anabaptists' moral superiority, Heisey sought to underscore the fact that Christians from many traditions have worked to enact the ideal that Dirk incarnated. This acknowledgement of enemy-love as a shared Christian commitment, she later wrote, also made its way into a formal statement she read in the pope's presence, a statement that referenced Benedict's very first encyclical, *Deus caritas est* (God is love).

Heisey later came to regret the emphasis she had placed on love of enemy, however. Her regret grew from a conversation with James Juhnke, who twenty years earlier had written the play *Dirk's Exodus*. Juhnke's primary goal in writing his play was to humanize Dirk, but he also wanted to humanize Dirk's inquisitor, a man with "generous impulses," asserted Juhnke, a "good man whose decisions were quite understandable" in light of his context.[81] *Martyrs Mirror*, Juhnke told Heisey, had no interest in granting any measure of humanity to Catholic authorities. To the contrary, the book abounded with anti-Catholic sentiment, and it was therefore insensitive of Heisey to present the pontiff with a remnant

Fig. 11.6. Mennonite World Conference president Nancy Heisey presenting an icon portraying Dirk Willems to Pope Benedict XVI, at the Vatican in 2007.
Copyright Servizio Fotografico–L'Osservatore Romano.

from it. Although Heisey remained unconvinced that giving Dirk to the pope was inappropriate, she did wish in retrospect that she had used different language in the course of her presentation. "Rather than naming [the icon] the picture of love of enemy," she said, "I would [now] call it a sketch of reaching out to the other," for the latter phrase, while less explicitly biblical, is more invitational and thus more suited for ecumenical dialogue. To identify Dirk as an enemy-lover may be appropriate in some settings, she concluded, but to do so in the presence of the pope could easily be perceived as an act of moral one-upmanship.[82]

Heisey's reflections on Dirk, which she published in 2012 in the *Journal of Ecumenical Studies,* represented the culmination of her thinking on the role of memory in ecumenical relations. As the president of the MWC and a professionally trained historian, Heisey was acutely aware of the challenges involved in making Dirk useful for the twenty-first century. She knew, of course, that Anabaptists had been slaughtered in the sixteenth century, but she also knew that van Braght's chronicling of those events was not objective. She realized that, while contemporary North American Anabaptists were far removed from the kind of suffering described in *Martyrs Mirror,* Mennonites in some regions of the world were not. Finally, she knew that claiming a martyr heritage was a common way for a group to establish its moral superiority, a posture that hindered relations with other groups. Despite these challenges, Heisey forged ahead, aided, she said, by her encounter with a new book that incorporated Dirk's image in a most unusual way.

Defacing Dirk: Iconoclasm in an Anabaptist Key

In 2010 Herald Press, longtime publisher of *Martyrs Mirror,* released an anthology of poems and essays inspired by *Martyrs Mirror.* Edited by Kirsten Eve Beachy, the anthology included reflections from Anabaptists of various stripes, with the bulk of contributions from assimilated Mennonites. A few contributors cited the martyrs as unassailable role models, though in more cases the martyrs and their legacy were uneasily embraced. James Lowry's "Meditation on Dirk Willems" appeared in the book, but so did Debra Gingerich's "Migraine" poem and Jeff Gundy's "The Martyr & the Child." One blurb-writer, favorably disposed to the collection, described it as a "conversation among writers alternately inspired and bewildered by [their] spiritual ancestors."[83] A less favorable assessment of the book, advanced in private by an Amish historian, dismissed it as making light of martyrdom.

Accompanying the seventy poems and essays were eight visual images, each of them launching a section of the book and each of them featuring Dirk. One of the eight images was Luyken's original, but the other seven were modifications of Luyken's image, drawn by the Mennonite-raised artist Ian Huebert. In one of Huebert's drawings, Dirk stands upright, reading a how-to manual while ignoring the drowning man's pleas. In another drawing, Dirk crouches behind an American soldier sighting a high-powered rifle. In still another drawing, Dirk offers his pursuer an electric space heater. Huebert's aim, of course, was to help his viewers imagine responses that diverged from Dirk's canonical response. Could it be that contemporary Mennonites, rather than extending themselves to others, only ponder how to do it? Could it be that Mennonites, rather than loving their enemies, hide behind their nations' militaries? Could it be that contemporary Mennonites are naive do-gooders who treat symptoms of a problem but fail to address its cause?

In an artist's statement, first published in 2009 and included in Beachy's anthology, Huebert explained his work by citing a deeply rooted Anabaptist principle: iconoclasm.[84] Images "have always been held at arm's length" in Anabaptist circles, wrote Huebert, for the tendency of those who revere them is to do so too highly, or at least unreflectively. Huebert surely knew that Anabaptists who revered Luyken's image did not plant their lips on it. At the same time, he realized that Dirk's sacrificial response was typically deemed the faithful response, the one to which all serious Anabaptists should aspire. In that regard, Huebert's iconoclastic artwork (he called it "defacing the image") was his way both to challenge the dogma that had accrued around Dirk and to show that other responses, more common among contemporary Mennonites, were equally suspect. One reviewer of Huebert's work noted that Anabaptists who encounter Luyken's image often ask "What would I have done?" but they too often stop there, consoled by the assumption that they will never face such a daunting dilemma. But, the reviewer continued, "the appropriate question is not so much how we might behave when faced with the threat of execution, but simply how we behave when faced by the 'other.'" Huebert's artwork was helpful, the reviewer concluded, be-

Fig. 11.7. "Dirk the Patriot," a pen-and-ink drawing by Ian Huebert (2009).
Courtesy of Ian Huebert.

cause it forced contemporary Anabaptists to consider Dirk anew and apply his self-sacrificing ethic in relevant ways.[85] Another commentator, similarly impressed, concluded that Huebert's illustrations, while humorous, provided "a well-focused reflection of our contemporary Anabaptist aberrations, warts and all." Perhaps, this second commentator implied, Huebert's reflective material provides a better mirror for modern-day Mennonites than does van Bracht's.[86]

The chances that tradition-minded Anabaptists would find Huebert's drawings humorous, let alone find them more edifying than Luyken's original, are exceedingly slim. Adding details to Dirk's story is one thing—as recently as 2008 one Old Order poet divined Dirk's thoughts on the problem of evil—but modifying Dirk's fundamental response is another.[87] For tradition-minded Anabaptists, the conventional understanding of Dirk, who, in the words of *Martyrs Mirror*, provided an "instructive example to all pious Christians," is more than sufficient. Indeed, for many Anabaptists who continue to consider Dirk the premier representative of sixteenth-century Anabaptism, satirizing Luyken's image or second-guessing Dirk's decision making is closer to desecration than to iconoclasm, closer to making fun of the martyrs than to making sense of them. For them, anything less than full-throated affirmation of Dirk's noble deed dishonors the sacrifice he performed "for all of us."[88]

Of course, to claim that Dirk performed his noble deed for all of us assumes the universal relevance of his historically situated exploits. Clearly his self-sacrificing actions struck a nerve, or perhaps scratched an itch, in North American Anabaptist circles, but would his actions do the same for Anabaptist enclaves in Africa, Asia, and South America? This question, which extended beyond the illustrious Dirk to encompass *Martyrs Mirror* as a whole, assumed newfound urgency as the twentieth century gave way to the twenty-first, as North Americans who had sustained the martyrs' witness for so long relinquished their majority status in the Anabaptist world.

CHAPTER 12

Going Global

Martyrs Mirror *in the Twenty-First Century*

The history of *Martyrs Mirror* is largely a European-American story. Produced in the Netherlands by a Dutch minister, the bulk of the volume's material, and all of the martyr accounts in the volume's second part, derive from Europe. This, of course, was where Anabaptist Christianity first took root, and where its opponents sought to stamp it out by bloody means. When, in the seventeenth and eighteenth centuries, Anabaptists sought relief from hardship, many emigrated to North America, where William Penn and others promised them safe havens in which to practice their faith, plow their fields, and ply their trades. By the middle of the nineteenth century, and even more so by the nineteenth century's close, the center of Anabaptist gravity was shifting relentlessly to North America, where Mennonites, Hutterites, and Amish, by 1950, outnumbered the Anabaptists who stayed behind in Europe.[1] Correspondingly, the production of new editions and translations of *Martyrs Mirror* moved from European to North American locales: Ephrata in the eighteenth century; Lancaster, Lewistown, and Elkhart in the nineteenth century; and Scottdale and Aylmer in the twentieth century. A few exceptions notwithstanding, *Martyrs Mirror*, which located the apex of Christian faithfulness in western Europe, was a book produced by persons of western European heritage for readers who looked like them and lived as they lived.

By the late nineteenth century, however, some North American Anabaptist groups had begun looking farther afield for potential converts.

Although even today some Anabaptist groups eschew evangelism, others hopped aboard the world missions train that roared out of the station more than a century ago. According to a study published by Edmund G. Kaufman in 1931, North American Mennonites founded sixteen different foreign missions programs between 1880 and 1930, programs that employed more than four hundred missionaries, including Kaufman himself.[2] These missionary endeavors, which took Mennonites to China, India, Nigeria, and elsewhere, only gathered steam as the twentieth century ran its course. Some of the endeavors fell flat, underscoring the challenge of translating Mennonite religious assumptions into non-ethnic Mennonite settings. Still, the church planting efforts undertaken in the last quarter of the nineteenth century and reinforced in the twentieth continue to bear fruit. According to one recent consideration of global Anabaptism, the typical member of a twenty-first-century Anabaptist-Mennonite congregation is no longer a German- or English-speaking Caucasian. Rather, the typical Anabaptist-Mennonite person has dark skin, lives in the southern hemisphere, and speaks neither English nor German.[3]

North American Anabaptists offer various perspectives on this demographic shift: whereas some celebrate it as the renewal of a lethargic movement, others worry that important Anabaptist-Mennonite convictions will get lost in translation.[4] Among the anxious are those who worry that the Anabaptist commitment to nonresistance will be abandoned or at least downplayed, relegated to optional status in the realm of Christian discipleship.[5] In that respect, these contemporary observers are much like the eighteenth-century Pennsylvania Mennonites who feared that the next generation of Mennonites would abandon their church's commitment to nonresistance—and who, in response to that fear, employed the Ephrata communitarians to produce a German-language edition of *Martyrs Mirror*. Like their eighteenth-century forebears, some modern-day Anabaptists have fixed upon *Martyrs Mirror* as a means to cultivate Anabaptist commitments in a new generation of adherents; only now they consider potential readers in far-flung regions of the globe. In many ways, *Martyrs Mirror* remains a Euro-American volume, with European stories taking center stage and North American publishers running the presses. Today, however, considerable sections of *Martyrs Mirror* can be found in more than a dozen languages, sometimes for people whose encounters with persecution have been much more recent than the seventeenth century.

Translating this venerable martyr book for global contexts has raised a host of questions for those on the sending side. Some of the questions are obvious. Which stories should be translated? What form should they take, and into which languages should they be rendered? But along with these obvious questions come more subtle ones. How should non-European Anabaptists be encouraged to think about the sixteenth-century European martyrs? Are they to consider these martyrs the pinnacle of Christian faithfulness? How do these early Anabaptist martyrs compare with Christian heroes from the readers' homelands, some of whom have also suffered on account of their faith? Although some European-American purveyors of *Martyrs Mirror* have given little thought to these issues, others worry about making western European heroes the measuring stick for Christians at all times and places. In some cases, these curators of the Anabaptist story find themselves asking the same questions that Thieleman van Braght and his predecessors asked hundreds of years ago. Should the literary canon of faithful martyrs once again be opened? If so, what criteria should be used to decide who belongs?

Tradition-Minded Anabaptists and the Hope of Translation

Tradition-minded Anabaptists found themselves well positioned to globalize the martyrs' witness at the close of the twentieth century. More than their assimilated counterparts, tradition-minded Anabaptists had worked hard to place sections of *Martyrs Mirror* into reader-friendly formats for home and devotional use. As early as 1943, the eccentric Menno Sauder—eccentric because he was both a plain-dressing Mennonite and uncommitted to any particular church—recognized the virtue of abridging *Martyrs Mirror* for easier access. Sauder's works, which included *A Description of the True and of the False Church as Outlined in . . . "The Bloody Theatre" or "Martyrs Mirror"* (1944) and *Companion of a Solution to World Problems; or, The Christian Faith as Portrayed throughout "The Bloody Theatre" or "Martyrs Mirror"* (1945), reprinted stories and other portions of *Martyrs Mirror* verbatim, complementing them with early Anabaptist writings and his own editorial comments.[6] Sauder's efforts forged a path that Joseph Stoll and Pathway Publishers later traveled in a more refined way with *The Drummer's Wife and Other Stories from "Martyrs' Mirror"* (1968), a 250-page story collection that transformed van Bracht's narratives into elaborated accounts of historical fiction.[7] Thirteen years later, in 1981, conservative Mennonite scholar James Lowry published his own abridgment, *In the Whale's Belly and Other Martyr Stories,* which retold in simple language eleven stories from *Martyrs Mirror.*[8] With shorter stories, larger print, and more illustrations than Stoll's volume, Lowry's book was the easiest abridgment to navigate, but the goal of all three men was precisely the same: to make it easier for twentieth-century readers to encounter the contents of *Martyrs Mirror.*[9]

These abridgments were not produced with cross-cultural witness in mind, but some tradition-minded Mennonites soon seized upon that prospect. In the second half of the twentieth century, a variety of conservative Mennonite groups, less acculturated than assimilated Mennonites but more evangelical than Old Order Anabaptists, undertook missionary endeavors, many of which were located in Spanish-speaking regions of the Western Hemisphere. The Beachy Amish in El Salvador and Costa Rica, the Eastern Pennsylvania Mennonite Church in Guatemala and Paraguay, and the Nationwide Mennonite Fellowship in the Dominican Republic and Mexico—these were just a few of the conservative Anabaptist groups that, beginning in the 1950s, launched missionary work in Latin America.[10] Unlike assimilated Anabaptists, who increasingly opted for relief and development work as their method of cross-cultural witness, these conservative groups gave priority to church planting, often seeking to replicate their own ecclesial practices, particularly with respect to dress and nonresistance. Accompanying this missionary impulse was the development of missions-minded publishing houses, among them Lamp and Light Publishers of Farmington, New Mexico. Founded in 1974 by members of the Conservative Mennonite Fellowship, though now associated with the Nationwide Fellowship Churches, Lamp and Light attends to domestic needs, but it also aims to provide "sound, Scriptural, original, and translated literature for mission outreaches."[11] Today, Anabaptist resources in Spanish, French, German, and Portuguese appear in Lamp and Light's catalog alongside its English-language resources.

Among the earliest of Lamp and Light's Spanish-language works were two that recounted stories in *Martyrs Mirror*. In 1984 it published a Spanish translation of Lowry's *In the Whale's Belly*.[12] Five years later, it published Dallas Witmer's *La fe por la cual vale morir* (The faith worth dying for), a study guide that Witmer first developed while serving as a missionary in the Dominican Republic in the 1980s.[13] According to Lamp and Light's catalog, Witmer's guide introduces students to "the faith that moved the apostles and many other Christians to give their lives" and "challenges the student to live the same faith."[14] Still in print today, *La fe por la cual vale morir* may be ordered in bulk for less than $1.50 per copy, making it possible for teachers to provide copies gratis to their students.[15]

More recently another Nationwide Fellowship publisher has taken the lead in translating *Martyrs Mirror* abridgments into a new language, although in this case the former Soviet Union provides the regional focus. Grace Press, located in Ephrata, Pennsylvania, just miles from where the first North American edition of *Martyrs Mirror* was produced in 1749, operates out of a modest block building adorned with bold, blue letters: "And the Gospel Must First Be Published among All Nations (Mark 13:10)."[16] To advance that mission, Grace Press specializes in producing Russian-language literature, which has included three *Martyrs Mirror* abridgments: Lowry's *In the Whale's Belly* (1997), Stoll's *The Drummer's Wife* (2001), and more recently *The Sacrifice of the Lord* (2013).[17] This latter volume, which replicates the sixteenth-century precursor to *Martyrs Mirror,* is particularly significant, for it did not originate as an English-language abridgment. Rather, the publisher identified the core martyr accounts in the English edition of *Martyrs Mirror* and, employing an able translator, rendered them directly into Russian.[18] All told, Grace Press has produced nearly two hundred thousand of these three Russian-language works, a number that climbs by thousands each year.

The process of printing and distributing the Russian-language abridgments involves a network of conservative Mennonites and Russian-speaking pastors that traces its roots to the 1970s. Inspired by the work of Beachy Amish bishop David A. Bontrager, who launched his *Jesus to the Iron Curtain Newsletter* in 1976, conservative Anabaptists have worked to cultivate a "preferential option for the suffering church," first in eastern Europe and more recently in Muslim countries.[19] This preference, which draws on the historical Anabaptist notion that the true church is a suffering church, led conservative Anabaptists in the 1970s and 1980s to view Protestant evangelicals behind the Iron Curtain as their spiritual kin. These evangelical-Baptist churches were not Anabaptist churches per se. Still, Bontrager and his allies sought to support their "suffering brethren" through empathy-building efforts in the United States and gifts of material aid abroad.[20] Toward that end, Beachy Amish leaders and others formed Christian Aid Ministries (CAM) as a means to distribute aid throughout eastern Europe. CAM, which promotes itself as a "trustworthy and efficient channel for Amish, Mennonite, and other conservative Anabaptist groups and individuals to minister to physical and spiritual needs around the world," has since grown into the leading parachurch organization in the conservative Anabaptist world. Today its multimillion-dollar budget enables the distribution of material aid and Christian literature in nearly one hundred countries.[21]

These interchurch connections, both at home and abroad, have proved critical for Grace Press, enabling and expediting its distribution of *Martyrs Mirror* abridgments. On the North American end, Grace Press relies on Mennonite and Beachy Amish laypersons to support its work, inviting them via bimonthly newsletters to make monetary contributions.[22] Once printed, the abridgments are loaded into shipping containers along with clothing and blankets and sent to various locations throughout the former Soviet Union. In the Ukraine, one key recipient location, Mennonite and Beachy Amish missionaries steer the material into the hands of Russian-speaking pastors, many of whom are part of the Council of Churches of Evangelical Christians-Baptists, an association of evangelical churches that, more than other Baptists, forswore cooperation with governing authorities under Communism.[23] Since the collapse of the Soviet bloc, conservative Mennonites have established strong relationships with these pastors, who appreciate the modest dress, clear-cut gender roles, and conservative theology of the Mennonite missionaries, as well as the material aid they provide. Many of these Baptist churches also receive materials from CAM, which operates a large warehouse just a few hundred yards from Grace Press. CAM's shipments consist largely of food, medicine, and other material items, but CAM also distributes literature that, according to its website, aims to "bring the Gospel to a lost and dying world."[24] In some places CAM has distributed Russian-language abridgments of *Martyrs Mirror.*[25]

That conservative Anabaptists would employ *Martyrs Mirror* to minister to non-Anabaptist Christians in Latin America and the former Soviet Union corresponds with a set of assumptions held by this segment of North American Anabaptists. First, conservative Anabaptists, much more than assimilated ones, consider suffering—whether it be persecution, material want, or social stigma—to be an integral element of authentic Christianity. Second, conservative Anabaptists continue to see Anabaptism, particularly as expressed in their conservative communities, to be the optimal form of Christianity.[26] Correspondingly, conservative Anabaptists tend to view Catholics and Orthodox Christians, with their reliance on infant baptism and other priestly sacraments, as falling well short of being truly Christian.[27] With these dynamics in view, Spanish- and Russian-language *Martyrs Mirror* abridgments must be seen as more than vehicles for imparting inspirational stories. They are, in fact, guidebooks for practicing the correct form of Christianity, which means eschewing the culturally entrenched Catholic or Orthodox faiths of these regions. In other words, these books constitute invitations to Latin Americans, eastern Europeans, and central Asians to replicate the example of the Swiss and Dutch Anabaptists, who in the sixteenth century renounced the compromised churches of their era. As in the sixteenth century, this commitment may result in hardship, but that is where the martyrs' witness is most compelling, for the faith they adopted was not just any faith. It was, in Witmer's words, "the faith worth dying for."

Of course, some eastern European and central Asian readers of these abridgments would find an additional point of connection to the Anabaptist martyrs, having witnessed firsthand the government-sponsored persecution of Christians during the Soviet era. In these cases, the *Martyrs Mirror* abridgments function as narrative bridges between the spiritual heritage of the Mennonite missionaries and the painful history of former Soviet subjects, many of whom know nothing about Anabaptist history and theology. Rightly used, the abridgments help to validate the Mennonites' missionary credibility, assuring the recipients that the Mennonite distributors are not interlopers, but are rather Christian brothers and sisters who share with them a history of religious persecution.

And the benefits of these spiritual connections extend back to North America, for they help to buttress the martyrological mentality of conservative Mennonites, those who support the work of Grace Press, Lamp and Light, and CAM. Despite having a keen sense of history, conservative Anabaptists are hard pressed to maintain a martyrological mentality in the comforts of twenty-first-century America, a mentality that, as we have seen, conservative churches draw on to preserve their countercultural ways. Being cognizant of more recent rounds of persecution helps in this regard, for it reminds conservative Mennonites that the world is still a dangerous place, filled with forces that wish to destroy the Christian faith. To accentuate this battle, CAM has recently begun to produce contemporary martyrologies that offer stories of Christians suffering under Communist or Islamic rule.[28] Published in English, these books are intended to inspire CAM's North American supporters to greater faithfulness, nurture their martyrological mentality, and raise funds that can further enhance CAM's work. CAM has also established a program it calls its Christian Martyrs Fund, which provides money to Christian workers who suffer (or suffered) persecution in the former Soviet Union and other regions of the world. The benefits of the Christian Martyrs Fund run both ways: the persecuted workers receive money for food, clothing, and other necessities, and CAM's supporters receive words of blessing from the fund's recipients. One pastor, whose letter was reprinted on CAM's website, noted that his wife was imprisoned for distributing religious literature, an activity that, not coincidentally, constitutes a key part of CAM's ministry. "Our communion through the blood of Jesus Christ . . . has made you remember such a brother [as me]," wrote the pastor, who then offered a hearty endorsement of CAM's missionary work: "May the Lord bless your efforts and reward you."[29]

In the conservative Anabaptist world, it is hard to imagine a better endorsement than one flowing from the pen of a persecuted pastor. Such words confirm both the importance of CAM's work and also the sense that CAM's supporters sit on the right side of the battle between good and evil. In some ways, this dividing line is a different one from the one that runs through *Martyrs Mirror*'s second half, for it no longer assumes that Anabaptist church members sit on one side and the rest of the world sits on the other. At the same time, the line remains definitive, falling sharply between conservative, adult-baptized followers of Jesus Christ and their determined enemies. In that sense, the dualistic construal of the world that runs through *Martyrs Mirror* remains an emphasis in the conservative Mennonite world.

Assimilated Mennonites and the Hope of Translation

Assimilated Mennonites have been less inclined to make *Martyrs Mirror* abridgments than their tradition-minded counterparts. Correspondingly, they have demonstrated less interest in translating those abridgments into other languages. The most significant abridgment that emerged from the assimilated Mennonite world in the late twentieth century was *Mirror of the Martyrs*, produced in 1990 by John S. Oyer and Robert S. Kreider to complement their *Mirror of the Martyrs* traveling exhibit.[30] Like tradition-minded Anabaptists, Oyer and Kreider produced their abridgment, twenty-eight paraphrased accounts, with North American readers in mind. Only later did Mennonites from various quarters decide that the book held promise for non-English-speaking audiences. Since then *Mirror of the Martyrs* has been translated into eight other languages: Spanish (1997), Indonesian (1999), Japanese (2002), Romanian (2002), Russian (2002), German (2002), French (2003), and Hindi (2010).

Compared to the efforts of conservative Mennonites, the *Mirror of the Martyrs* translations were less missions-minded printing endeavors, directed by North Americans, than cooperative ventures with Mennonite churches in other parts of the world. Some of these churches' roots reach back to the twentieth century's first half, when Mennonite missionaries pioneered cross-cultural evangelism in Africa, Asia, and Latin America. By the late twentieth century, the leadership of almost all of these churches had been assumed by nationals, with North Americans providing assistance in areas such as teaching, health care, and economic development. For instance, Mennonite missionaries first arrived in central Africa in 1911, where they planted churches in the Belgian Congo. By 1950 the transition to national leadership had begun, a changeover that reached completion after the Congo gained independence in 1960.[31] In Colombia, General Conference Mennonites began missionary work in 1943; twenty-five years later, in 1968, missionary leaders ceded formal control to Colombian nationals.[32] Today, Mennonite denominations in the Democratic Republic of Congo, Colombia, and many other nations are independent entities. Along with a variety of North American Mennonite denominations, they constitute the Mennonite World Conference, a filial organization of Anabaptist-related churches worldwide.[33]

These international Mennonite partnerships held implications for the translation of *Mirror of the Martyrs*, for in most cases the production process engaged persons or agencies outside of North America.[34] In the case of the Spanish translation, for instance, primary oversight came from Centro Latinoamericano de Recursos Anabautistas (CLARA), an Anabaptist resource center located in Bogotá, Colombia. Directed by Elizabeth Soto and later by Columbian-born Marco Guete, CLARA made arrangements for funding the project and contracted with a local print shop to produce one thousand copies of the book. In time, many of these copies were shipped to SEMILLA (Seminario Anabautista Latinamericano), an Anabaptist seminary in Guatemala City, where they were used in Anabaptist history and theology courses.[35] The translation of *Mirror of the Martyrs* into Hindi developed differently, though again the work of foreign-born Mennonites was central to the process. In this case, Jai Prakash Masih, an Indian Mennonite who came to the United States to attend seminary, took the initiative to translate the book for Hindi-speaking communities, both in the United States and in India.[36] For Masih, making these old martyrs' stories available to Indian Mennonites held potential to increase appreciation for the faith that Mennonite missionaries first took to India in the late nineteenth century.[37] "Even though [Indians] have had the Mennonite faith for so many years, people only know sporadically these [martyr] stories," Masih told a reporter shortly after the book was released.[38] His new translation, he hoped, would remedy that ignorance and thereby foster esteem for Mennonite values.

More than simply sustaining Mennonitism in general, however, the goal of translating *Mirror of the Martyrs* into new languages was to strengthen readers' commitment to nonviolence, even in the face of suffering. At least four of the new translations held potential for use in nations or regions plagued by ethnic, religious, or political violence: Spanish (Colombia and other Latin American countries), Hindi (India), Indonesian (Indonesia), and French (the Congo). In all of these places, Mennonites had themselves been victims of violence and, at least in some cases, had been persecuted on account of their faith. In Colombia, for instance, Mennonites found themselves in the crossfire between various military and paramilitary factions that wanted access to natural resources, factions that were willing to kill or displace civilians who would not support their causes. In India, violence ensued primarily from interreligious tensions between Hindus, Muslims, and Christians. In some regions of India, most notably in Orissa in 2008, Hindu extremists burned churches, attacked pastors, and set fire to Christians' homes as way to discourage Christian evangelistic efforts. Anabaptist church members were not immune to this wave of violence.[39]

With these circumstances in mind, the producers of the Spanish and Hindi translations envisioned their work as a way to promote what they considered a genuinely Christian response to the prospect of suffering and death. According to Masih, the Hindi translator, stories from *Martyrs Mirror* would resonate particularly well with Indians, given their familiarity with Mahatma Gandhi. More than that, the book would help Indians see that Gandhi actually "picked up" many of his ideas about nonviolence from the Bible.[40] The volume's publisher, also an expatriate Indian, saw the Hindi version of *Mirror of the Martyrs* as a means to encourage Indian Christians of all stripes, but particularly those who might face persecution, for its stories evinced "the strongest kind of faith" for which Christians continue to "give their lives today."[41] Elizabeth Soto, who superintended the translation of the Spanish edition, had similar hopes for the kind of work the book could do among Spanish-speaking Mennonites.[42] According to Soto, the political turmoil that enveloped Columbia and other Latin American nations in the 1990s placed Mennonites in situations that tested their faith and made the choice between violence and nonviolence a pressing one. In Columbia, some Mennonites undertook perilous peacemaking work, most notably through Justapaz (Just peace), a conflict-transformation ministry of the Columbian Mennonite Church that was sometimes on the receiving end of death threats.[43] In such situations, the martyrs' decision to die on account of their faith, but not kill on behalf of it, provided a meaningful template for faithful living.[44]

But even as some envisioned *Mirror of the Martyrs* as a way to promote peace, at least one person was aware of its capacity to generate ill will. Neal Blough, a Paris-based Mennonite educator who helped to produce the French edition in 2003, enjoyed close relationships with Catholics both personally and professionally: his wife was a Roman Catholic convert to Mennonitism, his in-laws were Catholics, and he collaborated with Catholics in his educational work. With these connections Blough was well suited to engage in Catholic-Mennonite dialogue, a process that began in a formal fashion at a gathering of Mennonite and Catholic theologians in Strasbourg, France, in 1998. The exchanges at that event awakened Blough to the fact that the Anabaptist martyrs, and the way van Braght memorialized them, held the potential to offend Roman Catholics. "If there was one issue that just kept coming up" at these Catholic-Mennonite gatherings, he later wrote, "sometimes stimulating angry reactions, . . . it was the martyrs."[45] Blough was of two minds on the issue. To excuse the Catholic persecutors on account of their medieval context ignored the more peaceful options that were available to them. On the other hand, to read Reformation history through martyrological lenses oversimplified the historical record and held the potential to nurture moral arrogance in the present.[46]

Blough's experience in the Catholic-Mennonite dialogue informed his work on the French edition of *Mirror of the Martyrs,* a volume intended for use in Africa as well as in France and Quebec. For Blough, the English edition of *Mirror of the Martyrs,* though more generous to the Anabaptists' enemies than *Martyrs Mirror* itself, did not go far enough in explaining the persecutors' perspectives. Therefore, as he crafted a new preface for the French edition, he endeavored to provide historical context to the martyr accounts that followed. In his preface Blough noted that sixteenth-century Europe was violent on many levels, with Catholics and Lutherans, not just Anabaptists, suffering martyrdom. Much of this violence, he conceded, came as a result of "schisms within Western Christianity," an admission that ascribed at least some responsibility for the conflict to Anabaptists. "The goal of this work is not to stigmatize or accuse," Blough continued, for contemporary Catholics and Lutherans are quite different from those who put the Anabaptists to death. Nonetheless, to ignore these stories would undercut the possibility of real reconciliation between Mennonites, Catholics, and Lutherans. Moreover, to pretend these events never happened would rob current generations of the chance to learn about Christians who, even under the threat of death, "refused to persecute or kill."[47]

The challenges Blough faced in producing a French translation of *Mirror of the Martyrs* were not unique to him, but unlike many Mennonites, he moved in a world where maintaining good relations with Catholics truly mattered. Committed as he was to Anabaptist theological principles, Blough nonetheless saw many opportunities to work with Catholics, opportunities that went far beyond teaching Reformation history. In 2003, the same year he produced his preface to *Mirror of the Martyrs*, Blough's name appeared on a report jointly produced by Catholics and Mennonites entitled "Called Together to Be Peacemakers." The report, a synthesis of the five-year dialogue that began in Strasbourg in 1998, highlighted many points of theological disagreement between Catholics and Mennonites, but it also included points of convergence, including the common conviction that "reconciliation, nonviolence, and active peacemaking belong to the heart of the Gospel."[48] Like other Mennonites who attended those gatherings, Blough believed that the witness of the Anabaptist martyrs could undergird that commitment to peacemaking, but only if the martyrs' witness was recalled in a way that tempered the stereotypes that van Braght had helped to create.

On this side of the Atlantic, similar conversations emerged in the context of Bridgefolk, a collection of sacramentally minded Mennonites and peace-minded Roman Catholics who gathered annually for worship and conversation.[49] Compared to the ecumenical dialogue in Strasbourg, which was coordinated by the Mennonite World Conference and the Vatican's Pontifical Council for Promoting Christian Unity, Bridgefolk was a ground-up initiative that welcomed anyone drawn to the intersection of the two traditions. At times Bridgefolk built on the European dialogue's work, as it did, for instance, in 2007, when it organized a conference to discuss the "Called Together to Be Peacemakers" report. In this setting and others, Bridgefolk participants, like the dialogue participants in Europe, found the Anabaptist martyrs and their memorialization to be an important but sometimes bewildering topic. Could Mennonites honor the Anabaptist martyrs in ways that avoided demonizing those who put them to death? Conversely, could contemporary Roman Catholics appreciate the Anabaptists' witness despite their complicity in fracturing the Catholic Church?

The most innovative attempts to address these questions fixed on Michael Sattler, the first-generation Swiss Anabaptist who was burned at the stake in 1527.[50] Prior to his conversion to Anabaptism, Sattler was a Benedictine monk, a detail that was not lost on Ivan and Lois Kaufman, Mennonite-born Catholics associated with Saint John's Abbey, a Benedictine monastery in Collegeville, Minnesota, that often hosted Bridgefolk gatherings.[51] With the abbey's support, the Kaufmans established the Michael Sattler House to extend "hospitality to those committed to making the world a better place."[52] In the Kaufmans' view, situating Sattler as a Christian committed to justice work was a way to bridge the divide between Sattler's Benedictine and Anabaptist identities. In time the Kaufmans sought to shape the memory of Sattler in a more expansive way, through the establishment of Michael Sattler Day on May 20, the date of his execution. In an open letter to their Mennonite and Catholic colleagues in 2012, the Kaufmans wrote that they had "come to believe that Catholics can now regard Michael Sattler as an early martyr witness to the values of social justice and freedom of conscience which became official Catholic doctrine at Vatican II." They had also come to believe that "Mennonites and Amish can now view Michael Sattler not only as one of their major founders, but also as one who brought with him the riches of the pre-Reformation tradition in which he was formed."[53] One Mennonite convert to Catholicism affirmed Sattler's commemoration. Convinced that Sattler had taken a more irenic approach toward his foes than most sixteenth-century Anabaptists, Julia Smucker concluded (only somewhat in jest) that "today we dare to say: Michael Sattler, Benedictine and Anabaptist, pray for us."[54] Another sympathetic Catholic entitled his news release about Michael Sattler Day, "Michael Sattler: Monk, Mennonite, Martyr."[55]

Not everyone was convinced. "Ol' Sattler seems like he was nice enough person," wrote one Catholic who was monitoring the developments, but "by deliberately leading people away from the Apostolic Church, he was working against God, the same way the heresiarchs of the Early Church did."[56] This statement from the Catholic side, affirmed by others who found Sattler's theological pilgrimage less than saintly, prompted one Mennonite to lament that Catholicism's true colors were now showing through. "As a Mennonite who at least HAD been seeking fuller communion with Rome," wrote Spencer Bradford, "these responses offer great insight into the . . . absence of Christ's charity that [drove] our spiritual ancestors out." In fact, Bradford continued, "I see no moral difference between the Middle-Eastern Muslim who will kill his cousin for converting to Christianity, and that Catholic who would condone executing Sattler and his spiritual descendants for leaving the barque of Peter."[57]

These competing statements, which ran counter to the reconciling hopes of those who initiated Michael Sattler Day, underscored the challenge of using martyr stories, even stories of defenseless Christians, to foster reconciliation. A few years later, a similar challenge—how to honor the martyrs' witness while refusing to stereotype their foes—marked yet another attempt by assimilated Mennonites to reinvigorate their church's martyrological heritage. This time, however, Sattler and his European contemporaries served mostly as the prologue to a conversation that took a new twist, pivoting away from the challenge of reciting old Anabaptist martyr stories to the possibility of writing new ones.

Reopening the Canon of Anabaptist Martyrs

For assimilated Mennonites who esteemed their martyr heritage, the prospect of translating *Martyrs Mirror* for readers across the globe held promise for sustaining the Anabaptist witness. It also produced disquiet. The stories in *Martyrs Mirror* were European stories, far removed from most of the world's Mennonites in terms of language, ethnicity, time, and space. Even in the twenty-first century, some North American Mennonites could open *Martyrs Mirror* and find their ancestors shedding family blood. Such was not the case, of course, for Mennonites living in Indonesia, India, Ethiopia, and Columbia. This genealogical distance did not make the sixteenth-century martyrs irrelevant to Mennonites in the global South, but it did make them less usable. Moreover, in many regions of the world, Mennonites and others had experienced their own forms religious of persecution, sometimes in the very immediate past. To think that sixteenth-century European martyrs were best positioned to teach lessons of faithfulness at all times and places struck some Mennonites as a dubious assumption. To some assimilated Mennonites, it smacked of ethnocentrism.

Was it possible to preserve the early martyrs' witness and avoid this exclusionary sin? That was the question that troubled some early-twenty-first-century Mennonite leaders, those who both valued *Martyrs Mirror* as a gift from the past and also wished to make Mennonites worldwide full partners in an Anabaptist future. In some respects, an affirmative answer to that question was easy to locate, residing as it did in the literary practices of early Anabaptist martyrologists. For these early martyrologists, the canon of Anabaptist martyrs was an open one, with additional martyrs enlarging the canon and its geographical scope as the years went by. From the initial edition of *The Sacrifice of the Lord,* published in 1562, to van Braght's *Bloody Theatre,* published in 1660, the canon of Anabaptist martyrs grew by leaps and bounds, and its geographical expanse reached beyond the Netherlands to include Anabaptists in other regions of Europe. This literary expansion was not lost on John D. Roth, director of the Institute for the Study of Global Anabaptism at Goshen College. In an opinion piece he published in 2012, Roth reminded his Mennonite readers of this process that produced ever-larger martyrologies, and he further noted that there was no good reason to consider the canon closed once and for all.[58] Why not reopen the canon and thereby produce "a new *Martyrs Mirror* for the twenty-first century"?[59] With his North American audience in mind, Roth argued that an updated *Martyrs Mirror* would do more than advance the cause of inclusiveness: it would challenge the "spiritual complacency" of comfortable North American Mennonites, and it would help North Americans empathize more deeply with the burdens of their spiritual kin.[60]

This goal, to update *Martyrs Mirror,* was the driving force behind a consultation held in Goshen, Indiana, in 2012. Sponsored by the Mennonite Historical Society and the Institute for the Study of Global Anabaptism, the 2012 consultation sprang from the same source as Kirsten Eve Beachy's *Tongue Screws and Testimonies* literary collection, that is, from two "Gifts of the Martyrs" consultations coordinated by Bluffton University professor Gerald Mast in 2009.[61] These earlier consultations, consisting mostly of assimilated Mennonite academics, posited a host of ways to reinvigorate or at least wrestle with the martyrs' witness, ways that ranged from a new-and-improved translation of *Martyrs Mirror,* to better educational resources for use in local congregations, to a published collection of literary engagements with the text, the latter of which Beachy undertook. Whereas Beachy's project gave priority to the ways Anabaptists have struggled to make sense of their martyr-pocked history, the 2012 Goshen College consultation gave priority to chronicling more recent experiences of Anabaptist-Mennonite suffering. Moderated by Mast and Roth, the 2012 consultation included nearly forty persons, most of them church leaders, missions personnel, and academics from assimilated churches in North America, but also representatives from

Africa and South America.[62] In addition to hearing presentations on the development of sixteenth- and seventeenth-century Anabaptist martyrologies, participants heard accounts of Mennonite persecution in the more recent past, including some during the first decade of the twenty-first century. Throughout the three-day meeting, facilitators invited participants to reflect on the virtue of producing an addendum to *Martyrs Mirror* that would expand the scope of van Braght's text. Responses to this proposition ranged widely, from enthusiastic endorsement to considerable skepticism, with most participants offering measured support. The devil, all admitted, lay in the details.[63]

Most of the difficult challenges revolved around three questions. The first question was the boundary question: who belongs in the canon of martyrs, and who does not? Answering this question was hard enough in the seventeenth century, as Anabaptists fragmented into competing groups with modest yet critical differences. These differences forced all the Anabaptist martyrologists—Twisck, de Ries, van Braght, and others—to answer the same question: who suffered and died on account of the *true* Christian faith? In subsequent centuries, the Anabaptist world had become even more diverse. Indeed, long before the end of the twentieth century, some Anabaptists had developed a greater affinity to non-Anabaptists than to their own theological kin. Just how widely should the canon of faithful martyrs be opened? Should it include nonviolent evangelicals such as the missionary Jim Elliot? Should it find room for peaceable Catholics like the El Salvadoran archbishop Óscar Romero? Was it arrogant to include only those whose names appeared on membership rosters of Anabaptist churches? In contrast, was it presumptuous to include persons who lived like Anabaptists but did not identify as such?

The second question, perhaps more vexing than the first, was one to which van Braght paid little mind: who controls the martyrs' stories? This question was in fact a series of questions: Who decides whether a particular story is told? Who decides how the story is told? And who decides when and in what medium the story is communicated? In van Braght's case, many of his chosen narratives had long histories, orally and in print, before they ended up in his volume. In that sense van Braght was primarily a compiler of previously published accounts, which he contextualized with his own commentary. As far as we know, van Braght did not make efforts to get permission from the martyrs' descendants or their home communities to retell their stories. With persecution in the Netherlands a thing of the past, van Braght assumed that the goodness of publishing the martyrs' stories far outweighed any negative effects his book might engender.

Many people today take a similar approach, publishing martyrs' stories without compunction, but participants at the Goshen consultation warned against that practice, particularly if the stories derived from communities with less money, less power, and less security.[64] These stories, most participants agreed, should be considered the possession of the martyrs' home communities, which were better positioned to decide whether, how, and when stories should be published for broader consumption. Participants from the global South, some of whom said little throughout the three-day gathering, entered into this conversation, noting that, in some places, telling stories of persecution could come back to haunt people who had already suffered enough. Of course, deciding that home communities should retain control over particular stories of suffering did not settle the control question once and for all; in some instances, it was not clear which stories belonged to which communities. At the same time, the conversation demonstrated a degree of sensitivity among the conference participants that many North Americans, including some Anabaptists, frequently lacked.

If the question of control is one that van Braght seemed to ignore, the third question is one that his historiographical methods raised: is it possible to tell the martyrs' stories without vilifying their persecutors? Some participants, concerned about ecumenical relations in the present, complained that *Martyrs Mirror* was a hindrance to that work, for it painted Catholics and other opponents of the Anabaptists in the worst possible light. If the Anabaptist tradition was truly committed to the principle of enemy-love, might there be a way to honor the victim's faithfulness and, at the same time, lovingly represent the persecutors and their concerns? As we have seen, some assimilated Mennonites had raised this concern previously with respect to *Martyrs Mirror*, encouraging readers to understand and empathize with the persecutors' perspectives. This undertaking, which sometimes met resistance from readers who preferred a more dualistic version of history, was admittedly a difficult one, though some consultants argued that an Anabaptist martyrology, to be truly Anabaptist, should make it a priority.

In the end, the consultation's organizers determined that there was enough support for updating the Anabaptist martyr tradition to proceed with gathering stories, not simply stories of martyrdom, but stories of "costly discipleship" more broadly, and not as a published addendum to *Martyrs Mirror*, but for entry into an electronic database that could inform future publishing ventures. The story criteria, as summarized by Roth at the consultation's close, were ones that van Braght could have affirmed: stories about people "from the Anabaptist community of faith," who "willingly suffered, died, or experienced some significant deprivation," not for just any reason, but "for the cause of Christ," and who suffered "in the manner of the defenseless Christ." In a further elaboration of these criteria, somewhat less van Braght–like, Roth wrote that the project should "be open to including stories from beyond the Anabaptist tradition" but at the same time should demonstrate caution "about presuming to tell the stories of other Christian groups." Roth's caveats, which fixed on concerns raised throughout the consultation, also urged story gatherers to "be attentive to broad inclusion" in the realms of gender, group identity, geography, and historical era.[65] Yes, stories from the contemporary global Anabaptist church were most welcome, but so too were stories of costly discipleship from centuries past that never received their due, such as those deriving from the Russian Mennonite experience under Stalin.[66]

Roth's provisos also sought to address the challenging questions of control and enemy-love. "Be attentive to the potential of the project to endanger individuals in some contexts," advised Roth. "Test stories with local communities before allowing them to go public." As for how to represent the persecutors, Roth sought to split the difference between truth-telling and compassion toward the enemy. Because "stories have the capacity to divide as well as unite," a "commitment to compassion and love of the 'enemy' should characterize the tone and content of our stories," and the perpetrators' perspectives should neither be ignored nor misrepresented. At the same time, storytellers should not "shy away too much from strong language when confronting evil." In other words, "we must be able to name the reality in the world of opposition to the way of Jesus."[67]

Eighteen months after the conference closed, the "Bearing Witness" wiki (a website that allows for collaborative content editing) was up and

running, part of a larger wiki that included other resources about martyrdom, including some pertaining to *The Bloody Theater*.[68] In many
ways it was still too early to tell what would come of this endeavor to
expand the Anabaptist martyr canon, which stories would eventually
make their way onto the wiki, and how these stories would be employed
for use in other venues. Early returns, however, demonstrated that expanding the chronological scope of Anabaptist martyrdom would be
more easily accomplished than expanding its geographical reach, for the
bulk of the stories that appeared in the first two years focused on European and North American Anabaptists. To be sure, one could find names
that were relatively new to the Anabaptist tradition, such as Mthom-
beni and Singh, but from the beginning African and Asian names were
far outnumbered by names like Hofer, Lapp, Dyck, and Klaassen.[69] One
contributor even saw fit to post the Dirk Willems account, perhaps misunderstanding the point of the project, though perhaps thinking that
no collection of Anabaptist martyr stories could be considered valid if
it failed to include Dirk.[70] If nothing else, Dirk's appearance symbolized
that any consideration of Anabaptist suffering would eventually touch
base with the saints who suffered long ago, the illustrious martyrs who
launched the Anabaptist movement in the first place.

Martyrology and the Challenge of Telling the Truth

Despite being invited to the Goshen consultation, tradition-minded Anabaptists were conspicuously underrepresented.[71] At first blush this might
seem peculiar, since tradition-minded Anabaptists reference *Martyrs
Mirror* more regularly than do assimilated Mennonites, and they also
take greater initiative in broadcasting its contents to the wider world. On
second thought, however, it is hardly surprising that tradition-minded
Anabaptists might view a new-and-improved *Martyrs Mirror* with some
reserve. It is one thing to publish Christian martyr stories from various
corners of the world. It is quite another to imagine these new stories
as enhancements to *Martyrs Mirror*. For tradition-minded Mennonites,
the stories in *Martyrs Mirror* are more than just representative samples
of Christian suffering. They are archetypal examples, drawn from the
primordial past that gave birth to the Anabaptist movement. To append
other stories to it—to create "a new *Martyrs Mirror* for the twenty-first

century"—would strike many tradition-minded Anabaptists as lacking in humility.

Of course, given the consultation's outcome, which stressed gathering discrete stories more than updating *Martyrs Mirror,* anxieties about slighting tradition may have been unfounded. Nonetheless, there are other reasons why most tradition-minded Anabaptists would have felt uneasy at the consultation. First, the recurrent call to complicate the historical record—to give persecutors' perspectives their due—would have struck many tradition-minded Anabaptists as a way of excusing evil. Second, the call from some participants to memorialize Catholic martyrs would have offended those for whom the Catholic-Protestant divide continues to be decisive. Finally, the recurring theme that stories of victimization are often ploys to leverage power would have been lost on many tradition-minded Anabaptists, who tend to think of their martyrologists as nonresistant truth-tellers in a power-hungry world. However inclusive the organizers tried to be, the Goshen consultation was largely a venue for assimilated Anabaptists to meet and talk with one another on their own terms.

This is not to say that conservative and assimilated Anabaptists have nothing in common when it comes to updating the Christian martyrological record. Above all, Anabaptists of both types affirm the process of gathering and publishing these accounts as a way to enter into solidarity with those who suffer on account of the faith.[72] As noted, conservative Mennonites have demonstrated a "preferential option for the suffering" since the 1970s, when they first took interest in the plight of Christians behind the Iron Curtain. From these early efforts in the 1970s to the work of CAM today, conservative Mennonites have devoted great energy to gathering and publishing persecution accounts from regions of the world unfriendly to the Christian faith. In the vast majority of cases, this has meant publishing stories about Christians in Communist lands and, more recently, in Islamic countries. By focusing on select stories from regions such as these, conservative Mennonites have been able to inscribe onto the contemporary world a dualism they see both in the Bible and in *Martyrs Mirror,* with God's people on one side and Satan's minions on the other. These contemporary stories, like the ones van Braght and his predecessors told, were never intended to be conceptually complicated or ideologically nuanced. They were meant, above all, to be inspiring.[73]

Many assimilated Mennonites are similarly content with this sort of storytelling, though many are not. Indeed, the conviction that the world and its evils cannot be organized so neatly, with innocent Christians on one side and ungodly persecutors on the other, is what makes some assimilated Mennonites skeptical of the entire martyrological project. Even at the Goshen consultation, which affirmed the process of gathering stories of costly discipleship, some participants raised voices of caution. In one case, a Mennonite leader from Colombia took pains to remind his fellow participants that in his community, the persecutors included forces aligned with multinational mining companies, some of which send their profits to the United States to enhance the investment portfolios of ordinary Americans. The Colombian leader admitted that stories such as his, which exposed the complicity of North American Christians in the suffering of their spiritual kin, were not the kind that most North American Mennonites wanted to read. They were, however, precisely the ones he thought should be told in an ecclesial family that claimed both to oppose violence and to value truth.

The dilemma at the heart of the Anabaptist martyrological project—in fact, the dilemma that riddles all martyrological projects—is the problem of telling the truth. What does it mean for martyrologists to tell the truth? Which truths are most important to tell, and which can be elided or ignored? Measured against contemporary academic standards, martyrologists rarely qualify as evenhanded historians. They may not fabricate saints and villains from thin air, but their storytelling decisions are always subject to spiritual goals that override other considerations that professional historians deem necessary to writing good history.[74] Van Braght and his Anabaptist predecessors were not exceptional in this regard, a conclusion that some assimilated Anabaptists come to as they read *Martyrs Mirror* and find it to be two parts sermon and only one part history. Might not a history of early Anabaptism be truer to life, they wonder, if well-meaning but equivocal Anabaptists were given greater voice? One thinks, for instance, of Anabaptist parents whose unwillingness to relinquish their children led them back to state-sponsored churches. Would not van Braght's history be richer and more reflective of early Anabaptist experience if these men and women were allowed to explain themselves? And would not his history be more balanced if Rome's desire for Christian unity were awarded as much attention as the papacy's moral failings? Richer and more balanced, perhaps, but taking that approach would have surely muddied the spiritual message that van Braght wanted to mediate, a message he hoped would enable his readers to discern the essence of Christian faithfulness. Like any martyrologist worth his salt, van Braght decided it was best to tell some of the truth but not the whole of it.[75]

Centuries later, van Braght's spiritual heirs continue to make their own sets of choices with respect to his martyrological work. Should *Martyrs Mirror* be read in the first place, and if so, by whom? Should its contents be trusted as objective accountings of what actually happened, or are they better understood as hagiographical recollections set in a polemical frame? Beyond that, should the text be read theologically, with the martyrs' convictions counting as theological truth? Or might the text be better understood as a generative piece of literature that expresses the human predicament: the anguish of losing loved ones, the desire to make sense of suffering, the hope of religious certitude, and the horror that often accompanies it? As we have seen, Anabaptists across many generations have worked hard to make historical, theological, and emotional meaning of van Braght's blood-filled text, positing some meanings that van Braght could not have imagined, let alone blessed. Still, even if van Braght could not control the meanings his readers have made, the fact that his work has fueled so many conversations attests to its literary power. In many ways *Martyrs Mirror* has made the Anabaptist tradition what it is.

Conclusion

Many things go into the making of a religious tradition, and most of them have nothing to do with printed texts. The social milieu in which a tradition is birthed, the idiosyncrasies of its early leaders, the ethnic ties that reinforce connections and commitments, and the migration patterns that unfold over time—all of these nontextual realities contribute to the making of a tradition that could have turned out otherwise. This is true, of course, with the Anabaptist tradition, a movement that first took shape in the roiling religious world of sixteenth-century Europe, a movement that was led by a cadre of flawed but able leaders, a movement that somehow managed to survive and transplant itself into new generations and into new lands. To be sure, recent devotees of the Anabaptist tradition have sought to correct the assumption that Anabaptism's essence can be accessed only through genetic connections to its European past, thus making way for people in the global South, as well as persons in non-Anabaptist churches, to claim the tradition as their own. Even then, however, most of these efforts to identify a naked Anabaptism stripped of its ethnic garb take heed of the movement's sixteenth-century beginnings and the commitments of its earliest adherents, many of whom were martyred.[1]

Printed texts may not be essential to a religious tradition's making, but as we have seen with *Martyrs Mirror,* they often play important roles. More than any other text written or compiled by an Anabaptist, *Martyrs Mirror* has shaped the way Anabaptists conceive of Christian faithfulness. Thieleman van Braght may have wished to prompt more changes in his Mennonite contemporaries than he actually did, but his collection of martyr stories has nonetheless compelled many generations of readers to take stock of their own lives vis-à-vis those of the martyrs. Even today many Anabaptists are well aware of their church's martyrological heritage and, for good or ill, perceive church history according to van Braght's interpretation of it. Although Anabaptism is now more fragmented than ever, the fact that Amish, Mennonites, and Hutterites of various stripes still recognize one another as theological kin owes much to van Braght's ability to weave a narrative that threaded together diverse Anabaptist groups from many parts of Europe. Interpreting Christian history in a particular way, van Braght enabled his readers to read history in a similar fashion, an interpretation that has often shaped their commitments in the present.

For van Braght, two particular commitments, adult baptism and defenselessness, were the keys for distinguishing authentic forms of the Christian faith from inauthentic ones. Three and a half centuries later, these convictions continue to distinguish Anabaptism from other Christian traditions. Although other adult-baptizing traditions have emerged since the sixteenth century, few if any of these traditions have linked adult baptism to defenselessness as a matter of course. For van Braght, adult baptism and defenselessness were intrinsically linked, for together they represented a discipleship-oriented Christianity that countered more established forms of Christianity, those that downplayed distinctions between church and state, between church membership and civic citizenship, and between "rendering unto God" and "rendering unto Caesar." Again, van Braght considered the two practices of a piece: adult baptism symbolized the decision to honor Christ above all other masters, and the refusal to take up the sword validated the authenticity of that decision.

Subsequent generations of Anabaptists have continued to give priority to those commitments, often with the assistance of *Martyrs Mirror.* Especially with respect to defenselessness, which has remained a countercultural posture in nearly all times and places, Anabaptist churches have often found it difficult to sustain van Braght's vision of authentic Christianity. In fact, over the centuries, thousands of individuals and scores of congregations have left the Anabaptist fold because they were no longer convinced that nonresistance lies at the heart of Christ's gospel.

Nevertheless, no Christian tradition has maintained its commitment to nonresistance longer and with more success than the Anabaptist tradition. Nearly five hundred years after the Schleitheim Confession deemed the sword "outside the perfection of Christ," the Anabaptist tradition, taken as a whole, remains a peace tradition.[2]

To award *Martyrs Mirror* full credit for sustaining nonresistance in the Anabaptist world would be overstating the case, but it must be given some credit. Nearly every tradition relies on exemplars to instruct its adherents on the content of faithfulness and, moreover, to show them that faithfulness is possible in perilous circumstances. Therefore, if a tradition is to insist upon a definition of Christian faithfulness that includes defenselessness, then it behooves that tradition's leaders to show that defenselessness is possible when violence comes knocking. Granted, most Anabaptist Christians have never come face to face with a violent predator, let alone a bloodthirsty persecutor, but nearly all of them have imagined that possibility. For many of them, the martyrs have been their instructors, teaching them that nonresistance is possible, even in the face of death. One Anabaptist sympathizer has sought to underscore this reality by suggesting that authentic Christianity is a tradition of "martyrs, not heroes," his point being that a defenseless faith turns traditional understandings of heroism upside down.[3] With respect to the Anabaptist tradition, it may be better to call it a tradition shaped by "martyr-heroes" whose nonresistant lives are recorded in *Martyrs Mirror*. One can reasonably ask whether the Anabaptist tradition would still be a peace tradition if the narrative content of *Martyrs Mirror*—its hero stories—had been lost to history.[4]

Of course, granting *Martyrs Mirror* a central role in sustaining the Anabaptist tradition is different from asserting an Anabaptist consensus on questions pertaining to the martyrs' witness: what their witness represents, how it applies to contemporary life, and whether the martyrs' beliefs and practices should go unquestioned. Through the centuries Anabaptist groups and persons have found a wide range of meanings in *Martyrs Mirror*, some standing in tension with others. More recently, some Mennonite readers have found certain aspects of the text to be problematic with respect to living in the present. These problems, which include unsparing moral expectations, dualistic assumptions about good and evil, and portrayals of the past that nourish spiritual arrogance, have given many readers reason for pause. On occasion critics of *Martyrs Mirror* have called for a moratorium on reading the book, including one provocateur who suggested that Anabaptists would help themselves and everyone else if they destroyed all remaining copies.[5] Few would take that proposal seriously, not only readers who esteem the text highly, but also those who have registered concerns about its unwelcome effects. Indeed, for the vast majority of these more critical readers, the desire to forget the past or ignore the martyrs' witness is not at all the goal.[6] Rather, the goal is to assure that remembering the Anabaptist martyr past is done rightly.

In the Anabaptist world, the explicit notion of *right remembering* can be traced to at least 1989, when Dave and Neta Jackson published an abridgment of *Martyrs Mirror* titled *On Fire for Christ: Stories of Anabaptist Martyrs.*[7] In addition to reworking fifteen of van Braght's martyr accounts, the Jacksons, cradle evangelicals who had come to embrace the Anabaptist tradition, produced an introduction that offered standard fare about finding inspiration in the martyrs' steadfastness. But also in their introduction was a warning about remembering. "There is a 'wrong remembering' and a 'right remembering,'" the Jacksons wrote. Whereas wrong remembering "focuses on the injustices done and fans the flames of hatred," right remembering exists as "a testimony that even suffering and death cannot extinguish the victory that is ours in Jesus." Right remembering also requires readers of *Martyrs Mirror* to recognize that, on some occasions, the Anabaptists "unnecessarily mocked what others believed" and thereby incited "the fervor with which they were persecuted." For that reason, right remembering will also "lead us to repent for those attitudes—especially as they linger today."[8]

This emphasis on right remembering has continued in assimilated Mennonite circles in the years since the Jacksons' book appeared. In fact, *right remembering* has become something of a mantra in these circles, a mantra that is fluid enough for people to define it as they see fit.[9] Nearly all who invoke the mantra warn against self-righteousness, but beyond that the proposals for right remembering flow in various directions. For some it means little more than reading the martyrs' stories with a more nuanced understanding of sixteenth-century history, recognizing, for instance, that civil authorities found the Anabaptists' rejection of state-sponsored religion truly terrifying.[10] Others, more present-minded in their approach, have suggested the creation of a companion volume that would narrate the wounds inflicted by Anabaptists upon their own, a volume that would complicate the prevailing narrative of kindhearted Anabaptists enduring a vicious world.[11] In a related vein, some ecumenically minded Mennonites have urged the pairing of Anabaptist martyr stories with those from other Christian traditions, lest Anabaptists assume that their martyrs are somehow unique.[12] One Mennonite writer has gone a step further, suggesting that Mennonites "cease regarding [the] Anabaptists in *Martyrs Mirror* as martyrs unless and until we hear from other Christians that these deaths do bear a kind of witness for the whole church."[13] In this view right remembering would mean forswearing martyrological assertions until non-Anabaptists can say about the Anabaptist victims what Anabaptists have said about them for centuries: that their deaths witnessed to the Christian faith. Although few advocates of right remembering would go that far, the ecumenical sensitivity that animates the suggestion is now common currency among assimilated Mennonites who both value their martyrological legacy and have reservations about it.

This same sensitivity has undergirded recent efforts at reconciliation between contemporary Anabaptists and the heirs of the persecuting traditions, not just Catholics but Lutheran and Reformed Protestants as well. In these settings, which invariably recall the martyrs' experiences, assimilated Mennonite participants have been careful to say, contra van Braght, that the true Christian church includes many kinds of Christians, including Christians from the traditions that hunted down the Anabaptists in the first place. Few statements expressed this conviction more clearly than the Mennonite response to a Statement of Regret offered by the Swiss Evangelical-Reformed Church at a conciliatory gathering in Zurich in 2004, the gathering at which Hans Landis's specter loomed so large. The Statement of Regret, read in the presence of Mennonite representatives from various parts of the world, confessed that the persecution of the Anabaptists by Swiss Reformed leaders was nothing less than a "betrayal of the Gospel."[14] The Mennonite recipients expressed appreciation for the Reformed apology but noted that it felt strange to receive it, for contemporary Mennonites "no longer feel as victims."[15] To the contrary, their response continued, Reformed and Mennonite churches have long sought to recognize one another as members of "the same body of Christ." In other words, rather than underscoring distinctions between Anabaptists and other Christians, the Mennonite response sought to soften them and, in the words of the response itself, "reinforce our common witness to Jesus Christ."[16] For the Mennonites who attended the gathering, remembering the martyrs rightly demanded as much.

Old Order Amish representatives were invited to the Zurich gathering, but in keeping with their church's proscription against air travel, they opted not to attend. Still, the letter they forwarded to the gathering reminds us that, in the twenty-first-century Anabaptist world, remembering the martyrs remains a contested enterprise. Unlike their assimilated counterparts, tradition-minded Anabaptists did not invoke the right-remembering mantra, but they nonetheless expressed strong opinions about what it means to remember the past in ways that advance Christ's kingdom in the present—which, by their lights, means maintaining a strict separation from the larger world. Nowhere in the Amish ministers' letter did words of gratitude for the Reformed apology appear, and although the Amish leaders avowed that they held no grudge, the Reformed request for reconciliation was largely disregarded. This disregard was no accident, much less a veiled threat. Rather, it was a product of how the Amish read the past, a reading that runs straight from Paul to Tertullian through van Braght to the Old Order Amish today, a reading that makes marginalization a virtue and persecution the clearest sign of God's approval. "History teaches us that a church is made stronger by persecution," continued the letter-writers, coming precariously close to thanking the Reformed leaders for their ancestors' complicity in Europe's bloody theater. Indeed, they concluded, "we wonder if there would be any Amish, Mennonite, or Hutterite churches today if there had not been any persecution."[17]

This question, posed nearly four hundred years after Hans Landis lost his head, is an interesting one to ponder, though like all counterfactual queries, its answer lies mostly in the realm of speculation. What we can assert with confidence is this: the nature of North American Anabaptism would be very different if its constituent communities had no martyrs to recall and no book by which to recall them. Divergent readings of *Martyrs Mirror* may have reinforced divisions in the Anabaptist world, but the book's presence in conversations about faithful living is a common thread connecting contemporary Anabaptists who, in many respects, have little in common. By invoking *Martyrs Mirror*, and by caring enough to wrestle with its contents, twenty-first-century Anabaptists reveal themselves to be members of the same religious tradition. Van Braght surely would have wished to shape that tradition more fully than he did, but these continuing references to his martyrological message—typically affirming, occasionally critical, almost always impassioned—attest to the power of his work.

Acknowledgments

I n his invocation to *The Bloody Theater*, Thieleman van Braght
thanked God for sparing him long enough to complete his book.
Unlike van Braght, I was never encompassed by the "snares of death,"
nor did my physicians urge me to stop writing, but I did sometimes wonder if this book would ever get done. Thanks to the people mentioned
below, it did.

I begin where I must: by acknowledging those whose scholarship enabled mine. Of the names that appear in the notes, none appears more
often than Brad Gregory, James Lowry, David Luthy, and Gerald Mast.
Their thoughtfulness characterizes the work of so many people who
have written about the Anabaptist tradition, its martyrs, and the book
that tells their stories.

A host of people read at least portions of my manuscript: Neal Blough,
Edsel Burdge Jr., Julie Byrne, Susanna Caroselli, Crystal Downing, Philip
Goff, Jeff Gundy, Douglas Jacobsen, James Juhnke, Julia Kasdorf, Karl
Koop, Robert Kreider, James Lowry, David Luthy, Richard Thomas, and
two anonymous readers for the Johns Hopkins University Press. I owe a
special debt of thanks to the Johns Hopkins readers, as well as to Edsel
Burdge Jr., James Lowry, and Julia Kasdorf, for providing detailed critiques of the entire manuscript. The remaining errors are my responsibility, but thanks to these capable readers, my misstatements, overstate-
ments, and foolish statements are more sporadic than they would have
been.

A few people were indispensable to me as go-to sources for information: Jeff Bach, Edsel Burdge Jr., Joseph Huffman, Gerald Mast, Steven Nolt, John Roth, and Joe Springer. None of them autoblocked my e-mail, but I suspect they are happy I have moved on to other things.

Other friends and colleagues provided much needed help along the way: John Beaney, Lois Beck, Dale Burkholder, Perry Bush, David Downing, Patrick Erben, Susan Falciani, John Fea, Philipp Gollner, Leonard Gross, Marco Guete, Jeff Gundy, Amos Hoover, Marshall King, Gerald Kraybill, Jim LaGrand, Jennifer McFarlane-Harris, Keith Graber Miller, Levi Miller, Wendell Miller, David Morgan, Glen Pierce, Adriaan Plak, Ben Riehl, Ken Sensenig, Elaine Shenk, Mary Sprunger, Richard Stevick, John Thiesen, Diane Zimmerman Umble, Piet Visser, Erik Wesner, and Norman Wilson.

This sort of book would have been impossible without good libraries staffed by first-rate librarians. Special thanks go to the staff at Messiah College's Murray Library in Grantham, Pennsylvania, and especially to Barb Syvertson, who filled dozens of interlibrary loan requests for me. I am also grateful for the Lancaster Mennonite Historical Society Library in Lancaster, Pennsylvania (especially Steve Ness); the Muddy Creek Farm Library in Ephrata, Pennsylvania (especially Amos Hoover and Jonathan Martin); the Heritage Historical Library in Aylmer, Ontario (especially David Luthy); the Mennonite Historical Library in Goshen, Indiana (especially Joe Springer); the Franklin and Marshall College Library in Lancaster, Pennsylvania; the Mennonite Church USA Archives in Goshen, Indiana; and the Mennonite Library and Archives in North Newton, Kansas. Most of the images that appear in this book were photographed at the Lancaster Mennonite Historical Society or, in a few cases, at the Muddy Creek Farm Library. It is hard to imagine two libraries being more generous with their resources.

I could not have asked for better work-study students than the ones who helped me these past few years. Eric Kehs is an excellent researcher (a great science teacher, too!); Alisha Stoner is a better proofreader than she has a right to be at twenty years old; and Frances Miller can work wonders with digital images, even those produced by a novice photographer like me.

The Young Center for Anabaptist and Pietist Studies at Elizabethtown College provided me with a semester-long Kreider Fellowship and a comfortable office. Better yet, it provided congenial colleagues with whom to drink coffee and share ideas. As always, it has been a pleasure working with Donald B. Kraybill and Cynthia Nolt, both at the Young Center, in the course of preparing this book. I continue to be grateful for Don's professional support and his friendship.

My home institution, Messiah College, graced me with a sabbatical and research funding. My supervisors—Kim Phipps, Randy Basinger, Peter Powers, and Brian Smith—are great people to work for, and my colleagues in the Department of Biblical and Religious Studies are, to a person, both generous and bright. While working on this book, I served on a college task force with six exceptional colleagues from across campus. They knew little about my research, but their hard work and good humor reminded me that working at Messiah College is more a privilege than a chore.

I continue to thank my lucky stars for having pursued a PhD at the University of North Carolina at Chapel Hill, where Grant Wacker served as my dissertation adviser. Twenty years and hundreds of pages later, I still ask myself "WWGT?"—"What Would Grant Think?"—when I craft a sentence or choose a verb. Much of what I know about writing I learned, or stole, from Grant, including the use of a WW-question to thank one's adviser.

Getting paid to be a college professor is a blessing, but as Grant always told me, having a loving family is even better. My mother, Alice Grace Zercher, and my in-laws, Richard and Ruth Weaver, are unfailingly supportive. Together Richard and Ruth raised a daughter who demonstrates almost all of their good qualities and adds some of her own. Circumstantial evidence to the contrary, I did not marry Valerie because she is a great writer and a skillful editor, but you won't find me complaining that she is.

And finally, my three boys: Samuel, Isaiah, and Henry. It seems as if I spend most of my energy trying to embarrass them or impress them. I am much better at the former than the latter, but I hope this book will someday make them say, "Not too bad, Dad. Not too bad."

Notes

MARTYROLOGIES, IN CHRONOLOGICAL ORDER

Spelling and punctuation of names and titles have varied over time. In the right-hand column, I have tried to be faithful to names and titles as they originally appeared. In the left-hand column, I have given priority to consistency, using the English word *Martyrs* instead of *Martyrs'*, and using the German word *Martyrer* instead of *Märtyrer*.

All complete editions of *Martyrs Mirror* include book 1 and book 2. In some editions, the two books are paginated separately. To refer to pages in the separately paginated editions, I use the volume–page number convention, such as "2:380" for page 380 in book 2.

This is not a comprehensive list of *Martyrs Mirror* editions, but is rather a list of the editions I cite most frequently and which I therefore abbreviate in the notes.

De Ries (1631)	[Hans de Ries et al.], *Martelaers Spiegel der Werelose Christenen t'zedert A°. 1524* . . . (Haerlem, Netherlands: Hans Passchiers van Wesbusch, 1631[–32]).
Van Braght (1660)	T. J. V. B[raght], *Het Bloedigh Tooneel der Doops-gesinde, en Weereloose Christenen* . . . (Dordrecht, Netherlands: Jacob Braat voor Jacobus Savry, 1660).
Van Braght (1685)	T. J. V. Braght [and Jan Luyken], *Het Bloedig Tooneel, of Martelaers Spiegel der Doops-gesinde of Weereloose Christenen* . . . (Amsterdam: By J. vander Deyster et al., En Compagnie, 1685).
Martyrer Spiegel (1749)	T. J. V. Braght, *Der Blutige Schau-Platz oder Martyrer-Spiegel der Tauffs Gesinnten oder Wehrlosen-Christen* . . . , [trans. Johann Peter Miller] (Ephrata, PA: 1748–49).
Martyrer Spiegel (1814)	T. J. V. Braght, *Der Blutige Schau-Platz, oder Martyrer Spiegel der Tauffs-Gesinnten, oder Wehrlosen Christen* . . . (Lancaster, PA: Joseph Ehrenfried, 1814[–15]).

Martyrs Mirror (1837)   Thielem J. von Bracht, *The Bloody Theatre, or Martyrs'*
                          Mirror, of the Defenceless Christians . . . , trans. I. Daniel
                          Rupp (Near Lampeter Square, Lancaster County, PA:
                          David Miller, 1837).

Martyrer Spiegel (1849)   Thielem. J. v. Braght, *Der Blutige Schauplatz, oder Märtyrer*
                          Spiegel der Taufs-Gesinnten oder Wehrlosen Christen . . .
                          (Near Lewistown, Mifflin County, PA: Shem Zook, 1849).

Martyrer Spiegel (1870)   Thielem J. v. Braght, *Der Blutige Schauplatz, oder Märtyrer*
                          Spiegel der Taufs-Gesinnten oder Wehrlosen Christen . . .
                          (Elkhart, IN: John F. Funk und Bruder, 1870).

Martyrs Mirror (1886)   Thielem J. van Braght, *The Bloody Theatre, or Martyrs Mirror*
                          of the Defenseless Christians . . . , trans. Joseph F. Sohm
                          (Elkhart, IN: Mennonite Publishing Company, 1886).

Martyrs Mirror (1938)   Thieleman J. van Braght, *The Bloody Theater or Martyrs*
                          Mirror of the Defenseless Christians . . . , trans. Joseph
                          F. Sohm (Scottdale, PA: Mennonite Publishing
                          House / Herald Press, 1938–present.

Martyrer Spiegel (2011)   Thielem J. v. Braght, *Der Blutige Schauplatz, oder Märtyrer-*
                          Spiegel der Taufgesinnten oder Wehrlosen Christen . . .
                          (Aylmer, ON: Pathway, 2011).

OTHER ABBREVIATIONS

ME   *Mennonite Encyclopedia* (Scottdale, PA: Mennonite
                          Publishing House / Herald Press, 1955–90). 5 volumes.
MPH   Mennonite Publishing House
MQR   *Mennonite Quarterly Review*

Preface

1. *Martyrs Mirror* (1938), 1103–5. Most of the *Martyrs Mirror* quotations in this book come from Joseph F. Sohm's English translation of the work, first published in 1886. Since the pagination of Sohm's translation has remained the same since 1938, I cite the publisher's 1938 edition, hereafter cited as *Martyrs Mirror* (1938).

2. Van Braght (1660). The complete title of van Braght's book, translated into English, reads as follows: *The Bloody Theater of the Baptism-Minded and Defenseless Christians, Who for the Testimony of Jesus Their Savior Have Suffered and Were Slain, from the Time of Christ to These Our Last Times. Along with a Description of Holy Baptism and Other Elements of Worship as Practiced by Them throughout All Ages. Contained in Two Books. Being an Enlargement of the Earlier "Martyrs Mirror," from Many Authentic Chronicles, Memorials, Testimonies, etc.* For the full Dutch title, see chapter 3.

3. The words *Martyrs Mirror* did appear in the title of van Braght's *Bloody Theater,* but only near the title's end. Because van Braght's martyr book was an expansion of a martyrology titled *Martyrs Mirror* (*Martelaers Spiegel*) published in 1631, van Braght included the following phrase near the end of his lengthy title: "Being an Enlargement of the Earlier *Martyrs Mirror.*" For more details, see chapter 3.

4. The term *nonresistance* derives from Jesus's instructions in the Sermon on the Mount: "You have heard that it was said, 'An eye for an eye and a tooth for a tooth.' But I say to you, Do not resist an evildoer" (Matthew 5:38–39, NRSV). In his martyrology's title, van Braght refers to "defenseless Christians" (*Weereloose Christenen*) to signify the Anabaptist commitment to defenselessness.

5. Quoted in Ferne Burkhardt, "Confession and Forgiveness Mark Historic Anabaptist-Reformed Gathering in Zurich," *Courier* 19, no. 3 (2004): 12.

6. Peter Dettwiler, "Mennonites and Reformed—A Process of Reconciliation," in *Steps to Reconciliation: Reformed and Anabaptist Churches in Dialogue*, ed. Michael Baumann (Zurich: Theologischer Verlag Zurich, 2007), 19–20.

7. John Landis Ruth, *The Earth Is the Lord's: A Narrative History of the Lancaster Mennonite Conference* (Scottdale, PA: Herald Press, 2001). For the Psalm 24:1 quotation, see "Document 13," in *Hans Landis: Swiss Anabaptist Martyr in Seventeenth Century Documents*, trans. James W. Lowry, ed. David J. Rempel Smucker and John L. Ruth (Millersburg, OH: Ohio Amish Library, 2003), 137.

8. Even persons who have left the Anabaptist tradition sometimes exploit this cachet. After recounting Hans Landis's martyrdom, one ministry website proclaimed that revivalist Raymond Landis was "a descendant of this rich heritage." The website then pointed to the "many trials and tribulations" that Raymond Landis faced, even as he remained steadfast in his evangelistic work. Significantly, Raymond Landis was neither Mennonite nor Amish, but rather a Oneness Pentecostal with Anabaptist family roots. His website proceeded to make connections between the way the early Anabaptists were persecuted and the way Oneness Pentecostals were reviled by their fellow Pentecostals in the twentieth century. It even claimed a dubious theological kinship between the two groups: "In the 16th century, many of the Anabaptists were also known to be anti-Trinitarian and they were modalistic monarchians. In other words, they were 'Oneness Pentecostals.' " From www.colmww.org/founders.html, accessed September 21, 2010 (website discontinued).

9. In *Martyrs Mirror* (1938), the word *Doopsgesinde* is typically rendered "Anabaptists," not "the baptism-minded." See the footnote in *Martyrs Mirror* (1938), 16.

10. For Amish beginnings, see Donald B. Kraybill, Karen Johnson-Weiner, and Steven M. Nolt, *The Amish* (Baltimore: Johns Hopkins University Press, 2013), 22–33.

11. In addition to Amish, Mennonites, and Hutterites, the North American Anabaptist family includes a variety of groups that carry the name *Brethren*. For an overview of these groups and their relative sizes, see Donald B. Kraybill, *Concise Encyclopedia of Amish, Brethren, Hutterites, and Mennonites* (Baltimore: Johns Hopkins University Press, 2010), 215–58.

12. Ibid., xv–xvi.

13. De Ries (1631).

Chapter 1. Anabaptism

1. The phrase *the German Reformation* fails to express two things: the multiplex nature of sixteenth-century religious reform and the absence at the time of a political

entity called *Germany*. For that reason, it may be better to speak of the "reformers and reformations in German-speaking regions of Europe." For simplicity's sake, however, I refer both to *Germany* and to *the German Reformation*, shorthand practices that place me in good company. See, for instance, Michael G. Baylor, *The German Reformation and the Peasants' War: A Brief History with Documents* (Boston: Bedford / St. Martin's, 2012).

2. For a consideration of the term *early modern*, see Euan Cameron's introduction to *Early Modern Europe: An Oxford History*, ed. Euan Cameron (Oxford: Oxford University Press, 1999), xvii–xix.

3. Alison Rowlands, "The Conditions of Life for the Masses," in Cameron, *Early Modern Europe*, 32. Cameron estimates a total European population in 1500 of 60 million to 85 million. See Euan Cameron, *The European Reformation* (Oxford: Oxford University Press, 1991), 4.

4. Cameron, introduction to *Early Modern Europe*, xix.

5. Steven Gunn, "War, Religion, and the State," in Cameron, *Early Modern Europe*, 103.

6. Cameron, *European Reformation*, 10.

7. Keith Thomas, *Religion and the Decline of Magic* (New York: Scribner's, 1971), 5. Even among the nobility, life expectation for boys was less than thirty years.

8. Ibid., 668.

9. Cameron, *European Reformation*, 79.

10. Desiderius Erasmus, *The Handbook of the Christian Soldier*, trans. Charles Fantazzi, in *Collected Works of Erasmus: Spiritualia* (Toronto: University of Toronto Press, 1988), 1–127.

11. Desiderius Erasmus, *The Praise of Folly*, in *Middle Ages, Renaissance, and Reformation*, vol. 2 of *Classics of Western Thought*, ed. Karl F. Thompson (New York: Harcourt Brace Jovanovich, 1980), 290–91.

12. See Carlos M. N. Eire, *War against the Idols: The Reformation of Worship from Erasmus to Calvin* (Cambridge: Cambridge University Press, 1986), 45–53.

13. Martin Luther, Theses 36 and 49, in *Ninety-Five Theses, or Disputation on the Power and Efficacy of Indulgences, 1517*, trans. C. M. Jacobs, in *Luther's Works*, ed. Harold J. Grimm (Philadelphia: Muhlenberg Press, 1957), 31:28–30.

14. Martin Luther, "Two Kinds of Righteousness, 1519," trans. Lowell J. Satre, in *Luther's Works*, 31:298.

15. Selected passages from Martin Luther, "Commentary on Galatians (1538)," trans. and quoted by Herbert J. A. Bouman, "The Doctrine of Justification in the Lutheran Confessions," *Concordia Theological Monthly* 26 (1955): 801.

16. Hans-Jürgen Goertz, "The Reformation of the Commoners," in *A Companion to Anabaptism and Spiritualism, 1521–1700*, ed. John D. Roth and James M. Stayer (Leiden: Brill, 2007), 4. The following accounts of Müntzer's and Karlstadt's reforms draw heavily from Goertz.

17. Ibid., 7.

18. Quoted in ibid., 8.

19. William W. McNiel, "Andreas Karlstadt and Thomas Müntzer: Relatives in Theology and Reformation" (PhD diss., Queens University, 1999), 253.

20. Thomas Müntzer, "Prague Manifesto," ed. and trans. Michael G. Baylor, *MQR* 63 (1989): 30–57 (quotation on 46). Müntzer wrote, "In our time God wants to separate the wheat from the tares so that one can grasp . . . who it is that seduced the church for such a long time" (56).

21. Quoted in Goertz, "Reformation of the Commoners," 34.

22. Thomas Müntzer, "Thomas Müntzer to His Followers in Allstedt, 27 April 1525," in *Martin Luther*, ed. E. G. Rupp and Benjamin Drewery (New York: St. Martin's Press, 1970), 121.

23. Martin Luther, "Letter to the Princes of Saxony concerning the Rebellious Spirit, 1524," trans. Conrad Bergendoff, in *Luther's Works*, ed. Conrad Bergendoff (Philadelphia: Muhlenberg Press, 1958), 40:49–59.

24. Martin Luther, *Against the Robbing and Murdering Hordes of Peasants, 1525*, trans. Charles M. Jacobs, in *Luther's Works*, ed. Robert C. Schultz (Philadelphia: Fortress Press, 1967), 46:49, 52.

25. This account of Anabaptist origins draws from C. Arnold Snyder, "Swiss Anabaptism: The Beginnings, 1523–1525," in Roth and Stayer, *Companion to Anabaptism and Spiritualism*, 45–81.

26. In late 1523, for instance, Grebel wrote, "Whoever thinks, believes, or declares that Zwingli acts according to the duty of a shepherd thinks, believes, and declares wickedly." See "Grebel to Vadian, Zurich, December 18, 1523," in *The Sources of Swiss Anabaptism*, ed. Leland Harder (Scottdale, PA: Herald Press, 1985), 276.

27. "The Mantz Petition of Defense, Zurich, between December 13 and 28, 1524," in Harder, *Sources of Swiss Anabaptism*, 312. By December 1524, "the radicals had come to understand baptism in the essential form that it would later retain: a visible sign of inner faith and a commitment to live a new life in the community of faith." Snyder, "Swiss Anabaptism," 63.

28. See "Council Mandate for Infant Baptism, Zurich, January 18, 1525" and "Council Decree against Anabaptists, Zurich, January 21, 1525," in Harder, *Sources of Swiss Anabaptism*, 336–38.

29. This quotation is from the *Hutterian Chronicle*'s account of these first baptisms. The *Chronicle* comprises some of the earliest historical writing by Anabaptists. See *The Chronicle of the Hutterian Brethren*, trans. and ed. Hutterian Brethren (Rifton, NY: Plough, 1987), 1:45.

30. Snyder, "Swiss Anabaptism," 64.

31. Harold S. Bender, "The Anabaptist Vision," *Church History* 13 (1944): 17–21.

32. Ibid., 21, 22.

33. James M. Stayer, *Anabaptists and the Sword*, 2nd ed. (Lawrence, KS: Coronado Press, 1976), 104–7. For the continuing debate on the centrality of nonresistance in early Anabaptism, see C. Arnold Snyder, "The Birth and Evolution of Swiss Anabaptism, 1520–1530," *MQR* 80 (2006): 501–645, and the responses to the article in the same issue.

34. James M. Stayer, Werner O. Packull, and Klaus Deppermann, "From Monogenesis to Polygenesis: The Historical Discussion of Anabaptist Origins," *MQR* 49 (1975): 83–121.

35. Klaus Deppermann, *Melchior Hoffman: Social Unrest and Apocalyptic Visions in*

the Age of Reformation, ed. Benjamin Drewery, trans. Malcolm Wren (Edinburgh: T. & T. Clark, 1987), 72–75, 321–48.

36. Ralf Klötzer, "The Melchiorites and Münster," in Roth and Stayer, *Companion to Anabaptism and Spiritualism,* 217–56.

37. For a summary of shared Anabaptist convictions, see C. Arnold Snyder, introduction to *Sources of South German / Austrian Anabaptism,* ed. C. Arnold Snyder, trans. Walter Klaassen, Frank Friesen, and Werner O. Packull (Kitchener, ON: Pandora Press, 2001), xiii–xiv.

38. Brad S. Gregory, *Salvation at Stake: Christian Martyrdom in Early Modern Europe* (Cambridge, MA: Harvard University Press, 1999), 86.

39. Quoted in ibid., 89.

40. For an account of these revolutionary activities, see Japp Geraerts, "The Prosecution of Anabaptists in Holland, 1530–1566," *MQR* 86 (2012): 5–47.

41. Michael Driedger, "Anabaptists and the Early Modern State," in Roth and Stayer, *Companion to Anabaptism and Spiritualism,* 515.

42. Harry Loewen, *Luther and the Radicals: Another Look at Some Aspects of the Struggle between Luther and the Radical Reformers* (Waterloo, ON: Wilfred Laurier University, 1974), 140–41.

43. Mob violence against Protestants in France took nearly twenty thousand lives. Also, compared to the number of Anabaptists executed in the sixteenth century, more women were executed for being witches. But the Anabaptists were a "real dissident sect," whereas the witches were a "largely fictitious creation of two centuries' worth of polemical discourse and inquisitorial and judicial compulsion." Gary K. Waite, *Eradicating the Devil's Minions: Anabaptists and Witches in Reformation Europe* (Toronto: University of Toronto Press, 2007), 4.

44. For the spectrum of Anabaptist responses to persecution, see John S. Oyer, "Nicodemites among Württemberg Anabaptists," *MQR* 71 (1997): 487–514.

45. Gregory estimates "between two and three thousand, about one thousand from central Europe (Switzerland, south and central Germany, Austria, Bohemia, and Moravia) and somewhat more than this from the Low Countries, with a smaller number of executions having occurred elsewhere." Brad S. Gregory, "Anabaptist Martyrdom: Imperatives, Experience, and Memorialization," in Roth and Stayer, *Companion to Anabaptism and Spiritualism,* 478.

46. Gregory, *Salvation at Stake,* 198.

47. Ibid., 201. Gregory cites figures from Claus-Peter Clasen, "Executions of Anabaptists, 1525–1618: A Research Report," *MQR* 47 (1973): 118–19.

48. Gregory, *Salvation at Stake,* 200. "Even to ponder becoming an Anabaptist," writes Gregory, "was ipso facto to think about martyrdom" (198).

49. "Grebel to Müntzer, Zurich, September 5, 1524," in Harder, *Sources of Swiss Anabaptism,* 290.

50. "The Trial of Grebel, Mantz, and Blaurock, Zurich, between November 9 and 18, 1525," in Harder, *Sources of Swiss Anabaptism,* 440.

51. All quotations in this paragraph are from *The Schleitheim Confession,* trans. and ed. John H. Yoder (Scottdale, PA: Herald Press, 1973), 11–12.

52. Ibid., 15–16, 19.

53. Quoted in Gregory, *Salvation at Stake*, 203. Gregory notes that the song, though attributed to Sattler, may not have been written by him, then adds, "Whether written by Sattler or not, the song illustrates separatism wedded to a martyrological mentality in Anabaptism's formative years" (444n26).

54. Ibid., 211. This connection draws on a reference to water and blood in 1 John 5:6.

55. Geraerts, "Prosecution of Anabaptists in Holland," 13. Freerks is sometimes called Sicke Snyder.

56. For details on Menno Simons's life, see Harold S. Bender, "A Brief Biography of Menno Simons," in *The Complete Writings of Menno Simons, c. 1496–1561*, trans. Leonard Verduin, ed. J. C. Wenger (Scottdale, PA: Herald Press, 1956), 4–29.

57. Nanne van der Zijpp, "Mennist," in *ME*, 3:574.

58. Menno Simons, "Foundation of Christian Doctrine, 1539," in Wenger, *Complete Writings of Menno Simons*, 109–10.

59. Ibid., 188. The reference here is to 2 Timothy 3:12.

60. Menno Simons, *Brief Confession on the Incarnation, 1544*, in Wenger, *Complete Writings of Menno Simons*, 425. See also Simons, "The Cross of the Saints, c. 1554," in ibid., 581–622. This latter piece is sometimes called "A Comforting Admonition," shorthand for "A Comforting Admonition concerning the Sufferings, the Cross, and the Persecution of the Saints Because of the Word of God and His Testimony" (580).

61. Gregory, *Salvation at Stake*, 201.

Chapter 2. Memorializing Martyrdom before *The Bloody Theater*

1. See Brad S. Gregory, *Salvation at Stake: Christian Martyrdom in Early Modern Europe* (Cambridge, MA: Harvard University Press, 1999), 3–4.

2. The status of the Apocrypha was contested among Protestant reformers and was eventually deemed of lower authority than the Old and New Testaments by Anabaptist churches. Early on, however, and in contrast to other Protestant reformers, "the Anabaptists considered the Apocrypha to be of equal authority as the rest of scripture." Jonathan R. Seiling, "Solae (Quae?) Scripture: Anabaptists and the Apocrypha," *MQR* 80 (2006): 30.

3. "The entire New Testament Scripture is full of such passages," wrote Felix Mantz in reference to adult baptism. "Whoever says or teaches otherwise does something which he cannot prove with Scripture." See "The Mantz Petition of Defense, Zurich, between December 13 and 28, 1524," in *The Sources of Swiss Anabaptism*, ed. Leland Harder (Scottdale, PA: Herald Press, 1985), 313–14.

4. "Hear the Scripture," says the 1527 *Schleitheim Confession* as it outlines the Anabaptists' stance on swearing oaths. *The Schleitheim Confession*, trans. and ed. John H. Yoder (Scottdale, PA: Herald Press, 1973), 17. For a relatively early Anabaptist doctrinal formula, see Leonard Gross, "'Whether the Writings of the Old Testament Are as Valid for Christians as Those of the New': Swiss Brethren Perspectives," *MQR* 88 (2014): 373–92.

5. Matthew 23:35, NRSV.

6. For the Anabaptists' frequent use of Maccabees and other apocryphal texts, see

Loren L. Johns, "Reading the Maccabean Literature by the Light of the Stake: Anabaptist Appropriations of the Apocrypha," *MQR* 86 (2012): 151–73.

7. 2 Maccabees 7:20, NRSV.

8. Susanna 1:1–64, NRSV.

9. In his treatise "The Cross of the Saints," Menno Simons begins with an account of Jesus's suffering, then proceeds to argue that this suffering will be shared by his followers. Menno Simons, "The Cross of the Saints," in *The Complete Writings of Menno Simons, c. 1496–1561,* trans. Leonard Verduin, ed. J. C. Wenger (Scottdale, PA: MPH, 1956), 581–82.

10. In the words of one writer, Jesus died "in order to sanctify the people by his own blood" (Hebrews 13:12, NRSV).

11. Romans 8:17, NRSV.

12. 2 Corinthians 4:8–10, NRSV.

13. Acts 8:3, NRSV.

14. 2 Timothy 3:12, NRSV. See Eldon T. Yoder and Monroe D. Hochstetler, comps., *Biblical References in Anabaptist Writings* (Alymer, ON: Pathway, 1969), 328–29.

15. Hebrews 11:38, 35, NRSV.

16. Revelation 7:9–17, NRSV.

17. Van Braght (1660), 1:sig. [**4]v. "Hence the whole volume of holy Scriptures, especially the Old Testament, seems to be almost exclusively, a book of martyrs." *Martyrs Mirror* (1938), 13. Note: citations including "sig." point to specially paginated sections ("signatures") in the front or back matter of certain versions of *Martyrs Mirror.* In the case of van Braght (1660), the signatures are sometimes signed with letters (a, b, . . .), and are sometimes signed with characters (* and ‡) or combinations of characters.

18. For a summary of early Christian persecution, see Candida Moss, *The Myth of Persecution: How Early Christians Invented a Story of Martyrdom* (New York: HarperOne, 2013). As the title of her book suggests, Moss argues that the extent of Christian persecution has often been exaggerated.

19. Geoffrey Dipple, *"Just as in the Time of the Apostles": Uses of History in the Radical Reformation* (Kitchener, ON: Pandora Press, 2005), 168.

20. See Eusebius, *The Church History,* trans. Paul L. Maier (Grand Rapids, MI: Kregel, 1999). Eusebius wrote his history in ten "books," though in some ways the books are more akin to what modern readers call chapters. According to Paul Maier, the first edition of *Ecclesiastical History,* consisting of books 1–7, was likely published before 300. Books 8–10 were added by 316, and book 10 was revised sometime around 325.

21. Eusebius, *Church History,* 22.

22. This was the case long before van Braght produced *The Bloody Theater* in 1660. For instance, the third song in the *Ausbund,* a sixteenth-century Swiss Brethren hymnal, draws from Eusebius as it recounts martyrs in the early church; see *Songs of the "Ausbund": History and Translations of "Ausbund" Hymns* (Millersburg, OH: Ohio Amish Library, 1998), 1:25–42. Also, Menno Simons refers to Eusebius's parade of martyrs in his 1554 treatise "The Cross of Christ," in Wenger, *Complete Writings of Menno Simons,* 595.

23. Maier titles chapter 9 of Eusebius's history "The Great Deliverance" (286).

24. Eusebius, *Church History*, 329.

25. Ibid., 331–32.

26. Charles Freeman, *A New History of Early Christianity* (New Haven, CT: Yale University Press, 2009), 225.

27. For Constantine's involvement at Nicaea, see Roger E. Olson, *The Story of Christian Theology: Twenty Centuries of Tradition and Reform* (Downers Grove, IL: InterVarsity Press, 1999), 151–57.

28. Ibid., 265–67. The Donatists considered unworthy those bishops who had cooperated with Roman authorities during times of persecution. Correspondingly, they rejected the efficacy of the sacraments administered by those bishops.

29. St. Augustine, "A Treatise concerning the Correction of the Donatists (Epistle CLXXXV)," trans. J. R. King, www.ccel.org/ccel/schaff/npnf104.v.vi.v.html, accessed January 29, 2015.

30. For instance, "Sermon 335C, On the Feast of a Martyr," in *Augustine: Political Writings*, ed. E. M. Atkins and R. J. Dodaro (Cambridge: Cambridge University Press, 2001), 54.

31. Cyriac K. Pullapilly, *Caesar Baronius: Counter-Reformation Historian* (Notre Dame, IN: University of Notre Dame Press, 1975), 50–52, 173–76.

32. Song 5, in *Songs of the "Ausbund,"* 1:50–56.

33. Michael Sattler, "When Christ with His Teaching True," trans. John H. Yoder, in Yoder, *The Legacy of Michael Sattler* (Scottdale, PA: Herald Press, 1973), 140–45.

34. Robert A. Riall, introduction to *The Earliest Hymns of the "Ausbund": Some Beautiful Christian Songs Composed and Sung in the Prison at Passau, Published in 1564*, ed. Galen A. Peters (Kitchener, ON: Pandora Press, 2003), 19.

35. Song 113, trans. Robert A. Riall, in *Earliest Hymns*, 313–18.

36. This definition of martyr ballads comes from Victor G. Doerksen, "The Anabaptist Martyr Ballad," *MQR* 51 (1977): 5–21. For Doerksen, the martyr ballad *"tells the story of a particular martyrdom.* They are, thus, not merely songs dealing with the theme of martyrdom, or songs by martyrs, but martyr ballads in a stricter sense" (8, emphasis in original).

37. Quotations from "A Song of Elisabeth," in *"Elisabeth's Manly Courage": Testimonials and Songs of Martyred Anabaptist Women in the Low Countries*, ed. and trans. Hermina Joldersma and Louis Grijp (Milwaukee: Marquette University Press, 2001), 114–21. Joldersma and Grijp translated this song from the 1570 edition of a Dutch martyrology, *Het Offer des Heeren (The Sacrifice of the Lord)*, which is considered later in this chapter.

38. "Song of Elisabeth," 121.

39. Ibid., 117.

40. C. Arnold Snyder, "Orality, Literacy, and the Study of Anabaptism," *MQR* 65 (1991): 371–92.

41. Gregory, *Salvation at Stake*, 214, who cites Ursula Lieseberg, *Studiem zum Märtyrerlied der Täufer im 16. Jahrhundert* (Frankfurt am Main: Peter Lang, 1991). Gregory notes that other martyr hymns, such as one detailing the death of Felix Mantz, were

composed by hymnists who drew from previously written accounts in pamphlets or letters (214).

42. For instance, Hans Landis, the last Anabaptist executed in Switzerland, was memorialized in a lengthy song sometime after his death in 1614. The ballad appears as Hymn 132 in the *Ausbund* (Lancaster, PA: Amish Book Committee, 1996), 771–83.

43. Christoph Erhard, quoted in Gregory, *Salvation at Stake*, 215.

44. The other early Anabaptist martyr memorialized in print was Jörgen Wagner; see Gregory, *Salvation at Stake*, 213. Strictly speaking, Wagner was not an Anabaptist, since he did not undergo rebaptism. He did, however, repudiate infant baptism, so many early Anabaptists embraced him as one of their own. See Johann Loserth and Harold S. Bender, "Wagner, Georg," in *ME*, 4:869.

45. The pamphlet may have been written by von Graveneck's brother-in-law, Balthasar Maler, a printer in Zurich. See Gustav Bossert Jr., Harold S. Bender, and C. Arnold Snyder, "Sattler, Michael (d. 1527)," in *Global Anabaptist Mennonite Encyclopedia Online* (1989), http://gameo.org/index.php?title=Sattler,_Michael_(d._1527)&oldid=121298, accessed January 29, 2014.

46. An edited version of von Graveneck's pamphlet can be found in Yoder, *Legacy of Michael Sattler*, 67–76.

47. Anabaptist refugees fled eastward to Moravia from places like Switzerland, Tyrol, and Austria in the mid-1520s. In 1527, one faction of these Moravian refugees began practicing a communal sharing of goods as outlined in the New Testament book of Acts. Two years later, an Anabaptist pastor from Tyrol, Jacob Hutter, began visiting the Moravian communalists to provide spiritual counsel. In time Hutter became the group's leader, and the group eventually took his name. They continue today as a distinct North American Anabaptist group, located primarily in the western United States and Canada. See Werner O. Packull, *Hutterite Beginnings: Communitarian Experiments during the Reformation* (Baltimore: Johns Hopkins University Press, 1995), 54–76.

48. *The Chronicle of the Hutterian Brethren*, trans. and ed. Hutterian Brethren (Rifton, NY: Plough, 1987), 1:145.

49. James W. Lowry, *The "Martyrs' Mirror" Made Plain: How to Study and Profit from the "Martyrs' Mirror*," rev. ed. (Aylmer, ON: Pathway, 2011), 131n1; and Riall, introduction to *Earliest Hymns*, 13. The oldest surviving edition of the *Ausbund* derives from 1583, though Gregory says that the hymnal was "likely published around 1570." *Salvation at Stake*, 214, 450n82.

50. Gregory, *Salvation at Stake*, 214.

51. Nanne van der Zijpp, "Punishment of the Anabaptists in the Low Countries," in *ME*, 4:232–34.

52. See Piet Visser, "Mennonites and Doopsgezinden in the Netherlands, 1535–1700," in *A Companion to Anabaptism and Spiritualism, 1521–1700*, ed. John D. Roth and James M. Stayer (Leiden: Brill, 2007), 314–17.

53. Ibid., 301–11. The phrase "management problems" is from 307. The Waterlanders' name came from the many rivers and lakes in the region where they lived, north of Amsterdam.

54. Visser, "Mennonites and Doopsgezinden," 310, 317. According to James W. Lowry, the Biestkens Bible was valued by Anabaptists because "it was the first Dutch Bible with numbered verses and had an index of scripture passages especially relating to their doctrine." James W. Lowry, "*Het Offer des Heeren* (The Sacrifice of the Lord)," *Pennsylvania Mennonite Heritage* 33, no. 1 (January 2010): 13n18.

55. Visser, "Mennonites and Doopsgezinden," 317; Nanne van der Zijpp, "Veelderhande Liedekens (Various Songs)," in *ME*, 4:799–800.

56. Hendricksz is also known as Jan Hendricks van Schoonrewoerd. See Lowry, "*Het Offer des Heeren*," 12n11; and Brad Gregory, "Anabaptist Martyrdom: Imperatives, Experience, and Memorialization," in Roth and Stayer, *Companion to Anabaptism and Spiritualism*, 492.

57. Paul Valkema Blouw, "Een onbedende doperse drukkerij in Freisland," *Doopsgezinde Bijdragen* 15 (1989): 37–63. Blouw's work is summarized in Lowry, "*Het Offer des Heeren*," 12–13.

58. The quotations in this paragraph come from the title translation in Irvin B. Horst, "The Dutch Background of the *Martyrs' Mirror*," *Christian Monitor* 42, no. 4 (April 1950): 114.

59. The book concludes with the same cost-benefit analysis of present suffering versus eternal reward. For a translation of the book's conclusion, see Lowry, "*Martyrs' Mirror" Made Plain*, 93–94.

60. Ibid., 76.

61. Gregory, *Salvation at Stake*, 225. In the 1563 edition, the prose section constituted 80 percent of the book's pages and the songbook only 20 percent. This 4:1 ratio stayed relatively constant throughout the book's history. Lowry, "*Het Offer des Heeren*," 11n6.

62. "The last ten editions print the songbook continuously as part of the signatures of the main body of the book." Lowry, "*Het Offer des Heeren*," 11n6.

63. Gregory, "Anabaptist Martyrdom," 493.

64. There were exceptions to the book's chronological predilection for the 1550s, but they were few (1539, 1544, 1549, 1564, and 1569). Not only were the martyrs in *The Sacrifice of the Lord* relatively monolithic in their church affiliation; so too were their adversaries in their own affiliation. In other regions of Europe, Anabaptists suffered persecution at the hands of Protestants and Catholics alike, but the persecuting church in the sixteenth-century Netherlands was the Catholic Church. Correspondingly, the martyrs' tormentors in *The Sacrifice of the Lord* are Catholics.

65. Gregory, "Anabaptist Martyrdom," 494. Gregory's observations draw on Piet Visser, "Het bedrieglijk onbewogen bestaan van brieven: Een editorische vergelijking tussen de geschreven en de gedrukte martelaarsteksten van Jeronimus en Lysken Segers," *Doopsgezinde Bijdragen*, n.s., 29 (2003): 65–87.

66. English translations of the preface and conclusion to *The Sacrifice of the Lord* can be found in Lowry, "*Martyrs' Mirror" Made Plain*, 90–92, 93–94 (translations by Lowry).

67. Gregory, *Salvation at Stake*, 244. The dimensions of the 1599 edition were approximately five and a half inches high, four inches wide, and an inch and two-thirds thick.

68. The persecution of European Anabaptists did not end with the close of the six-

teenth century. In Switzerland, for instance, the last Anabaptist martyr was not put to death until 1614, and even after that date some Anabaptists died as they lingered in Swiss prisons. The persecution of Anabaptists, especially in the form of social and economic discrimination and civic banishment, continued in some regions of Europe for centuries.

69. The emphasis on church discipline among Anabaptists "was related to the assumption that the church, as the body of Christ, must show real signs of spiritual regeneration. . . . To maintain the purity of the body of Christ, those who committed serious moral offenses were disciplined, which often involved separating or removing the guilty person from the fellowship of the church until repentance and visible change had occurred." Karl Koop, *Anabaptist-Mennonite Confessions of Faith: The Development of a Tradition* (Kitchener, ON: Pandora Press, 2004), 50.

70. Ibid., 50–51. One Mennonite leader, Leonard Bouwens, called the Waterlanders the "garbage wagon" because of their lenient disciplinary standards. For Bouwens's quotation, see Cornelius J. Dyck, *An Introduction to Mennonite History: A Popular History of the Anabaptists and the Mennonites*, 3rd ed. (Scottdale, PA: Herald Press, 1993), 123.

71. For instance, the Flemish faction divided into Old Flemish and Young Flemish in 1586. For a more detailed exploration of these various groups, see Visser, "Mennonites and Doopsgezinden," 313–28; and Samme Zijlstra, "Anabaptism and Tolerance: Possibilities and Limitations," in *Calvinism and Religious Toleration in the Dutch Golden Age*, ed. R. Po-Chia Hsia and Henk F. K. Van Nierop (New York: Cambridge University Press, 2002), 112–31.

72. [Hans de Ries, Jacques Outerman, et al.], *Historie der Martelaren ofte Waerachtighe Getuygen Jesu Christi . . .* (Haerlem, Netherlands: Jacob Pauels Hauwert for Daniel Keyser, 1615).

73. Gregory, *Salvation at Stake*, 237.

74. This entire paragraph draws from Gregory, *Salvation at Stake*, 237.

75. Nanne van der Zijpp, "Ries, Hans de," in *ME*, 4:330–31.

76. For instance, de Ries's martyrology included many German-speaking martyrs from Anabaptism's first two decades, martyrs who did not appear in *The Sacrifice of the Lord*. See Gregory, "Anabaptist Martyrdom," 497.

77. [De Ries, Outerman, et al.], "Voor-reden," in *Historie der Martelaren*, sig. **1; English translation in Gregory, *Salvation at Stake*, 240.

78. Ibid., sig. **1; English translation in Gregory, *Salvation at Stake*, 240.

79. Gregory, *Salvation at Stake*, 240–41.

80. [Pieter Jans Twisck et al.], *Historie der Warachtighe Getuygen Jesu Christi . . .* (Hoorn, Netherlands: Zacharias Cornelis, 1617).

81. Ibid., "Tot den Leser," sig. [*1]v; English translation from Gregory, *Salvation at Stake*, 241.

82. For instance, with respect to shunning a disciplined spouse, the Old Frisian confession insisted on it. See "Thirty-Three Articles (1617)," trans. Gary K. Waite, in *Confessions of Faith in the Anabaptist Tradition, 1527–1660*, ed. Karl Koop (Kitchener, ON: Pandora Press, 2006), 169–261; see especially Article 29 (247–50).

83. [Pieter Jans Twisck et al.], *Historie van de Vrome Getuygen Jesu Christi* . . . (Hoorn, Netherlands: Isaac Willems for Zacharias Cornelis, 1626).

84. For the importance of this doctrine to early Dutch Mennonites, see Gerald J. Mast, "Jesus' Flesh and the Faithful Church in the Theological Rhetoric of Menno Simons," in *The Work of Jesus Christ in Anabaptist Perspective*, ed. Alain Epp Weaver and Gerald J. Mast (Telford, PA: Cascadia, 2008), 173–90.

85. Gregory, *Salvation at Stake*, 241–42.

86. De Ries (1631).

87. "Voor-reden tot den Leser," in de Ries (1631), 3.

88. Ibid., 3–4.

89. See Piet Visser, *Broeders in de Geest* (Deventer, Netherlands: Uitgeverij Sub Rosa, 1988), 1:43–45; and Keith L. Sprunger, "Dutch Anabaptists and the Telling of the Martyr Stories," *MQR* 80 (2006): 171.

90. "Voor-reden," in de Ries (1631), 3–4; English translation from Gregory, *Salvation at Stake*, 243. Even though van Braght included in *The Bloody Theater* nearly all of the 1631 preface, he excised the editors' argument about the martyrs' theological diversity; cf., van Braght (1660), 2:sig. [*4]v. In *Martyrs Mirror* (1938), 355, this deleted material would have fallen after the third paragraph.

91. With respect to the essentials of the faith, the Waterlander editors wrote that there was "conformity of the ancient, apostolic church with the church of these martyrs." With respect to the treatment of faithful Christians, they contended there was "lasting persecution . . . from the time of Christ to the beginning of this *Martyrs Mirror*." De Ries (1631), 21; English translation from Gregory, *Salvation at Stake*, 243.

92. Cornelius J. Dyck, "Hans de Ries and the Legacy of Menno," *MQR* 62 (1988): 401–2.

93. According to Gregory, the cost of de Ries's 1615 martyrology was three guilders, about half a week's salary for a journeyman bricklayer. The cost of de Ries (1631) was likely similar. See Gregory, *Salvation at Stake*, 239, 464n211.

94. "Voor-reden," in de Ries (1631), 17. Because van Braght quoted most of the 1631 preface in his later work, these phrases appear in van Braght (1660), 2:sig. ***3. For the English translation, see *Martyrs Mirror* (1938), 361.

95. Lowry, *"Martyrs' Mirror" Made Plain*, 130–32.

96. Herbert Grabes, *The Mutable Glass: Mirror-Imagery in Titles and Texts of the Middle Ages and the English Renaissance*, trans. Gordon Collier (Cambridge: Cambridge University Press, 1982).

97. Lowry, *"Martyrs' Mirror" Made Plain*, 130–31.

98. Quotation from de Ries (1631), 157. This account appears in van Braght (1660), 2:209. The English translation is from *Martyrs Mirror* (1938), 522.

Chapter 3. Thieleman van Braght and the Publication of *The Bloody Theater*

1. The *Ausbund* has remained in print and is still used in Amish congregations. Although specific martyr accounts appear in the *Ausbund*, it is more typically considered a hymnal than a martyrology.

2. In chapter 5 we will examine a particularly significant revision of *The Bloody Theater,* when it was illustrated with 104 copper etchings.

3. Van Braght (1660), 2:590–91; *Martyrs Mirror* (1938), 871.

4. "It seemed that the country and at the same time also this city should before long change government and religion, which about two years afterwards [1572] was accomplished through the coming of William I, prince of Orange; and thus the constraint over the faith and conscience ceased at the same time, at said place." Van Braght (1660), 2:590; *Martyrs Mirror* (1938), 871.

5. Charles Wilson, *The Dutch Republic and the Civilisation of the Seventeenth Century* (New York: McGraw-Hill, 1968), 7–12.

6. Article 13 of the Union of Utrecht (1579), quoted in Jeremy Dupertuis Bangs, "Dutch Contributions to Religious Toleration," *Church History* 79 (2010): 591–92.

7. See Nanne van der Zijpp, "Netherlands," in *ME,* 3:829–30. Mary Sprunger notes that "in the first half of the seventeenth century, Reformed synods tried to block construction of Mennonite meeting houses in Franeker, Haarlem, and Leeuwarden, but the city magistrates had little interest in aggravating respectable and profitable segments of the population." Mary S. Sprunger, "The Dutch Golden Age: Prosperity and the Martyr Tradition," *Mennonite Life* 45, no. 3 (September 1990): 29.

8. Descartes is quoted in Wilson, *Dutch Republic,* 42. Descartes spent much of his adult life in the Dutch Republic, including the period from 1628 to 1649.

9. Michael North, *Art and Commerce in the Dutch Golden Age* (New Haven, CT: Yale University Press, 1997), 19–61.

10. Simon Schama, *The Embarrassment of Riches: An Interpretation of Dutch Culture in the Golden Age* (New York: Alfred A. Knopf, 1987), 289–371.

11. Mary Sprunger, "Waterlanders and the Dutch Golden Age: A Case Study on Mennonite Involvement in Seventeenth-Century Dutch Trade and Industry as One of the Earliest Examples of Socio-Economic Assimilation," in *From Martyr to Muppy: A Historical Introduction to Cultural Assimilation Processes of a Religious Minority in the Netherlands: The Mennonites,* ed. Alastair Hamilton, Sjouke Voolstra, and Piet Visser (Amsterdam: Amsterdam University Press, 1994), 138.

12. Ibid., 136. Some historians have suggested that Rembrandt was a member of this congregation, and while that claim has not been substantiated, he likely had warm friendships with some of its members. See Julia Kasdorf, "The Master and the Mennonites or 'Did Anslo Make It?'" *Mennonite Historical Bulletin* 57, no. 1 (January 1996): 1–5. "Anslo" in Kasdorf's title refers to Mennonite minister Cornelius Anslo, whom Rembrandt painted in 1641.

13. Sprunger, "Waterlanders and the Dutch Golden Age," 147.

14. Quoted in ibid., 133–34.

15. North, *Art and Commerce,* 1.

16. In Dutch the book's complete title was *Lusthof des Gemoets inhoudende verscheyden geestelijcke Oeffeningen met noch twee Collatien der wandelende Ziele met Adam en Noach* [A pleasure garden of the mind containing various spiritual exercises with two dialogues of the wandering soul with Adam and Noah]. The English title, *The Wander-*

ing Soul, derives from a 1717 High German translation of the work, which was titled *Die wandlende Seel*.

17. Piet Visser, "Jan Philipsz Schabaelje (1592–1656), a Seventeenth Century Dutch Mennonite, and His *Wandering Soul*," in Hamilton, Voolstra, and Visser, *From Martyr to Muppy*, 99–109.

18. For economic classes in the Golden Age, see North, *Art and Commerce*, 48.

19. This Flemish-Frisian division had various causes. The Flemish Mennonites, composed mostly of people who had migrated north from Flanders to escape persecution, found the Frisians worldly, and the Frisians found their Flemish counterparts strange, particularly in matters of dress. Squabbles, both theological and nontheological in nature, compromised their ability to work and worship together. After 1567 many Dutch towns with Mennonite populations had two churches, one Flemish and the other Frisian. See Christian Neff and Nanne van der Zijpp, "Flemish Mennonites," in *ME*, 2:337–40; and Gerald C. Studer, "The Dordrecht Confession of Faith, 1632–1982," *MQR* 58 (1984): 507–8.

20. For the importance of church discipline in the Anabaptist tradition, see Karl Koop, *Anabaptist-Mennonite Confessions of Faith: The Development of a Tradition* (Kitchener, ON: Pandora Press, 2004), 50.

21. Piet Visser, "Mennonites and Doopsgezinden in the Netherlands, 1535–1700," in *A Companion to Anabaptism and Spiritualism, 1521–1700*, ed. John D. Roth and James M. Stayer (Leiden: Brill, 2007), 321.

22. Visser writes that, in the 1590s, "at least ten different [Mennonite] groups existed and many hardly acknowledged the legitimacy of the others." Visser, "Jan Philipsz Schabaelje," 99.

23. Christian Neff and Nanne van der Zijpp, "Olijftacxken (Olive Branch)," in *ME*, 4:54–55.

24. The text of the Olive Branch Confession, also called "Scriptural Instruction," can be found online at http://gameo.org/index.php?title=Olive_Branch_Confession _of_Faith_(1627), accessed January 29, 2015. This English version, translated by Joseph F. Sohm, first appeared in *Martyrs Mirror* (1886), 26–32.

25. Visser, "Mennonites and Doopsgezinden," 326.

26. Koop, *Anabaptist-Mennonite Confessions of Faith*, 56. The text of the Jan Cents Confession, translated by Walter Klaassen, can be found in *Confessions of Faith in the Anabaptist Tradition, 1527–1660*, ed. Karl Koop (Kitchener, ON: Pandora Press, 2006), 269–84.

27. John C. Wenger, "Dordrecht Confession of Faith," in *ME*, 2:92–93. The text of the Dordrecht Confession, translated by Irvin B. Horst, can be found in Koop, *Confessions of Faith in Anabaptist Tradition*, 288–310.

28. Koop, *Anabaptist-Mennonite Confessions of Faith*, 56.

29. Visser, "Mennonites and Doopsgezinden," 327.

30. Koop, *Anabaptist-Mennonite Confessions of Faith*, 57.

31. James W. Lowry, "Thieleman van Braght (1625–1664): A Preliminary Study of His Life and Thought," presented at the conference "*Martyrs Mirror*: Reflections across

Time," at the Young Center for Anabaptist and Pietist Studies, Elizabethtown College, Elizabethtown, PA, June 8, 2010.

32. H. Westra and Nanne van der Zijpp, "Braght, Tieleman Jansz van," in *ME*, 1:400–401.

33. Nanne van der Zijpp, "Aemilius, Gerardus," in *ME*, 1:20.

34. Koop, *Anabaptist-Mennonite Confessions of Faith*, 57. According to Koop, the Waterlanders proposed that "each group could retain the freedom to formulate its own beliefs, and that unity would be based on the Word of God in the Bible" (57). This leniency the united group could not abide.

35. One of the chief anticonfessionalists, Galenus Abrahamsz, was a minister at the Church of the Lamb (Lam) in Amsterdam. The dispute split the congregation, and when the confessionalist faction began meeting in a building with the sign of the sun, the confessionalist faction became known as the Zonists. See Nanne van der Zijpp, "Lamist Mennonite Church," in *ME*, 3:270.

36. Quoted in Koop, *Anabaptist-Mennonite Confessions of Faith*, 78.

37. Nanne van der Zijpp, "Leidsche Synode (Synod of Leiden)," in *ME*, 3:317–18.

38. Van Braght (1660), 1:sig. [b4]–f2; and *Martyrs Mirror* (1938), 27–44. The Waterlanders had produced their own confessions (in 1577, 1610, and 1626), but van Braght did not include them in *The Bloody Theater*. For these confessions, see Koop, *Confessions of Faith*, 123–63.

39. Van Braght (1660), 1:sig. [b4]; and *Martyrs Mirror* (1938), 27. See Samme Zijlstra, "Anabaptism and Tolerance: Possibilities and Limitations," in *Calvinism and Religious Toleration in the Dutch Golden Age*, ed. R. Po-Chia Hsia and Henk F. K. Van Nierop (New York: Cambridge University Press, 2002), 126–27.

40. Quoted in Willem Frijhoff and Marijke Spies, *Dutch Culture in a European Perspective* (New York: Palgrave Macmillan, 2004), 1:404.

41. Westra and van der Zijpp, "Braght," 1:401.

42. Van Braght (1660), 1:sig. [*4]v–**3; and *Martyrs Mirror* (1938), 8–11.

43. Van Braght (1660), 1:sig. ***[1]v–***2; and *Martyrs Mirror* (1938), 14–15.

44. Van Braght (1660), 2:865–80; and *Martyrs Mirror* (1938), 1108–25. In these decades Swiss Anabaptists were not executed, but some died in prison as a result of disease, physical abuse, or bad food.

45. Van Braght (1660), 1:sig. [***4]; and *Martyrs Mirror* (1938), 18. While acknowledging that a commitment to adult baptism was impossible to confirm in every pre-Reformation martyr he included in *The Bloody Theater*, van Braght argued that it was at least possible that they held this view, for "there have been persons in every century, from the beginning of the Gospel all along, who have believed and taught the article of holy baptism" (18).

46. Van Braght (1660), 1:sig. ***3v–[***4]; and *Martyrs Mirror* (1938), 17.

47. An ornamented page with a slightly different title precedes the actual title page of van Braght's 1660 work.

48. Thanks to Leonard Gross and James W. Lowry for their translating assistance.

49. The Catholic martyrology, which condemned the cruelties of Protestant authori-

ties in England, France, and elsewhere, was Richard Verstegan's *Theatrum Crudelitatum Haereticorum Nostri Temporis* [Theater of the cruelties of the heretics of our time] (Antwerp, Belgium: Adrien Hubert, 1587). Verstegan's martyrology, also published in French, went through many editions in the sixteenth and seventeenth centuries.

50. Keith L. Sprunger, "Dutch Anabaptists and the Telling of the Martyr Stories," *MQR* 80 (2006): 164.

51. For the persecution of Christians in the Roman Empire as a spectacle, see Elizabeth A. Castelli, *Martyrdom and Memory: Early Christian Culture Making* (New York: Columbia University Press, 2004), 104–33. For later forms of spectacle, see Mitchell B. Merback, *The Thief, the Cross and the Wheel: Pain and the Spectacle of Punishment in Medieval and Renaissance Europe* (Chicago: University of Chicago Press, 1999).

52. See, for instance, Linda A. Huebert Hecht, "Anabaptist Women in Tirol Who Recanted," in *Profiles of Anabaptist Women: Sixteenth-Century Reforming Pioneers*, ed. C. Arnold Snyder and Linda A. Huebert Hecht (Waterloo, ON: Wilfred Laurier University Press, 1996), 156–63.

53. For a more extensive consideration of the martyrs' performances, see Gerald J. Biesecker-Mast, "'Bloody Theater' and Christian Discipleship," *Mennonite Historical Bulletin* 62, no. 4 (October 2001): 1–10.

54. Sprunger, "Dutch Anabaptists," 174–80.

55. The distinction between Christians who are put to death as a consequence of their confession of faith and Christians who die in the course of taking heroic action has been captured by the Latin phrases *in odium fidei* (out of hatred for the faith) and *in odium caritatis* (out of hatred for love). For van Braght, martyrs were those who died *in odium fidei*. See Lawrence Cunningham, "Christian Martyrdom: A Theological Perspective," in *Witness to the Body: The Past, Present, and Future of Christian Martyrdom*, ed. Michael L. Budde and Karen Scott (Grand Rapids, MI: Eerdmans, 2011), 14–15.

56. See Nanne van der Zijpp, "Doopsgezind," in *ME*, 2:86. Van der Zijpp notes a use of this term as early as 1578, in a letter written by William of Orange.

57. Van Braght (1660), 1:sig. ***2v–***3; and *Martyrs Mirror* (1938), 16.

58. The MPH/Herald Press translation of *Martyrs Mirror* translates *Doopsgesinde* as "Anabaptist." The word *Anabaptist*, which literally means "rebaptizer," is the Greek equivalent to the German word *Wiedertäufer*, a term of opprobrium used in German-speaking settings to label those who underwent adult baptism. As noted, however, a literal translation of *Doopsgesinde* is "baptism-minded," not rebaptizer. See Harold S. Bender, "Anabaptist," in *ME*, 1:113–14.

59. Van Braght (1660), 1:sig. ***3–***3v; and *Martyrs Mirror* (1938), 16–17.

60. Van Braght (1660), 1:145; and *Martyrs Mirror* (1938), 174.

61. Van Braght (1660), 1:sig. [***4]; and *Martyrs Mirror* (1938), 17.

62. Van Braght (1660), 1:1; and *Martyrs Mirror* (1938), 63.

63. Binding sizes vary, of course, but the point remains that van Braght's *Bloody Theater* was larger than de Ries's *Martyrs Mirror*. In addition to having a slightly larger printed area on each page, *The Bloody Theater* ran four hundred more pages than *Martyrs Mirror*.

64. Producing a book of *The Bloody Theater*'s size would have taken an early modern printer and his workforce months to set, proofread, correct, and print. Each page had to be typeset letter by letter; not only did the typesetters need to select the correct letters (an A instead of a B, for instance), but they also needed to select from their type compartments the correct size and style of type and space their selections appropriately across each line. The various textual features, from page headers and section headings to registers and marginal comments, called for different types. In the case of *The Bloody Theater*, these selections resulted in a book that exhibits no less than fifteen different styles or sizes of type, nine on the title page alone.

65. The other martyrology, published in 1657, was Johannes Gysius's revision of a century-old Calvinist martyrology compiled by Adriaen van Haemstede in 1559. Gysius's revised work was titled *Historie der Martelaren* [History of the martyrs]. See W. G. Goeters, "Haemstede, Adriaen Cornelis van," in *ME*, 2:620–21.

66. The Latin reads, "Spera in Domino et fac bonitatem et inhabita terram et pasceris in divitiis eius." The English translation is from the Douay-Rheims Bible (Psalm 36:3).

67. As Julia Kasdorf has pointed out, it is possible that some Europeans would have associated the digging man with Adam, the first human being and the archetypical laborer. See Julia Kasdorf, " 'Work and Hope': Tradition and Translation of an Anabaptist Adam," *MQR* 69 (1995): 178–204.

68. Van Braght (1660), 1:sig. *2; and *Martyrs Mirror* (1938), 5.

69. In the 1685 edition, the words *Het Bloedig Tooneel* appear at the top of the title page, but they are immediately followed by the words *Of Martelaers Spiegel*, with *Spiegel* in a larger font. See figure 5.1 in chapter 5.

Chapter 4. *The Bloody Theater*

1. Van Braght (1660), 2:745–46; and *Martyrs Mirror* (1938), 1005–7.

2. Two of the poems were written anonymously, and one was written by van Braght's brother Peter. See van Braght (1660), 1:sig. i3-[i4]v. Peter van Braght's poem appears in Dutch in *Martyrs Mirror* (1938), 61, and in English on 1139. According to a footnote that accompanies the poem, the poem's translator was A. B. Kolb, who produced his translation at the time Joseph F. Sohm was translating the entire work.

3. The first four registers are lists of sources. The five subsequent registers are akin to modern-day indexes, pointing readers to specific pages and columns in book 1 where they can find the following information for the church's first fifteen centuries: names of persons who correctly practiced baptism; the circumstances under which people were baptized; statements on various ecclesiastical matters, including baptism; accounts of persecutions that occurred; and names of persons who suffered martyrdom. See van Braght (1660), 1: sig. k[1]–m3v.

4. Van Braght (1660), 1:sig. *3, **3v; and *Martyrs Mirror* (1938), 6, 11. The first part of van Braght's preface, directed to Anabaptist readers, was dated July 25, 1659. The second part, directed to general readers, was dated July 27, 1659.

5. Gerald Studer writes that van Braght lists 356 books in his lists of sources. See Gerald C. Studer, "A History of *Martyrs Mirror*," *MQR* 22 (1948): 169.

6. Nanne van der Zijpp, "Twisck, Pieter Jansz," in *ME*, 4:757–58. According to James Lowry (correspondence with author), van Braght cites Twisck more than two hundred times in book 1.

7. See Cornelius Krahn and Nanne van der Zijpp, "Franck, Sebastian," in *ME*, 2: 363–67.

8. See Nanne van der Zijpp, "Mellin, Abraham Philippus," in *ME*, 3:566. Mellin's and Gysius's martyrologies were both published in Dordrecht. Gysius's work, a revised edition of Adriaen van Haemstede's sixteenth-century martyrology, *De Gheschiedenisse ende den doodt der vromen Martelaren* [A history of the killing of the pious martyrs], was printed by Jacob Braat, who printed *The Bloody Theater* three years later.

9. See Otto Schowalter, "Mehrning, Jakob," in *ME*, 3:561.

10. Van Braght (1660), 2:sig. [*4]; and *Martyrs Mirror* (1938), 354.

11. Van Braght (1660), 2:sig. [*4]v–[***4]v; and *Martyrs Mirror* (1938), 355–62.

12. Van Braght (1660), 2:1; and *Martyrs Mirror* (1938), 363.

13. Van Braght (1660), 2:7–14, 17–75; and *Martyrs Mirror* (1938), 367–71, 373–410.

14. Lloyd M. Weiler, "Thomas von Imbroich and His Writings," *Muddy Creek Review* 5 (2014): 4–5. Weiler notes that van Imbrœck's confession draws heavily on the writing of Dutch Mennonite leader Dirk Philips.

15. For a list of martyr accounts in *The Bloody Theater* that appeared in the 1562 edition of *The Sacrifice of the Lord*, see James W. Lowry, *The "Martyrs' Mirror" Made Plain: How to Study and Profit from the "Martyrs' Mirror,"* rev. ed. (Aylmer, ON: Pathway, 2011), 92–93.

16. James W. Lowry, introduction to *Hans Landis: Swiss Anabaptist Martyr in Seventeenth Century Documents,* ed. David J. Rempel Smucker and John L. Ruth (Millersburg, OH: Ohio Amish Library, 2003), 9–10. The Hans Landis material appears in de Ries (1631), 934–35; van Braght (1660), 2:859–60; and *Martyrs Mirror* (1938), 1103–5.

17. The seventeenth-century material appears in van Braght (1660), 2:855–92.

18. Van Braght (1660), 2:888; and *Martyrs Mirror* (1938), 1135.

19. For the de Roore disputation, see de Ries (1631), 558–74. In van Braght (1660), 2:503, van Braght writes that he has decided to omit the disputations because of Cornelis's crude language and slanderous accusations against the Anabaptists. However, at the end of the 1660 edition, which would have been printed later, van Braght explains that people had approached him in the meantime and encouraged him to include the disputations, because they contained useful refutations of the charges leveled against Anabaptists. The disputations appear in van Braght (1660), 2:sig. ‡[1]–‡‡‡2v; and in *Martyrs Mirror* (1938), 774–98. In some copies of van Braght (1660), the disputations run four additional pages, concluding on 2:sig. [‡‡‡4]v. The footnote in *Martyrs Mirror* (1938), 774, is incorrect, for it suggests the disputations did not appear anywhere in the 1660 edition. I am indebted to James W. Lowry for his translation of van Braght's explanations. James W. Lowry to David Weaver-Zercher, March 5, 2011.

20. James Clifton, preface to *Scripture for the Eyes: Bible Illustration in Netherlandish Prints of the Sixteenth Century,* ed. James Clifton and Walter S. Melion (New York: Museum of Biblical Art, 2009), 11.

21. Ibid., 12. De Ries's *History of the Martyrs* (1615) launched the practice, and its ornamental page was modified only slightly for use in the two Old Frisian martyrologies (1617 and 1626). A new ornamental page appeared in de Ries (1631); see figure 2.1.

22. Revelation 7:9–17, NRSV.

23. Van Braght (1660), 1:sig. a3-i2; and *Martyrs Mirror* (1938), 21–60.

24. Van Braght (1660), 1:sig. a3; and *Martyrs Mirror* (1938), 21.

25. Van Braght (1660), 1:sig. a3v; and *Martyrs Mirror* (1938), 22.

26. Enoch appears briefly in Genesis 5, but a description of his preaching office is mentioned only in the New Testament (Jude 14–15).

27. Van Braght (1660), 1:sig. [a4]–b2; and *Martyrs Mirror* (1938), 22–24.

28. Van Braght (1660), 1:sig. b[1]v; and *Martyrs Mirror* (1938), 24. Jesus's promise can be found in Matthew 28:20.

29. Van Braght (1660), 1:sig. b3; and *Martyrs Mirror* (1938), 25–26.

30. Van Braght (1660), 1:sig. b3; and *Martyrs Mirror* (1938), 26.

31. Van Braght (1660), 1:sig. b3v; and *Martyrs Mirror* (1938), 26.

32. Van Braght (1660), 1:sig. b3v; and *Martyrs Mirror* (1938), 26–27.

33. Van Braght (1660), 1:sig. [b4]–f2; and *Martyrs Mirror* (1938), 27–44. See chapter 3 for a brief consideration of these confessions.

34. Van Braght (1660), 1:sig. f2; *Martyrs Mirror* (1938), 44.

35. Van Braght (1660), 1:sig. f3v; and *Martyrs Mirror* (1938), 46.

36. In particular, van Braght explores Matthew 16:18, Matthew 16:19, and John 21:15–17, concluding that none of them support the Catholic Church's claim that Jesus named Peter the supreme head of the apostolic church. Van Braght (1660), 1:sig. f3v–g2; and *Martyrs Mirror* (1938), 46–49.

37. Van Braght (1660), 1:sig. g2; and *Martyrs Mirror* (1938), 49.

38. Van Braght (1660), 1:sig. h[1]v–i2.; and *Martyrs Mirror* (1938), 52–59.

39. Van Braght (1660), 1:sig. i[1]v, i2; and *Martyrs Mirror* (1938), 59.

40. Van Braght (1660), 1:sig. i2v; and *Martyrs Mirror* (1938), 59. The quotation is from Zechariah 2:8.

41. Some of the interrogations recorded in *The Bloody Theater* are rather mundane, focusing on the details of baptisms administered and worship services attended. Other interrogations are very short, examining only a few basic beliefs. In this section, I consider more thoroughgoing inquisitions in which court or church officials asked a variety of questions about the martyrs' convictions.

42. Van Braght (1660), 2:313–14; and *Martyrs Mirror* (1938), 612.

43. Van Braght (1660), 2:313; and *Martyrs Mirror* (1938), 612.

44. The books were Matthew, Mark, 1 Corinthians, 2 Corinthians, 1 Peter, and James. See van Braght (1660), 2:222; and *Martyrs Mirror* (1938), 533.

45. Van Braght (1660), 2:sig. ‡[1]v; and *Martyrs Mirror* (1938), 776.

46. Sarah Covington, "Paratextual Strategies in Thieleman van Braght's *Martyrs' Mirror,*" *Book History* 9 (2006): 18.

47. Van Braght (1660), 2:224; and *Martyrs Mirror* (1938), 535.

48. Van Braght (1660), 2:380–81; and *Martyrs Mirror* (1938), 667.

49. Van Braght (1660), 2:90; and *Martyrs Mirror* (1938), 423.

50. Van Braght (1660), 2:162; and *Martyrs Mirror* (1938), 482. This particular interrogation account can be traced to an earlier martyr ballad about Elisabeth; see chapter 2.

51. Van Braght (1660), 2:sig. ‡[1]–‡‡‡2v; see also note 19 above.

52. For instance, *Martyrer Spiegel* (1749), 2:494; *Martyrs Mirror* (1837), 694–98; and *Martyrs Mirror* (1938), 776–79. For an explanation of this decision, see the footnote in *Martyrs Mirror* (1938), 774. Thanks to Edsel Burdge Jr. for these citations.

53. Van Braght (1660), 2:sig. ‡[1]v; and *Martyrs Mirror* (1938), 776.

54. The invective Cornelis launches at de Roore is *botten muyl,* which literally means "stupid mouth." Joseph F. Sohm translated the phrase "blockhead." Van Braght (1660), 2:sig. ‡2v; and *Martyrs Mirror* (1938), 778.

55. Van Braght (1660), 2:sig. ‡‡‡2; and *Martyrs Mirror* (1938), 797.

56. See M. J. Reimer-Blok, "The Theological Identity of Flemish Anabaptists: A Study of the Letters of Jacob de Roore," *MQR* 52 (1988): 320. Reimer-Blok cites Cramer's rejection of their authenticity in 1899 (S. Cramer, "De geloofwaardigheid van Van Braght," *Doopsgezinde Bijdragen,* 1899, 94–95).

57. Van Braght (1660), 2:182–83; and *Martyrs Mirror* (1938), 499–500.

58. Brad S. Gregory, *Salvation at Stake: Christian Martyrdom in Early Modern Europe* (Cambridge, MA: Harvard University Press, 1999), 123. Gregory continues, "To prefer the short-lived agony that led to eternal joy over the repudiation of Christ that portended damnation was not insanity; it was simply clear thinking" (124).

59. Van Braght (1660), 2:675; and *Martyrs Mirror* (1938), 945.

60. Jenifer Hiett Umble makes this point in "Women and Choice: An Examination of the *Martyrs' Mirror,*" *MQR* 64 (1990): 139–40. On the other hand, *The Bloody Theater* contains stories of Anabaptists who escaped from prison when they had a chance; for instance, van Braght (1660): 2:126–27; 163; and *Martyrs Mirror* (1938), 452–53; 483.

61. Van Braght (1660), 2:676; and *Martyrs Mirror* (1938), 947.

62. Ibid.

63. Gerald J. Mast, "Research Note: Epistolary Rhetoric and Marital Love in the *Martyrs Mirror,*" *MQR* 82 (2008): 174.

64. One Anabaptist, Jan Wouterss, wrote eleven letters that made their way into *The Bloody Theater:* (1) to his brother-in-law and sister; (2) to his brother and sisters; (3) to the Anabaptist church at Dordrecht; (4) to his wife; (5) to his wife and daughter; (6) to his daughter; (7) to his father and mother; (8) to his Roman Catholic sister-in-law; (9) to his youngest three sisters; (10) to his oldest brother-in-law and sister; and (11) to his youngest brother-in-law. Van Braght (1660), 2:621–50; and *Martyrs Mirror* (1938), 901–25.

65. For instance, Jan Wouterss's letter to his sister-in-law, "mother in the convent." Wouterss concludes his letter by writing, "Finally, I declare unto you once more in the name of my Lord: 'Amend your life and ways, believe the Gospel, and flee idolatry.' " Van Braght (1660), 2:644; and *Martyrs Mirror* (1938), 920. See also the letter from Janneken Munstdorp to her father and mother, in van Braght (1660), 2:724–25; and *Martyrs Mirror* (1938), 987–89.

66. Mast, "Research Note," 177.

67. Van Braght (1660), 2:702–9; and *Martyrs Mirror* (1938), 969–75.

68. Van Braght (1660), 2:653; and *Martyrs Mirror* (1938), 927.

69. "Hold fast that which you have, for it is the only and unadulterated truth, that no one take your crown." Van Braght (1660), 2:653; and *Martyrs Mirror* (1938), 927.

70. Van Braght (1660), 2:686; and *Martyrs Mirror* (1938), 955.

71. Jacob van den Wege wrote to his wife that he was "far too simple and ignorant to write anything profitable for your exhortation." Van Braght (1660), 2:703; and *Martyrs Mirror* (1938), 970. For his part, Jan Hendrickss wrote, "Not . . . that I have not the confidence that you will walk in the fear of God: oh, no! I am confident that you will do nothing but what is good." Van Braght (1660), 2:660; and *Martyrs Mirror* (1938), 933.

72. For reference to biblical injunctions, see van Braght (1660), 2:570; and *Martyrs Mirror* (1938), 854. For reference to soul love, see van Braght (1660), 2:660; and *Martyrs Mirror* (1938), 933.

73. For instance, van Braght (1660), 2:279, 686; and *Martyrs Mirror* (1938), 585, 955. Adriaenken Jans addresses her husband as "my most beloved husband and dearest brother in the Lord" and refers to herself as "your cordial and dearest wife and sister in the Lord." Van Braght (1660), 2:653; and *Martyrs Mirror* (1938), 927.

74. Mast, "Research Note," 183.

75. For a particularly poignant example, see Hendrick Verstralen's letter to his wife in van Braght (1660), 2:596–97; and *Martyrs Mirror* (1938), 877–78.

76. Van Braght (1660), 2:278–82; and *Martyrs Mirror* (1938), 584–88.

77. Van Braght (1660), 2:350–51; and *Martyrs Mirror* (1938), 642–43. For another testament to a very young child, see Anna of Rotterdam's testament to her son Isaiah, in van Braght (1660), 2:127–29; and *Martyrs Mirror* (1938), 453–54. Anna's letter to Isaiah, written in 1539, circulated among other Anabaptists. It was so highly regarded that a later martyr, Maeyken van Deventer, copied parts of it into a letter to her children in advance of her execution thirty-four years later. See Lowry, *"Martyrs' Mirror" Made Plain*, 121.

78. Van Braght (1660), 2:716; and *Martyrs Mirror* (1938), 981.

79. Van Braght (1660), 2:427; and *Martyrs Mirror* (1938), 705.

80. Van Braght (1660), 2:771; and *Martyrs Mirror* (1938), 1027.

81. Van Braght (1660), 2:596; and *Martyrs Mirror* (1938), 877.

82. For examples of their ongoing teaching function, see Lowry, *"Martyrs' Mirror" Made Plain*, 61–64; and Joseph Isaac, ed., *"Martyrs Mirror" Excerpts: Selections from "Martyrs Mirror"* (Moundridge, KS: Gospel, 2002), 269–94.

Chapter 5. *The Bloody Theater* Illustrated

1. Ernst Müller, *History of the Bernese Anabaptists,* trans. John A. Gingerich, ed. Joseph Stoll (Aylmer, ON: Pathway, 2010), 183–214.

2. James W. Lowry, *"Martyrs' Mirror* Picture Albums and Abridgements: A Surprising Find," *Pennsylvania Mennonite Heritage* 25, no. 1 (October 2002): 3. Lowry cites Gilles Dionysius Jacobus Schotel, *Kerkelijk Dordrecht; eene bijdrage tot de geschiedenis der vaderlandsche hervormde kerk, sedert het jaar 1572* (Utrecht, 1841–45), 1:359.

3. Schotanus titled his book *Van de Gronden der Mennisterij, ofte Waerschouwinghe over 't Bloed-tooneel der Doopsgesinde van Thieleman Jans van Bracht* [Concerning the foundation of Mennonitism, or warnings against the Bloody Theater of the Baptism-minded, by Thieleman Jans van Bracht].

4. Nanne van der Zijpp, "Schotanus, Christianus," in *ME*, 4:479.

5. I base this sales estimate on conversations with collectors who have purchased copies of the 1660 edition.

6. The publishers mentioned in the 1685 edition were Hieronymus Sweerts, Jans ten Hoorn, Jan Bouman, and Daniel van den Dalen (in some copies); and J. vander Deyster, H. vanden Berg, Jan Blom, Wed. S. Swart, S. Wybrands, and A. Oossaan (in other copies). For their Reformed connections and their entrepreneurial goals, see Piet Visser, "De pelgrimage van Jan Luyken door de Doopsgezinde boekenwereld," *Doopsgezinde Bijdragen*, n.s., 25 (1999): 167–79, esp. 170. According to James W. Lowry (correspondence with author), Andries Vinck, who later joined the publishing group, might have been a Mennonite.

7. Sarah Covington, "Jan Luyken, the *Martyrs Mirror*, and the Iconography of Suffering," *MQR* 85 (2011): 454–56. First published in 1559, van Haemstede's work went through numerous editions. It was first illustrated in 1604 but became more richly illustrated in its 1657 and 1659 incarnations. These new editions, assembled by Johannes Gysius, were both titled *Historie der Martelaren* [History of the martyrs].

8. Keith L. Sprunger, "Dutch Anabaptists and the Telling of the Martyr Stories," *MQR* 80 (2012): 161.

9. Maarten Prak, *The Dutch Republic in the Seventeenth Century: The Golden Age* (Cambridge: Cambridge University Press, 2005), 130; see also Jaap Jacobs, *New Netherland: A Dutch Colony in Seventeenth-Century America* (Leiden: Brill, 2005), 343–44.

10. For instance, whereas in book 1 of the 1660 edition the baptism material for each century precedes the martyr material, in the 1685 edition the martyr material precedes the baptism material. Also, the two disputations that conclude the 1660 edition have been moved to the middle of book 2 in the 1685 edition (pp. 425–52), where they also appear in *Martyrs Mirror* (1938), 774–98.

11. The formal title of the Mennonite Publishing House's (later Herald Press's) English edition begins with the words *The Bloody Theater*, but the title on the spine says *Martyrs Mirror*. Similarly, the formal title of Pathway Publisher's German edition begins with the words *Die blutige Schauplatz*, but the title on the spine says *Märtyrer Spiegel*.

12. For general information on Haslibacher, see Harold S. Bender, "Haslibacher, Hans," in *ME*, 2:675–76.

13. Van Braght (1685), 2:830; *Martyrs Mirror* (1938), 1128.

14. For instance, the German translation published in 1748–49 in Ephrata, Pennsylvania, included the last twelve stanzas of the thirty-two-stanza hymn; see *Martyrer Spiegel* (1749), 2:939. The entire hymn appears in *Martyrs Mirror* (1938), 1128–29, and the last twelve stanzas appear in Pathway Publisher's *Martyrer Spiegel* (2011), 2:621.

15. Van Braght (1660), 2:889–92.

16. Van Braght (1685), 2:838–40; and *Martyrs Mirror* (1938), 1139–41.

17. This new poem appears at the place where three other poems appeared in the 1660 edition (i.e., right after van Braght's account of the false church). Correspondingly, the three older poems were bumped back to book 2 in the 1685 edition, where they appear right after the preface to the Old Book. *Martyrs Mirror* (1938) does not include the newer poem, but the newer poem does appear in the front matter of some German editions, including *Martyrer Spiegel* (1749), 55–56; and *Martyrer Spiegel* (2011), 57.

18. H. Westra and Nanne van der Zijpp, "Braght, Tieleman Jansz van," in *ME*, 1:401.

19. The quotations are from Bill Osterman's translation, which can be found in the holdings of the Muddy Creek Farm Library, Ephrata, Pennsylvania.

20. Visser, "De pelgrimage van Jan Luyken," 172.

21. The entire title of the 1685 edition reads, *Het Bloedig Tooneel, of Martelaers Spiegel der Doops-Gesinde of Weereloose Christenen, die om't getuygenis van Jesus haren Saligh-maker geleden hebben ende gedood zijn van Christi tijd af tot desen tijd toe. Versamelt uyt verscheyde geloofweerdige Chronijken, Memorien, en Getuygenissen.* Translated into English it reads, "The bloody theater, or martyrs mirror of the baptism-minded and defenseless Christians, who for the testimony of Jesus their Savior suffered and were slain, from the time of Christ to the present time. Collected from various authentic chronicles, memorials, and testimonies."

22. Unlike the 1660 edition, the 1685 edition features the words "of Martelaers-Spiegel der Doops-Gesinde" as the heading on each recto page.

23. Michael Twyman, *The British Library Guide to Printing History and Techniques* (Toronto: University of Toronto Press, 1998), 35–38.

24. Jan is sometimes rendered "Joannes," and Luyken is sometimes rendered "Luiken."

25. Irvin B. Horst, "Jan Luiken: Devout Poet and Printmaker," *Eastern Mennonite College Bulletin,* February 1976, 3–10. John Oyer writes that the poems were "erotic enough to support the impression of a dissolute life." John S. Oyer, "Jan Luyken, Mennonite Artist in the Netherlands' 'Golden Century,'" in *"They Harry the Good People Out of the Land": Essays on the Persecution, Survival and Flourishing of Anabaptists and Mennonites,* ed. John D. Roth (Goshen, IN: Mennonite Historical Society, 2000), 75.

26. Some scholars, following the lead of Luyken's anonymous biographer, identify Luyken's conversion as occurring in 1675. James Lowry is likely correct, however, to date it to 1673, just before Luyken was baptized into the Mennonite church. See James W. Lowry, "A Search for Jan Luyken," *Pennsylvania Mennonite Heritage* 29, no. 1 (January 2006): 5.

27. See Oyer, "Jan Luyken, Mennonite Artist," 77.

28. This number is from Covington, "Jan Luyken," 442.

29. The history of the Bible was entitled *De Schriftuurlyke Geschiedenissen en Gelykenissen van het Oude in Nieuwe Verbond* [Scriptural histories and illustrations of the old and new covenants]. For information on Luyken's contribution to *Pilgrim's Progress,* see Paul Raasveld, "The Long and Winding Road: The Dutch Emblematic Adaptation of Elizabeth Jocelin's *The Mothers Legacie, to Her Unborn Childe* (1624)," in *Anglo-Dutch Relations in the Field of the Emblem,* ed. Bart Westerweel (Leiden: Brill, 1997), 283–86.

30. Oyer, "Jan Luyken, Mennonite Artist," 75.

31. Lowry, "Search for Jan Luyken," 3.

32. H. W. Meihuizen, "Galenus Abrahamsz de Haan," in *ME*, 2:431–35.

33. Cornelis B. Hylkema writes that Luyken was "heterodox" in his theology, a claim that Lowry and others have successfully called into question. Irvin Horst is probably closest to the mark when he calls Luyken's religious orientation a "Jesus-spiritualism" that emphasized "fellowship with Christ and following in His footsteps" over doctrinal precision. See Cornelis B. Hylkema, "Luyken, Jan," in *ME*, 3:423–24; Lowry, "Search for Jan Luyken," 9; and Horst, "Jan Luiken," 6.

34. Lowry, "Search for Jan Luyken," 8.

35. Horst, "Jan Luiken," 8.

36. Oyer, "Jan Luyken, Mennonite Artist," 76.

37. Forty-nine of the 104 images (47 percent) appear in book 1, even though book 1 is less than half the length of book 2.

38. Van Braght (1685), 1:1, 5, 6 (Jesus, John the Baptist, and Stephen); and *Martyrs Mirror* (1938), 68, 71 (Jesus and Stephen; the image of John the Baptist was not included).

39. Another explanation for the plethora of early images is that Luyken got a head start on fashioning the plates. Once the printing began, he was hard pressed to keep up with the typesetters and therefore needed to illustrate scenes more selectively. See James W. Lowry, *The "Martyrs' Mirror" Made Plain: How to Study and Profit from the "Martyrs' Mirror,"* rev. ed. (Aylmer, ON: Pathway, 2011), 122.

40. In counting the number of executions depicted, I include images of people being led to their executions, even if the mode of execution is not apparent from the image itself.

41. Van Braght (1685), 2:641; and *Martyrs Mirror* (1938), 962–63.

42. Many of the seventy-four execution scenes also depict physical torture prior to the martyr's death. My reference to nine torture scenes counts only those scenes in which a victim's impending execution is not visually apparent.

43. Van Braght (1685), 1:35; and *Martyrs Mirror* (1938), 97.

44. Van Braght (1685), 2:661; and *Martyrs Mirror* (1938), 980.

45. Van Braght (1685), 1:74; this Luyken image does not appear in *Martyrs Mirror* (1938).

46. Van Braght (1685), 1:168–69; and *Martyrs Mirror* (1938), 200–201.

47. Van Braght (1685), 2:149; quotation in *Martyrs Mirror* (1938), 540, but the Luyken image does not appear.

48. Van Braght (1685), 2:385–86; and *Martyrs Mirror* (1938), 739.

49. Van Braght (1685), 2:387; and *Martyrs Mirror* (1938), 741.

50. Ibid.

51. Foxe and Day did not make the woodcuts themselves; they were likely designed and cut by a variety of artists. Evidence exists, however, that Foxe provided guidance in the design of some of the woodcuts. Moreover, some of the cuts that appear in Foxe's martyrology were owned by Day, who had used them in previous publications. John N. King, *Foxe's "Book of Martyrs" and Early Modern Print Culture* (Cambridge: Cambridge University Press, 2006), 166–67.

52. Margaret Aston and Elizabeth Ingram, "The Iconography of *Acts and Monuments*," in *John Foxe and the English Reformation*, ed. David Loades (Aldershot, UK: Scolar Press, 1997), 66. Given the efficacy of Foxe's illustrated work, it is hardly surprising that the Catholic apologist Richard Verstegan countered with an illustrated Catholic martyrology, *Theatrum Crudelitatum Haereticorum Nostri Temporis* [Theater of the cruelties of the heretics of our time], published in Antwerp in 1587.

53. Unlike copper etchings, which demanded a second printing step after the type had been printed, woodcuts could be printed with the type matter. This means that "woodcutting was relatively crude but was quick at the multiplication stage . . . ; copperengraving [and etching] was refined but was slow at the multiplication stages." Twyman, *British Library Guide*, 37.

54. King, Foxe's "*Book of Martyrs*," 201. For instance, the image of the martyrdom of John Hooper places the words, "Lord Jesus rescue my soul" on the lips of the burning Hooper. The image of William Tyndale's execution includes the words, "Lord open the king of Englands eies."

55. It is tempting to conclude that the inclusion of generic images was a matter of convenience or profit-mindedness. That may be the case, though it is also arguable that these generic images served a broader purpose, providing those who perused Foxe's book with standard referents that marked their memories and shaped their responses in other contexts. For instance, "the martyr-figure in the flames" became a sort of icon in the mental world of English Protestants, catalyzing antipapal sentiments among those who encountered similar images outside the bounds of *Acts and Monuments*. See Aston and Ingram, "Iconography of *Acts and Monuments*," 79–80.

56. Mitchell B. Merback, *The Thief, the Cross and the Wheel: Pain and the Spectacle of Punishment in Medieval and Renaissance Europe* (Chicago: University of Chicago Press, 1999), 15.

57. Ibid., 16.

58. According to Sarah Covington, it is likely that Rembrandt, who had close associations with Dutch Mennonites, also contributed to the "visual mood" that Luyken reflected in his martyrological illustrations. See Covington, "Jan Luyken," 454–55.

59. Ibid., 455–67. This entire paragraph, including the reference to Cranach and the comparative illustrations, draws upon Covington's work.

60. The pole arguably appears in six additional Luyken etchings, though it appears only in part or in a different form. Of the pole's twenty-nine definite appearances, only four occur in book 1: in the questioning of Tharacus (290 CE), in the execution of Clement the Scotsman (756 CE), and in two pictures depicting mass burnings of Waldensians in the thirteenth century.

61. For instance, see van Braght (1685), 2:10; and *Martyrs Mirror* (1938), 421.

62. James W. Lowry, "The Rod of Justice in the *Martyrs' Mirror*," *Mennonite Life* 54, no. 3 (September 1999): 23.

63. As Lowry has suggested, it is possible that Luyken derived the theme of perverted justice from the text itself, where the phrases "servants of justice," "lords of justice," and "ministers of justice" appear in one of the martyr accounts. See van Braght (1685), 2:566–69; *Martyrs Mirror* (1938), 897–901; and Lowry, "Rod of Justice," 24.

64. See, for instance, van Braght (1685), 1:102; and *Martyrs Mirror* (1938), 148. By *figuratively* I mean that Luyken sometimes places a different sort of pole in the authorities' hands. This is how the pole sometimes appears in book 1, though it does at times appear in book 1 in the same fashion as it appears in book 2 (see note 60 above).

65. Van Braght (1685), 2:539; and *Martyrs Mirror* (1938), 873.

66. Van Braght (1685), 2:283; this image does not appear in *Martyrs Mirror* (1938).

67. Van Braght (1685), 2:691, 788; and *Martyrs Mirror* (1938), 1006, 1090.

68. Van Braght (1685), 2:605; and *Martyrs Mirror* (1938), 930.

69. Van Braght (1685), 2:750; and *Martyrs Mirror* (1938), 1058.

70. Van Braght (1685), 2:47; this image does not appear in *Martyrs Mirror* (1938).

71. Van Braght (1685), 2:387; and *Martyrs Mirror* (1938), 741.

72. Van Braght (1685), 2:750; and *Martyrs Mirror* (1938), 1058.

73. Van Braght (1685), 2:235; this image does not appear in *Martyrs Mirror* (1938).

74. For instance, van Braght (1685), 2:540; and *Martyrs Mirror* (1938), 875.

75. Sarah Covington, "Paratextual Strategies in Thieleman van Braght's *Martyrs' Mirror*," *Book History* 9 (2006): 22.

76. Quoted in ibid.

77. Van Braght (1685): 2:143; this image does not appear in *Martyrs Mirror* (1938).

78. Van Braght (1685), 2:371; and *Martyrs Mirror* (1938), 725.

79. Van Braght (1685), 2:661; *Martyrs Mirror* (1938), 980.

80. Van Braght (1685), 2:812; *Martyrs Mirror* (1938), 1111.

81. Van Braght (1685), 2:47; this image does not appear in *Martyrs Mirror* (1938).

82. Van Braght (1685), 2:173–74; quotation in *Martyrs Mirror* (1938), 560, but the image does not appear.

83. Van Braght (1685), 2:235; quotation in *Martyrs Mirror* (1938), 611, but the image does not appear.

84. For a summary of this debate and its relevance to martyrological writing, see Sprunger, "Dutch Anabaptists," 169–74.

85. Julia Kasdorf, "Work and Hope: Tradition and Translation of an Anabaptist Adam," *MQR* 69 (1995): 194. Kasdorf attributes this insight to Joe Springer.

86. Nanne van der Zijpp, "Vinne, van der," in *ME*, 4:829.

87. At some point in the publication process Luyken fashioned an ornamental title page, but for reasons unknown the publishers opted to use van der Vinne's offering instead. Horst, "Jan Luiken," 7.

88. All quotations in this paragraph are from van de Roer's poetic key; English translation by Jeff Bach.

89. For the growing prevalence of German speakers among eastern Pennsylvania Mennonites, see John L. Ruth, *Maintaining the Right Fellowship: A Narrative Account of Life in the Oldest Mennonite Community in North America* (Scottdale, PA: Herald Press, 1984), 94–133.

Chapter 6. A North American Edition

1. Gerald J. Mast has warned against overstating the case that *Martyrs Mirror* was a Dutch Mennonite book, noting the "multiplicity of voices and postures and purposes" in the text. In many respects, however, and especially in its pretranslated state, it makes sense to consider the work a Dutch martyrology. See Gerald J. Mast, "Swiss Brethren Spirituality in the *Martyrs Mirror*," presented at the conference "*Martyrs Mirror*: Reflections across Time," at the Young Center for Anabaptist and Pietist Studies, Elizabethtown College, Elizabethtown, PA, June 8, 2010; available at www.bluffton.edu/~mastg /Swiss Brethren Spirituality in the Martyrs Mirror.htm, accessed February 2, 2014.

2. Published in Venice by Girolamo Albrizzi, the book's more complete title was *Il Teatro Della Crudelta Praticata nelli più severi Tormenti del Mondo, cioè sin dalla Crocifissione di nostro Signore Giesu Cristo* [The theater of cruelty practiced in torments, the most ruthless in the world since the crucifixion of our Lord Jesus Christ]. For more information, see James W. Lowry, "*Martyrs' Mirror* Picture Albums and Abridgements: A Surprising Find," *Pennsylvania Mennonite Heritage* 25, no. 4 (October 2002): 3–4.

3. The years 1748 and 1749 appear on the book's title pages as the publication dates for book 1 and book 2, respectively. Complete copies may not have been finished until 1750.

4. Van Braght (1660), 2:881–83; and *Martyrs Mirror* (1938), 1130–31.

5. See *Documents of Brotherly Love: Dutch Mennonite Aid to Swiss Anabaptists*, ed. David J. Rempel Smucker and John L. Ruth, trans. James W. Lowry (Millersburg, OH: Ohio Amish Library, 2007), 12–13.

6. Because early Anabaptist leaders called themselves *Brüder* (brothers), the term *Swiss Brethren* became the common label for many Swiss Anabaptists. In time the Swiss Brethren identified themselves as Mennonite or Amish.

7. John D. Roth, introduction to *Letters of the Amish Division: A Sourcebook*, 2nd ed., trans. and ed. John D. Roth (Goshen, IN: Mennonite Historical Society, 2002), 6.

8. John D. Roth, "Marpeck and the Later Swiss Brethren, 1540–1700," in *A Companion to Anabaptism and Spiritualism, 1521–1700*, ed. John D. Roth and James M. Stayer (Leiden: Brill, 2007), 377.

9. Roth, introduction to *Letters of the Amish Division*, 10–12.

10. James W. Lowry, "The Amish Reception of the *Martyrs' Mirror*: A History of Encounters with the Book," *Pennsylvania Mennonite Heritage* 33, no. 1 (January 2010): 20, 22.

11. Writing in 1694, Gut may have used van Braght (1660) or van Braght (1685) as his source for Servaes's letters, though it is also possible that Gut used a German translation of Servaes's letters that appeared in an undated pamphlet prior to 1694. Thanks to Joe Springer and Edsel Burdge Jr. for alerting me to this possibility.

12. "Jakob Gut to the Congregation at Baldenheim (ca. 1694)," quoted in Roth, *Letters of the Amish Division*, 53–54. The account of Servaes's arrest and execution can be found in van Braght (1660), 2:407; van Braght (1685), 2:327–28; and *Martyrs Mirror* (1938), 688–89. The letter in which he discusses shunning can be found in van Braght (1660), 2:407–11; van Braght (1685), 2:328–31; and *Martyrs Mirror* (1938), 689–91.

13. Lowry, "Amish Reception," 22–23.

14. In his German-language copy of *Martyrs Mirror*, which he purchased in 1944, Ohio Amish bishop Menno Mast made his own index of the book's references to shunning, which he handwrote on his copy's endpaper. Photocopy in author's possession.

15. Harold S. Bender, "Amish Division," in *ME*, 1:90–92. It has also been known as the Ammann-Reist division, which references Hans Reist, Ammann's primary opponent in the conflict.

16. A few German-speaking Mennonites arrived in the last decades of the seventeenth century, but most of the Mennonites settling in Germantown prior to 1700 spoke Dutch. See Harold S. Bender, "Germantown (Pa.) Mennonite Settlement," in *ME*, 2: 482–83.

17. See C. Henry Smith, *The Mennonite Immigration to Pennsylvania in the Eighteenth Century* (Norristown, PA: Norristown Press, 1929), 221. Smith estimates that twenty-five hundred Mennonite immigrants came to Pennsylvania in the years 1683–1754 and that most of them spoke German.

18. For immigration numbers and destinations, see Donald B. Kraybill, Karen M. Johnson-Weiner, and Steven M. Nolt, *The Amish* (Baltimore: Johns Hopkins University Press, 2013), 38.

19. Richard K. MacMaster, *Land, Piety, Peoplehood: The Establishment of Mennonite Communities in America, 1683–1790* (Scottdale, PA: Herald Press, 1985), 138–48.

20. Heinrich Funck, *Ein Spiegel der Tauffe mit Geist, mit Wasser, und mit Blut* (Germantown, PA: Gedruckt [by Christoph Saur], 1744). For an English reprint, see Henry Funk, *A Mirror of Baptism: With the Spirit, with Water, and with Blood* (Moundridge, KS: Gospel, 2000), 68. The first English translation, produced by Joseph Funk and Sons in Mountain Valley, Virginia, appeared in 1851.

21. John L. Ruth, *Maintaining the Right Fellowship: A Narrative Account of Life in the Oldest Mennonite Community in North America* (Scottdale, PA: Herald Press, 1984), 118–19; Rodney James Sawatsky, *History and Ideology: American Mennonite Identity Definition through History* (Kitchener, ON: Pandora Press, 2005), 15.

22. For a brief account, see Joseph J. Kelley, *Pennsylvania: The Colonial Years, 1681–1776* (Garden City, NY: Doubleday, 1980), 209–14.

23. Richard K. MacMaster, *Conscience in Crisis: Mennonites and Other Peace Churches in America, 1739–1789: Interpretation and Documents,* with Samuel L. Horst and Robert F. Ulle (Scottdale, PA: Herald Press, 1979), 61–72.

24. For documentation of this assistance, see Rempel Smucker and Ruth, *Documents of Brotherly Love.*

25. All quotations in this paragraph are from an English translation of the 1745 letter, in MacMaster, *Conscience in Crisis,* 84–87.

26. "So soon as the believer has the witness of the spiritual baptism and has received the baptism with water, he should yield himself willingly to receive the baptism of the shedding of his blood for the name of Christ." Funk, *Mirror of Baptism,* 83.

27. The quotation is from the English translation of the 1745 letter, in MacMaster, *Conscience in Crisis,* 86.

28. The Dutch finally responded in February 1748, though even then the response only kicked the project back into Pennsylvania Mennonite hands. See Samuel W. Penny-

packer, "A Noteworthy Book: *Der Blutige Schau-Platz Oder Martyrer Spiegel*: Ephrata, Pa., 1748," *Pennsylvania Magazine of History and Biography* 5 (1881): 281.

29. The community along the Wissahickon, called the Society of the Woman in the Wilderness, was founded by Johann Kelpius, who, like Beissel, was influenced by the writing of the radical pietist Jacob Boehme. See "Kelpius, Johann," in Robert S. Fogarty, *Dictionary of American Communal and Utopian History* (Westport, CT: Greenwood Press, 1980), 62–63.

30. Jeff Bach, *Voices of the Turtledoves: The Sacred World of Ephrata* (University Park: Pennsylvania State University Press, 2003), 13–19.

31. Ibid., 19.

32. Ibid., 113. Bach concludes, "Ephrata pursued a heterosexually oriented bridal mysticism of the soul" (113), an intimacy with the divine that exceeded sexual intimacy between men and women.

33. Donald B. Kraybill, "Ephrata Cloister," in *Concise Encyclopedia of Amish, Brethren, Hutterites, and Mennonites* (Baltimore: Johns Hopkins University Press, 2010), 78.

34. John Hruschka, *How Books Came to America: The Rise of the American Book Trade* (University Park: Pennsylvania State University Press, 2012), 45. Sauer's press went into operation in 1738; see Stephen L. Longenecker, *The Christopher Sauers: Courageous Printers Who Defended Religious Freedom in Early America* (Elgin, IL: Brethren Press, 1981), 40.

35. Hruschka calls it "a self-contained, comprehensive book publishing enterprise in the middle of the wilderness." Hruschka, *How Books Came to America*, 47.

36. Bach, *Voices of the Turtledoves*, 19–21. *Güldene Aepffel* is a devotional book that includes testimonies and prayers by early Anabaptists. *Die Ernsthafte Christenpflict* is a prayer book that dates to the early 1700s. Both works have since been translated into English.

37. Although some historians have highlighted the divergence of these two traditions, Anabaptism and pietism shared common emphases on ethical living, love toward neighbor, disciplined community life, and in some cases heartfelt devotional practices. According to Jan Stievermann, some pietists had found inspiration in Anabaptist martyrological writings, including *Martyrs Mirror*. See Stievermann, "A 'plain, rejected little flock': The Politics of Martyrological Self-Fashioning among Pennsylvania's German Peace Churches, 1739–65," *William and Mary Quarterly* 65 (2009): 297. For an example of conflict historiography, see Robert Friedmann, *Mennonite Piety through the Centuries: Its Genius and Its Literature* (Goshen, IN: Mennonite Historical Society, 1949). For the complementary nature of Anabaptism and pietism, see MacMaster, *Land, Piety, Peoplehood*, 157–82.

38. Mennonite family names among the Ephrata membership included Graff (Groff), Funk, Guth (Good), and Wenger. See Bach, *Voices of the Turtledoves*, 29.

39. The letter quotation is from MacMaster, *Conscience in Crisis*, 86.

40. Mack's abridgment, which included only three small sections from *Martyrs Mirror*, was titled *Das Andencken einiger heiligen Martyrer* [The memorial of some holy martyrs] and appeared as an appendix to *Die Ernsthafte Christenpflict*. See James W.

Lowry, *The "Martyrs' Mirror" Made Plain: How to Study and Profit from the "Martyrs' Mirror,"* rev. ed. (Aylmer, ON: Pathway, 2011), 80. According to Lowry, the material Mack included in *Das Andencken* can be found in *Martyrs Mirror* (1938), 486–94, 726–31, and 1128–29.

41. Patrick M. Erben makes a case for the volunteer to have been the Germantown printer Christopher Sauer, but given the Skippack letter's reference to "the establishment of a new German printing office," I think an Ephrata connection is more likely, since Sauer's business was established in 1738. See Patrick M. Erben, *A Harmony of the Spirits: Translation and the Language of Community in Early Pennsylvania* (Chapel Hill: University of North Carolina Press, 2012), 257–59.

42. See note 28 above.

43. It is unclear when and on what terms Miller entered the picture as the new translator. For his part, Mack, the son of German Baptist Brethren founder Alexander Mack Sr., left the Ephrata Community around 1748. He later rejoined the German Baptist Brethren. Lowry, *"Martyrs' Mirror" Made Plain*, 80–81.

44. See Dielman Kolb and Heinrich Funck, "Kurtze Nachrede," in *Martyrer Spiegel* (1749), n.p., where the publishing arrangement is outlined.

45. David D. Hall and Elizabeth Carroll Reilly, "Customers and the Market for Books," in *A History of the Book in America*, vol. 1, *The Colonial Book in the Atlantic World*, ed. Hugh Amory and David D. Hall (Chapel Hill: University of North Carolina Press, 2007), 387.

46. The launch date of the project is uncertain. The Ephrata Community's internal history says that "three years were spent on this book," which carries two publication dates, 1748 (book 1) and 1749 (book 2). Assuming that book 2 was finished in 1749, three years of work would place the start date in 1746. At another point in the community's history, however, the chroniclers write that the Mennonites approached the community for its assistance "shortly before the mill burnt down," an event that took place on September 5, 1747. The chroniclers also write that the printing of *Martyrs Mirror* began only after the community rebuilt its mill. It is therefore likely that the project was launched in 1747 and extended into 1750, even though book 2 identifies the publication date as 1749. See Brother Lamech and Brother Agrippa (Jacob Goss and Peter Miller), *Chronicon Ephratense: A History of the Community of Seventh Day Baptists at Ephrata, Lancaster County, Penn'a, by "Lamech and Agrippa,"* trans. J. Max Hark (Lancaster, PA: S. H. Zahm, 1889), 209–10, 213.

47. For an excellent account of Miller's role, see Erben, *Harmony of the Spirits*, 259–61.

48. Ibid., 195–202.

49. This quotation is from the Skippack ministers' 1745 letter to the Dutch Committee for Foreign Needs; see MacMaster, *Conscience in Crisis*, 86.

50. Miller made the claim to Israel Acrelius, who visited the Ephrata Community in 1753. See Israel Acrelius, *A History of New Sweden*, trans. William M. Reynolds (Philadelphia: Historical Society of Pennsylvania, 1874), 383. Acrelius's history was first published in Sweden in 1759.

51. Lamech and Agrippa, *Chronicon Ephratense* (Hark translation), 213.

52. According to Hruschka, *How Books Came to America*, some of the paper used for *Martyrs Mirror* was purchased from other suppliers (47).

53. Ibid., 46.

54. The *Ephrata Chronicle* says 1,300 copies were printed; see Lamech and Agrippa, *Chronicon Ephratense* (Hark translation), 213. Acrelius, in his *History of New Sweden*, places the print run at 1,200 copies (383).

55. The phrase *geistl. Marterthum*, short for *geistlichen Marterthum*, is used twice in the *Chronicon*'s description of the community's production of *Martyrs Mirror*. For the German, see Brother Lamech and Brother Agrippa (Jacob Goss and Peter Miller), *Chronicon Ephratense, Enthaltend den Lebens-Lauf des ehrwürdigen Vaters in Christo Friedsam Gottrecht, . . .* (Ephrata, PA, 1786), 183.

56. Lamech and Agrippa, *Chronicon Ephratense* (Hark translation), 210.

57. Peter Miller, "Kurtzer Vorbericht," *Martyrer Spiegel* (1749), 4, translated and quoted in Erben, *Harmony of the Spirits*, 260–61.

58. The term *printer's device* (or *printer's mark*) assumes that an emblem identifies a particular printer, who employs the device in different books to mark them as his work. By this time, however, the digging-man emblem is being included as a vital feature of van Braght's martyrology, not as a clue to the printer's identity. Although the emblem is an important visual device, it is not, literally speaking, the Ephrata Community's printer's device. I am grateful to Joe Springer for bringing this distinction to my attention. See also John Carter, *ABC for Book Collectors*, 7th ed., rev. Nicolas Barker (New Castle, DE: Oak Knoll Press, 1995), 78.

59. That the device appears in reverse and in a rougher form relative to the 1685 edition "suggests a derivative copying process such as a woodblock cut directly from an oil-paper tracing of the original." Julia Kasdorf, " 'Work and Hope': Tradition and Translation of an Anabaptist Adam," *MQR* 69 (1995): 180.

60. According to Kasdorf, translating the phrase into German also "strengthened a connection between the book and the image" that persisted for most of the book's German-language publication history in America. Ibid.

61. Miller, "Kurtzer Vorbericht," 4, translated and quoted in Erben, *Harmony of the Spirits*, 261.

62. The Ephrata edition's frontispiece includes numbers and letters that suggest the existence of an explanatory key. However, no copies of the key have been located.

63. For the Ephrata Community's views on baptism, see Bach, *Voices of the Turtle-doves*, 70–75.

64. One collector estimates that nearly one-half of the copies sold were bound with the frontispiece. See David Luthy, "German Printings of the *Martyrs' Mirror*," in the back matter of *Martyrer Spiegel* (2011), 9.

65. Stievermann notes that the immersion image on the frontispiece would have appealed to other Pennsylvania-German sectarians who practiced baptism by immersion. It therefore may have been a strategy to widen the book's market appeal beyond the Mennonite realm. See Stievermann, " 'Plain, rejected little flock,' " 313–15.

66. MacMaster, *Land, Piety, Peoplehood*, 229–48.

67. Kolb and Funck, "Kurtze Nachrede," n.p. The English translation of this German afterword is from Pennypacker, "Noteworthy Book," 286. Kolb and Funck admitted, "[We] have indeed found a number of words about which [we] have hesitated and doubted, and which might have been improved both in the Dutch and German . . . but nobody ought to complain for this reason, for we are all human and often err" (286).

68. Quoted in ibid., 287.

69. Acrelius, *History of New Sweden*, 383–84.

70. The chronicle writers identify the price, then note that the modest price "ought to be proof that other causes than eagerness for gain led to the printing." Lamech and Agrippa, *Chronicon Ephratense* (Hark translation), 213. Acrelius identifies the price as twenty-two shillings, then quotes Miller as saying, "We do not propose to get rich," to justify the price; see Acrelius, *History of New Sweden*, 384. In *How Books Came to America,* Hruschka observes that the undertaking was "most likely a financial disaster" (47).

71. Hall and Reilly, "Customers," 387. For wages in the 1750s, see Thomas L. Purvis, *Colonial America to 1763* (New York: Facts on File, 1999), 117.

72. Population statistics can only be estimated, but immigration records suggest that the Mennonite-Amish population in Pennsylvania in 1750 was approximately five thousand men, women, and children (see notes 17 and 18 above).

73. "For Marylanders and, we may suppose, for Americans in general, the typical household library was tiny in size. . . . Three fourths contained fewer than ten books." Hall and Reilly, "Customers," 388. See also Purvis, *Colonial America to 1763,* 248–49.

74. Quoted in John Landis Ruth, *The Earth Is the Lord's: A Narrative History of the Lancaster Mennonite Conference* (Scottdale, PA: Herald Press, 2001), 305.

75. Ibid., 320. For more on "nonassociators," see MacMaster, *Conscience in Crisis,* 220–23; and also 250–53, which reprints the names of nonassociators in Earl Township, Lancaster County.

76. Ruth, *Earth Is the Lord's,* 305.

77. Ruth, *Maintaining the Right Fellowship,* 176.

78. Christian Burkholder placed the following information in his copy of *Martyrs Mirror:* the names and birth years of his siblings, the date of his marriage, the dates of his children's births, and the date of his wife's death. His death in 1809 was recorded in the book by his son Daniel, who then recorded his own family's history as well as the date of his own ordination. H. Romaine (Burkholder) Stauffer, "Bishop Christian Burkholder and His Swiss Family," *Pennsylvania Mennonite Heritage* 34, no. 3 (July 2011): 23.

79. Paul C. Gutjahr, *An American Bible: A History of the Good Book in the United States, 1777–1880* (Stanford, CA: Stanford University Press, 1999), 143–46.

80. Christian Burkholder's copy was "passed to his son Daniel in 1809, grandson Christian in 1858, and great-grandson Daniel in 1868." At that point, the book was passed to a cousin, Ezra G. Burkholder. Stauffer, "Bishop Christian Burkholder," 23, 23n58.

81. See MacMaster, *Land, Piety, Peoplehood,* 229–48.

82. J. C. Wenger, preface to Thieleman J. van Braght, *The Bloody Theater, or Martyrs Mirror of the Defenseless Christians . . . ,* trans. Joseph F. Sohm (Scottdale, PA: MPH, 1950), [2].

83. The details in this paragraph are drawn from two sources: a brief account in the *Chronicon Ephratense*, written in the 1780s, and an account on the flyleaf of an extant copy of the Ephrata *Martyrs Mirror*, written sometime in the eighteenth century by owner Joseph von Gundy. For both accounts I rely on English translations done by David Luthy, which appear in Luthy, "The Ephrata *Martyrs' Mirror*: Shot from Patriots' Muskets," *Pennsylvania Mennonite Heritage* 9, no. 1 (January 1986): 4–5. Von Gundy's copy of *Martyrs Mirror* is now housed in the Heritage Historical Library in Aylmer, ON.

84. Quotations in this paragraph are from David Luthy's translation of the *Chronicon Ephratense* account, in Luthy, "Ephrata *Martyrs' Mirror*," 4. For the original German, see Lamech and Agrippa, *Chronicon Ephratense*, 182n.

85. According to Luthy, von Gundy was Amish for some of his life but later joined the Mennonites. See Luthy, "Ephrata *Martyrs' Mirror*," 5.

86. The *Chronicon Ephratense* account restricts its comments on the book's postwar return to one sentence, noting that "some sensible persons" returned the remaining copies. See Lamech and Agrippa, *Chronicon Ephratense* (Hark translation), 214n.

87. The English translation and the original German are from Luthy, "Ephrata *Martyrs' Mirror*," 5. Von Gundy's *Martyrs Mirror* was a formerly captive copy, and he gratefully noted that it was "not lacking a single page." The completeness of his copy distinguished it from many other redeemed copies, he said, many of which had missing pages or were otherwise damaged.

88. For instance, Daniel K. Cassel, *History of the Mennonites* (Philadelphia: Daniel K. Cassel, 1888), 214; Martin G. Weaver, *Mennonites of Lancaster Conference* (Scottdale, PA: MPH, 1931), 29; John C. Wenger, *History of the Mennonites of the Franconia Conference* (Telford, PA: Franconia Mennonite Historical Society, 1937), 322; and Daniel R. Heatwole, "The Ephrata *Martyrs' Mirror*: Past and Present," *Mennonite Community*, October 1949, 6–13.

89. David Luthy, "The Ephrata *Martyrs' Mirror*: Shot from Patriots' Muskets," *Family Life*, January 1986, 21–23; and Luthy, "Ephrata *Martyrs' Mirror*," *Pennsylvania Mennonite Heritage* 9, no. 1 (January 1986): 2–5.

90. 2 Chronicles 36:22, NRSV.

Chapter 7. *Martyrs Mirror* in Nineteenth-Century America

1. For an account of the book's production, see James W. Lowry, "The Amish Reception of the *Martyrs' Mirror*: A History of Encounters with the Book," *Pennsylvania Mennonite Heritage* 33, no. 1 (January 2010): 24–26.

2. Ibid., 24n21. For biographical information on Brechbill, see Christian Neff and Ira D. Landis, "Brechbill, Benedikt," in *ME*, 1:411–12.

3. David Luthy, "German Printings of the *Martyrs Mirror*," in the back matter of *Martyrer Spiegel* (2011), 9–10.

4. This indebtedness was not the case, however, for Isaac van Dühren's 1787 German-language abridgment of *Martyrs Mirror*, which he titled *Geschichte der Märtyrer, oder: Kurze Historisch Nachricht von der Verfolgungen der Mennonisten* [History of the martyrs, or a brief historical account of the persecutions of the Mennonites] (Königsberg:

Gottlieb Lebrecht Hartung, 1787). Van Dühren's uniquely organized, prefaced, and in-dexed abridgment, the excerpts of which he translated directly from the Dutch, was published about the time Prussian Mennonites were preparing to migrate to Russia. It was, wrote Robert Friedmann, "just the right material for a flock ready for a large-scale emigration with unknown hardships ahead." Robert Friedmann, *Mennonite Piety through the Centuries: Its Genius and Its Literature* (Goshen, IN: Mennonite Historical Society, 1949), 138. Some Prussian families carried the book with them to their new home. Later, the Prussian emigrant Klaas Reimer cited the martyrs' experiences and commitments as he sought to reinvigorate Russia's Molotschna Mennonite settlement. Unhappy with the state of spirituality he found there, Reimer eventually founded a new Mennonite group, the Kleine Gemeinde, which republished van Dühren's abridgment in 1863. See Friedmann, *Mennonite Piety*, 137–40; and Cornelius J. Dyck, *An Introduction to Mennonite History*, 3rd ed. (Scottdale, PA: Herald Press, 1993), 179.

5. The exception was an English edition produced in London at midcentury. Unlike the nineteenth-century North American editions, the London edition, titled *A Martyr-ology of the Churches of Christ, Commonly Called Baptists, during the Era of the Reforma-tion,* was never completed. This edition is discussed later in this chapter.

6. German Baptist Brethren (Dunkers) and other Brethren groups may also be in-cluded in the family of North American Anabaptists at this time. Generally speaking, however, they demonstrated less interest in *Martyrs Mirror*. For that reason, and also for simplicity's sake, I do not include them in this summary of nineteenth-century Ana-baptism.

7. At the time the term used for this subculture was *Pennsylvania Dutch,* not *Pennsyl-vania German*. In the twentieth century, some scholars opted for the term *Pennsylvania German,* which more clearly reflected the community's use of the German language. In this paragraph I employ *Pennsylvania German* to underscore the distinction between Swiss-German Anabaptists, on the one hand, and Dutch-Russian Mennonites on the other. See Aaron Spencer Fogleman, *Hopeful Journeys: German Immigration, Settlement, and Political Culture in Colonial America, 1717–1775* (Philadelphia: University of Penn-sylvania Press, 1996), 197n23; and Don Yoder, "Pennsylvania German," in *Harvard Ency-clopedia of American Ethnic Groups,* ed. Stephan Thernstrom (Cambridge, MA: Harvard University Press, 1980), 770–72.

8. James O. Lehman and Steven M. Nolt, *Mennonites, Amish, and the American Civil War* (Baltimore: Johns Hopkins University Press, 2007), 9, 14, 246n29.

9. James C. Juhnke, "Mennonite History and Self Understanding: North American Mennonitism as a Bipolar Mosaic," in *Mennonite Identity: Historical and Contemporary Perspectives,* ed. Calvin Wall Redekop and Samuel J. Steiner (Lanham, MD: University Press of America, 1988), 83–99.

10. For an example, see John Landis Ruth, *The Earth Is the Lord's: A Narrative His-tory of the Lancaster Mennonite Conference* (Scottdale, PA: Herald Press, 2001), 308–15.

11. Richard K. MacMaster, *Conscience in Crisis: Mennonites and Other Peace Church-es in America, 1739–1789: Interpretation and Documents,* with Samuel L. Horst and Rob-ert F. Ulle (Scottdale, PA: Herald Press, 1979), 354–56.

12. For accounts of the Funk controversy, see ibid., 360–69; John L. Ruth, *Maintaining the Right Fellowship: A Narrative Account of Life in the Oldest Mennonite Community in North America* (Scottdale, PA: Herald Press, 1984), 150–55; and Richard K. MacMaster, *Land, Piety, Peoplehood: The Establishment of Mennonite Communities in America, 1683–1790* (Scottdale, PA: Herald Press, 1985), 267–74.

13. Albert N. Keim, foreword to Theron F. Schlabach, *Peace, Faith, Nation: Mennonites and Amish in Nineteenth-Century America* (Scottdale, PA: Herald Press, 1988), 11.

14. The term "sorting out" is from Schlabach, *Peace, Faith, Nation,* 214.

15. See Beulah Stauffer Hostetler, "The Formation of the Old Orders," *MQR* 66 (1992): 5–25; and Paton Yoder, *Tradition and Transition: Amish Mennonites and Old Order Amish, 1800–1900* (Scottdale, PA: Herald Press, 1991), 115–71.

16. For a summary of this variety, see Donald B. Kraybill, *Concise Encyclopedia of Amish, Brethren, Hutterites, and Mennonites* (Baltimore: Johns Hopkins University Press, 2010), 215–58.

17. *Martyrer Spiegel* (1814). The two title pages in the Ehrenfried edition indicate an 1814 publication date. Although the book's introduction ("Kurtzer Vorbericht") is dated May 1815, the introduction does not appear in some copies and is simply inserted unbound into other copies. According to collector Amos Hoover, the introduction may have been an afterthought, produced to help boost lagging sales.

18. See Ira D. Landis, "Ehrenfried, Joseph," in *ME,* 2:164–65.

19. Luthy, "German Printings," 10.

20. All quotations in this paragraph are from "Kurtzer Vorbericht," *Martyrer Spiegel* (1814), n.p., trans. Noah G. Good, in *"Martyrs Mirror* Introduction, 1814 Style," *Mennonite Research Journal* 16, no. 2 (April 1975): 20–22.

21. For an instance of this rhetoric, see the anonymous work "A Dialogue between the Devil and George III, Tyrant of Britain," in *Political Sermons of the American Founding Era, 1730–1805,* ed. Ellis Sandoz (Indianapolis, IN: Liberty Press, 1991), 689–710.

22. See Gerald C. Studer, "A History of the *Martyrs' Mirror,*" *MQR* 22 (1948): 177.

23. David Sehat, *The Myth of American Religious Freedom* (New York: Oxford University Press, 2011).

24. The "Kurtzer Vorbericht" quotations in this paragraph are from *"Martyrs Mirror* Introduction," 20–22.

25. Ibid., 22.

26. Dietrich Philips, *Enchiridion: Oder Handbüchlein, von der christlichen Lehre und Religion* [Handbook of the Christian doctrine and religion] (Lancaster, PA: Joseph Ehrenfried, 1811).

27. Emanuel Swedenborg (1688–1772), the inspiration for the Swedenborgians, "saw heaven as open to all those, inside or outside the church, who sustained their love of God and active benevolence toward their neighbors." Leigh Eric Schmidt, *Restless Souls: The Making of American Spirituality* (San Francisco: HarperSanFrancisco, 1995), 46. Of course, Anabaptists also emphasized ethical living and love toward neighbor, which means that Mennonites may have been the source of that material.

28. The "Kurtzer Vorbericht" quotation in this paragraph is from *"Martyrs Mirror*

Introduction," 20. For the possibility that the introduction was produced to boost lagging sales, see note 17 above.

29. Luthy, "German Printings," 10.

30. John Foxe, *Allgemeine Geschichte des Christlichen Marterthums* (Philadelphia: Wm. G. Mentz, 1831). See also David Luthy, "The Overlooked Martyr Book of 1833," *Family Life*, November 1992, 17–19. According to Luthy, the copyright for the book was registered in 1831, but the book was first printed in 1833.

31. Luthy, "Overlooked Martyr Book," 18.

32. J. Newton Brown and Joseph Belcher, eds., *Memorials of Baptist Martyrs: With a Preliminary Historical Essay* (Philadelphia: American Baptist Publication Society, 1854).

33. J. Newton Brown, "Preliminary Historical Essay," in *Memorials of Baptist Martyrs*, 6.

34. The author does note that the Baptists refused to retaliate against their foes, but his claim pertains to the Baptists' commitment to liberty of conscience (i.e., their refusal to persecute other religious sects when they held the seats of power) as opposed to a comprehensive commitment to nonresistance. Ibid., 19–20.

35. The Muddy Creek Farm Library, near Ephrata, Pennsylvania, possesses a copy of this edition that carries an 1836 publication date, but the 1837 publication date appears in more copies. See Edsel Burdge Jr., "Pattern for the True Church: The *Martyrs Mirror* and the Reformed Mennonite Church," delivered at the conference "*Martyrs Mirror*: Reflections across Time," Elizabethtown College, Elizabethtown, PA, June 9, 2010. In the 1840s, the Old Mennonite majority in Lancaster County numbered about six thousand members, whereas the Reformed Mennonites numbered less than one thousand. I. Daniel Rupp, *History of Lancaster County: To Which Is Prefixed a Brief Sketch of the Early History of Pennsylvania* (Lancaster, PA: Gilbert Hills, 1844), 456, 463.

36. Ruth, *Earth Is the Lord's*, 355. In the decades following the Revolutionary War, many Lancaster County Mennonites voted, and some even held civic office.

37. The Reformed Mennonite historian Daniel Musser wrote, "So far as I know, they did not themselves assume this name, but being given to them, they have no objection to the appellation." Daniel Musser, *The Reformed Mennonite Church: Its Rise and Progress, with Its Principles and Doctrines* (Lancaster, PA: Elias Barr, 1873), 9. In this and subsequent chapters, the term *Old Mennonites* refers to the largest body of Swiss-German Mennonites in the nineteenth and twentieth centuries. Informal conference affiliations eventually gave way to a denominational structure, which became known as the (Old) Mennonite Church. The Old Mennonites should not be confused with *Old Order Mennonites*, who are discussed in chapters 8 and 9.

38. Ruth, *Earth Is the Lord's*, 357. See also C. Henry Smith and Harold S. Bender, "Reformed Mennonite Church," in *ME*, 4:267–70; and Harold S. Bender, "Herr, John," in *ME*, 2:712–13.

39. John Herr, *The Way to Heaven, Which Leadeth beneath the Cross; or, A True Doctrine from the Word of God*, in *John Herr's Complete Works* (Buffalo, NY: Peter Paul, 1890), 127. First published as Johannes Herr, *Der Wahre und selige Weg der mitten unter*

dem Creuss gen Himmel geht, oder, Eine gründliche Lehre aus Gottes Wort (Lancaster, PA: Joseph Ehrenfried, 1815).

40. John Herr, *A Brief and Apostolic Answer: To a Letter Addressed to Him by a Minister of the Moravian Church,* in *John Herr's Complete Works,* 418–19. First published as Johannes Herr, *Eine Kurze und apostolische Antwort* (n.p., 1819).

41. *Martyrs Mirror* (1938), 9.

42. Echoing van Braght, Herr wrote, "For the devil does not only go about like a roaring lion, but also as a subtle serpent, and before we are aware of it he may wound us with his hellish fangs, and thereby infuse his subtle poison into our souls." Herr, *Way to Heaven,* 157. For van Braght's reference to this principle, see *Martyrs Mirror* (1938), 8.

43. Herr, *Way to Heaven,* 107.

44. Ibid., 11–12.

45. Ibid., 13, 107. Herr considered the Old Mennonites not much different from other nominal Christians. He encouraged his readers to "view the present Mennonite church . . . with a spiritual eye, and observe their carnal life, their proud and haughty mood, their cold and sluggish heart in divine things, their insatiable worldliness, [and] their walk and conversation which, with most of them, is in many ways vain and carnal" (107).

46. Musser, *Reformed Mennonite Church,* 298.

47. Ibid., 305, 314, 315.

48. *Martyrs Mirror* (1837).

49. Burdge, "Pattern for the True Church."

50. Menno Simons, *A Foundation and Plain Instruction of the Saving Doctrine of our Lord Jesus Christ, Briefly Compiled from the Word of God,* trans. I. Daniel Rupp ([Lancaster, PA]: John Herr, 1835).

51. Rupp's history of Lancaster County, published in 1844, attests that all the Old Mennonite ministers at the time continued to preach in German, whereas the Reformed Mennonite ministers sometimes preached in English. See Rupp, *History of Lancaster County,* 456, 463.

52. A partial English translation of *Martyrs Mirror* was produced in London, England, in 1850–53 (see note 5 above).

53. In his history of the Reformed Mennonite Church, Daniel Musser cited the 1837 English translation, often referencing the page numbers.

54. For the print run, see William H. Egle, "I. Daniel Rupp," *Historical Magazine* 9 (1871): 113.

55. Steven M. Nolt, *A History of the Amish,* rev. ed. (Intercourse, PA: Good Books, 2003), 72–95. The letter quotation is from 78.

56. Ibid., 103.

57. David Beiler, "Memoirs of an Amish Bishop," trans. and ed. John Umble, *MQR* 22 (1948): 101–2.

58. For the story of this sorting-out process among the Amish, see Yoder, *Tradition and Transition,* 115–260; and Schlabach, *Peace, Faith, Nation,* 210–20.

59. Bishop Elias Riehl to John Stoltzfus, January 20, 1860; and "Letter from One Bishop to Another Bishop," August 24, 1862, in *Tennessee John Stoltzfus: Amish Church-*

Related Documents and Family Letters, ed. Paton Yoder, trans. Noah Good (Lancaster, PA: Lancaster Mennonite Historical Society, 1987), 54, 90. The first letter cites the example of the sixteenth-century deacon Jan de Swarte, which can be found in *Martyrs Mirror* (1938), 664–65. The second letter cites a letter written by sixteenth-century martyr Jacob de Roore, which can be found in *Martyrs Mirror* (1938), 815.

60. This quotation is from a letter written by Solomon K. Beiler to John Stoltzfus, September 6, 1864, in Yoder, *Tennessee John Stoltzfus,* 117. The comments by Friar Cornelis in this regard can be found in *Martyrs Mirror* (1938), 785, 789–90.

61. Yoder, *Tradition and Transition,* 121–30.

62. See *Martyrs Mirror* (1938), 847.

63. Beiler's reference to Dircks and other Anabaptist martyrs can be found in his book *Das Wahre Christenthum: Eine Christliche Betrachtung nach den Lehren der Heiligen Schrift* [True Christianity: A Christian meditation on the teachings of the holy scripture] (Lancaster, PA: Johann Bär's Söhnen, 1888), 40, 69. Beiler's book was first published in 1888, but he wrote it in 1857.

64. So involved was Zook in the world's affairs that, at least according to legend, Pennsylvania railroad officials asked him to run for Pennsylvania governor. Zook declined, but he nonetheless valued his relationships with people in high places. At the same time, Zook enjoyed considerable esteem among the Pennsylvania Amish, many of whom valued his thoughtful perspectives and his ability to get things done. John A. Hostetler, "Memoirs of Shem Zook (1798–1880)," *MQR* 38 (1964): 280–87.

65. The quotations are from an English translation of Zook's 1880 publication *Eine wahre Darstellung von Dem, welches uns das Evangelium in der Reinheit lehrt* [A true exposition of that which the gospel in purity teaches us], in Hostetler, "Memoirs of Shem Zook," 291–92. Zook's comment on Beiler's disregard of scripture may refer to a letter from Beiler to an Amish bishop in Ohio. See David Beiler et al. to Moses Miller, October 14, 1851, in Yoder, *Tennessee John Stoltzfus,* 33–37.

66. *Martyrer Spiegel* (1849).

67. Mark 1:9–10.

68. Luthy suggests that the setting looks more like the Rhine River in Switzerland than the Jordan River in Palestine. Luthy, "German Printings," 11.

69. According to John A. Hostetler, Zook left two thousand dollars to each of his eight surviving children. His sizable estate also included a forty-five-acre farm in Mifflin County and land in Tennessee. See Hostetler, "Memoirs of Shem Zook," 284.

70. Zook planned to sell the book for $5.50 per copy, and it is possible that he secured a thousand more subscriptions before the book was printed. See Abrm. Hunsicker to John Oberholtzer, January 15, 1849; letter reprinted in *Mennonite Historians of Eastern Pennsylvania Quarterly* 1, no. 4 (December 1998): 6–7.

71. "Vorbericht zur dritten hochdeutschen Auflage," in *Martyrer Spiegel* (1849), 4. Translated phrases are from Luthy, "German Printings," 10.

72. See "Vorbericht zur dritten hochdeutschen Auflage," in *Martyrer Spiegel* (1849), 4. Also, Luthy, "German Printings," 11.

73. Lowry, "Amish Reception," 28.

74. For the details of this division, see Yoder, *Tradition and Transition*, 113–203. Yoder identifies the year 1865 as "the point of no return" (153), but his account of the division concludes with events in 1878.

75. The biographical details in this paragraph are drawn from Helen Kolb Gates, John Funk Kolb, J. Clemens Kolb, and Constance Kolb Sykes, *Bless the Lord O My Soul: A Biography of Bishop John Fretz Funk, 1835–1930, Creative Pioneer for Christ and Mennonite Leader,* ed. J. C. Wenger (Scottdale, PA: Herald Press, 1964), 15–63; and Joseph Liechty and James O. Lehman, "From Yankee to Nonresistant: John F. Funk's Chicago Years, 1857–1865," *MQR* 59 (1985): 203–47.

76. John A. Hostetler, *God Uses Ink: The Heritage and Mission of the Mennonite Publishing House after Fifty Years* (Scottdale, PA: Herald Press, 1958), 26. Hostetler quotes Funk: "My father and mother, and the whole number of grand, great-grand, and great-great-grandfathers and mothers were all Mennonites" (26). According to Hostetler, only three of Funk's seven siblings who grew to maturity remained Mennonites. The other four became either Presbyterians or Methodists (27).

77. Kathryn Teresa Long, *The Revival of 1857–58: Interpreting an American Religious Awakening* (New York: Oxford University Press, 1998).

78. Gates et al., *Bless the Lord,* 45.

79. John F. Funk, *Warfare: Its Evils, Our Duty; Addressed to the Mennonite Churches throughout the United States, and All Others Who Sincerely Seek and Love the Truth* (Chicago: Chas. Hess, printer, 1863).

80. Under the banner "The Herald of Truth" were these words: "Devoted to the Interests of the Denomination of Christians known as 'The Mennonites.'" In 1882 the *Herald of Truth* became a semimonthly periodical, and in 1903 it became a weekly periodical.

81. In the first issue of *Herald of Truth,* Funk acknowledges but counters his adversaries' complaints: "I do not pretend to show that [a periodical] is a duty positively enjoined upon us by the word of God—that would be folly—but the Bible contains nothing against it, but rather encourages us in such a work." John F. Funk, "Shall We Have a Religious Paper?" *Herald of Truth,* January 1864, 1. His fellow advocate, John M. Brenneman, was even more explicit: "I am well aware that we have many good-meaning brethren in our church, who are opposed to a religious paper . . . [but] we hope that our brethren will, by and by, become more favorably inclined, with regard to its usefulness in the church." John M. Brenneman, "Ought We to Have a Religious Paper?" *Herald of Truth,* January 1864, 2–3.

82. Hostetler, *God Uses Ink,* 48–51, 59–63.

83. Ibid., 52–54.

84. *Martyrer Spiegel* (1870).

85. Luthy, "German Printings," 11.

86. "The Martyrs' Mirror," *Herald of Truth,* April 1870, 56; and "Der Märtyrer Spiegel," *Herold der Wahrheit,* April 1870, 56.

87. Delbert F. Plett, *The Golden Years: The Mennonite Kleine Gemeinde in Russia, 1812–1849* (Steinbach, MB: D. F. P., 1985), 327–28.

88. John B. Toews, *Perilous Journey: The Mennonite Brethren in Russia, 1869–1910* (Winnipeg, MB: Kindred Press, 1988), 11–13.

89. Plett, *Golden Years*, 327–28. Plett cites letters that Toews wrote to Funk in August 1872 and December 1872.

90. Thielem J. van Braght, *The Bloody Theatre, or Martyrs Mirror, of the Defenseless Christians . . .* , trans. Joseph F. Sohm (Elkhart, IN: Mennonite Publishing Company, 1886). Although the book includes an 1886 publication date, the printing and binding were completed in 1887; see *Herald of Truth*, March 15, 1887, 88.

91. Luthy, "Overlooked Martyr Book," 18–19.

92. *A Martyrology of the Churches of Christ, Commonly Called Baptists, during the Era of the Reformation*, 2 vols. (London: J. Haddon, 1850–53). James W. Lowry writes that the Hanserd Knolleys edition was "possibly unknown" to Funk; see "Research Note: Joseph F. Sohm's Translation of the *Martyrs Mirror*," *MQR* 86 (2012): 380.

93. Edward B. Underwood, introduction to *Martyrology of the Churches*, 1:xii. Underwood and Benjamin Millard served as translators for this new edition.

94. Funk cites this shift in his preface to *Martyrs Mirror* (1886). "As the English language, year by year, becomes more prevalent among our Mennonite people, the necessity of presenting [literature] to them in that language . . . becomes apparent to every reflecting mind" [3]. The shift from German to English was not universal, however. Tradition-minded Mennonites held onto the German language much more vigorously than did change-minded Mennonites. Also, late-nineteenth-century immigrant Mennonites bolstered the ranks of German-speaking Mennonites in North America.

95. "The *Martyrs' Mirror* in the English Language," *Herald of Truth*, December 1880, 218. A year earlier Funk had floated the idea to his readers, asking them to respond with their views on the matter; see "The *Martyrs' Mirror* in English," *Herald of Truth*, November 1879, 210.

96. John F. Funk, "Biographical Sketch of Joseph Sohm," reprinted in the *Mennonite Historical Bulletin* 18, no. 4 (October 1957): 1. This sketch, the original of which is housed in the Mennonite Church U.S.A. Archives in Goshen, Indiana, was penned by Funk circa 1919 and edited for publication by John C. Wenger. For more on Sohm, see Lowry, "Research Note," 371–81.

97. "The English *Martyrs Mirror*," *Herald of Truth*, August 15, 1882, 248.

98. *Herald of Truth*, March 15, 1885, 88. For the challenges of producing the translation, see Joseph F. Sohm, "Translator's Preface," *Martyrs Mirror* (1886), [4]. See also "The Copy of the *Martyrs Mirror*," *Herald of Truth*, April 1, 1887, 105.

99. Funk, "Biographical Sketch of Joseph Sohm," 7.

100. The Herald Press edition that is reprinted every few years uses Sohm's translation.

101. For Funk's claim of the new translation's superiority, see "The Translation of the *Martyrs' Mirror*," *Herald of Truth*, March 1, 1884, 65–66. "If any one may chance to think that . . . we have gone to unnecessary trouble and expense in retranslating the work, they will, no doubt, conclude that after all, it would not only have been folly to republish a work containing so many and such great incorrections, but, positively wrong" (65).

102. "*Martyrs' Mirror* in the English Language," 218. In an effort to print only the number of copies that would be sold, Funk sold the book by subscription, a sales process that urged buyers to order copies in advance. By mid-1882, Funk announced that he had a list of 1,004 subscribers, surpassing his prepublication goal of one thousand subscribers. See "English *Martyrs Mirror*," *Herald of Truth*, July 15, 1882, 216.

103. For instance, Jonathan Kolb, "The *Martyrs' Mirror*," *Herald of Truth*, March 1, 1882, 74.

104. Many of the images are unattributed, but some are attributed to Joe K. French, some to Anthony Sohm, and still others to the Chicago-based Acme Engraving Company.

105. Funk placed the 1685 ornamental title page, revised with English text, at the beginning of book 1; see *Martyrs Mirror* (1886), 60. The image of van Braght appeared as the frontispiece to the entire volume.

106. Funk, publisher's preface to *Martyrs Mirror* (1886), [3].

107. Ibid. See George M. Marsden, *Fundamentalism and American Culture*, 2nd ed. (New York: Oxford University Press, 2006), 72–80. Marsden notes that D. L. Moody popularized this concept by holding so-called *consecration meetings*.

108. Funk, publisher's preface to *Martyrs Mirror* (1886), [3].

109. Even though *Martyrs Mirror* (1886) included only thirty-six narrative images, the first twenty-two images that appear are the same twenty-two images that first appear in van Braght (1685), from the crucifixion of Jesus to the execution of Phocas in 118 CE.

110. The six images, as identified in *Martyrs Mirror* (1886), are Leonhard Keyser (406), two girls in Bamburg (482), Andries Langedul (609), Dirk Willems (710), Mattheus Mair (1032), and Catharina Mulerin (1052).

111. Funk, publisher's preface to *Martyrs Mirror* (1886), [3].

112. Musser, *Reformed Mennonite Church* (see note 37 above).

113. John F. Funk, *The Mennonite Church and Her Accusers: A Vindication of the Character of the Mennonite Church of America, from Her First Organization in This Country to the Present Time* (Elkhart, IN: Mennonite Publishing Company, 1878.)

114. Ibid., 6.

115. Ibid., 38–39, 124–25.

116. Ibid., 181.

117. Musser, *Reformed Mennonite Church*, 314.

118. Funk, *Mennonite Church and Her Accusers*, 183–84.

119. Ibid., 184.

120. Ibid., 206.

Chapter 8. *Martyrs Mirror* in Twentieth-Century America

1. Excerpting selections from *Martyrs Mirror* for distribution occurred prior to the twentieth century, but the scope of that activity increased dramatically as the twentieth century ran its course.

2. In this chapter the term *Mennonite Church* refers to the largest North American Mennonite denomination throughout the twentieth century. Composed largely of

people of Swiss-German ancestry, the Mennonite Church, sometimes called the *(Old) Mennonite Church*, was the result of Old Mennonites joining together in a formal denominational structure.

3. James C. Juhnke, *Vision, Doctrine, War: Mennonite Identity and Organization in America, 1890–1930* (Scottdale, PA: Herald Press, 1989), 34, 36.

4. Ibid., 40–52.

5. Ibid., 50.

6. Benjamin Wetzel, "Fundamentalists, Modernists, and a Mennonite 'Third Way': Reexamining the Career of Bishop Daniel Kauffman," in *The Activist Impulse: Essays on the Intersection of Evangelicalism and Anabaptism*, ed. Jared S. Burkholder and David C. Cramer (Eugene, OR: Pickwick, 2012), 104–28. Kauffman served as editor of *Gospel Herald* from 1908 to 1943.

7. Cornelius H. Wedel, *Abriss der Geschichte der Mennoniten* [Summary of the history of the Mennonites], 4 vols. (Newton, KS: Bethel College, 1900–1904).

8. J. Denny Weaver, *Keeping Salvation Ethical: Mennonite and Amish Atonement Theology in the Late Nineteenth Century* (Scottdale, PA: Herald Press, 1997), 81.

9. Ibid., 79–81. For the beginning of the General Conference Mennonite Church, see Theron F. Schlabach, *Peace, Faith, Nation: Mennonites and Amish in Nineteenth-Century America* (Scottdale, PA: Herald Press, 1988), 117–40.

10. Rodney James Sawatsky, *History and Ideology: American Mennonite Identity Definition through History* (Kitchener, ON: Pandora Press, 2005), 39–94.

11. Paul Toews, *Mennonites in American Society, 1930–1970: Modernity and the Persistence of Religious Community* (Scottdale, PA: Herald Press, 1996), 93–94.

12. C. Henry Smith, *Mennonites in History* (Scottdale, PA: Mennonite Book and Tract Society, 1907), 35. Smith delivered his address at First Mennonite Church of Philadelphia. For the congregation's progressive ways, see Ross L. Bender, "It Was Large and Fancy," *Mennonite*, May 13, 1986, 212–13.

13. C. Henry Smith, *The Mennonites of America* (Goshen, IN: C. Henry Smith, 1909), 17–18. See also C. Henry Smith, *The Mennonites: A Brief History of Their Origin and Later Development in Both Europe and America* (Berne, IN: Mennonite Book Concern, 1920); and C. Henry Smith, *The Story of the Mennonites* (Berne, IN: Mennonite Book Concern, 1941).

14. Susan Fisher Miller, *Culture for Service: A History of Goshen College, 1894–1994* (Goshen, IN: Goshen College, 1994), 87–122.

15. Albert N. Keim, *Harold S. Bender, 1897–1962* (Scottdale, PA: Herald Press, 1998), 160–66. Previously Bender had studied theology at Princeton Theological Seminary, where he enjoyed the mentorship of the fundamentalist theologian J. Gresham Machen (123).

16. John Horsch, *The Mennonite Church and Modernism* (Scottdale, PA: MPH, 1924), 104–6. Had early Mennonites compromised their convictions, writes Horsch, "there would never have been a Mennonite Church nor a single Mennonite martyr" (105).

17. Keim, *Harold S. Bender, 1897–1962*, 205–6.

18. For a midcentury history of the publishing house, see John A. Hostetler, *God Uses*

Ink: The Heritage and Mission of the Mennonite Publishing House after Fifty Years (Scottdale, PA: Herald Press, 1958). After 1950, many of the books published at the Mennonite Publishing House were issued under the Herald Press trade name. Others, however, continued to carry the Mennonite Publishing House trade name. *Martyrs Mirror* carried the Mennonite Publishing House trade name in 1938, 1950, and 1951. It assumed the Herald Press trade name beginning in 1968.

19. Harold S. Bender, "What Can the Church Do for Her Historical Work?" *Gospel Herald,* May 26, 1927, 170.

20. Guy F. Hershberger, "To Keep Alive Our Scriptural Peace Testimony: On Being True to the Faith of the Fathers," *Youth's Christian Companion,* September 11, 1938, 296. A year later, an entire issue of the periodical was devoted to promoting the church's nonresistant position. See *Youth's Christian Companion,* November 5, 1939, 769–76.

21. Publishers' preface to *Martyrs Mirror* (1938), [3]. The most outdated line, more appropriate for the 1886 edition than the 1938 edition, spoke of the English language as becoming "more prevalent" each year in the Mennonite Church. This preface was removed from later MPH / Herald Press editions.

22. Ibid.

23. In 1970, one Mennonite Publishing House employee, Jan Gleysteen, claimed that the images omitted from the 1938 edition were excluded because they were "too gruesome." Although this assumption regarding their exclusion was common in the late twentieth century, I have not found evidence from the 1930s to support Gleysteen's claim. See [John L. Ruth and Jan Gleysteen], "Resume on the *Martyrs' Mirror* Study and Products," unpublished report sent to Art Smoker, secretary for youth ministry of the Mennonite Church. Smoker's response to Gleysteen and Ruth was dated April 15, 1970. Copies of both are in author's possession.

24. Mirjam M. Foot, *Bookbinders at Work: Their Roles and Methods* (London: British Library and Oak Knoll Press, 2006), 56–57. "All this was done not just for aesthetic reasons," writes Foot, "but because a coloured or sprinkled edge would not show the dirt" (57). Some copies of the nineteenth-century Hanserd Knolleys edition of *Martyrs Mirror* also had a red sprinkled edge.

25. This assertion is based on conversations with Amish ministers in Pinecraft, Florida, in February 2011; see also Julia Spicher Kasdorf, "Mightier Than the Sword: *Martyrs Mirror* in the New World," *Conrad Grebel Review* 31, no. 1 (Winter 2013): 44. Levi Miller, who worked in the MPH's book division from 1995 to 2009, acknowledges that MPH executives eventually came to see the sprinkled edges as signifying the martyrs' blood. Levi Miller, e-mail message to author, February 25, 2011.

26. Initial advertisements for *Martyrs Mirror* appeared in the following issues of *Gospel Herald* in 1938: November 3 (p. 680); November 10 (p. 712), and November 17 (p. 728).

27. In addition to publishing the 1938 English edition, the Mennonite Publishing House printed a German edition in 1915. Financed by Amish clients, the 1915 German edition drew heavily from *Martyrer Spiegel* (1870), published by John F. Funk. The 1915 edition is discussed in this chapter's next section.

28. Guy Franklin Hershberger, *The Mennonite Church in the Second World War* (Scottdale, PA: MPH, 1951), 39; and Perry Bush, *Two Kingdoms, Two Loyalties: Mennonite Pacifism in Modern America* (Baltimore: Johns Hopkins University Press, 1998), 97–99.

29. H. S. Bender, "Forward into the Postwar World with Our Peace Testimony," *Christian Missions*, a supplement to *Gospel Herald*, June 1946, 220. See also Bush, *Two Kingdoms, Two Loyalties*, 99–100.

30. J. C. Wenger, preface to Thieleman J. van Braght, *The Bloody Theater or Martyrs Mirror of the Defenseless Christians . . .* , trans. Joseph F. Sohm (Scottdale, PA: MPH, 1950), [2].

31. Ford Berg to A. J. Metzler and David Alderfer, July 20, 1950; copy in author's possession.

32. See also the advertisement at the end of Daniel R. Heatwole, *The Ephrata "Martyrs' Mirror": Past and Present* (Scottdale, PA: MPH, [1950]).

33. "A Publishing Event," *Gospel Herald*, June 13, 1950, 555.

34. For Mennonite responses to military service in the 1950s, see Bush, *Two Kingdoms, Two Loyalties*, 153–87.

35. Gerald C. Studer, "You Can Afford a *Martyrs Mirror*," *Youth's Christian Companion*, July 1950, 247. Ironically, the story of the drowned teenager is not from *Martyrs Mirror* but is rather from Smith, *Mennonites: A Brief History*, 26. Some of the story's details are similar to those in a *Martyrs Mirror* account in which some Anabaptist women are drowned in a horse pond. There is no indication in the *Martyrs Mirror* account that any of the women are teenagers. See *Martyrs Mirror* (1938), 437.

36. Studer, "You Can Afford a *Martyrs Mirror*," 247. Here Studer quotes Philippians 3:10 (KJV).

37. Ibid., 247.

38. David Alderfer to Katie Yoder, July 25, 1950; copy in author's possession.

39. The four periodicals were *Gospel Herald*, *Youth's Christian Companion*, *Mennonite Community*, and *Christian Monitor*.

40. *Budget*, August 17, 1950, [5].

41. John A. Hostetler, "Book Review Column," *Budget*, November 16, 1950, [3]. Hostetler also noted that the price "is not too high when one considers the cost of one volume in 1814 was ten dollars."

42. *Der blutige Schauplatz oder Märtyrer-Spiegel oder Taufgesinnten oder Wehrlosen Christen . . .* (Scottdale, PA: Mennonitischen Verlagshaus, 1915).

43. David Luthy, *A History of the Printings of the "Martyrs' Mirror"* (Alymer, ON: Pathway, 2013), 51–52.

44. Hans E. Bornträger, "Eine neue Auflage des *Märtyrer Spiegel*," *Herold der Wahrheit*, December 1, 1914, 393–94.

45. L. A. Miller, "Die neue Auflage des *Märtyrer Spiegel*," *Herold der Wahrheit*, February 1, 1915, 50.

46. *Der blutige Schauplatz oder Märtyrer-Spiegel oder Taufgesinnten oder Wehrlosen Christen . . .* (Berne, IN: Licht und Hoffe, 1950).

47. Alderfer to Yoder, July 25, 1950.

48. Luthy notes that the printing cost for the 1950 edition was $4.15 per book. See Luthy, *History of the Printings*, 52.

49. Alderfer to Yoder, July 25, 1950.

50. For information on Pathway, see Pathway Publishers, http://pathway-publishers .com/, accessed February 4, 2015.

51. Pathway now employs two dozen people in the United States and Canada, and it sells, among other things, a quarter million books per year. David Luthy to David Weaver-Zercher, September 2, 2014.

52. "We at [Pathway] feel very strongly that our church is not becoming a 'dead' culture," said Pathway cofounder Joseph Stoll. "Therefore, we try to instruct our young people in the whys and wherefores of all practices." Quoted in John A. Hostetler, *Amish Society*, 3rd ed. (Baltimore: Johns Hopkins University Press, 1980), 369.

53. David Luthy, "What's a *Martyrs' Mirror*?" in *Step by Step* (Aylmer, ON: Pathway, 1968), 213–20. Since then, this particular textbook has been reprinted ten times and has sold nearly sixty thousand copies, a total that pales in comparison to the number of children who have used the text, since the readers are used year after year in the schools that adopt them. For sales numbers, see David Luthy to James Lowry, February 16, 2010; Heritage Historical Library, Aylmer, ON.

54. [Elmo Stoll], "Dirk Willems and the Thief Catcher," in *Our Heritage* (Aylmer, ON: Pathway, 1968), 20–24. According to David Luthy, more than forty-five thousand copies of *Our Heritage* were in print in 2011. See Luthy, *Dirk Willems: His Noble Deed Lives On* (Aylmer, ON: Pathway, 2011), 55.

55. Joseph Stoll, preface to *The Drummer's Wife and Other Stories from "Martyrs' Mirror"* (Aylmer, ON: Pathway, 1968), [5].

56. David Luthy, "Half-Way Baptism," *Family Life*, January 1968, 25–26.

57. Joseph Stoll, "Chats about the Anabaptists," *Family Life*, February 1968, 35–39; Joseph Stoll, "Chats about the Anabaptists: Felix Manz Is Drowned," *Family Life*, August 1968, 35–37; Joseph Stoll, "Chats about the Anabaptists: Michael Sattler, the Unshakeable Martyr," *Family Life*, September 1968, 37–39; and Joseph Stoll, "Chats about the Anabaptists: Anabaptist Hunts in the Emmental," *Family Life*, October 1968, 35–37.

58. David Luthy, "The Death of a Church," *Family Life*, October 1968, 37–39.

59. The Mennonite Publishing House printed the 1962 German-language edition, which was financed by Amish layperson Lester C. Byler. See Luthy, *History of the Printings*, 54–55.

60. For Dutch-Russian Mennonites who continue to speak a Low German dialect, see Royden Loewen, "To the Ends of the Earth: An Introduction to the Conservative Low German Mennonites in the Americas," *MQR* 82 (2008): 427–48.

61. The current production editor at MennoMedia, which produces Herald Press titles, estimates that the 1968 retail price for *Martyrs Mirror* was twelve dollars. Amy Gingerich, e-mail message to author, May 14, 2012.

62. For the use of *Martyrs Mirror* in Low German Mennonite history, and especially as a resource to remind migrating Mennonites that God's people are refined through material privation, see Loewen, "To the Ends of the Earth," 433–34.

63. Some tradition-minded Anabaptists objected to Jan Luyken's images, finding them ostentatious, impiously gruesome, or both. Others, however, concluded that Luyken's images could help to convey important messages. See, for instance, Noah Zook, *Seeking a Better Country* (Gordonville, PA: Old Order Book Society, 1963), 30–31, which includes two Luyken images.

64. From 1964 to 1969, the Pathway catalog was associated with the privately owned Pathway Bookstore, which was founded and owned by one of Pathway Publisher's founders, David Wagler, but was not part of the Pathway Publishing Corporation. In February 1970, the corporation purchased Pathway Bookstore from Wagler and assumed publication of the catalog. David Luthy to David Weaver-Zercher, June 4, 2012.

65. In 1976, when Scottdale's list price for the English edition was $17.95, Pathway sold copies for $14.95. In 1993, when Scottdale's list price was $39.95, Pathway's was $35.00. Luthy to Weaver-Zercher, June 4, 2012.

66. David Luthy to Maurice Martin, June 17, 1998; and David Luthy to Paul Schrock, February 1, 1999; both letters in Heritage Historical Library.

67. In 1999 the Mennonite Publishing House's suggested retail price for *Martyrs Mirror* was $45.00 US, which means that Pathway could acquire copies for $22.50. Pathway then sold those copies for $30.00 including shipping. See David Luthy to Robert Kreider, February 26, 1999, Heritage Historical Library.

68. Although the destination of English-language copies is harder to discern than the destination of German-language copies, English copies were likely being purchased as much by tradition-minded Anabaptists as by change-minded Anabaptists. An MPH sales list from 1997 identifies both individual purchasers and a list of distributors, along with the number of copies sold. Most of the distributors that purchased twenty or more copies were enterprises operated by or oriented to traditional Anabaptists. Pathway led the way in 1997 by purchasing 630 of the 2,000 copies. This pattern continued into the twenty-first century. From 1998 to 2012, Herald Press produced 20,000 copies of *Martyrs Mirror;* Pathway purchased more than one-third of those copies for resale. Luthy to Weaver-Zercher, October 5, 2012.

69. Toews, *Mennonites in American Society,* 213.

70. Ibid., 110–21.

71. For an account of the conference, see Leo Driedger and Donald B. Kraybill, *Mennonite Peacemaking: From Quietism to Activism* (Scottdale, PA: Herald Press, 1994), 84–87.

72. Ibid., 85. See Ervin R. Stutzman, *From Nonresistance to Justice: The Transformation of Mennonite Church Peace Rhetoric, 1908–2008* (Scottdale, PA: Herald Press, 2011).

73. Paul Peachey, "Nonviolence in the South," *Gospel Herald,* February 19, 1957, 177. In *Mennonite Peacemaking,* Driedger and Kraybill note that 114 articles on race relations appeared in *Gospel Herald* during the years 1957–69 (127).

74. See Tobin Miller Shearer, *Daily Demonstrations: The Civil Rights Movement in Mennonite Homes and Sanctuaries* (Baltimore: Johns Hopkins University Press, 2010), 98–129. See also Bush, *Two Kingdoms, Two Loyalties,* 210–17; and Stutzman, *From Nonresistance to Justice,* 125–29.

75. Guy F. Hershberger, "Nonresistance, the Mennonite Church, and the Race Question," *Gospel Herald,* June 28, 1960, 577–78, 581–82.

76. For the advancing use of this phrase, see Stutzman, *From Nonresistance to Justice*, 125–52. Stutzman cites the Mennonite Church's statement "The Christian Witness to the State," adopted by the denomination in 1961, as "a pivotal point in the move toward greater peace activism" in the Mennonite Church (137).

77. Quoted in Driedger and Kraybill, *Mennonite Peacemaking*, 128.

78. *Mennonite Life* 22, no. 2 (April 1967): 49–96.

79. Ibid., 51–52. Krahn was also the editor of *Mennonite Life*.

80. Ibid.

81. Vincent Harding, quoted in Shearer, *Daily Demonstrations*, 102.

82. David Janzen, quoted in Bush, *Two Kingdoms, Two Loyalties*, 246–47.

83. Melissa Miller and Phil M. Shenk, *The Path of Most Resistance: Stories of Mennonite Conscientious Objectors Who Did Not Cooperate with the Vietnam War Draft* (Scottdale, PA: Herald Press, 1982), 48.

84. Mennonite Church, "Response to Conscription and Militarism," 1969, at http://anabaptistwiki.org/mediawiki/index.php?title=Response_to_Conscription_and_Militarism_Mennonite_Church,_1969, accessed January 26, 2015.

85. Krahn's decision to cast his message into this format appears to have been successful. The image-rich periodical sold out quickly, and it was republished under the title *The Witness of the "Martyrs Mirror" for Our Day* (North Newton, KS: Bethel College, n.d.).

86. [Ruth and Gleysteen], "Resume on the *Martyrs' Mirror*."

87. John L. Ruth, *Branch: A Memoir with Pictures* (Lancaster, PA: TourMagination; Harleysville, PA: Mennonite Historians of Eastern Pennsylvania, 2013), 208; Julia Kasdorf, e-mail message to author, July 23, 2014.

88. Ruth, *Branch*, 196; Ruth notes that parts of the oratorio were developed and rehearsed as early as 1967.

89. *The Drama of the Martyrs: From the Death of Jesus Christ up to the Recent Times* (Lancaster PA: Mennonite Historical Associates, 1975).

90. [Ruth and Gleysteen], "Resume on the *Martyrs' Mirror*."

91. The introduction that accompanied *The Drama of the Martyrs*, written by Gerald C. Studer, poked fun at *Ms.* magazine, which had used Luyken's image of Anneken Hendricks to illustrate an article on witch burnings. "I strongly suspect that Ms. Hendricks would not have considered either witchcraft or the women's lib movement as sufficient reason to sacrifice her life," remarked Studer.

92. Curated by the Kauffman Museum, the exhibit is supported by the Martyrs Mirror Trust, a collaborative effort of the Mennonite Historical Library in Goshen, Indiana, and the Kauffman Museum at Bethel (KS) College. See The Mirror of the Martyrs, www .bethelks.edu/kauffman/martyrs/, accessed January 30, 2015.

93. For a discussion of the Albrizzi picture album, see James W. Lowry, "*Martyrs' Mirror* Picture Albums and Abridgements: A Surprising Find," *Pennsylvania Mennonite Heritage* 25, no. 4 (October 2002): 2–8.

94. Amos B. Hoover, "Jan Luyken's Lost *Martyrs Mirror* Engravings," *Pennsylvania Mennonite Heritage* 1, no. 1 (July 1978): 2–5. According to Hoover, the plates' previous

owner, Christian Wolf, attested that he owned only 90 of the 104 originals. The whereabouts of the other fourteen at that time is unknown (5).

95. Gerald C. Studer, "A History of the *Martyrs' Mirror*," *MQR* 22 (1948): 171.

96. Hoover, "Luyken's Lost *Martyrs Mirror* Engravings," 2–5.

97. Hoover's comment is cited in John S. Oyer and Robert S. Kreider, *Mirror of the Martyrs* (Intercourse, PA: Good Books, 1990), 86.

98. According to his own account, Hoover paid 3,900 Deutsche Marks (about $1,600) for each of the seven plates, retaining two for his own Muddy Creek Farm Library collection and selling the others to five different Anabaptist persons or institutions in the United States. Hoover, "Luyken's Lost *Martyrs Mirror* Engravings," 5.

99. Robert Kreider, "A *Martyrs' Mirror* Invitation," *Mennonite Life*, September 1990, 4. Kreider does not explicitly call Anabaptists the rightful heirs to the Luyken plates, though he does assert that "we *claimed*" the plates, in reference to his group's purchase of them. Oyer and Kreider, *Mirror of the Martyrs*, 7 (emphasis added).

100. Robert Kreider, e-mail message to author, July 31, 2014.

101. Kreider, "*Martyrs' Mirror* Invitation," 4.

102. Oyer and Kreider, *Mirror of the Martyrs*, 7.

103. Information about the exhibit that appears in this paragraph was taken from the exhibit's website, The Mirror of the Martyrs, www.bethelks.edu/kauffman/martyrs /creation.html, accessed January 30, 2015.

104. Kreider, "*Martyrs' Mirror* Invitation," 5.

105. Oyer and Kreider, *Mirror of the Martyrs*, 9, 15. Oyer and Kreider concluded their catalog with a more contemporary vignette, the "odyssey of the lost copper plates." In Kreider and Oyer's telling, the plates, like the martyrs themselves, had demonstrated a high level of faithfulness, for they "survived wars, plundering, and neglect to carry the memory of martyrs long past, but living still" (86–87).

106. Ibid., 14.

107. See Marlin Jeschke, *Believers Baptism for Children of the Church* (Scottdale, PA: Herald Press, 1983), 139. Jeschke rejected the argument that all adult believers who had been baptized as infants needed to be rebaptized. In Jeschke's view, baptism signified "the act of accountable entrance upon the way of faith," and it therefore made no sense to baptize, say, a forty-year-old person who had embraced the Christian faith as a young adult.

108. Oyer and Kreider, *Mirror of the Martyrs*, 14.

109. By reading *Martyrs Mirror*, "we become aware that those magistrates who killed and tortured perceived themselves to be good people, engaging in painful chores for the public good." Ibid., 12.

110. Photocopied note in *Mirror of the Martyrs* file in Heritage Historical Library.

111. David Luthy to Robert Kreider, December 11, 2003, Heritage Historical Library. In his letter, Luthy is responding to a previous letter from Kreider, who acknowledged that some people had complained that the *Mirror of the Martyrs* exhibit was "too gentle on the persecutors." Kreider to Luthy, December 5, 2003, Heritage Historical Library.

Chapter 9. Tradition-Minded Anabaptists and the Use of *Martyrs Mirror*

1. For details of the restructuring, see John E. Sharp, "End of an Era," *Mennonite,* June 2011, 12–17.

2. The total includes approximately 30,000 copies in English produced by Herald Press and approximately 6,500 in German produced by Pathway Publishers.

3. James C. Juhnke, *Vision, Doctrine, War: Mennonite Identity and Organization in America, 1890–1930* (Scottdale, PA: Herald Press, 1989), 304. Juhnke's numbers, drawn from the Census Bureau's report *Religious Bodies: 1936* (Washington, DC: Government Printing Office, 1941), show about 73,000 members in the Mennonite Church and General Conference Mennonite Church combined, and about 15,000 members in Old Order Amish, Old Order Mennonite, and Beachy Amish churches.

4. See Donald B. Kraybill and C. Nelson Hostetter, *Anabaptist World USA* (Scottdale, PA: Herald Press, 2001), 67, 105. The growth of traditional churches has been fueled by high birthrates and high retention rates, which far exceed the corresponding rates in assimilated churches.

5. Steven Nolt, "The Mennonite Eclipse," *Festival Quarterly,* Summer 1992, 8. In one fifteen-year period alone, 1974–89, the Old Order Amish doubled in membership, whereas the Mennonite Church's membership grew only 9 percent and the General Conference Mennonite membership declined by 3 percent (9).

6. Donald B. Kraybill, "Overview," in Donald B. Kraybill, *Concise Encyclopedia of Amish, Brethren, Hutterites, and Mennonites* (Baltimore: Johns Hopkins University Press, 2010), xv.

7. Donald B. Kraybill, "Traditional Groups," in Kraybill, *Concise Encyclopedia,* 201.

8. Donald B. Kraybill, "Assimilated Groups," in Kraybill, *Concise Encyclopedia,* 19.

9. Kraybill, "Overview," xvi.

10. This table is adapted from Kraybill and Hostetter, *Anabaptist World USA,* 56. In that book, Kraybill and Hostetter used the labels *transformational* (instead of assimilated), *transitional* (instead of conservative), and *traditional* (instead of Old Order).

11. Information in this section derives largely from advertisements I placed in Amish and Mennonite periodicals, which asked readers to provide me with details of their families' uses of *Martyrs Mirror.*

12. Martha Hofer to David Weaver-Zercher, December 17, 2009.

13. Mrs. Rube Wickey to David Weaver-Zercher, December 28, 2009.

14. Ruby Burkholder to David Weaver-Zercher, December 2009.

15. Keith Gingerich, "Family Worship," *Pilgrim Witness,* August 2012, 9; and Keith Gingerich, e-mail message to author, August 22, 2012. The *Pilgrim Witness* is the periodical of the Pilgrim Mennonite Conference, a conservative Mennonite group. For similar testimonies, see also Noah Renno to David Weaver-Zercher, March 4, 2012; and Mahlon Bontrager to David Weaver-Zercher, February 14, 2010.

16. The most tradition-minded groups, such as the Swartzentruber Amish, continue to buy and use only German-language editions.

17. Some tradition-minded Anabaptists do, in fact, avoid reading the book to young

children on these grounds. One Old Order Amish grandfather told me that all his children own a copy, but they do not read the stories to his grandchildren because of their gruesome nature. John Whetstone, interview by the author, February 23, 2011. For an assimilated Mennonite case for telling *Martyrs Mirror* stories to children, see Elizabeth Miller, interview by Carrie Mast, "Is the *Martyrs Mirror* a Book for Children?" in *Bearing Witness Stories Project* (blog), January 26, 2015, www.martyrstories.org/is-the-martyrs-mirror-a-book-for-children/.

18. Burkholder to Weaver-Zercher, December 2009.

19. Johnny Zook, e-mail message to author, June 4, 2012.

20. Dale Burkholder to David Weaver-Zercher, December 28, 2009.

21. Hofer to Weaver-Zercher, December 17, 2009.

22. Anna Stoltzfus to David Weaver-Zercher, March 31, 2012.

23. Hofer to Weaver-Zercher, December 17, 2009.

24. Bontrager to Weaver-Zercher, February 14, 2010.

25. Hofer to Weaver-Zercher, December 17, 2009.

26. Stoltzfus to Weaver-Zercher, March 31, 2012.

27. For instance, *Martyrs Mirror* "stressed that serving God does not mean wealth and comfort, but it does mean being happy." Zook e-mail message, June 4, 2012.

28. LeRoy Beachy, *Unser Leit: The Story of the Amish* (Millersburg, OH: Goodly Heritage Books, 2011), 2:471. Another Amish leader, writing in 1987, observed, "We are so busy with our daily work that we seldom find either the time or the interest to read this monumental book." Elmo Stoll, "Views and Values: Children of Martyrs," *Family Life*, August–September 1987, 7.

29. Stoltzfus to Weaver-Zercher, March 31, 2012.

30. For instance, David Graber, interview by author, February 24, 2011.

31. Joseph Stoll, *The Drummer's Wife and Other Stories from "Martyrs Mirror"* (Aylmer, ON: Pathway, 1968).

32. Some Amish settlements use a Swiss dialect rather than Pennsylvania Dutch.

33. David Kline, quoted in Donald B. Kraybill, Steven M. Nolt, and David L. Weaver-Zercher, *The Amish Way: Patient Faith in a Perilous World* (San Francisco: Jossey-Bass, 2010), 67.

34. For background on the Amish style of singing, see Hedwig T. Durnbaugh, "The Amish Singing Style: Theories of Its Origin and Description of Its Singularity," *Pennsylvania Mennonite Heritage* 22, no. 2 (April 1999): 24–31.

35. The quotation is in Donald B. Kraybill, Steven M. Nolt, and David L. Weaver-Zercher, *Amish Grace: How Forgiveness Transcended Tragedy* (San Francisco: Jossey-Bass, 2007), 100. A Canadian Amish man, writing in 1987, concurred: "Hardly a sermon is preached in our churches today without some mention being made of our forefathers and what they suffered." Stoll, "Views and Values," 7.

36. Chester Miller, interview by author, February 23, 2011.

37. Ben Riehl to David Weaver-Zercher, March 6, 2011.

38. These two stories appear in *Martyrs Mirror* (1938), 112–14 (Polycarp) and 129 (Irenaeus).

39. These two stories appear in *Martyrs Mirror* (1938), 420–22 (Keyser) and 1128–30 (Haslibacher). The details of Haslibacher's death also appear in a well-known *Ausbund* hymn, which contributes to Haslibacher's renown in Amish communities.

40. This comment was made at a meeting of eight Amish church leaders from various regions of the country in Pinecraft, Florida, February 23, 2011.

41. This was, in fact, a common sentiment in at the ministers' gathering in Pinecraft, Florida, February 23, 2011.

42. Riehl to Weaver-Zercher, March 6, 2011. This notion of Satan as both a lion and an angel of light combines two biblical allusions to Satan (2 Corinthians 11:14 and 1 Peter 5:8) and echoes a comment by van Braght in his preface to *The Bloody Theater*. See *Martyrs Mirror* (1938), 8.

43. Freeman Beachy, Pinecraft ministers' gathering, February 23, 2011.

44. See Robert L. Kidder, "The Role of Outsiders," in *The Amish and the State*, ed. Donald B. Kraybill, rev. ed. (Baltimore: Johns Hopkins University Press, 2003), 213–33.

45. This notion was widely shared in the aftermath of the Nickel Mines school shooting. See Kraybill, Nolt, and Weaver-Zercher, *Amish Grace*, 49–52.

46. Kraybill and Hostetter, *Anabaptist World USA*, 58–59. In this work, published in 2001, Kraybill and Hostetter used the term *transitional* instead of *conservative* in reference to these groups. Kraybill and Hostetter's membership estimate of transitional Anabaptists in 2001 was 70,000 adult members.

47. Ibid., 59–60.

48. These course titles can be found in the 2009–10 catalog for the Ashland Mennonite Bible School and the Numidia Mennonite Bible School, two winter Bible schools coordinated by the Eastern Pennsylvania Mennonite Church (EPMC). The use of *Martyrs Mirror* at one of these schools is considered later in this chapter.

49. 2 Timothy 3:16–17 (KJV).

50. The following account is based on my visit to the Churchtown Mennonite Church near Boiling Springs, Pennsylvania, on October 3, 2010. The EPMC began in 1969, when about fifty conservative leaders withdrew from the Lancaster Mennonite Conference over issues "related to dress, television, and other cultural changes." In other words, these leaders sensed that congregations in the Lancaster Mennonite Conference were becoming too worldly and sought to resist those changes. In 2010 the EPMC consisted of about forty-five hundred members in fifty-six congregations in thirteen states. See Kraybill, *Concise Encyclopedia*, 71.

51. The afternoon session was the second of three sessions—Sunday morning, afternoon, and evening—that together constituted the congregation's annual Bible meeting. According to EPMC member Gerald Kraybill, most EPMC congregations hold annual Bible meetings, which bring in speakers from a distance and visitors from nearby EPMC congregations. Gerald Kraybill to David Weaver-Zercher, July 11, 2012.

52. For the text of this hymn, see *Church Hymnal, Mennonite: A Collection of Hymns and Sacred Songs Suitable for Use in Public Worship, Worship in the Home, and All General Occasions*, ed. J. D. Brunk and S. F. Coffman (Scottdale, PA: MPH, 1927), 358.

53. The nine points were "Trusted in God," "Encouraged Others," "Suffered Willing-

ly," "True Peace," "In Love They Forgave," "Many Sang," "Often Prayed," "Never Ashamed of Their Lord," "Yearned for Their Heavenly Home."

54. One of the preachers, Darvin Martin, was at the time a minister at Harleton Mennonite Church, an EPMC congregation. The other preacher, Clifford Martin, was a minister at Stouffers Mennonite Church, which is a member congregation of another conservative Mennonite group, the Washington-Franklin Mennonite Conference. Edsel Burdge Jr., e-mail message to author, May 20, 2011.

55. My reflections in this section were aided by listening to an audio recording of the two sermons. Unlike Old Order Anabaptist churches, some conservative Anabaptist churches use electronic sound systems for voice amplification and recording.

56. The story of Mamus appears in *Martyrs Mirror* (1938), 142–43.

57. The story of Eulalia appears in *Martyrs Mirror* (1938), 176–78.

58. The story of this unnamed teenager appears in *Martyrs Mirror* (1938), 179.

59. The Ashland Mennonite Bible School, which meets annually in Ashland, Pennsylvania, is a regional winter Bible school coordinated by the EPMC. In 2009–10, it included five three-week terms that ran from early December through mid-March. The simple, stapled catalog for the Bible school, which identified 2009–10 as the Bible school's forty-third year, listed forty-eight different course options in the areas of biblical studies, theology, church history, and practical Christian living. In each case, the course instructor was male.

60. The information in this paragraph and the one that follows is taken from photocopied study guides that students completed each day. Wendell Miller provided me with one student's completed study guides, enabling me to see not only the questions Miller provided, but also the answers given by one of his students.

61. I infer this from the fact that the study guide was largely completed in green ink, but a few of the answers had additional information in black ink. My assumption is that the student filled out the study guide in green ink, but as the instructor went over the guide in class, the student added more information in black ink. Because students took an exam on the last day of class, they would have been advised to complete their study guides as fully and correctly as possible.

62. For a brief consideration of this phenomenon, see Donald B. Kraybill, "Plotting Social Change across Four Affiliations," in *The Amish Struggle with Modernity*, ed. Donald B. Kraybill and Marc A. Olshan (Hanover, NH: University Press of New England, 1994), 72–74.

63. In the following pages, I give priority to two recent church histories written by tradition-minded historians. These works are representative of tradition-minded historiography. Other works produced by tradition-minded historians are also cited. Although some of the works cited were written decades ago, they can be used as supporting evidence, because they would not be considered out-of-date in tradition-minded circles, where works are frequently reprinted. For instance, Noah Zook's history text *Seeking a Better Country* (Gordonville, PA: Old Order Book Society), was first published in 1963. Reprinted for the eighth time in 2003, it is still listed for sale in the Pathway Publishers catalog.

64. [Ben Blank], *Resurrection to Reformation and Beyond: A Historical View of the Christian Church* (Parkesburg, PA: Blank Family, 2010), 133–209.

65. Ibid., 155–56. For a similar point, see Joseph Stoll, "Chats about the Anabaptists: Anabaptist Hunts in the Emmental," *Family Life*, October 1968, 35–37. "But killing the Anabaptists did not seem to work very well," writes Stoll. "Even the authorities had to admit it" (36). See also Zook, *Seeking a Better Country*, 74.

66. *Martyrs Mirror* (1938), 21–60.

67. [Blank], *Resurrection to Reformation and Beyond*, 39. See also Stoll, "Chats about the Anabaptists," *Family Life*, February 1968, 35–38. "When Constantine the emperor professed to have become a Christian, a very important milestone was reached. But for true Christians . . . it was a time of sadness" (36). See also Zook, *Seeking a Better Country*, 56.

68. The textbook *The Price of Keeping the Faith*, which carries no publication date or place, was used in a regional Bible school course offered by the EPMC in winter 2009–10. For a similar approach, featuring the same conservative verb in its title, see the EPMC's authorized history: Kenneth Auker, *Keeping the Trust: Issues Surrounding the Formation of the Eastern Pennsylvania Mennonite Church* (Ephrata, PA: Eastern Mennonite Publications, 2013).

69. *Price of Keeping*, 24.

70. Ibid., 25–26. See also Stoll, "Chats about the Anabaptists," February 1968. "From a simple brotherhood of godly believers, the church became a large and powerful organization that accepted many pagan (or heathen) ideas, and was no longer true to the teachings of the Bible" (36).

71. See *Price of Keeping*, 28–30. For a similar narrative that gives a central role to the faithful remnant, see Lester Bauman, *Wolves in the Flock* (Crockett, KY: Rod and Staff, 2001), 12–13, 184–85.

72. According to Blank, they acted "more like scheming bureaucrats and politicians than like shepherds of a Christian flock," and they thereby "made a mockery of the Christianity they were to represent." [Blank], *Resurrection to Reformation and Beyond*, 41.

73. *Price of Keeping*, 36–38. For a similar critique, see David G. Burkholder, *Distinctive Beliefs of the Anabaptists* (Ephrata, PA: Eastern Mennonite Publications, 2009), 14–18.

74. [Blank], *Resurrection to Reformation and Beyond*, 127. See also Stoll, "Chats about the Anabaptists," February 1968. "As a spiritual reform, Luther's work was a failure. In fact, it was often said the common people lived more wickedly than ever" (38).

75. *Price of Keeping*, 55–56. In *Keeping the Trust*, Auker titles his second and third chapters "Mennonite Apostasy" and "Drift in the Lancaster Mennonite Conference" (27–57).

76. *Price of Keeping*, 56–57; see also *Keeping the Trust*, 27–38.

77. *Price of Keeping*, 53.

78. [Blank], *Resurrection to Reformation and Beyond*, 235.

79. Ibid., 208–9. For a similar argument from an Old Order Amish historian, see David Luthy, "The Death of a Church," *Family Life*, October 1968, 37–39. At the end of

this piece, Luthy draws a direct line from Dutch Mennonitism to contemporary North American Mennonites, who, according to Luthy, are "follow[ing] the Dutch Mennonites on the road downhill" (39). Burkholder, *Distinctive Beliefs of the Anabaptists,* also compares the spiritual decline of North American Mennonitism to the decline of Dutch Mennonitism, lamenting that today many North American Mennonites "cannot be recognized as a distinctive people" (84).

80. [Blank], *Resurrection to Reformation and Beyond,* 208.

81. Although they had much to gain by renouncing their faith, they "esteemed it greater riches to suffer with the same reproach of Christ . . . than to enjoy the pleasures of sin for a season." Clifford Martin sermon, "The Account of Holy Baptism," October 3, 2010.

82. Brad Gregory, *Salvation at Stake: Christian Martyrdom in Early Modern Europe* (Cambridge, MA: Harvard University Press, 1999), 208.

83. Article 18 of the "Dordrecht Confession of Faith," in *In Meiner Jugend: A Devotional Reader in German and English,* ed. Joseph Stoll (Aylmer, ON: Pathway, 2000), 59.

84. Mary M. Miller, comp., *Our Heritage, Hope, and Faith,* rev. ed. (Topeka, IN: Mary M. Miller, 2008), 115; original in *Ausbund, Das ist: Etlich schone christlicher Lieder* (Lancaster, PA: Lancaster Press, 1984), 770.

85. The Old Order Amish are well known for their refusal to claim assurance of their own salvation since, in their view, only God knows for sure who will be saved. See Kraybill, Nolt, and Weaver-Zercher, *Amish Way,* 38–39.

86. Tom Shachtman, *Rumspringa: To Be or Not to Be Amish* (New York: North Point Press, 2006), 142; and Richard A. Stevick, *Growing Up Amish: The Teenage Years* (Baltimore: Johns Hopkins University Press, 2007), 238.

87. *Price of Keeping,* 62. "Mennonite General Conference was proposed as a way to unify and strengthen the church. Instead it became a tool of the liberals to promote their agenda" (57). Also, "blurred fellowship lines resulted from the homogenizing of the church in cooperative relief efforts sponsored by Mennonite Central Committee" (57).

88. Ibid., 64.

89. See, for instance, Donald B. Kraybill, *The Riddle of Amish Culture,* rev. ed. (Baltimore: Johns Hopkins University Press, 2001), 202–6.

90. David Belton, "New York Amish in Court over Smoke Alarms," *BBC News Magazine,* May 19, 2012, www.bbc.co.uk/news/magazine-18108197.

91. Quoted in Paton Yoder, "The Amish View of the State," in Kraybill, *Amish and the State,* 30.

92. Stoll, "Views and Values," 8.

Chapter 10. Assimilated Mennonites and the Dilemma of *Martyrs Mirror*

1. These national denominations had combined memberships of approximately 125,000 members in 2015. The Mennonite Church USA number (95,000) is from Hannah Heinzekehr, e-mail message to author, February 6, 2015; the Mennonite Church Canada number (31,000) is from www.mennonitechurch.ca/about/membership.htm, accessed February 6, 2015.

2. The merger decision took several years to finalize and implement. By 2002 the two new denominations, Mennonite Church USA and Mennonite Church Canada, were distinct operational entities.

3. For information on MennoMedia, see its website, www.mennomedia.org/, accessed February 6, 2015.

4. For instance, *Hymnal: A Worship Book* (Elgin, IL: Brethren Press; Newton, KS: Faith and Life Press; Scottdale, PA: MPH, 1992).

5. See Michael A. King, ed., *Stumbling toward a Genuine Conversation on Homosexuality* (Telford, PA: Cascadia, 2007).

6. Donald B. Kraybill, *Concise Encyclopedia of Amish, Brethren, Hutterites, and Mennonites* (Baltimore: Johns Hopkins University Press, 2010), 251–52, 256–58. For instance, the only reference to Anabaptism I could find on the website of the Fellowship of Grace Brethren Churches occurs in the early stages of the denomination's history (see http://fgbc.org/about/our-story, accessed November 18, 2014). Correspondingly, the group's statement of faith is shaped more by American fundamentalism than it is by Anabaptism.

7. I include in my consideration of Mennonite scholars persons who were born into Anabaptist church–attending families or were themselves members of Anabaptist churches but who no longer identify themselves as religiously Mennonite.

8. This chapter focuses on assimilated Mennonites associated with the Mennonite Church and the General Conference Mennonite Church (before their merger) and with the Mennonite Church USA and the Mennonite Church Canada (after the subsequent division into national bodies). There are other assimilated Mennonite denominations in North America, and still other assimilated Anabaptist denominations that are not Mennonite, but the ones featured here have demonstrated the most sustained interest in *Martyrs Mirror*.

9. Robert Wuthnow, *The Restructuring of American Religion: Society and Faith since World War II* (Princeton, NJ: Princeton University Press, 1988), 83–96.

10. The evidence for soft denominational loyalty is abundant. For instance, while 34 percent of Mennonite Church USA members in a 2006 survey indicated they were strongly committed to the denomination, almost as many agreed that "church denominations do not matter to me; one is as good as another." Correspondingly, nearly half of the church members surveyed in 2006 agreed that "too much emphasis on Mennonite beliefs gets in the way of the true message of the gospel." Conrad L. Kanagy, *Road Signs for the Journey: A Profile of Mennonite Church USA* (Scottdale, PA: Herald Press, 2007), 148–49.

11. Ibid., 27.

12. For evidence, see John D. Roth, ed., *Engaging Anabaptism: Conversations with a Radical Tradition* (Scottdale, PA: Herald Press, 2001); and Stuart Murray, *The Naked Anabaptist: The Bare Essentials of a Radical Faith* (Scottdale, PA: Herald Press, 2010), 21–31.

13. Kanagy, *Road Signs for the Journey*, 28–29.

14. John S. Oyer and Robert S. Kreider, *Mirror of the Martyrs* (Intercourse, PA: Good Books, 1990), 15.

15. The Anabaptist Network website can be found at www.anabaptistnetwork.com/, accessed January 21, 2015.

16. Alan Kreider, "The Relevance of *Martyrs Mirror* to Our Time," *Mennonite Life* 45, no. 3 (September 1990): 9.

17. Ibid., 12, 15.

18. Ibid., 11. Kreider cites here the confession of Adrian Corneliss, which includes his account of singing Isaiah 59:14; see *Martyrs Mirror* (1938), 531.

19. Ibid., 16.

20. John D. Roth, "The Significance of the Martyr Story for Contemporary Anabaptists," *Brethren Life and Thought* 37 (1992): 97–106. Roth's piece began as a lecture at Elizabethtown (PA) College, which at the time (March 1992) was hosting the *Mirror of the Martyrs* exhibit.

21. Ibid., 104, 105, 106.

22. Mark 9:19, NRSV.

23. Roth, "Significance of the Martyr Story," 105–6.

24. Melvin Goering, "Dying to Be Pure: The Martyr Story," *Mennonite Life* 47, no. 4 (December 1992): 9–15. The occasion for Goering's reflection was the opening of a play, written by Bethel College historian James Juhnke, about Dirk Willems, the Anabaptist martyr who rescued his pursuer from drowning only to be arrested and burned at the stake. Juhnke's play, titled *Dirk's Exodus,* is considered at length in chapter 11.

25. Ibid., 12.

26. Ibid., 12–14.

27. Roth, "Significance of the Martyr Story," 105.

28. Goering, "Dying to Be Pure," 13.

29. John K. Sheriff, "*Dirk's Exodus:* Morality Play and Modern Tragedy," *Mennonite Life* 47, no. 4 (December 1992): 20.

30. Sheriff's article was a review of Juhnke's play (see note 24), which Sheriff feared might buttress the superiority myth. At the same time, Sheriff held out hope that Juhnke's play could be viewed as tragedy that would help to refute the myth. See ibid.

31. Ibid.

32. For a brief consideration of the literary renaissance by one of its participants, see Julia Spicher Kasdorf, "Sunday Morning Confession," *MQR* 87 (2013): 7–10. See also John D. Roth and Ervin Beck, eds., *Migrant Muses: Mennonite/s Writing in the U.S.* (Goshen, IN: Mennonite Historical Society, 1998).

33. Julia Kasdorf, "Catholics," in Julia Kasdorf, *Sleeping Preacher* (Pittsburgh: University of Pittsburgh Press, 1992), 32–33.

34. Jan Gerrits's letter can be found in *Martyrs Mirror* (1938), 681–85.

35. Ibid., 683.

36. Esther Stenson, "No Apologies," in *Tongue Screws and Testimonies: Poems, Stories, and Essays Inspired by the "Martyrs Mirror,"* ed. Kirsten Eve Beachy (Scottdale, PA: Herald Press, 2010), 244–45.

37. "We ask for forgiveness—from God and from our Mennonite sisters and brothers—for the harm that our forebears in the sixteenth century committed to Anabaptists, for forgetting or ignoring this persecution in the intervening centuries, and for all in-

appropriate, misleading and hurtful portraits of Anabaptists and Mennonites made by Lutheran authors, in both popular and scholarly forms, to the present day." "Action on the Legacy of Lutheran Persecution of 'Anabaptists,'" approved by the Lutheran World Federation Eleventh Assembly, July 22, 2010; http://ecumenism.net/archive/docu/2010 _lwf_action_legacy_lutheran_persecution_anabaptists.pdf, accessed January 19, 2015.

38. Bender's father was Ross T. Bender, who taught in Mennonite seminaries over a thirty-four-year span. From 1984 to 1990, the senior Bender served as president of the Mennonite World Conference.

39. Ross L. Bender's piece, titled "Writing for Mennos or Not," was originally published in 1997. It was republished in Beachy, *Tongue Screws and Testimonies*, 260–61.

40. Ibid., 261.

41. Stephanie Krehbiel, "Staying Alive: How Martyrdom Made Me a Warrior," in Beachy, *Tongue Screws and Testimonies*, 133–44. Krehbiel's essay first appeared in *Mennonite Life* 61, no. 4 (December 2006); online at http://archive.bethelks.edu/ml/issue /vol-61-no-4/.

42. Ibid., 134–35.

43. Ibid., 136. The story of Maeyken Wens can be found in *Martyrs Mirror* (1938), 979–80. See figure 5.3 for the image of Wens's sons searching for her tongue screw.

44. Julia Spicher Kasdorf, *The Body and the Book: Writing from a Mennonite Life* (Baltimore: Johns Hopkins University Press, 2001), 169.

45. Jeff Gundy, "Cathedrals, Churches, Caves: Notes on Architecture, History, and Worship," in Jeff Gundy, *Scattering Point: The World in a Mennonite Eye* (Albany: State University of New York Press, 2003), 17.

46. Krehbiel, "Staying Alive," 140. "As a young woman in this misogynist, pornography-drenched culture, . . . I'm at no loss for narratives that depict splayed, exploited bodies that look like mine" (140–41). The most obvious imagistic parallels between the violence depicted in *Martyrs Mirror* and in contemporary sadomasochistic pornography are the torture images of Ursel van Essen and Geleyn Corneliss; see *Martyrs Mirror* (1938), 843, 930. For a similar argument using nineteenth-century sources, see Karen Halttunen, "Humanitarianism and the Pornography of Pain in Anglo-American Culture," *American Historical Review* 100 (1995): 303–34.

47. Miriam Toews, *A Complicated Kindness: A Novel* (New York: Counterpoint, 2004), 5.

48. Krehbiel, "Staying Alive," 142. For a similar point, see Jeff Gundy, *Songs from an Empty Cage: Poetry, Mystery, Anabaptism, and Peace* (Telford, PA: Cascadia, 2013), 225.

49. Krehbiel, "Staying Alive," 144.

50. Ibid., 143.

51. The quotation in this paragraph is from Gerald J. Mast, "How the *Martyrs Mirror* Helped Save Me: A Response to Krehbiel and Goering," *Mennonite Life* 62, no. 1 (Spring 2007), which can be found online at http://archive.bethelks.edu/ml/issue/vol -62-no-1/. Mast's most important work of history is *Separation and the Sword in Anabaptist Persuasion: Radical Confessional Rhetoric from Schleitheim to Dordrecht* (Telford, PA: Cascadia, 2006).

52. Krehbiel, "Staying Alive," 142, 144.

53. Di Brandt, "scapegoat," in Beachy, *Tongue Screws and Testimonies,* 146.

54. Becca J. R. Lachman, "When Red Rushes Up," in Beachy, *Tongue Screws and Testimonies,* 163–64.

55. The conference, coordinated by Diane Zimmerman Umble, took place on June 8–11, 1995, at Millersville (PA) University. Using *Martyrs Mirror* as a source or conversation partner, at least eight conference papers focused on the experiences of sixteenth-century Anabaptist women, as did some poetry and creative nonfiction readings.

56. These quotations are from the published version of the conference presentation. Linda A. Huebert Hecht, "Speaking Up and Taking Risks: Anabaptist Family and Household Roles in Sixteenth-Century Tirol," in *Strangers at Home: Amish and Mennonite Women in History,* ed. Kimberly D. Schmidt, Diane Zimmerman Umble, and Steven D. Reschly (Baltimore: Johns Hopkins University Press, 2002), 238, 251–52.

57. C. Arnold Snyder, introduction to *Profiles of Anabaptist Women: Sixteenth-Century Reforming Pioneers,* ed. C. Arnold Snyder and Linda A. Huebert Hecht (Waterloo, ON: Wilfred Laurier University Press, 1996), 10.

58. Ibid., 11–12.

59. Jean Kilheffer Hess, "Women's Words in the *Martyrs Mirror,*" presented at the "*Martyrs Mirror:* Reflections across Time" conference at the Young Center for Anabaptist and Pietist Studies, Elizabethtown College, Elizabethtown, PA, June 9, 2010.

60. The story of Janneken can be found in *Martyrs Mirror* (1938), 583–84; the story of Claesken can be found in *Martyrs Mirror* (1938), 611–12; the story of Kalleken can be found in *Martyrs Mirror* (1938), 652–54.

61. Quotations in the paragraph are from the sermon transcript in my possession. The sermon was preached on January 16, 2011.

62. This was James Lowry's response to my summary of Kilheffer Hess's sermon, a summary I included in a lecture at Elizabethtown College, March 22, 2011.

63. Some examples in this section and the next derive from advertisements I placed in assimilated Mennonite periodicals, asking readers to provide me with details of their use of *Martyrs Mirror.*

64. For instance, "I have many memories of reading *Martyrs Mirror* as a boy. . . . It is a book I need to review again." Sam Augsburger, e-mail message to author, October 27, 2011.

65. "Other kids got fairy tales at night; we got *Martyrs Mirror.*" Susan Mark Landis, e-mail message to author, October 20, 2011. Similarly, in a report about an assimilated congregation that explored *Martyrs Mirror* during Sunday school, the correspondent noted, "We discussed how *Martyrs Mirror* was read to Mennonite children as bedtime stories." See Stephanie Nance, "Dallas: Peace Mennonite," *Mennonite Weekly Review,* January 10, 2011, 8.

66. LeRoy Beachy, *Unser Leit: The Story of the Amish* (Millersburg, OH: Goodly Heritage Books, 2011), 2:471.

67. Steven Lantz, e-mail message to author, November 25, 2011. This is one of many messages I have received from teachers or students from assimilated Mennonite

churches. The story of Dirk Willems appears in *Martyrs Mirror* (1938), 741–42; the story of Anneken Heyndricks appears in *Martyrs Mirror* (1938), 872–74.

68. Nance, "Dallas," 8. In anticipation of her execution, Anna of Rotterdam wrote a testament to her infant son, admonishing him to "strive for righteousness unto death." For Anna's letter, see *Martyrs Mirror* (1938), 453–54.

69. Barry Kreider, e-mail message to author, September 29, 2011.

70. Amy Showalter, "A Story Seeking to Understand My Denominational Heritage," an excerpt from Showalter's senior thesis, "Stories Almost My Own: A Personal Narrative Theology;" Goshen College, April 13, 2009. Copy of excerpt in author's possession.

71. For Cordero's rap, see "Onward Martyrdom Rap: Peacemaking," www.youtube.com/watch?v=XImiokalAVE, accessed February 6, 2015.

72. For information about the movie, which was produced by D. Michael Hostetler and directed by Raul Carrera, see *The Radicals Movie*, www.theradicalsmovie.com/, accessed February 6, 2015. For the account of Michael Sattler's martyrdom, see *Martyrs Mirror* (1938), 416–18.

73. Jeanne Grieser and Carol Duerksen, *Adventures with the Anabaptists* (Newton, KS: Faith and Life Resources, [2001]). Faith and Life Resources, a General Conference Mennonite agency, was absorbed by MennoMedia following the merger of the General Conference Mennonite Church and the Mennonite Church.

74. Jeanne Grieser and Carol Duerksen, "Blessed Are the Picked On," in ibid., 41–49. The three martyr stories can be found in *Martyrs Mirror* (1938), 415–16, 430–32, 481–83.

75. The *Journeys with God* curriculum is located at Mennonite Education Agency, www.mennoniteeducation.org, accessed February 6, 2015. The two lessons are titled "The Executioners" and "To Die For."

76. "Lesson 8: To Die For," in *Journeys with God*, 139.

77. For instance, the second *Journeys with God* lesson, "To Die For," includes these discussion questions: "What difficult choices are Christians asked to make today?"; "How do they compare to the choices that the Anabaptists had to make?"; and "What personality qualities do you think made it possible for the martyrs to make the decisions they did?" (140).

78. To help teens grasp the topic's contemporary relevance, "Blessed Are the Picked On" advises teachers to have their students talk about times when they were teased, since such an experience, according to the lesson, is "a type of torture." See Grieser and Duerksen, "Blessed Are the Picked On," 41–42.

79. "Lesson 8: To Die For," 140.

80. "Lesson 7: The Executioners," in *Journeys with God*, 128.

81. Ibid.

82. Grieser and Duerksen, "Blessed Are the Picked On," 45. The popularity of the adjective *upside-down* owes in part to Donald B. Kraybill's book *The Upside-Down Kingdom* (Scottdale, PA: Herald Press, 1978). Herald Press issued revised editions of Kraybill's book in 1990, 2003, and 2011.

83. "Lesson 8: To Die For," 151.

84. Grieser and Duerksen, "Blessed Are the Picked On," 43. In keeping with the more

politically engaged approach of assimilated Anabaptists, the *Adventures* lesson offers one example: the story of Carla, who kept her Anabaptist faith to herself during high school, but later "got real involved in protesting against the death penalty" (44).

85. Deborah-Ruth Ferber, e-mail message to author, November 21, 2011.

86. The Masts' booklet is downloadable via a link within "How Jacques d'Auchy Became a Household Name," at www.martyrstories.org/jacques-dauchy-drama/, accessed February 6, 2015.

87. For an additional example of using *Martyrs Mirror* as a resource for teaching peace, see Carrie Mast, "How Jacques d'Auchy Became a Household Name," at www .martyrstories.org/jacques-dauchy-drama/, accessed February 6, 2015.

88. Nance, "Dallas," 8. The story of Simon the Shopkeeper appears in *Martyrs Mirror* (1938), 540.

89. The congregation's website can be found at Peace Mennonite Church, www .peacemennonitedallas.org/, accessed January 22, 2014.

90. Nance, "Dallas," 8.

91. Goering, "Dying to Be Pure," 12.

92. Angela Moore, e-mail message to author, October 20, 2011.

93. Jared L. Peifer, e-mail message to author, March 24, 2011.

94. Ibid.

95. Troy Schlabach to David Weaver-Zercher, January 21, 2010.

96. Miriam [Hess] Kreider to David Weaver-Zercher, October 29, 2011. The story of Hans Jacob Hess and his unnamed wife appears in *Martyrs Mirror* (1938), 1115.

97. Landis, e-mail message to author, October 20, 2011.

98. Showalter, "Story Seeking to Understand."

99. Ibid.

100. Ibid.

Chapter 11. The Most Usable Martyr

1. The quotation is from a petition introduced in 1940 at the Lancaster Mennonite Conference fall meeting, which identified five reasons for starting a Mennonite high school; quoted in Donald B. Kraybill, *Passing on the Faith: The Story of a Mennonite School* (Intercourse, PA: Good Books, 1991), 14.

2. The school's belief statement says, "The theological foundation of the school is based on the authority of the Bible as understood in the *Confession of Faith in a Mennonite Perspective.*" See Lancaster Mennonite School, http://lancastermennonite.org /about/mission.php, accessed January 15, 2014. See also *Confession of Faith in a Mennonite Perspective* (Scottdale, PA: Herald Press, 1995).

3. J. Richard Thomas, interview by author, August 12, 2013.

4. In Dutch editions, the word used for Dirk's pursuer is *Diefleyder*, which Joseph F. Sohm translated in 1886 as "thief-catcher." There is no indication in the text that Dirk was being pursued because he had stolen something, though it is likely that the person employed to catch thieves was also charged to arrest Anabaptists.

5. *Martyrs Mirror* (1938), 741–42.

6. For instance, the 1988 high school yearbook, *Laurel Wreath,* includes a picture of Dirk above an article titled "Classes Dig Below the Surface to the Roots" (39).

7. John S. Oyer and Robert S. Kreider, *Mirror of the Martyrs* (Intercourse, PA: Good Books, 1990), 36.

8. [Pieter Jans Twisck et al.], *Historie der Warachtighe Getuygen Jesu Christi . . .* (Hoorn, Netherlands: Zacharias Cornelis, 1617), 410–11. The account also appeared in [Pieter Jans Twisck et al.], *Historie van de Vrome Getuygen Jesu Christi . . .* (Hoorn, Netherlands: Isaac Willems for Zacharias Cornelis, 1626), 521–22, and in de Ries (1631), 481–82, before it appeared in van Braght (1660), 2:469–70.

9. The transcription, which follows the narrative, concludes with the following statement: "Extracted from the records of the town of Asperen, and after collation this copy was found to agree [with the original]." Dated October 15, 1606, this statement is attributed to T'Sheerenbergh, the Asperen town clerk. See [Twisck et al.], *Historie der Warachtighe Getuygen Jesu Christi . . . ,* 411; van Braght (1660), 2:470; and *Martyrs Mirror* (1938), 742.

10. The additional account first appeared in van Braght (1660), 2:470.

11. Van Braght (1660), 2:470; *Martyrs Mirror* (1938), 742.

12. Matthew 27:46; Luke 23:46.

13. Van Braght (1660), 2:470; *Martyrs Mirror* (1938), 741. The Dutch word translated as "papists" in this passage is *Paus-gesinden,* literally, "pope's servants."

14. "Were they angry at how [Dirk] had just changed the rules? Did they realize that they had been checkmated? Were they aware that Dirk had escaped his own double bind and placed it on them?" W. Benjamin Myers, "The Stage and the Stake: 16th-Century Anabaptist Martyrdom as Resistance to Violent Spectacle," *Liminalities* 5, no. 3 (September 2009): 10.

15. Luyken produced pen sketches of his images before he etched them onto copper plates. Luyken's pen sketch of the Dirk Willems scene, which is housed in a museum in Amsterdam, is very similar to the etching, foregrounding Dirk and his pursuer with the three observers in the background. In the pen sketch, a fourth man stands farther in the background. See David Luthy, *Dirk Willems: His Noble Deed Lives On* (Aylmer, ON: Pathway, 2011), 8.

16. *Martyrs Mirror* (1886), 710. The artist's name is not incorporated into this new engraving, though many of the knockoff images in the 1886 edition are attributed to Joe K. French.

17. David Luthy to Joseph Stoll, April 16, 1990, Heritage Historical Library, Aylmer, ON. In a letter to Julia Kasdorf, who did groundbreaking research on the digging-man image, Luthy took the "credit or discredit" for the change, noting that he was "a big Dirk Willems fan." Luthy continued, "I have in a way tampered with history, but we know who Dirk was and the other man was fictional yet symbolic." David Luthy to Julia Kasdorf, December 7, 1993, quoted in Julia Kasdorf, *The Body and the Book: Writing from a Mennonite Life* (Baltimore: Johns Hopkins University Press, 2001), 112.

18. Thielem J. v. Braght, *Der blutige Schauplatz, oder Märtyrer-Spiegel der Taufgesinnten oder Wehrlosen Christen . . .* (Aylmer, ON: Pathway, 1996).

19. The phrase "noble deed" appears in William Boyd Carpenter's poem "Dirk Willemzoon," published in the December 1885 issue of the *English Illustrated Magazine*. Amish historian David Luthy has more recently used this phrase in various places, including his book *Dirk Willems*.

20. Tollens's poem, "Dirk Willemsz, van Asperen," which appeared in the *Nederlandsche Muzen-Almanak* (Rotterdam: J. Immerzeel Jr., 1819), adds the following details to the original: (1) Dirk is in prison before he makes his escape; (2) Dirk escapes from prison by braiding together bedsheets and lowering himself out of a window; (3) Dirk's pursuer is a prison watchman who carries heavy weapons in pursuit of Dirk; and (4) the captured Dirk is beheaded, not burned. Tollens's prison-window escape detail, which appeared in visual form in a later volume of Tollens's poetry, may be responsible for the detail's presence in subsequent retellings. For two recent examples, see Rebecca Seiling, *Plant a Seed of Peace* (Scottdale, PA: Herald Press, 2007), 40–41; and Malcolm Gladwell, *David and Goliath: Underdogs, Misfits, and the Art of Battling Giants* (New York: Little, Brown, 2013), 254–55. For Pieter Velthove's English translation of Tollens's poem, see Luthy, *Dirk Willems*, 19–21.

21. W. S., "Dirk Willemzoon: An Incident of Dutch History, A.D. 1569," *Sunday at Home* (London: Religious Tract Society, 1879), 256; and W. B. Ripon [Carpenter was the bishop of Ripon], "Dirk Willemzoon," *English Illustrated Magazine*, December 1885, 227–29. The second of these two poems began with a headnote excerpted from John Lothrop Motley's *The Rise of the Dutch Republic* (New York: Harper, 1855), which identified Dirk as an Anabaptist who "instinctively obey[ed] the dictates of a generous nature" (2:280–81). For ready access to these two poems, see Luthy, *Dirk Willems*, 22–25.

22. Ripon, "Dirk Willemzoon," 228.

23. The basis for many of the prose retellings was probably Motley, *Rise of the Dutch Republic*, 2:280–81. Subsequent retellings include Mary Barrett, *The Story of William the Silent and the Netherland War, 1555–1584* (Boston: American Tract Society, 1869), 256–57; and R. T. S., "Noble Revenge," *Sunday School Teacher* 3 (1870): 413–14.

24. The story of Dirk Willems was not entirely absent from Anabaptist instructional literature in the nineteenth century; it appeared in 1899 in C. H. Wedel, *Bilder aus der Kirchengeschichte für Mennonitische Gemeindeschulen* [Sketches of Christian history for Mennonite community schools] (Newton, KS: Schulverlag von Bethel College, 1899), 56. Wedel was the first president of Bethel College, a General Conference Mennonite college located in North Newton, Kansas.

25. W. S., "Dirk Willemzoon: An Incident," 256.

26. John C. Wenger, *Glimpses of Mennonite History* (Scottdale, PA: MPH, 1940), 68–69.

27. John Horsch, *Mennonites in Europe* (Scottdale, PA: MPH, 1942), 332–33.

28. *Words of Cheer*, January 3, 1943, 1; and *Youth's Christian Companion*, May 19, 1949, 1. The latter image was a reproduction of the Luyken image painted by C. Norman Kraus.

29. *Mennonite Community*, June 1950, 34.

30. This quotation is from the MPH advertising flyer.

31. The first of these plates measured 4⅝×5¾ inches. The second plate measured 3¾×4⅝ inches.

32. R. T. S., "Noble Revenge," 3:414. This story was reprinted as "Saving an Enemy" in *The New Cyclopædia of Illustrative Anecdote, Religious and Moral, Original and Selected* (London: Elliot Stock, 1872), 887; and "Noble Revenge," in *The Sabbath School Magazine, Designed for the Use of Teachers, Adult Scholars, and Parents*, ed. William Keddie (Glasgow: John M'Callum, 1875), 192.

33. Horsch, *Mennonites in Europe*, 332–33.

34. *Mennonite Community*, June 1950, 34.

35. Two Hutterite brothers, Joseph and Michael Hofer, died in Fort Leavenworth after suffering various forms of mistreatment. See Duane Stoltzfus, "Armed with Prayer in an Alcatraz Dungeon: The Wartime Experiences of Four Hutterite C.O.'s in Their Own Words," *MQR* 85 (2011): 259–92.

36. *Gospel Herald*, January 23, 1919, 761.

37. For accounts of physical and psychological abuse, see J. S. Hartzler, *Mennonites in the World War; or, Nonresistance under Test* (Scottdale, PA: MPH, 1922).

38. Section 5(g) of the Selective Training and Service Act of 1940, quoted in Albert N. Keim, *The CPS Story: An Illustrated History of Civilian Public Service* (Intercourse, PA: Good Books, 1990), 24.

39. Perry Bush, *Two Kingdoms, Two Loyalties: Mennonite Pacifism in Modern America* (Baltimore: Johns Hopkins University Press, 1998); and A. J. Klassen, ed., *Alternative Service for Peace in Canada during World War II, 1941–1946* (Abbotsford, BC: Mennonite Central Committee, 1998).

40. One Mennonite smokejumper expressed hope that his work would help people realize "that I was serious about my stand against war and was not just a 'yellow belly.'" James R. Brunk, quoted in Robert C. Cottrell, *Smokejumpers of the Civilian Public Service in World War II: Conscientious Objectors as Firefighters for the National Forest Service* (Jefferson, NC: McFarland, 2006), 191.

41. For a critique of Niebuhr's use of this word, see John H. Yoder, "Reinhold Niebuhr and Christian Pacifism," *MQR* 29 (April 1955): 101–17.

42. For an account of the conference, see Leo Driedger and Donald B. Kraybill, *Mennonite Peacemaking: From Quietism to Activism* (Scottdale, PA: Herald Press, 1994), 84–87.

43. Story collections include John C. Wenger, *Even unto Death: The Heroic Witness of the Sixteenth-Century Anabaptists* (Richmond, VA: John Knox Press, 1963), 101; and Ben Hoeppner, ed., *Know These People* (Steinbach, MB: Evangelical Mennonite Board of Education, 1974).

44. Edna K. Wenger, "The Man Who Saved His Enemy," in Edna Wenger, *Happy Life Stores: Third Grade Reading Lessons* (Lancaster, PA: Textbook Committee of the Lancaster Mennonite Conference, 1954), 78–83.

45. La Vernae J. Dick, "Anabaptist Dirk and the Thiefcatcher," *Christian Living*, February 1971, 20–24.

46. Noah Zook, *Seeking a Better Country* (Gordonville, PA: Old Order Book Society, 1963). The Dirk image appears in an insert between pages 30 and 31.

47. The Luyken image in Zook's text includes credits to both *Martyrs Mirror* (1938) and Horsch's *Mennonites in Europe*.

48. Elmo Stoll, "Dirk Willems and the Thief-Catcher," in *The Drummer's Wife and Other Stories from "Martyrs' Mirror,"* ed. Joseph Stoll (Aylmer, ON: Pathway, 1968), 247–51.

49. [Elmo Stoll], "Dirk Willems and the Thief Catcher," in *Our Heritage* (Aylmer, ON: Pathway, 1968), 20–24.

50. The sales numbers are from Luthy, *Dirk Willems,* 54–55. My claim that readership outpaces sales numbers is based on the fact that most schools use copies more than one year.

51. John 15:13, KJV.

52. [Stoll], "Dirk Willems and the Thief Catcher," in *Our Heritage,* 24–25.

53. Ibid., 25–26.

54. For a detailed accounting of this surge, see Luthy, *Dirk Willems,* 48–52.

55. Ibid., 11.

56. John Horsch, *Mennonites in Europe,* rev. ed. (1950; repr., Crockett, KY: Rod and Staff, 1995).

57. Above the flailing teen were the words, "For the church today and the generations of tomorrow." David Luthy to Amos Hoover, August 3, 2001; copy in author's possession.

58. C. D. Wenger, *Why I Am a Conscientious Objector* (Harrisonburg, VA: Christian Light, [1977]).

59. For instance, in Oyer and Kreider's *Mirror of the Martyrs,* the Dirk Willems image is titled "Compassion for the Enemy" (36).

60. The sermon, given by Joel Miller of the Cincinnati (OH) Mennonite Fellowship in 2006, is quoted in Luthy, *Dirk Willems,* 64. In a similar fashion, the carving of Dirk at Lancaster Mennonite High School is simply captioned, "Tradition of Love."

61. Stoll, "Dirk Willems and the Thief-Catcher," in *Drummer's Wife,* 251.

62. Jeff Gundy's "How to Write the New Mennonite Poem" first appeared in *Mennonot* 1 (Fall 1993): 10. It has been republished numerous times, including in *A cappella: Mennonite Voices in Poetry,* ed. Ann Hostetler (Iowa City: University of Iowa Press, 2003), 86–87.

63. Other evidence that Dirk had become a cliché can be found in the emergence of parodies of Luyken's image. On the front cover of a tongue-in-cheek primer for new Mennonites, a modified image shows Dirk with a baseball glove on his left hand, reaching out to catch a ball. See Craig Haas and Steve Nolt, *The Mennonite Starter Kit: A Handy Guide for the New Mennonite* (Intercourse, PA: Good Books, 1993).

64. James Juhnke, *Dirk's Exodus,* in *Four Class Acts: Kansas Theatre,* ed. Repha J. Buckman and Robert N. Lawson (Topeka, KS: Woodley Memorial Press, 1992), 85–184. The play debuted at Bethel College in September 1990.

65. Quotations from Juhnke, *Dirk's Exodus,* 98, 157.

66. Debra Gingerich, "Migraines and Other Mennonite Pains," in Debra Gingerich, *Where We Start* (Telford, PA: DreamSeeker Books, 2007), 70. For a similar complaint about Dirk's example setting the bar too high, see Ann Hostetler, "Pearl Diver—Archetypes for Mennonite Artists," *Mennonite Literature* (blog) January 19, 2011,

http://mennoniteliterature.blogspot.com/2011/01/pearl-diver-archetypes-for-menno
nite.html.

67. Jeff Gundy, "Ancient Themes #14: The Martyrs & the Child," first published in *Mennonot* 12 (Summer 1999): 14. The poem can also be found in Gundy's essay "Churches, Cathedrals, and Caves: Notes on Architecture, History, and Worship," in Gundy, *Scattering Point: The World in a Mennonite Eye* (Albany: State University of New York Press, 2003), 5–35. In a later reflection on *Martyrs Mirror*, Gundy highlighted the theme "of running away, of living to carry on the work," a theme that is also present in *Martyrs Mirror*. Jeff Gundy, *Songs from an Empty Cage: Poetry, Mystery, Anabaptism, and Peace* (Telford, PA: Cascadia, 2013), 237.

68. James W. Lowry, *The "Martyrs' Mirror" Made Plain: How to Study and Profit from the "Martyrs' Mirror,"* rev. ed. (Aylmer, ON: Pathway, 2011), vii.

69. Lowry, "A Meditation on Dirk Willems: Upon a Visit to a Dutch Village," in Lowry, *"Martyrs' Mirror" Made Plain,* 118; van Braght (1938), 741.

70. Lowry, "Meditation on Dirk Willems," 119.

71. Ibid., 118.

72. *Martyrs Mirror* (1938), 422.

73. Lowry, "Meditation on Dirk Willems," 120.

74. Joseph Liechty, "A Meditation on Dirk Willems," *Mennonite Life* 45, no. 3 (September 1990), 18–23, online at http://archive.bethelks.edu/store/ml/files/1990sep.pdf.

75. Ibid., 21.

76. Ibid., 23.

77. Like Liechty, Lowry suggested that the Dirk account, read in full, can help readers humanize their enemies by reminding them that "the wolf is also a lost sheep, a helpless lamb floundering in the water." Lowry, "Meditation on Dirk Willems," 120. Nonetheless, the distance between the two men is significant. Whereas Liechty saw Dirk's actions as a corrective to the dualistic rhetoric that characterized much of early Anabaptism, Lowry believed that the dualistic rhetoric was an appropriate way to describe sixteenth-century realities.

78. This meeting took place on July 22, 2010. See Byron Rempel-Burkholder, "Lutherans and Anabaptists Reconcile in Service of Repentance and Forgiveness," July 27, 2010, online at Mennonite World Conference, www.mwc-cmm.org/joomla/index.php/news-releases/76-lutherans-and-anabaptists-reconcile-in-service-of-repentance-and-forgiveness.

79. Information in this paragraph and the next come from Nancy R. Heisey, "Remembering Dirk Willems: Memory and History in the Future of Ecumenical Relationships," *Journal of Ecumenical Studies* 47 (2012): 355–75. The quotation in this paragraph is from 355.

80. The painter was Bulgarian Jivko Donkov, who painted the icons at the request of Keith and Ann Graber Miller. For a photograph of Donkov's icon of Dirk, see the Found website at http://www.foundgoshen.com/anabaptist-icons/, accessed February 7, 2015.

81. James C. Juhnke, "Rightly Remembering a Martyr Heritage," *Mennonite Life* 58, no. 3 (September 2003), online at http://archive.bethelks.edu/ml/issue/vol-58-no-3/.

82. Heisey, "Remembering Dirk Willems," 374.

83. Hildi Froese Tiessen, back cover of Kirsten Eve Beachy, *Tongue Screws and Testimonies: Poems, Stories, and Essays Inspired by the "Martyrs Mirror"* (Scottdale, PA: Herald Press, 2010).

84. Ian Huebert, "Views from a Pond: The Dirk Willems Variations," *Pacific Journal* 4 (2009): 3, 5, 7; also, Huebert, "Artist's Statement," in Beachy, *Tongue Screws and Testimonies*, 289. By *iconoclasm* Huebert meant a wariness regarding religious imagery, not the forceful destruction of images that was common among other Protestant reform movements.

85. Kevin Enns-Rempel, "What *Might* Dirk Have Done?" *Pacific Journal* 4 (2009): 7, 9–10.

86. John Blosser, "Mirror for Reluctant Martyrs," *Pacific Journal* 4 (2009): 11.

87. "Dirk Willems' Sacrifice," *Family Life*, June 2008, 21–22. The poet wrote that Dirk "believed what God let happen was intended for his good." The poet also added a crowd of supporters to Dirk's execution scene, shouting, "No more persecution in our cherished Holland land!"

88. Lowry, "Meditation on Dirk Willems," 120.

Chapter 12. Going Global

1. Wilbert R. Shenk estimates Anabaptist-Mennonite membership in Europe and Russia in 1911 at around 150,000 and the Mennonite membership in the United States and Canada at about 75,000. By 1978 the Anabaptist membership in North America was more than 300,000, and the membership in Europe had dwindled to 96,000. Wilbert R. Shenk, "Mission and Service and the Globalization of North American Mennonites," *MQR* 70 (1996): 8–10.

2. Edmund G. Kaufman, *The Development of the Missionary and Philanthropic Interest among the Mennonites of North America* (Berne, IN: Mennonite Book Concern, 1931), 311. Kaufman's count includes mission work among Native Americans in the United States.

3. Hanspeter Jecker and Alle G. Hoekema, preface to Claude Baecher, Neal Blough, James Jakob Fehr, Alle G. Hoekema, and Hanspeter Jecker, *Testing Faith and Tradition: Global Mennonite History Series: Europe* (Intercourse, PA: Good Books, 2006), vii. According to Mennonite World Conference statistics, nearly 64 percent of the world's Anabaptists lived in Latin America, Asia, or Africa in 2009. This represented a 30 percent share increase since 1978, when the majority of the world's 613,000 Anabaptists lived in North America. Conrad L. Kanagy, Tilahun Beyene, and Richard Showalter, *Winds of the Spirit: A Profile of Anabaptist Churches in the Global South* (Scottdale, PA: Herald Press, 2012), 59.

4. For a positive assessment, see Kanagy, Beyene, and Showalter, *Winds of the Spirit*.

5. For one particular account of this challenge, see Felipe Hinojosa, "'Pool Tables are the Devil's Playground': Forging an *Evangelico-Anabautista* Identity in South Texas," in *The Activist Impulse: Essays on the Intersection of Evangelicalism and Anabaptism*, ed. Jared S. Burkholder and David C. Cramer (Eugene, OR: Pickwick, 2012), 237–61.

6. Menno Sauder, *A Description of the True and of the False Church as Outlined in a Certain History, Properly Named "The Bloody Theatre" or "Martyrs Mirror" by Thieleman J. van Braght 1660, and a Solution to World Problems* (Elmira, ON: Menno Sauder, 1944); and *Companion of a Solution to World Problems; or, The Christian Faith as Portrayed throughout "The Bloody Theatre" or "Martyrs Mirror" and Other Authors* (Elmira, ON: Menno Sauder, 1945). In addition to excerpting sections of *Martyrs Mirror*, Sauder included writings of Menno Simons, Dirk Philips, and others.

7. Joseph Stoll, *The Drummer's Wife and Other Stories from "Martyrs' Mirror"* (Aylmer, ON: Pathway, 1968).

8. James W. Lowry, *In the Whale's Belly and Other Martyr Stories* (Harrisonburg, VA: Christian Light, 1981). Lowry's abridgment has since been issued in ten other languages —Spanish, Telugu, Russian, German, Hungarian, Chinese, French, Romanian, Uzbek, and Georgian—by a variety of conservative Mennonite publishers.

9. A more recent example is Joseph Isaac, *"Martyrs Mirror" Excerpts: Selections from "Martyrs Mirror"* (Moundridge, KS: Gospel, Church of God in Christ Mennonite, 1988).

10. For a more complete list of missionary undertakings, see Stephen Scott, *An Introduction to Old Order and Conservative Mennonite Groups* (Intercourse, PA: Good Books, 1996), 214–16.

11. The quotation is from "The Purpose of Lamp and Light Publishers," www.australia.anabaptistmennonites.org/index_htm_files/LampAndLight2011.pdf, accessed February 6, 2015. The Conservative Mennonite Fellowship is now defunct; most of its congregations are now associated with the Nationwide Mennonite Fellowship, a loose association of conservative Mennonite congregations. For more information on the Nationwide Fellowship, see Scott, *Old Order and Conservative*, 167–69.

12. James W. Lowry, *En el vientre de la ballena*, trans. Maria Juana del Mejia (Farmington, NM: Publicadores Lampara y Luz, 1984). Rod and Staff, a conservative Mennonite publishing house in Crockett, Kentucky, translated Joseph Stoll's *Drummer's Wife* into Spanish three years earlier. José Stoll, *La esposa del tamborilero: Y otras historias*, trans. Marcos Gingerich, Norma González, Flora Patzán, and David Stutzman (Crockett, KY: Editorial Vara Y Cayado, 1981).

13. Dallas Witmer, *La fe por la cual vale morir* [The faith worth dying for] (Farmington, NM: Publicadora Lámpara y Luz, 1989); David Luthy, *A History of the Printings of the "Martyrs' Mirror"* (Alymer, ON: Pathway, 2013), 84. Witmer was a missionary with the Nationwide Mennonite Fellowship.

14. The recent Lamp and Light resource catalog can be found at "The Purpose of Lamp and Light Publishers," www.australia.anabaptistmennonites.org/index_htm_files/LampAndLight2011.pdf, accessed February 6, 2015.

15. Witmer's booklet has also been translated into Russian, French, and German; see Luthy, *History of the Printings*, 85.

16. For information on Grace Press, see Scott, *Old Order and Conservative*, 214.

17. Grace Press has since translated Stoll and Lowry's abridgments into other languages, including German, Hungarian, Chinese, and Uzbek, but the production of Russian-language copies has remained primary.

18. This work was enabled by James W. Lowry, who identified these core accounts in *The "Martyrs' Mirror" Made Plain: How to Study and Profit from the "Martyrs' Mirror,"* rev. ed. (Aylmer, ON: Pathway, 2011), 92–93.

19. Steven M. Nolt, "MCC's Relationship with 'Plain' Anabaptists in Historical Perspective," in *A Table of Sharing: Mennonite Central Committee and the Expanding Networks of Mennonite Identity,* ed. Alain Epp Weaver (Telford, PA: Cascadia, 2011), 144–45.

20. In 1980 a column entitled "Our Suffering Brethren" began appearing in the *Budget,* a correspondence newspaper read by many tradition-minded Amish and Mennonites. The column sought to highlight the plight of Christians suffering under Communist rule and to educate readers about ways to support persecuted Christians.

21. See Christian Aid Ministries, www.christianaidministries.org/about-cam/who -we-are, accessed February 6, 2015.

22. A 2013 edition of *Grace Press News* lists nine different books (64,000 total copies) to be included in a container bound for Kazakhstan, along with the cost of the shipment. Among the books are five thousand Russian-language copies of *The Sacrifice of the Lord.* "Container Shipment to Kazakhstan," *Grace Press News,* February 2013, 3.

23. Dale A. Burkholder, interview by author, January 17, 2014; and Dale Burkholder, "An Introduction to the Evangelical Christians-Baptists," *Grace Press News,* June 2015, 1–5.

24. See Christian Aid Ministries, www.christianaidministries.org/about-cam/who -we-are, accessed February 6, 2015.

25. The abridgments that CAM distributed were not printed by Grace Press, but were rather Russian and Romanian translations of John S. Oyer and Robert S. Kreider, *Mirror of the Martyrs* (Intercourse, PA: Good Books, 1990), which CAM itself published in 2002.

26. A recent article in *Grace Press News* criticized self-identified Christians of various sorts and concluded with a call to action: "We need to actively forge solid Biblical communities that bring into their folds 'those that should be saved' from every tribe and nation. And guess what? *More and more people are looking to the Amish and conservative Mennonites as an example of the way things ought to be!* Let us keep it that way! Let us help others establish truly Biblical churches and fellowships." "Pennsylvania without Plain People," *Grace Press News,* October 2013, 4.

27. For an example of a conservative Anabaptist critique of contemporary Catholicism, see David G. Burkholder, *Distinctive Beliefs of the Anabaptists* (Ephrata, PA: Eastern Mennonite Publications, 2009), 75. See also Dale A. Burkholder, "The Church at Laodicea," *Grace Press News,* August 2013, 2.

28. For instance, Harvey Yoder, *They Would Not Be Silent* (Berlin, OH: TGS International, 2001); and Harvey Yoder, *A Small Price to Pay* (Berlin, OH: TGS International, 2006).

29. "Christian Martyrs Fund," Christian Aid Ministries, https://christianaidminis tries.org/programs/7, accessed January 7, 2014.

30. Oyer and Kreider, *Mirror of the Martyrs.* The other prominent abridgment produced by assimilated Anabaptists was Dave and Neta Jackson, *On Fire for Christ: Stories of Anabaptist Martyrs* (Scottdale, PA: Herald Press, 1989).

31. Currently there are three different Mennonite denominations in the Democratic Republic of Congo, together comprising nearly 250,000 members. See Erik Kumedisa, "Mennonite Churches in Central Africa," in Alemu Checole, Samuel Asefa, Bekithemba Dube, et al., *Anabaptist Songs in African Hearts: Global Mennonite History Series: Africa* (Intercourse, PA: Good Books, 2006), 45–94.

32. Jaime Prieto Valladares, *Mission and Migration: Global Mennonite History Series: Latin America,* trans. and ed. C. Arnold Snyder (Intercourse, PA: Good Books, 2010), 143.

33. The Mennonite World Conference "exists to (1) be a global community of faith in the Anabaptist tradition, (2) facilitate relationships between Anabaptist-related churches worldwide, and (3) relate to other Christian world communions and organizations." See the Mennonite World Conference mission statement, at www.mwc-cmm.org /article/vision-and-mission, accessed January 14, 2015.

34. This was not the case with the Russian and Romanian translations, which were initiated and superintended by Christian Aid Ministries. See note 25.

35. Marco Guete, interview by author, February 4, 2014. Guete was born in Columbia and migrated to the United States in 1970. He and his wife returned to Columbia under the auspices of the Commission on Overseas Mission, an agency of the General Conference Mennonite Church. Marco Guete, e-mail message to author, February 4, 2014.

36. John D. Roth, now director of the Institute for the Study of Global Anabaptism at Goshen College, assisted in the translation and publication of the Hindi edition (and also the German and French editions), using funding provided by Pathway Publishers. John D. Roth, e-mail message to author, January 10, 2014.

37. Mennonite Brethren missionaries arrived in India in 1889, and General Conference Mennonite Church missionaries and (Old) Mennonite Church missionaries arrived in 1899. See I. P. Asheervadam, "The Mennonite and Brethren in Christ Churches of India," in I. P. Asheervadam, Adhi Dharma, Alle Hoekema, et al., *Churches Engage Asian Traditions: Global Mennonite History Series: Asia* (Intercourse, PA: Good Books, 2011), 125–219.

38. Masih, quoted in Sheldon C. Good, "Pastor Translates Anabaptist Martyr Stories into Hindi," *Mennonite Weekly Review,* October 18, 2010, 9.

39. See Kanagy, Beyene, and Showalter, *Winds of the Spirit,* 239–40. A pastor in India's Brethren in Christ Church, also a member of the Mennonite World Conference, was killed by Hindu extremists in 2001. In 2008 a Brethren in Christ hostel was set on fire by Hindu militants. See "Leader from BIC Church in India Reports on Violence in Orissa," at www.bic-church.org/news/churchwide/archives/08_09_24_mwc_india_rele ase.asp, accessed January 16, 2015.

40. Masih, quoted in Good, "Pastor Translates Anabaptist Martyr Stories," 9.

41. Sharovan, quoted in ibid.

42. John S. Oyer and Robert S. Kreider, *Espejo de los mártires: Historias de inspiración y coraje,* trans. Clara Helena Beltrán Suárez (Bogatá, Columbia: CLARA, 1997).

43. Valladares, *Mission and Migration,* 339–42. For the ministry's website, see www .justapaz.org/, accessed February 7, 2015.

44. Elizabeth Soto, interview by author, February 6, 2015.

45. Neal Blough, "Response of Neal Blough [to Brad Gregory]," in *Martyrdom in an Ecumenical Perspective: A Mennonite-Catholic Conversation,* ed. Peter C. Erb (Kitchener, ON: Pandora Press, 2007), 42. Blough's response was given at a subsequent Catholic-Mennonite dialogue that took place in Collegeville, Minnesota, in July 2003.

46. Ibid., 43–48.

47. Neal Blough, preface to John S. Oyer and Robert S. Kreider, *Miroir des martyrs: Histoires d'anabaptistes ayant donné leur vie pour leur foi au XVIe siècle,* trans. Lydie Hege Wiebe (Cléon d'Andran, France: Editions Excelsis), 7–8; English translation of the preface by Lois Beck.

48. "Called Together to Be Peacemakers: Report of the International Dialogue between the Catholic Church and Mennonite World Conference, 1998–2003," para. 179, www.oecumene.nl/files/Documenten/Called_together_to_be_Paecemakers.pdf, accessed January 31, 2015.

49. See Bridgefolk.net, www.bridgefolk.net/about, accessed January 7, 2015.

50. C. Arnold Snyder, *The Life and Thought of Michael Sattler* (Scottdale, PA: Herald Press, 1984); see also *Martyrs Mirror* (1938), 416–18.

51. For biographical information, see Ivan J. Kaufman, "On Being a Mennonite Catholic," *MQR* 77 (2003): 235–55.

52. The quotation is from the Michael Sattler House website, www.michaelsattlerhouse.org/index.html, accessed January 7, 2015.

53. Dated May 20, 2012, the letter is available for download at www.praytellblog.com/wp-content/uploads/2012/05/Sattler-open-letter.pdf; accessed January 7, 2015. The Kaufmans acknowledged the influence of Abbot Eoin de Bhaldraithe, who twenty-five years earlier had written an essay that highlighted Sattler's dual theological identity. See Eoin de Bhaldraithe, "Michael Sattler, Benedictine and Anabaptist," *Downside Review* 105 (1987): 111–31.

54. Julia Smucker, "Feasting Michael Sattler," *Vox Nova: Catholic Perspectives on Culture, Society, and Politics* (blog), May 20, 2012, http://vox-nova.com/2012/05/20/feasting-michael-sattler/.

55. Anthony Ruff, "Michael Sattler: Monk, Mennonite, Martyr," *Pray Tell: Worship, Wit & Wisdom* (blog), May 21, 2012, www.praytellblog.com/index.php/2012/05/21/michael-sattler-monk-mennonite-martyr/.

56. Robert Lennon, response to Smucker's blog, "Feasting Michael Sattler," posted May 20, 2012.

57. Spencer Bradford, response to Lennon's response, posted June 7, 2012.

58. John D. Roth, "Should We Update *Martyrs Mirror*?," *Mennonite,* June 2012, 9.

59. This was the subtitle of the consultation discussed in the following paragraphs: "'Bearing Witness': A New *Martyrs Mirror* for the Twenty-First Century?"

60. Roth, "Should We Update *Martyrs Mirror*?," 9.

61. The first gathering, which I attended, took place at Goshen College on May 22–23, 2009. The second consultation took place at Bluffton College on June 12–13, 2009. Beachy's book is discussed in the last section of chapter 11.

62. I attended the 2012 consultation. My account is drawn from my own notes, from

detailed minutes taken by Kate Yoder, and from a four-page summary produced by John D. Roth after the conference ended.

63. The letter of invitation to participants identified four goals for the consultation: (1) "To test the wisdom of initiating a collaborative project that would gather and disseminate stories of Christian faithfulness amid adversity in the Anabaptist-Mennonite tradition since 1685"; (2) "To clarify mutual understandings of the goals of the larger project, recognizing that a host of complex questions need to be addressed before any major initiative can move forward"; (3) "To discuss specific strategies for identifying, gathering, collecting, preserving, and disseminating such material"; and (4) "To develop a strategy . . . for moving the project along."

64. Jack Suderman, former general secretary of Mennonite Church Canada, spoke most eloquently about the dangers inherent in "speaking about victimization from a position of power." See Kaeli Evans, "Modern *Martyrs Mirror* Envisioned," *Mennonite World Review,* August 20, 2012, 20.

65. John D. Roth, "Bearing Witness: A New *Martyrs Mirror* for the 21st Century? An International Consultation at Goshen College, August 5–8, 2012," unpublished summary, August 12, 2012; copy in author's possession.

66. For one compilation, see Aaron A. Toews, *Mennonite Martyrs: People Who Suffered for Their Faith, 1920–1940,* trans. John B. Toews (Winnipeg, MB: Kindred Press, 1990).

67. Roth, "Bearing Witness" summary.

68. "Bearing Witness: Martyrdom and Costly Discipleship in the Anabaptist-Mennonite Tradition," www.anabaptistwiki.org/mediawiki/index.php?title=Bearing_Witness, accessed January 15, 2015.

69. A newer, more polished website, titled "Bearing Witness: Story Project," includes fewer stories but exhibits more geographical and ethnic balance. Managed by the Institute for the Study of Global Anabaptism, the website begins with these sentences: "Anabaptist witness in the face of suffering did not end in Europe in the 16th century. Read the stories of believers from around the world who have continued to bear witness to their faith at great cost." See www.martyrstories.org/, accessed February 6, 2015.

70. "Dirk Willems," www.anabaptistwiki.org/mediawiki/index.php/Dirk_Willems, accessed February 6, 2015.

71. Chester Weaver, a Beachy Amish church leader, attended the consultation, as did two members of the Bruderhof Communities, a communal society that shares some history with the Hutterites. Other tradition-minded Mennonites and Amish were invited but chose not to participate.

72. According to the minutes from the 2012 Goshen College consultation, one of the rationales for gathering new stories was "to honor the voices and experiences of the vulnerable . . . by being attentive to their stories [and] by standing in solidarity with them."

73. "Here at Christian Aid Ministries we feel compelled to capture at least some of these stories . . . to inspire us to new heights in our own spiritual experiences." David N. Troyer, foreword to Yoder, *They Would Not Be Silent,* viii. With respect to the "Bearing Witness" story-gathering project, John Roth has encouraged tradition-minded Ana-

baptists to submit stories, producing a two-page handout intended for distribution in tradition-minded communities. The handout quotes extensively from traditional Anabaptist sources, and it tells its readers that gathering stories of costly discipleship is particularly important in a context so similar to van Braght's, that is, during an era "undisturbed and untroubled by persecution" when many Mennonites "have grown lukewarm . . . and carnally attached to the world."

74. For a summary of these considerations, see Thomas Andrews and Flannery Burke, "What Does It Mean to Think Historically?" *Perspectives on History* 45, no. 1 (January 2007): 32–35. Andrews and Burke's inclusion of *complexity* as a consideration is pertinent here: "Reveling in complexity rather than shying away from it, historians seek to dispel the power of chronicle, nostalgia, and other traps that obscure our ability to understand the past on its own terms" (35).

75. I realize, of course, that no historian can tell the whole truth about the past and that all historians select, organize, and present pieces of the past according to their own interpretive judgments. My point is not that van Braght failed to be something that no historian can be, but rather that he, like other early modern martyrologists, wrote an account of church history that showed little interest in acknowledging or addressing evidence that might detract from his theological objectives.

Conclusion

1. Stuart Murray, *The Naked Anabaptist: The Bare Essentials of a Radical Faith* (Scottdale, PA: Herald Press, 2010), 135–59.

2. *The Schleitheim Confession,* trans. and ed. John H. Yoder (Scottdale, PA: Herald Press, 1973), 14.

3. Tripp York, "A Faith Worth Dying For: A Tradition of Martyrs Not Heroes," in *A Faith Not Worth Fighting For: Addressing Commonly Asked Questions about Christian Nonviolence,* ed. Tripp York and Justin Bronson Barringer (Eugene, OR: Cascade Books, 2012), 207–25.

4. For an argument in this regard, see Richard Beck, "Why the Church Needs Its Martyrs," *Mennonite World Review,* November 10, 2014, 4. For Christian traditions that once held but have largely abandoned a pacifist stance, see Michael W. Casey, "From Pacifism to Patriotism: The Emergence of Civil Religion in the Churches of Christ during World War I," *MQR* 66 (1992): 376–90; and Paul Alexander, *Peace to War: Shifting Allegiances in the Assemblies of God* (Telford, PA: Cascadia, 2009).

5. This was an online comment from Dale Welty at the end of Andre Gingerich Stoner, "Our Victim Mentality," *Mennonite World Review,* May 28, 2012; online conversation at www.mennoworld.org/archived/2012/5/28/our-victim-mentality/.

6. Here I depart from John Roth's suggestion that the "recent critics of 'martyr memory'" advocate the rejection of history and storytelling and thereby hope to "escape from the burden of memory." See John D. Roth, "The Complex Legacy of the *Martyrs Mirror* among Mennonites in North America," *MQR* 87 (2013): 310.

7. Dave and Neta Jackson, *On Fire for Christ: Stories of Anabaptist Martyrs* (Scottdale, PA: Herald Press, 1989).

8. Ibid., 26. Citing the Passover celebration, the Jacksons claimed that "the biblical record is a good example of right remembering." Of course, the Bible also includes calls to remember that sustain the cycle of violence (e.g., Deuteronomy 25:17–19).

9. For instance, James C. Juhnke, "Rightly Remembering a Martyr Heritage," *Mennonite Life* 58, no. 3 (September 2003), online at http://ml.bethelks.edu/issue/vol-58-no-3/. For a more recent use of this phrase, see Roth, "Complex Legacy of the *Martyrs Mirror*," 305–16, which draws on the work of Miroslav Wolf, *The End of Memory: Remembering Rightly in a Violent World* (Grand Rapids, MI: William B. Eerdmans, 2006).

10. Brad S. Gregory, *Salvation at Stake: Christian Martyrdom in Early Modern Europe* (Cambridge, MA: Harvard University Press, 1999), 82–90.

11. For instance, Jeff Gundy, "Some Inappropriate Thoughts about the Martyr Project," an unpublished response to a lecture by John D. Roth at Bluffton University in February 2013; copy in author's possession. For an example of the dominant narrative, see Joe Wittmer, *The Gentle People: Personal Reflections of Amish Life*, 3rd ed. (Minneapolis, MN: Educational Media Corp., 2001). For a challenge to this narrative, one that documents sexual abuse in Amish homes, see Nadya Labi, "The Gentle People," *Legal Affairs*, January–February 2005, at http://legalaffairs.org/issues/January-February-2005/feature_labi_janfeb05.msp.

12. Gingerich Stoner, "Our Victim Mentality."

13. Jeremy Bergen, "The Anabaptist *Martyrs Mirror* in the Past and for Today," presented at the 47th International Ecumenical Seminar, Institute for Ecumenical Research, Strasbourg, France, July 8, 2013. Online at www.strasbourginstitute.org/wp-content/uploads/2013/08/Bergen-Martyrs-Mirror-in-the-Past-and-for-Today.pdf.

14. "Statement of Regret," in *Steps to Reconciliation: Reformed and Anabaptist Churches in Dialogue*, ed. Michael Baumann (Zurich: Theologischer Verlag Zurich, 2007), 81.

15. "Mennonite Response," in *Steps to Reconciliation*, 83.

16. Ibid., 84.

17. John T. Petersheim, John S. Stoltzfus, Samuel K. Lapp, et al., "From the Old Order Amish Churches of the USA," in *Steps to Reconciliation*, 96.

Index

YOUNG CENTER BOOKS IN ANABAPTIST & PIETIST STUDIES

James A. Cates, *Serving the Amish: A Cultural Guide for Professionals*

D. Rose Elder, *Why the Amish Sing: Songs of Solidarity and Identity*

Brian Froese, *California Mennonites*

Charles E. Hurst and David L. McConnell, *An Amish Paradox: Diversity and Change in the World's Largest Amish Community*

Rod Janzen and Max Stanton, *The Hutterites in North America*

Karen M. Johnson-Weiner, *Train Up a Child: Old Order Amish and Mennonite Schools*

Peter J. Klassen, *Mennonites in Early Modern Poland and Prussia*

James O. Lehman and Steven M. Nolt, *Mennonites, Amish, and the American Civil War*

Mark L. Louden, *Pennsylvania Dutch: The Story of an American Language*

Steven M. Nolt and Thomas J. Meyers, *Plain Diversity: Amish Cultures and Identities*

Douglas H. Shantz, *A New Introduction to German Pietism: Protestant Renewal at the Dawn of Modern Europe*

Tobin Miller Shearer, *Daily Demonstrators: The Civil Rights Movement in Mennonite Homes and Sanctuaries*

Janneken Smucker, *Amish Quilts: Crafting an American Icon*

Richard A. Stevick, *Growing Up Amish: The Rumspringa Years* (second edition)

Duane C. S. Stoltzfus, *Pacifists in Chains: The Persecution of Hutterites during the Great War*

Susan L. Trollinger, *Selling the Amish: The Tourism of Nostalgia*

Diane Zimmerman Umble and David L. Weaver-Zercher, eds., *The Amish and the Media*

David L. Weaver-Zercher, *Martyrs Mirror: A Social History*

Valerie Weaver-Zercher, *Thrill of the Chaste: The Allure of Amish Romance Novels*